*SHELLEY AND BYRON*

# Shelley and Byron

## THE SNAKE AND EAGLE

## WREATHED IN FIGHT

## CHARLES E. ROBINSON

*The Johns Hopkins University Press*
*Baltimore and London*

The publication of this volume has been aided by a grant from
The Carl and Lily Pforzheimer Foundation, Inc.

Copyright © 1976 by The Johns Hopkins University Press
All rights reserved. No part of this book may be
reproduced or transmitted in any form or by any means,
electronic or mechanical, including photocopying,
recording, xerography, or any information storage and
retrieval system, without permission in writing
from the publisher.

Manufactured in the United States of America

The Johns Hopkins University Press, Baltimore, Maryland 21218
The Johns Hopkins University Press Ltd., London

Library of Congress Catalog Card Number 75-36927
ISBN 0-8018-1707-2

NEWTON PARK

COLLEGE

BATH

DISCARD

CLASS
NO. 821.7 SHE R

ACC.
NO. 77/1705

*For Peggy*

# CONTENTS

## ACKNOWLEDGMENTS

While preparing this study I have incurred many debts; and to all those Shelley and Byron scholars, past and present, who have made my task easier or more rewardingly difficult, I am grateful. For their special assistance, I wish to thank the following: Professor David V. Erdman for introducing me to the subject of Shelley and Byron's literary relations and for cautioning me against rushing an earlier version of this book into print; Professor Jerome J. McGann for criticizing my manuscript in its penultimate stage; Professors James Rieger, Truman Guy Steffan, and Marion K. Stocking for replying to my requests for information and assistance; and Professor Donald H. Reiman for encouraging me and faithfully answering innumerable letters.

I am also indebted to the American Council of Learned Societies for a grant-in-aid to study Shelley's manuscript notebooks at The Bodleian Library, Oxford; and to the University of Delaware General Research Fund for a grant-in-aid to prepare my final manuscript.

Quotations in my text from Bodleian MSS. Shelley e. 4, adds. d. 7, adds. e. 6-adds. e. 12, adds. e. 17, and adds. e. 19 are printed by permission of The Bodleian Library and The Clarendon Press, Oxford; quotations from *The Letters of Percy Bysshe Shelley*, ed. Frederick L. Jones, 2 vols., © 1964 Oxford University Press, by permission of The Clarendon Press, Oxford; and quotation of the manuscript "All hail, Mont Blanc," by the courtesy of the Humanities Research Center, The University of Texas at Austin.

For their professional and personal courtesies, I also thank my colleagues and the library staff at the University of Delaware; my many typists and proofreaders, particularly Sally Schwartz and Mary Loftus; Dennis Porter, whose kindnesses extended from The Bodleian to Appleton, Berkshire; and George and Mary Bird, whose affection for a young family on sabbatical will always be treasured.

My ultimate debt is to my parents, wife, and children: their patience and faith in my work have "lit/My midnight lamp" these many years.

Newark, Delaware                                                    C.E.R.
March 1975

*SHELLEY AND BYRON*

CREATORS AND CREATIONS:
THE SPIRITS AND FORMS OF SHELLEY
AND BYRON

In the Preface to *Prometheus Unbound,* Percy Bysshe Shelley
maintained that a poet was the combined product of both "internal
powers" and "external influences"; and to explain these external
influences, he added that "every man's mind is . . . modified by
all the objects of nature and art; by every word and every suggestion
which he ever admitted to act upon his consciousness; it is the mirror
upon which all forms are reflected, and in which they compose one
form." Because of these external influences, Shelley continued, poets
are in one sense "the creations, of their age" and there is "a similarity
between Homer and Hesiod, between Æschylus and Euripides, between
Virgil and Horace, between Dante and Petrarch, between Shakespeare
and Fletcher, between Dryden and Pope." By the same logic, we might
add that during the age of English Romanticism, there was at least some
similarity between Byron and Shelley himself. Such a conclusion,
however, can obscure the immediate influences that Byron and Shelley
provided for each other's poetry, because any similarities between
them might be traced only to the mediate "spirit of the age." Yet a
literary "age" is a nominal abstraction which has meaning only in
terms of its writers, and it is desirable, if possible, to articulate the
reciprocal influences between two contemporary poets who, in Shelley's
own terms, are "in one sense, the *creators,* and, in another, the
*creations,* of their age."[1]

To establish that a particular poet rather than an indefinite "age"
influenced another poet requires a number of circumstances rarely
available to the literary critic, for not only the "form" of the poem
but also the "spirit" of the poet must be demonstrably affected by the
influencing agent. In his same Preface to *Prometheus Unbound,* Shelley
distinguished between this "form" and "spirit":

> It is impossible that any one who inhabits the same age with such
> writers as those who stand in the foremost ranks of our own, can
> conscientiously assure himself that his language and tone of
> thought may not have been modified by the study of the produc-

*1*

tions of those extraordinary intellects. It is true, that, not the spirit of their genius, but the forms in which it has manifested itself, are due less to the peculiarities of their own minds than to the peculiarity of the moral and intellectual condition of the minds among which they have been produced. Thus a number of writers possess the form, whilst they want the spirit of those whom, it is alleged, they imitate; because the former is the endowment of the age in which they live, and the latter must be the uncommunicated lightning of their own mind.

Notwithstanding Shelley's implication here that the spirit or "the uncommunicated lightning" of a poet's mind is uniquely inviolable, he states elsewhere in the Preface that the mind, and hence the spirit, may be modified by external objects (including other minds). Only by means of such a modification whereby two spirits or minds engage each other is a study of the literary relations between two poets fruitful; otherwise, a critic is limited to paralleling passages or "forms" of the two authors. Although he might judge that one "form" influenced the other, what is described as immediate influence is often merely the mediate "endowment of the age."

The formal relations between the poetry of Byron and Shelley are due, however, not so much to the traditions of their age but to the influences each exerted on the other's "spirit" or mind. In this way, their literary association resembles that between Wordsworth and Coleridge; but unlike the latter pair, Byron and Shelley hardly ever agreed on matters concerning God, Man, and Nature, and their influences on each other were more negative than positive. That is, their frequently contradictory metaphysics, ethics, and aesthetics determined each poet to assert his point of view, his "spirit," to correct the misconceptions of the other. Had their ideas been more similar, we might not have been able to differentiate between the influencing and the influenced spirit. But because their literary association in more respects defined rather than changed their different conceptions of the human condition, the nature of their reciprocal influences is demonstrable through this effect, this definition of their antagonistic "spirits." By 1819, in *Julian and Maddalo*, Shelley succinctly distinguished his "spirit" of meliorism from that of Byron's fatalism; and, as we shall see, many other poems (including Shelley's *Two Spirits: An Allegory*) were written by the two poets to make this same distinction.

II

The requisite for any literary influence is proximity: the self must have experienced the other; the creative artist must have either known the influencing agent or have read his works. Byron and Shelley satisfy both requirements, for they were personally acquainted for six years, spent in excess of two hundred and fifty days together during that time, read and reacted to all of each other's major works, and exchanged fifty letters (most of which are extant). Although the most important periods of their association were the three months that began their friendship in Geneva during the summer of 1816 and the six months (November 1821 through April 1822) that concluded it in Pisa, the two poets also met occasionally in Venice from August through October 1818, and they were together daily for two weeks in Ravenna during August 1821. Their final meeting occurred a few days before Shelley's death on 8 July 1822.[2]

The duration and complex nature of Byron and Shelley's association captured the imagination of their contemporaries: the names of Claire Clairmont, Leigh Hunt, Thomas Medwin, Thomas Moore, Thomas Love Peacock, John Polidori, Mary Shelley, Edward Trelawny, and Edward Williams bring to mind a circle of literati who recorded their judgments about the two poets in letters, biographies, novels, recollections, editions, and diaries. Yet these admirers and apologists did not accurately present the literary relations between Byron and Shelley: personal bias or lack of historical perspective either limited the accounts to biographical details or obscured the poets' indebtedness to each other. The confusing result of early-nineteenth-century commentary on their association is typified by an emotional debate on their relative merits in November 1829, when the Cambridge Union journeyed to Oxford and espoused not Byron, the renowned alumnus of Cambridge, but Shelley. The Oxonians, who disassociated themselves from the avowed atheist who had been expelled from Oxford nearly twenty years before, championed Byron and won handily by a vote of ninety to thirty-three.[3] This debate was continued during the nineteenth century as Byron and Shelley were separately and then jointly championed and denounced in critical prose fraught with balance and antithesis but with little understanding of the two poets' relationships.[4] Even now, because most twentieth-century studies of Byron and Shelley have usually examined one to the exclusion of the other, we encounter only an occasional reference to their reciprocal influences. And the three comparative studies of the two poets have emphasized the biographical friendship between the men rather than the artistic and philosophical interaction of the "spirits." That no critic has attempted completely to analyze this more complex interaction probably results from the perilously intricate nature of an influence study. Even John Buxton, whose *Byron and Shelley: The History of a Friendship* is the finest of the three comparative studies on the two poets, observed that he "only briefly indicated" the effect of Byron and Shelley's friendship

*3*

on their poetry and confessed that the "interplay of these two poetic minds, so stimulating to both, is too complex to be altogether decipherable by us, who never listened to them talking."[5] Similarly, William J. Calvert, in *Byron: Romantic Paradox,* projected the inconclusiveness of an influence study:

> It is difficult and hazardous to demarcate exactly the reciprocal reactions of Byron and his fellow poet. That both came to have like views on some subjects is obvious. It is also true that there are echoes of the odes to the Skylark or the West Wind in the latter half of *Childe Harold,* or that the former lyrics echo the latter, and that certain unusual words, like "immedicable," spring up in both poets at about the same time. But whether the one affects the other or the other the one, or they both draw from the same source similar material, or arrive by like trains of thought or through similar reading at the same result, is in the separate case indeterminable.[6]

Notwithstanding these warnings, I propose that sufficient evidence can be employed to distinguish the reciprocal influences of the two poets from the "endowment of the age," which Calvert feared would obstruct such a study.

Byron and Shelley's letters to and about each other demonstrate the thoroughness of their literary association: in a very real sense, each was a student of the other, whose works he read, criticized, and remembered. Although neither poet publicly acknowledged the influence of the other, neither denied what might be politely called "literary borrowings" from his contemporaries. Byron, who occasionally credited his sources in the notes to his poetry but was nevertheless accused of plagiarism by his reviewers, acknowledged "that he was indebted to the hints of others for some of the most esteemed passages in his poetry. 'I never,' said he, 'considered myself interdicted from helping myself to another man's stray ideas.'"[7] Similarly, Shelley borrowed from his contemporaries, but unlike Byron he seldom provided any particular source for his ideas. Rather, as in his Preface to *Prometheus Unbound,* he credited the "endowment of the age" to escape charges of plagiarism.[8] However, Shelley's particular "endowment" from Byron, like Byron's from Shelley, is specifically demonstrable, but citing the parallel passages between the "forms" of their poetry is not so much the end of this study as the means to demonstrate their philosophical dialogue, which in part determined each poet's allusions to the other in his works. Shelley, generally more conscious of his complex relationship with the elder poet, incorporated portraits and praise of Byron and his "eagle spirit" in *Julian and Maddalo, Lines Written Among the Euganean*

*Hills, The Two Spirits: An Allegory, Epipsychidion, Adonais, Hellas,* and *Sonnet to Byron.* Byron for his part may not have so openly " 'puffed the Snake [Shelley],' "[9] but he at least alluded to Shelley, particularly in *Don Juan.*

However valuable these mutual allusions and borrowings may be in demonstrating the influences Byron and Shelley provided for the "form" of each other's poetry, their antagonistic philosophies and the record of this antagonism in their poetry written from 1816 through 1823 provide the more important evidence for a study of the interaction of their "two spirits." Shelley's *Julian and Maddalo* (1818/19) may be the only major poem that explicitly juxtaposes the melioristic Shelleyan and the fatalistic Byronic spirits, but after 1816 the two poets frequently used their major works to debate their philosophical differences. Their opposition may be traced not only in their lyrical poetry, in which each poet imaginatively objectified his personal hopes and fears, but also in their narrative and dramatic works, in which the "fictionalized" heroes directly reflect each poet's self-consciousness or his artistic struggle "to idealize and to unify" his imaginative prehension of the human condition.[10] This does not mean that Byron is in every respect Manfred or that Shelley is Prometheus, but it does mean that as imaginatively constructed perceptions of the real world that does or should exist, *Manfred* and *Prometheus Unbound* distinguish Byron's and Shelley's philosophies. If, as John Buxton regrets, we can never listen to Byron and Shelley "talking," we can at least experience the two poets' dialogue in their poetry.

Byron and Shelley's dialogue resulted from what C. E. Pulos in *The Deep Truth: A Study of Shelley's Scepticism* termed their different "varieties of the transcendental tendency." In both cases, according to Pulos, whose book devotes less than a paragraph to Byron, the two poets "pursued a non-dogmatic idealism compatible with scepticism,"[11] that is, compatible with the empirical limitations on man's senses and the consequent limitations on man's reason and his knowledge of ultimate reality. For Shelley, however, these limitations could be escaped by a "sceptical solution to doubt"—a faith in the existence and realization of the ideals created (or intuited) by the human imagination. Byron seldom experienced such a faith and he usually deemed these ideals to be the illusory products of a diseased mind. Nevertheless, Byron's belief that "human ideas have only a subjective validity"[12] meant that he could accept Shelley's definition of metaphysics as "the science of all that we know, feel, remember and believe: inasmuch as our knowledge, sensations, memory and faith *constitute the universe considered relatively to human identity.*"[13] Underlying this definition is Shelley's epistemological metaphor of the circle—that man's mind is "somehow/At once circumference and centre/Of all [man] might or feel or know."[14] In other words, as Shelley often expressed, "nothing exists but as it is perceived." And what ultimately distinguishes Byron's and Shelley's conceptions of man's circumferential existence (including ideals) is the nature of the center, the perceiving mind.

The difference between Byron's and Shelley's epistemologies is somewhat obscured by their common appeal to Sir William Drummond's *Academical Questions* (1805), a skeptical inquiry equally admired by both poets. Byron's first recorded reference to this volume is in a note to stanza cxxvii of *Childe Harold* IV in which he defends reason as "Our right of thought—our last and only place/Of refuge . . ./Though from our birth the Faculty divine/Is chained and tortured."[15] Shelley would agree with Drummond and Byron on the limited nature of human reason, but he did not rest his epistemology on reason. Instead he believed with Wordsworth that man's "vision and faculty divine" (*The Excursion* I.79) was the synthetical imagination rather than the analytical reason. And in his essay *On Life* (?1818), Shelley modified Drummond's "intellectual system" ("The view of life presented by the most refined deductions of the intellectual philosophy, is that of unity") by explaining this unity in terms of a child's synthetical and imaginative intuitions of the intimate relations between self and the universe. "As men grow up this power [intuition or imagination] commonly decays," and the subsequent "feelings and then reasonings [as] the combined result of a multitude of entangled thoughts, and . . . impressions"[16] inhibit the imaginative apprehension of what Wordsworth and Coleridge had called the "one life."[17] Shelley, however, believed that the divine faculty of the imagination could be restored to its former state; to the contrary, Byron believed that the divine faculty of reason was impaired "from our birth."

By means of the synthetical imagination Shelley could posit a faith in his idealism, a faith opposed to Byron's analytic denial of the illusory ideal, "the unreached Paradise of our despair" (*Childe Harold* IV.cxxii). Shelley's awareness of this philosophical opposition is evident from the following dialogue with Byron in *Julian and Maddalo*:

> "—it is our will
> That thus enchains us to permitted ill—
> We might be otherwise—we might be all
> We dream of happy, high, majestical.
> Where is the love, beauty and truth we seek,
> But in our mind? and if we were not weak,
> Should we be less in deed than in desire?"

"Aye if we were not weak,—and we aspire
How vainly to be strong!" said Maddalo:
"You talk Utopia." "It remains to know,"
I then rejoined, "and those who try may find
How strong the chains are which our spirit bind:
Brittle perchance as straw."                    (ll. 170-82)

Shelley's metaphysical hopes were based on a Coleridgean conception of the imagination as "that reconciling and mediatory power . . . incorporating the Reason in Images of the Sense, and organizing (as it were) the flux of the Senses by the permanence and self-circling energies of the Reason."[18] In other words, the imagination for Shelley was the mental power that integrated reason and sense, understanding and passion, head and heart, so that man might attain the object of both thought and love, or consciousness and desire. Although in the first paragraph of his *Defence of Poetry* Shelley seemingly opposed the synthetic imagination to the analytic reason, he observed that this was only "one mode of regarding those two classes of mental action" and that "reason is to imagination as the instrument to the agent, as the body to the spirit, as the shadow to the substance." Similarly, Shelley instructed Leigh Hunt in November 1819 that both the passions and the understanding serve "the Imagination, who is the master of them both, their God, and the Spirit by which they live and are."[19] And Shelley had mythically dramatized man's psychological unity a few months earlier when he represented Demogorgon as the divine power by which man, bipartitely conceived as Prometheus (head or thought) and Asia (heart or love), imaginatively reclaimed his lost paradise.

Whereas Shelley believed that virtuous love imaginatively complemented man's knowledge and promoted the happiness of life, Byron could not sustain a faith in imaginative fulfillment because, as Jerome McGann observed, he "never wholly stilled, or completely harmonized, the conflicting principles in himself (essentially, love and thought, or desire and consciousness)." The imagination could not reconcile what Robert Gleckner also called the "by now familiar Byronic duality of mind and heart"[20] because, as Byron told Lady Blessington, the imagination opposed both man's emotional and intellectual life:

our *imaginations* being warmer than our *hearts,* and much more given to wander, the latter have not the power to control the former; hence, soon after our passions are gratified, imagination again takes wing, and, finding the insufficiency of actual indulgence beyond the moment, abandons itself to all its wayward fancies, and during this abandonment becomes cold and insensible to the demands of affection.

7

> Great imagination is seldom accompanied by equal powers of
> reason, and *vice versâ*, so that we rarely possess superiority in
> any one point, except at the expense of another. . . . the excess
> of imagination . . . debars reason.[21]

For Byron, who did not share Shelley's views on the synthetical
imagination, the divided man could never successfully reintegrate:
"Sorrow is Knowledge"; "knowledge is not happiness" (*Manfred*
I.i.10; II.iv.61); "Alas! what else is Love but Sorrow" (*Heaven and
Earth* I.iii.461). Such Byronic sentiments provided the basis for
Maddalo's objection to Julian's "Utopia."

Lacking Shelley's faith in the imaginatively unified mind or
center which could enlarge and purify the circumference of experience,
Byron may be likened to Rousseau, who, according to Georges Poulet,
concluded that the "experience of the propagation of self by the
imagination can only end in the consciousness of the radical distance
which separates the soul from its desire and spreads out an immense
hostile and insurmountable space between the imaginative center and
its imaginary projections."[22] This radical separation between "the
circumferential self" and "the central self" was more characteristic of
Byron's heroes than of Shelley's, although in *Alastor* (1816) and
*Epipsychidion* (1821) Shelley himself dramatized the "error . . . in
seeking in a mortal image the likeness of what is perhaps eternal."[23]
Yet from 1816 until 1821, Shelley hoped that he could realize the
ideal beauty of his mind, that being the circumferential creation of the
imaginative center. In his major poetry, "at once the centre and
circumference of knowledge," Shelley based his hopes on "the ideal
prototype of every thing excellent or lovely that we are capable of
conceiving as belonging to the nature of man," and he believed that
there was "a soul within our soul that describes a circle around its
proper paradise, which pain, and sorrow, and evil dare not overleap."[24]
Shelley might be guilty of inverting his own metaphor of circle and
circumference here, but he did not, like Byron, conclude that "Of its
own beauty is the mind diseased,/And fevers into false creation"
(*Childe Harold* IV.cxxii).

Yet Byron's skeptical denial of imaginative fulfillment did not end
in nihilism, for he endured the human condition by relying on his
reason, the "last and only place/Of refuge." In mythic terms,
Prometheus had strengthened "Man with his own mind" by which he
could endure and defy his "funereal destiny" and "his sad unallied
existence" (*Prometheus*, ll. 38, 50, 52). Similarly, Manfred had been an
imaginative "Croesus in creation" before his knowledge destroyed his
love and happiness, but he still would not yield "The Mind—the
Spirit—the Promethean spark,/The lightning of [his] being" (II.ii.

142; I.i.154-55). Although Byron had expressed his philosophical skepticism as early as stanza vii of *Childe Harold* II ("Well didst thou speak, Athena's wisest son! / 'All that we know is, nothing can be known' "), and although he later perverted the function of Socrates' heuristic method by "holding up the Nothingness of life" (see *Don Juan* VII.5-6; *Cain* II.ii.418-22), he still upheld the "invulnerable mind" of man, whose "very knowledge that he lived in vain, / That all was over on this side the tomb, / Had made Despair a smilingness assume" (*Childe Harold* III.x, xvi). In his "Detached Thoughts," the skeptical Byron expressed a similar "conviction" that man could not improve his temporal condition: "All history and experience, and the rest, teaches us that the good and evil are pretty equally balanced in this existence, and that what is most to be desired is an easy passage out of it."[25]

Shelley, who hypothetically accepted the Manichaean (or Byronic) dualism as a personification of the struggle between good and evil both within and without man, opposed Byron's smiling "Despair" with the principle of hope: "the supposition that the good spirit is, or hereafter will be, superior, is a personification of the principle of hope, and that thirst for improvement without which, present evil would be intolerable."[26] Until 1821, when the younger poet accepted Byron's judgment that "The Tree of Knowledge is not that of Life" (*Manfred* I.i.12) in a canceled Preface to *Epipsychidion* and thus concluded that a second Eden for man was only an illusion, Shelley expressed his hope that imaginative knowledge and fulfillment in life were compatible and that man could transcend the physical limitations occasioned by the loss of the first Eden. Mythically, a Byron's Prometheus (or mind) could unbind himself through the sympathy of love and regain paradise. To Byron's "everlasting *to be* which *hath been*" (*Ode on Venice*, l. 59), Shelley would have responded as Christ did to Satan in the fragmentary "Prologue" to *Hellas*: "Obdurate spirit! / Thou seest but the Past in the To-come. / Pride is thy error and thy punishment" (ll. 160-62). Love, even a "Love in desolation masked" (as Shelley portrayed himself in *Adonais*), was the Shelleyan means to reclaim the Byronic mind, "Proud though in desolation" (*Childe Harold* III.xii).

As the "great secret of morals," Shelleyan love depends on the imagination—"the great instrument of moral good" by which love and thought are reconciled. And as the expression of the imagination, poetry in turn "enlarges the circumference of the imagination" and thus "strengthens that faculty which is the organ of the moral nature of man." Consequently, "Poetry redeems from decay the visitations of the divinity in Man" by ascending "to bring light and fire from those eternal regions where the owl-winged faculty of calculation dare not ever soar."[27] Shelley's emphasis here on the imagination as the source of poetry again distinguishes him from Byron, whose poetry "shows reflection and passion combined, though not [imaginatively] reconciled."[28] Had Byron had Shelley's faith in the synthetic imagination, he might have poetically employed beautiful idealisms of moral excellence to purify man, who, "in part divine," was a "troubled stream from a pure source" (*Prometheus*, ll. 47-48). In *The Prophecy of Dante*, he anticipated Shelley's Promethean image of poetry as a fire bringer, but since Byron there based poetry on the "o'ermastering Power" of "Intellect" *and* an "overfeeling Good or Ill" (IV.21, 12)—rather than on the imagination which would have reconciled "reflection and passion"—he characteristically undercut his most Shelleyan conception of the power and function of art:

> For what is Poesy but to create
> From overfeeling Good or Ill; and aim
> At an external life beyond our fate,
> And be the new Prometheus of new men,
> Bestowing fire from Heaven, *and then, too late,*
> *Finding the pleasure given repaid with pain,*
> *And vultures to the heart of the bestower,*
> *Who, having lavished his high gift in vain,*
> *Lies chained to his lone rock by the sea-shore?*
>
> (IV.11-19, my italics)

This same frustration "convinced" Byron that "the poetical temperament . . . precludes happiness";[29] yet in the *Defence of Poetry* Shelley was equally convinced that the poet was the happiest of all men.

Shelley's more optimistic aesthetic is made evident by comparing his and Byron's reactions in 1816 and 1817 to Rousseau's *Nouvelle Héloïse* and Plutarch's *Life of Nicius*. Of the former, which the two poets read while touring Lake Geneva together in June 1816, Byron wrote the following judgment to John Murray:

> I have traversed all Rousseau's ground, with the *Héloïse* before me; and am struck, to a degree, with the force and accuracy of his descriptions and the beauty of their reality.

At the same time Byron compared Rousseau's accurate descriptions and the sensible reality, Shelley contrasted the "fact" and the "fiction" in a letter to Thomas Love Peacock:

> I read Julie [*Nouvelle Héloïse*] all day; an overflowing, as it now seems, surrounded by the scenes which it has so wonderfully

peopled, of sublimest genius, and more than human sensibility. Meillerie, the Castle of Chillon, Clarens, the mountains of La Valais and Savoy, present themselves to the imagination as monuments of things that were once familiar, and of beings that were once dear to it. They were created indeed by one mind, but a mind so powerfully bright as to cast a shade of falsehood on the records that are called reality.

Unlike the fundamentally empirical Byron, Shelley saw in Rousseau's narrative the greater "reality" of the imaginative ideal.[30]

Byron's bias for empirical reality and Shelley's for the imaginative ideal also determined their different reactions to Plutarch's tale of the condemned slave's redemptive song in the *Life of Nicius*. Because the two poets were separated in 1817 when each employed this tale in his poetry, C. D. Locock conjectured that they discussed it the previous year in Switzerland.[31] Byron, in *Childe Harold* IV, wrote that

> When Athens' armies fell at Syracuse,
> And fettered thousands bore the yoke of war,
> Redemption rose up in the Attic Muse,
> Her voice their only ransom from afar:
> See! as they chant the tragic hymn, the car
> Of the o'ermastered Victor stops—the reins
> Fall from his hands—his idle scimitar
> Starts from its belt—he rends his captive's chains,
> And bids him thank the Bard for Freedom and his strains.   (xvi)

Shelley's Cythna tells the same tale to Laon in *The Revolt of Islam*:

> "Think'st thou that I shall speak unskilfully,
> And none will heed me? I remember now,
> How once, a slave in tortures doomed to die,
> Was saved, because in accents sweet and low
> He sung a song his Judge loved long ago,
> As he was led to death.—All shall relent
> Who hear me—tears as mine have flowed, shall flow,
> Hearts beat as mine now beats, with such intent
> As renovates the world; a will omnipotent!"           (II.xli)

In both instances, the two poets reveal their liberal political sympathies—Byron specifically applying the tale to the enchained and oppressed Venice; and Shelley's Cythna wanting to renovate the world. But Byron, whose frequently expressed desire for man's political liberation was never imaginatively sustained, limited this "beautiful idealism" of poetry as man's liberator by citing Venice's "choral

memory of the Bard divine,/Thy love of Tasso" as that which
"should have cut the knot/Which ties thee [Venice] to thy tyrants"
(IV.xvii), but which in fact did not. The consequent historical despair
even prompted the narrator of *Childe Harold* to prophesy England's
fall to tyrants; the redemption promised by the Attic Muse was a
practical impossibility. On the other hand, Shelley employed the tale
of the redeemed slave as an exemplum for man's future political
freedom. Even though Laon and Cythna's political and social ideals
were not fulfilled, the "thirst for a happier condition of moral and
political society survives" (Preface to *The Revolt*) and the poetical
representation of this hope will, for Shelley, legislate the future of
the world. Once more, the Byronic "Past" and the Shelleyan "To-
come" are opposed, this time in terms of their different conceptions
of poetry's function and power.

III

The literary influences that such fundamentally different poets
provided for each other were indeed of a complex nature: their
personal friendship and knowledge of each other's work determined
that each poet materially affected the "forms" of the other's work;
but more significantly, their philosophical and aesthetic antagonism
caused each poet to challenge dialectically the "spirit" of the other's
poetry. Shelley gave the fullest expression to this dialectic in *Julian
and Maddalo,* which he began in 1818 to distinguish his philosophical
principles from Byron's. But both poets were aware of these different
principles during their first summer together in 1816, and my next
chapter analyzes Byron's partial, and even unwilling, acceptance of
Shelley's metaphysics in *Childe Harold* III and other poems written in
Geneva; and the following two chapters document Byron's rejection of
these same metaphysics in *Manfred* and *Childe Harold* IV. Because
Byron's and Shelley's influences upon each other were reciprocal at all
times, these three chapters also discuss Byron's influence on Shelley's
poetry from 1816 to 1818. However, Byron's major influence on
Shelley occurred between their second meeting in Venice in August
1818 and their third meeting in Ravenna in August 1821; and
Chapters 5 and 6 explain Shelley's answers to Byron in *Julian and
Maddalo* and *Prometheus Unbound*. Chapter 7 develops Byron and
Shelley's self-conscious opposition to each other by contrasting their
different estimates of contemporary poetry, particularly as they relate
to Keats and *Adonais*; and their different dramatic principles, especially
in *The Cenci* and *Marino Faliero*.

After 1821, Byron and Shelley's philosophical antagonism had
somewhat lessened. Byron, whose post-Geneva poetry emphasized the

futility of the human condition and recorded a skeptical distrust of Shelley's meliorism, had not significantly changed, for even the "satiric" Byron was fundamentally the same as the "romantic" Byron: only his more extreme acceptance of the "sad truth" of all things turned "what was once romantic to burlesque" (*Don Juan* IV.3). As Edward Bostetter observed, "what in *Childe Harold* was cause for despair and aimless rebellion becomes in *Don Juan* a cause of laughter and vigorous creative activity."[32] But what for Shelley had been a source of hope—the effectuality of man's Promethean will to attain an earthly paradise, the object of both love and thought—had become an illusion. Shelley in fact rejected his former equations of the trees of knowledge and of life by writing *Epipsychidion, Adonais, Hellas,* and *The Triumph of Life*; and even though he idealistically transferred his hopes for man's fulfillment to a diviner clime and burning fountain transcending this world, he nevertheless depicted man's temporal limitations with a Byronic sense of frustration. This disillusionment is demonstrated in Chapter 8 through an analysis of Shelley's reactions to *The Prophecy of Dante, Don Juan, The Vision of Judgment,* and *Cain,* four works exhibiting both the consistency of Byron's thought and, in part, Shelley's prior influence on them. Finally, Chapter 9 and the Epilogue argue the startling effects that Shelley and Byron's six-year association had on their final poetry, particularly *The Triumph of Life* and *The Island.* Shelley had frequently rejected the "expressions of contempt & desperation" in Byron's poetry, but these same expressions are to be found in *The Triumph of Life*; and Byron just as frequently had complained that Shelley wrote "'Utopias and set himself up as a Reformer,'" but Shelley's Utopian vision is to be found in *The Island.*[33] This reversal of roles does not mean, however, that we should take seriously Byron's judgment that he and Shelley should be remembered as "two *important triflers,* and *eminent madmen.*"[34]

 WITH THE WORLD ALL BEFORE
THEM: BYRON AND SHELLEY IN GENEVA

When Byron and Shelley met for the second time in Venice in 1818, they descanted "Concerning God, freewill, and destiny./Of all that Earth has been, or yet may be;/All that vain men imagine or believe,/Or hope can paint or suffering may achieve" (*Julian and Maddalo,* ll. 42-45); and there is every reason to believe that they discussed similar subjects during their first summer together in 1816. With the exception of one week in July, when Shelley, Mary, and Claire Clairmont toured the Valley of Chamouni while Byron remained at Villa Diodati, the two poets were together daily from 27 May, when they met on the shore of Lake Geneva, until 29 August, when the Shelley party returned to England. The extent of the two poets' friendship is suggested by their tour around Lake Geneva from 22 until 30 June, by the number of their meetings recorded by Mary Shelley and John William Polidori, and by Mary Shelley's statement that "many and long were the conversations between Lord Byron and Shelley."[1] The eagerness with which the two poets engaged their friendship was a result of many circumstances. Shortly before they met, each had suffered from "Large codes of fraud and woe"—for Shelley, the failure of the Chancery suit; for Byron, separation from Lady Byron. And after Byron left England on 25 April, the Shelleys were directed to join him at Geneva by Claire Clairmont, she having conceived Byron's child (Allegra, born January 1817) in March or April of 1816. Because Claire had introduced Mary Shelley to Byron in London, she also may have arranged a meeting between the two poets before Byron left for the continent in April. Whether or not this pre-Geneva meeting ever took place,[2] Byron and Shelley were at least acquainted with each other's poetry before May 1816. By 1810, Shelley had read Byron's 1808 edition of *Poems: Original and Translated,* the volume that followed and differed slightly from the 1807 edition of *Hours of Idleness.* We know that Shelley read this particular volume because two of the six poems in *St. Irvyne; or, The Rosicrucean* (1810) contain lines plagiarized from poems included only in Byron's 1808 edition. By 1816, Shelley had also read *English Bards and Scotch Reviewers,*

*Childe Harold* I-II, *Lara,* and probably *The Giaour, The Bride of Abydos,* and *The Corsair.* Shelley's admiration for Byron's poetry (according to Claire, he was "Byron-mad" in 1815) was to some extent reciprocated by Byron when he read *Queen Mab* in 1813 and *Alastor* in early 1816. According to a note in the Appendix to *The Two Foscari,* Byron had judged *Queen Mab* "as a poem of great power and imagination" when he read it and showed it to William Sotheby in 1813. (For a documentation of Byron and Shelley's reading of each other's poetry at this time, see Appendix A.)

During their three-month residence together, Byron and Shelley undoubtedly compared their previous works: poetically innovative, politically liberal, religiously heterodox, and philosophically skeptical, they did share some common attitudes. As Maddalo/Byron somewhat sarcastically remarked to Julian/Shelley in Venice, " 'I think with you/ In some respects, you know' " (ll. 240-41). Yet the two poets' ideas were far from compatible. And if neither by 1816 had sufficiently systematized his ideas to the extent that Shelley could complain, as he did in *Julian and Maddalo,* that he "(for ever still/Is it not wise to make the best of ill?)/Argued against despondency, but pride/Made my companion take the darker side" (ll. 46-49), each nevertheless could sense his fundamental differences with the other.

These differences between Byron and Shelley may be illustrated by comparing their ostensibly similar liberalism and humanitarianism. Both poets had in the past championed the cause of the politically and socially oppressed, but consider, for example, their different actions in behalf of Irish emancipation in 1812. On 28 February of that year, Shelley addressed the Irish at Fishamble Street Theatre in Dublin, citing British abuses against the Irish and delivering, in part, the points he had made in his pamphlet *An Address, to the Irish People,* which had been distributed a few days before the speech. Byron's defense of the Irish took place seven weeks later, on 21 April 1812, when he addressed the House of Lords in favor of a motion to establish a committee on the Catholic claims against British oppression. As Shelley had done in February, Byron called for Irish freedom and deprecated the Act of Union which had joined Ireland to England in 1801. In the main, Byron's speech catalogued the Irish Catholics' grievances. From the reports of Shelley's speech, it would seem that he also displayed a specific knowledge of Ireland's economic and social problems in order to gain his audience's attention. But in his pamphlet *An Address, to the Irish People,* he "purposely avoided any lengthened discussion on [Irish] grievances"[3] and instead appealed to his reading audience by promulgating his melioristic theories of a perfected society. Admittedly, the place and circumstance of Byron's speech and Shelley's

*Address* were quite different, but a comparison of them reveals the different intellectual methods of the two poets. Byron addressed himself to the past and present injustices suffered by the Irish, and he mocked England's oppressive policies. But Shelley placed the Irish question in a larger context: he expounded his utopian theories of brotherly love, nondefiance, and the necessary supremacy of good, and he prophesied an idyllic future founded on a system of "wisdom and virtue" that would obviate the need for governmental restrictions. Even a cursory reading of Shelley's pamphlet and Byron's speech distinguishes the minds that later created *Prometheus Unbound* and *Don Juan.*

That two dissimilar minds or "spirits" met in Geneva is also apparent through a comparison of their two major works written prior to 1816. In *Childe Harold* I-II and *Queen Mab,* both Byron and Shelley rejected tyrannical governments and sympathized with oppressed peoples who suffered the ravages of fate and time. Yet the form and idea of these poetical expressions were quite different. In the first two cantos of *Childe Harold,* Byron's struggle for a coherent vision of reality led to a "Consciousness awaking to her woes" (I.xcii). For Byron, man was a "child of Doubt and Death" (II.iii)—his double inheritance suffered by the fall from Eden—and he was subject to a malevolent necessity: in Canto I, Vathek's decaying paradise was subject to "Time's ungentle tide" (xxiii) and revealed man's inability to reclaim his former place in Nature. And in Canto II, Greece's "shattered splendour," subject to vanquishing "Time and Fate" (lxxxiv), revealed that man and Nature were inevitably irreconcilable: "Art, Glory, Freedom fail, but Nature still is fair" (lxxxvii). On the other hand, Shelley's similar laments for the corruption of past and present were relieved by a faith that Necessity, as manifested in the "fixed and virtuous will,/The sacred sympathies of soul and sense" (IX.35-36), would prepare for the fall of time and the fulfillment of man in a natural paradise with a "loveliness/Surpassing fabled Eden" (IV.88-89). Mab's dream vision enabled Ianthe to transcend the empirical and Byronic limitations of past and present and to apprehend imaginatively man's glorious future, when "man, with changeless nature coalescing,/Will undertake regeneration's work" (VI.42-43).

Childe Harold's and Ianthe's journeys thus had quite distinct results: Byron, dealing in more descriptive and less polemic materials, chose to record the evidences of man's internal and external conflicts; Shelley, inculcating a moral philosophy into a visionary art form, predicted man's psychological and social integration. The given "fact" of Ianthe's imaginative vision revealed her psychological integrity, and with a "resolute mind" and "passion lofty, pure and unsubdued"

(IX.200, 202), she prefigured the new earth where "Reason and passion [would] cease to combat" (VIII.231). But for Byron in *Childe Harold* there existed no Shelleyan Ianthe to prompt a vision of "that high being, of cloudless brain,/Untainted passion, elevated will" (*Queen Mab* V.154-55). Instead, Byron saw man's fate in the "broken arch" and "ruined wall" of the skull: "The Dome of Thought . . ./And Passion's host, that never brooked control" (*Childe Harold* II.vi). Not until the seventh edition of *Childe Harold* in 1814, by which time Byron had read *Queen Mab*, does an "Ianthe" enter his poem (in the dedicatory stanzas). Even though this Ianthe was idealized like Shelley's, Byron quite clearly separated this vision of "Love's image" from the tone of *Childe Harold*:

> Not in those climes where I have late been straying,
>> Though Beauty long hath there been matchless deemed,
>> Not in those visions to the heart displaying
>> Forms which it sighs but to have only dreamed,
>> Hath aught like thee in Truth or Fancy seemed.[4]

Since neither Shelley nor Byron had forgone his fundamental hopes and fears for man as outlined above, their conversations in Geneva must have involved similarly antagonistic positions. And Queen Mab, who prophetically withdrew life's dark veil for Ianthe, might here be summoned to spread a figured curtain in order to characterize the probable nature of some of these conversations:

> *Man is of soul and body, formed for deeds*
> *Of high resolve,* on fancy's boldest wing
> To soar unwearied, fearlessly to turn
> The keenest pangs to peacefulness, and taste
> The joys which mingled sense and spirit yield.
> *Or he is formed for abjectness and woe,*
> To grovel on the dunghill of his fears,
> To shrink at every sound, to quench the flame
> Of natural love in sensualism, to know
> That hour as blest when on his worthless days
> The frozen hand of death shall set its seal,
> Yet fear the cure, though hating the disease.
> *The one is man that shall hereafter be;*
> *The other, man as vice has made him now.*
>> (IV.154-67, my italics)

II

Mab's separation of the Shelleyan time future from the Byronic time past and present provides the extremes by which to judge Byron and Shelley's reciprocal influences from 1816 until 1822. Of the two poets, Byron was the more noticeably affected by their first meeting in 1816, as Edward Williams later attested in a letter to Edward Trelawny: "I must tell you that the idea of the tragedy of 'Manfred,' and many of the philosophical, or rather metaphysical, notions interwoven in the composition of the fourth Canto [error for the third canto] of 'Childe Harold,' are of his [Shelley's] suggestion; but this, of course, is between ourselves."[5] Yet Byron himself was at least obliquely aware of this "metaphysical" influence, for he confessed to Thomas Moore, in January 1817, that his newly finished canto of *Childe Harold* was

> a fine indistinct piece of poetical desolation, and my favourite. I was half mad during the time of its composition, between metaphysics, mountains, lakes, love unextinguishable, thoughts unutterable, and the nightmare of my own delinquencies.[6]

The "metaphysics" and the "love unextinguishable" are quite apparent in *Childe Harold* III and they result, at least in part, from Byron's discussions with Shelley in Geneva. Some of these discussions, Byron acknowledged, were about Wordsworth: " 'Shelley, when I was in Switzerland, used to dose me with Wordsworth physic even to nausea; and I do remember then reading some things of his with pleasure.' "[7] That pleasure caused Byron in *Childe Harold* III to profess, at least temporarily, a Wordsworthian sympathy with Nature and in so doing to reveal what Jerome McGann regards as "the profound influence that Shelley had upon Byron's mind during their stay in Switzerland."[8] With the aid of McGann's careful dating of the MSS of *Childe Harold,* it is now possible to determine more accurately the extent of this influence after Byron met Shelley on 27 May.

Before his meeting with Shelley, Byron disliked poetry dictated by a transcendental vision of Nature, and even as late as October 1815 he believed Wordsworth to be unintelligible.[9] There were numerous occasions before 1816 when Byron described the beauties of Nature, but he had never apprehended a benevolent life force or Wordsworthian "presence" in the phenomenal world. In 1806, he had written *The Prayer of Nature,* but its imitatively deistical tone precluded any personal engagement with an immanent "presence." And in the first canto of *Childe Harold,* Byron disparaged, in the person of the Childe, the solitary "Meditation" prompted by the peaceful aspects of Nature (see stanzas xxvii-xxviii). A similar "Meditation" in the second canto (xxiii) occasioned, however, a more reflective desire to commingle with Nature:

To sit on rocks—to muse o'er flood and fell—
   To slowly trace the forest's shady scene,
   Where things that own not Man's dominion dwell,
   And mortal foot hath ne'er or rarely been;
   To climb the trackless mountain all unseen,
   With the wild flock that never needs a fold;
   Alone o'er steeps and foaming falls to lean;
   This is not Solitude—'tis but to hold
Converse with Nature's charms, and view her stores unrolled.

                                   (II.xxv)

Yet this meditative feeling, which recalls the mode of eighteenth-century descriptive poetry, was soon rendered functionless to Byron by the encroaching "world he had almost forgot" (xxvii).

    That Byron had not altered his judgment on the impossibility or at least ineffectuality of a Wordsworthian "fittedness" between man and Nature is evident from the first sixty-two stanzas of *Childe Harold* III, a record of Byron's wanderings through the fields of Waterloo and up the Rhine in May 1816 before he met Shelley. Byron's former reading of " 'How exquisitely . . ./The external World is fitted to the Mind' " and of how the " 'Chaldean Shepherds . . ./Looked on the polar star' " in Wordsworth's *Excursion* ("Prospectus," ll. 63-68; IV.694-717) probably inspired the following two stanzas, but Byron could not yet give Harold the confident hopes that Wordsworth and his imitators (including Shelley) possessed:

Where rose the mountains, there to him were friends;
   Where rolled the ocean, thereon was his home;
   Where a blue sky, and glowing clime, extends,
   He had the passion and the power to roam;
   The desert, forest, cavern, breaker's foam,
   Were unto him companionship; they spake
   A mutual language, clearer than the tome
   Of his land's tongue, which he would oft forsake
For Nature's pages glassed by sunbeams on the lake.

Like the Chaldean, he could watch the stars,
   Till he had peopled them with beings bright
   As their own beams; and earth, and earth-born jars,
   And human frailties, were forgotten quite:
   *Could he have kept his spirit to that flight*
   *He had been happy; but this clay will sink*
   *Its spark immortal,* envying it the light

*19*

> To which it mounts, as if to break the link
> That keeps us from yon heaven which woos us to its brink.
>
> (III.xiii-xiv, my italics)

In the first stanza above, Byron did little more than rephrase the "To sit on rocks" meditative stanza (xxv) from Canto II; there was no divine "presence" to be apprehended by the mind or embraced by the heart. And in the second stanza, Byron acknowledged the futility of a Wordsworthian "physic" or "metaphysic," for Harold could *not* keep "his spirit to that flight." All men's aspirations, Byron seems to be saying, are limited by the human condition: "but this clay will sink / Its spark immortal." Even if "Maternal Nature" (xlvi) offered promise, the "ripened rose" would eventually wither if man plucked it and "The star which rises o'er [the] steep" could never be attained (xi). This irreconcilability of man and Nature Byron made quite explicit in stanza lxii, written shortly before 27 May:

> Above me are the Alps,
> The Palaces of Nature, whose vast walls
> Have pinnacled in clouds their snowy scalps,
> And throned Eternity in icy halls
> Of cold Sublimity, where forms and falls
> The Avalanche—the thunderbolt of snow!
> All that expands the spirit, yet appals,
> Gather around these summits, as to show
> *How Earth may pierce to Heaven, yet leave vain man below.*
>
> (my italics)

This judgment on man's inevitable frustration, which Shelley would counter in *Mont Blanc,* was to be modified immediately after Byron met Shelley on 27 May.

In stanzas lxviii-lxxi of *Childe Harold* III (beginning with "Lake Leman woos me with its crystal face"), Byron "on or shortly after May 26-27"[10] once more began a "Meditation" on the benefit of solitude within Nature as opposed to "mingling with the herd" and the "crushing crowd." Similar meditations in *Childe Harold* had never been productive, but "within a day or two" after he met Shelley on 27 May, Byron professed a new Wordsworthian "fittedness" to Nature:

> I live not in myself, but I become
> Portion of that around me; and to me
> High mountains are a feeling, but the hum
> Of human cities torture: I can see
> Nothing to loathe in Nature, save to be

> A link reluctant in a fleshly chain,
> Classed among creatures, when the soul can flee,
> And with the sky—the peak—the heaving plain
> Of Ocean, or the stars, mingle—and not in vain. (lxxii)

Shelley's "doses" of Wordsworth had an immediate effect, for Byron, "not in vain," could now keep "his spirit to that flight" and achieve a metaphysical insight that was not before possible. Byron's next stanza makes his transformation even more apparent:

> And thus I am absorbed, and this is life:—
> I look upon the peopled desert past,
> As on a place of agony and strife,
> Where, for some sin, to Sorrow I was cast,
> To act and suffer, but remount at last
> With a fresh pinion; which I feel to spring,
> Though young, yet waxing vigorous as the Blast
> Which it would cope with, on delighted wing,
> Spurning the clay-cold bonds which round our being cling.
> (lxxiii)

A few weeks earlier, Harold could not keep "his spirit to that flight" and the narrator was left a "vain man" below the Alpine summits. Here however, Byron, as narrator, had a new experience: remounting "at last/With [the] fresh pinion" provided by Wordsworthian metaphysics, he had attained the imaginative means to transcend the empirically limiting "clay-cold bonds."

Byron continued to maintain this Wordsworthian perspective and like the Poet in *Alastor,* which Byron had read before he left England, he attempted to attain the Poet's "mystic sympathy/With nature's ebb and flow" (ll. 652-53):

> And when, at length, the mind shall be all free
> From what it hates in this degraded form,
> Reft of its carnal life, save what shall be
> Existent happier in the fly and worm,—
> When Elements to Elements conform,
> And dust is as it should be, shall I not
> Feel all I see less dazzling but more warm?
> The bodiless thought? the Spirit of each spot?
> Of which, even now, I share at times the immortal lot?
>
> Are not the mountains, waves, and skies, a part
> Of me and of my Soul, as I of them?
> Is not the love of these deep in my heart
> With a pure passion? should I not contemn

All objects, if compared with these? and stem
A tide of suffering, rather than forego
Such feelings for the hard and worldly phlegm
Of those whose eyes are only turned below,
Gazing upon the ground, with thoughts which dare not glow?

(III.lxxiv-lxxv)

Note, however, that Byron's rhetorically limiting questions here exhibit
what Shelley feared in *Alastor*: that the mind might never apprehend
the ultimately unknowable power or beauty or spirit of the universe.
Yet Shelley, in *Hymn to Intellectual Beauty,* could still approach
Nature for its shadowing embodiment of that "unknown and awful"
spirit of Beauty. On the other hand, Byron's "conversion" to this
metaphysic was as yet incomplete: he had inverted the Wordsworthian
and to some extent Shelleyan formula that love of Nature led to love
of man (Byron had approached Nature in order to "fly from . . .
mankind" [lxix]); and he quickly sought to "return/To that which is
immediate" (lxxvi).

But this immediacy (a portrait of Rousseau), which reminded
Byron of man's self-destructiveness, could not satisfy his new aspirations, and he once more appeared in Wordsworthian garb. Contrasting
"Clear, placid Leman" to the "wild world" of man (lxxxv) and at first
uncertain if "Our destinies [could] o'erleap their mortal state"
(lxxxviii), Byron began a metaphysical ascent that surpassed the first
evidences of Shelley's influences on him:

All Heaven and Earth are still—though not in sleep,
But breathless, as we grow when feeling most;
And silent, as we stand in thoughts too deep:—
All Heaven and Earth are still: From the high host
Of stars, to the lulled lake and mountain-coast,
All is concentered in a life intense,
Where not a beam, nor air, nor leaf is lost,
But hath a part of Being, and a sense
Of that which is of all Creator and Defence.

Then stirs the feeling infinite, so felt
In solitude, where we are *least* alone;
A truth, which through our being then doth melt,
And purifies from self: it is a tone,
The soul and source of Music, which makes known
Eternal harmony, and sheds a charm
Like to the fabled Cytherea's zone,

> Binding all things with beauty;—'twould disarm
> The spectre Death, had he substantial power to harm.
>
> (III.lxxxix-xc)

Written after one or perhaps two weeks of Byron's residence with Shelley, by which time the Geneva circle according to Polidori "talked, till the ladies' brains whizzed with giddiness, about idealism,"[11] these two stanzas rhetorically affirm the transcendental experience that Byron had hesitantly questioned in stanzas lxxiv-lxxv (ca. 27 May); consequently, they offer evidence of Shelley's increasing influence upon *Childe Harold* III. Although Wordsworth's poetry probably inspired these lines, it is possible that Shelley's similar poetical sentiments influenced Byron here; thus Byron's expression of the unity of Being in the first stanza above might have been occasioned by such lines as the following from *Queen Mab,* which Byron had read in 1813 and which he probably reread in Geneva:[12]

> Spirit of Nature! here!
> In this interminable wilderness
> Of worlds, at whose immensity
> Even soaring fancy staggers,
> Here is thy fitting temple.
> Yet not the lightest leaf
> That quivers to the passing breeze
> Is less instinct with thee:
> Yet not the meanest worm
> That lurks in graves and fattens on the dead
> Less shares thy eternal breath.
> Spirit of Nature! thou!
> Imperishable as this scene,
> Here is thy fitting temple. (I.264-77)

This newly acquired "feeling infinite" caused Byron to affirm that *"Not vainly* did the early Persian make/His altar the high places, and the peak/Of earth-o'ergazing mountains . . ./. . . to seek/The Spirit" (xci, my italics). Contrasting Byron's earlier lament that the "Palaces of Nature" left "vain man below" (lxii), these lines foreshadow Byron's concluding desire to "quit Man's works, again to read/His Maker's":

> The clouds above me to the white Alps tend,
> And I must pierce them, and survey whate'er
> May be permitted, as my steps I bend
> To their most great and growing region, where
> The earth to her embrace compels the powers of air. (III.cix)

This metaphysical imperative, the antepenultimate stanza in Byron's original hundred-stanza MS of *Childe Harold* III (finished by 12 June and lacking the storm [xcii-xcvii] and Clarens [xcix-civ] sequences), reveals Byron's dedication to a Wordsworthian quest for meaning in Nature. However, the remaining two stanzas in Byron's original peroration give little hope that this imperative will be fulfilled:

> Thus far have I proceeded in a theme
>     Renewed with no kind auspices:—to feel
>     We are not what we have been, and to deem
>     We are not what we should be,—and to steel
>     The heart against itself.                    (cxi; originally c)

But among Byron's additions to his poem after 12 June is a stanza in which he affirmed his faith in man's imaginative fulfillment:

>                 I do believe,
>     Though I have found them not, that there may be
>     Words which are things,—hopes which will not deceive,
>     And Virtues which are merciful . . . . . . . . .
>     That Goodness is no name—and Happiness no dream.     (cxiv)

The intensity of this rediscovered "faith" in *Childe Harold* III had its correlative and perhaps its origin in an unusually violent thunderstorm witnessed by Byron on the night of 12 June. That very evening and the next morning while the storm raged and then passed,[13] Byron recorded his hope to become one with the night and the tempest (xciii), but also his fear that the "far roll/Of [the storm's] departing voices" (xcvi) presaged the diminishing intensity of the metaphysical insight he consciously desired; in other words, he did not welcome a "return/To that which is immediate." Instead, he asked for the psychological integration of "Soul—heart—mind—passions—feelings" to give form to his experience, that is to "embody and unbosom now/ That which is most within me . . ./. . . into *one* word,/And that one word were Lightning" (xcvii); but he failed. Nevertheless, the return of morning promised future "food for *meditation*" by which the "march of our existence" might be directed (xcviii, my italics).

Byron discovered that direction or meditation within two weeks following the evening of the storm sequence. Writing to Hobhouse on 23 June that he had finished one hundred and eleven stanzas of the new canto of *Childe Harold,* Byron was then with Shelley, touring Lake Geneva. Within the next four days, Byron wrote the six famous Clarens stanzas[14] in which he addressed the scene of Rousseau's *Julie; ou, La Nouvelle Héloise* (which both poets read during their tour) and apprehended the ideal of Love manifest within the beauty of Nature. What

24

Byron called "Love," Shelley (whose *Hymn to Intellectual Beauty* "was conceived during his voyage round the lake with Lord Byron"[15]) called the "Spirit of BEAUTY." Due credit must be given to Rousseau's influence on these complementary expressions by Byron and Shelley, but I can't but see Shelley's forming hand on Byron's newly acquired faith in the existence of Love as a metaphysical power. Shelley had been developing his theories of the regenerative power of Love since *Queen Mab*, and the "awful LOVELINESS" of Intellectual Beauty inspired him, while with Byron, to "love all human kind" (ll. 71, 84). Shelley's intense faith in the power of Love (later judged to be "the sole law which should govern the moral world" in the Preface to *The Revolt of Islam* and also embodied in the person of Asia in *Prometheus Unbound*) unquestionably influenced Byron's note to these Clarens stanzas:

> But this is not all; the feeling with which all around Clarens, and the opposite rocks of Meillerie, is invested, is of a still higher and more comprehensive order than the mere sympathy with individual passion; it is a sense of the existence of love in its most extended and sublime capacity, and of our own participation of its good and of its glory: it is the great principle of the universe, which is there more condensed, but not less manifested; and of which, though knowing ourselves a part, we lose our individuality, and mingle in the beauty of the whole.

If indeed this note was not written by Shelley,[16] it certainly reveals the cumulative effect of Byron's daily discussions with the younger and more confidently idealistic poet.

Notwithstanding the metaphysical ascent by which Byron, in June 1816, could "lose [his] individuality, and mingle in the beauty of the whole," in little more than three months he reexperienced the frustrations of the pre-Shelleyan Childe; that is, he could admire the beauty of Nature but could not believe in Nature's restorative effect:

> I am a lover of Nature and an admirer of Beauty. I can bear fatigue and welcome privation, and have seen some of the noblest views in the world. But in all this—the recollections of bitterness, and more especially of recent and more home desolation, which must accompany me through life, have preyed upon me here; and neither the music of the Shepherd, the crashing of the Avalanche, nor the torrent, the mountain, the Glacier, the Forest, nor the Cloud, have for one moment lightened the weight upon my heart, nor enabled me to lose my own wretched identity in the majesty, and the power, and the Glory, around, above, and beneath me.[17]

*25*

These observations, which conclude Byron's journal to Augusta and were written on 29 September during his tour with Hobhouse, do not impugn Byron's sincerity in *Childe Harold* III. Rather, written one month after Shelley left Switzerland carrying Byron's Geneva poems to John Murray, they suggest that Byron's metaphysical union with the forces of Nature in his third canto were due to Shelley's daily influences from June through August.

The extent of Shelley's influence in Geneva is also apparent in Byron's minor poetry written during that summer of 1816. Byron, who could then judge Wordsworth a "great poet . . . of whom there can exist few greater admirers than myself,"[18] continued to imitate Wordsworth in such poems as *Monody on the Death of Sheridan,* which opens with another instance of man's "fittedness" to Nature:

> While Nature makes that melancholy pause—
> Her breathing moment on the bridge where Time
> Of light and darkness forms an arch sublime—
> Who hath not shared that calm, so still and deep,
> The voiceless thought which would not speak but weep,
> A holy concord, and a bright regret,
> A glorious sympathy with suns that set? (ll. 6-12)

Byron's developing "sympathy" with Nature is also apparent through a comparison of his three poems to Augusta Leigh, praised for her constancy during Byron's separation and self-exile. In the first *Stanzas to Augusta* ("When all around grew drear and dark"), probably the last poem Byron wrote before leaving England, she is portrayed in terms of the conventional metaphors of "star" and "lovely tree." In the second *Stanzas to Augusta* ("Though the day of my Destiny's over"), written on 24 July while Byron was at Diodati and Shelley toured the Valley of Chamouni, she is linked to the "fountain," "tree," and "bird" after Byron had explained that "Nature around me is smiling" (l. 9). In the final *Epistle to Augusta,* not published in 1816 out of Byron's deference to his half sister,[19] the former conventional metaphors for Augusta are replaced by a new reverence for Nature itself: "the Alpine landscapes" provided Byron a "fund for contemplation" and he could "worship Nature with a thought profound" (viii, xv). Believing that he was at a critical point in his development, Byron simultaneously echoed the conclusion to *Paradise Lost* ("The World was all before them" [XII.646][20]) and asked to be redeemed by Wordsworth's Nature:

> The world is all before me; I but ask
> Of Nature that with which she will comply—

> It is but in her Summer's sun to bask,
> To mingle with the quiet of her sky,
> To see her gentle face without a mask,
> And never gaze on it with apathy. (xi)

Like Wordsworth, who reversed the meaning of Milton's lines when he
enthusiastically wrote that "The earth is all before me" (*The Prelude*
I.14), Byron hoped that the earthly paradise was not altogether lost.
Yet Byron's allusion to Milton works both ways: if Nature did not
"comply" with his request in the *Epistle to Augusta,* then he would
never escape the inheritance of Adam and Eve.

With "The world . . . all before" him in Geneva, Byron was
momentarily suspended between hope for fulfillment and despair from
frustration, and the *Epistle to Augusta* helps to explain the contradictions between his poems written during the summer of 1816.[21]
Even after being influenced by Wordsworthian Nature and Shelleyan
Love, Byron occasionally reverted to a darker vision of the human
condition. However, Wordsworth's and Shelley's metaphysical struggles
for universals had at least taught Byron the need to "idealize and
unify" his experiences with a more cosmic vision. That is, the microcosmic darkness which always reappeared in Byron's poetry was to be
dressed in macrocosmic forms. If Byron adopted in part Shelley's
"spirit" of metaphysical idealism in *Childe Harold* III and other poems,
he also renounced that same "spirit" in poetry influenced by the
Shelleyan poetic "forms" of dream and myth. This Byronic "spirit"
contained in the Shelleyan "form" is most apparent in *Manfred,* "a
very wild, metaphysical, and inexplicable" drama begun during the
"summer in Switzerland,"[22] but *The Dream, Darkness, The Prisoner of
Chillon,* and *Prometheus* (all written in June and July 1816) also
demonstrate Byron's exchange of the empirically "immediate" for a
visionary structure in which " 'beings more intense' act out more
intensely than in 'real life' the misery and lostness of man, the eternal
death of love, and the repetitive ruination of paradise."[23]

Before meeting Shelley, Byron in *Childe Harold* III had explained
the function of his narrative art:

> 'Tis to create, and in creating live
>   A being more intense that we endow
>   With form our fancy, gaining as we give
>   The life we image, even as I do now— (vi)

This intensity, Byron suggests, was the poet's to experience: his reality,
hopes, and fears were put into a new and more pleasurable form.
But after meeting Shelley and reacquainting himself with *Queen Mab*

and *Alastor,* Byron began to write less immediately personal poetry. In *The Dream,* for example, Byron was not intensifying his experiences with Mary Chaworth solely by writing a poem. Instead, he judged that a dream intensified experience in the same manner that a poem did,

> What are [dreams]?
> Creations of the mind?—The mind can make
> Substance, and people planets of its own
> With beings brighter than have been, and give
> A breath to forms which can outlive all flesh;　　　(ll. 18-22)

and he sought a double intensification by writing a poem about a dream of his experiences with Mary Chaworth. By twice removing himself from the memory of his experiences, Byron was not necessarily falsifying them or making them any less personal. But by such a distancing (through the dream and then the poem about the dream), he was necessarily giving his experiences a universal and symbolic significance.

In *Queen Mab,* the opening lines of which have a "curieuse ressemblance"[24] to those in *The Dream,* Ianthe's waking dream gave her access to both the past and the future. Byron in *The Dream* argues the same point:

> [Dreams] leave a weight upon our waking thoughts,
> They take a weight from off our waking toils,
> They do divide our being; they become
> A portion of ourselves as of our time,
> And look like heralds of Eternity;
> They pass like spirits of the past,—they speak
> Like Sibyls of the future; they have power—
> The tyranny of pleasure and of pain;
> They make us what we were not—what they will,
> And shake us with the vision that's gone by.　　　(ll. 7-16)

Despite the Shelleyan separation of the dream into the frustrating past and the fulfilling future, Byron in this poem concerns himself mainly with the past. He might idealize his present experiences in Geneva into a passage that resembles lines 20-29 of Shelley's *Alastor,*

> 　　　　　　　he lived
> Through that which had been death to many men,
> And made him friends of mountains: with the stars
> And the quick Spirit of the Universe
> He held his dialogues; and they did teach
> To him the magic of their mysteries;

> To him the book of Night was opened wide,
> And voices from the deep abyss revealed
> A marvel and a secret—Be it so,     (*The Dream*, ll. 193-201)

but these Shelleyan "forms" merely provided a vehicle for universalizing
Byron's distinct vision of a fallen world: the "two beings in the hues of
youth" are rudely transported to a final "reality—the one/To end in
madness—both in misery" (ll. 27, 205-6). And when Byron took up
the question of the future at the same time in *Darkness* (July 1816),
his "dream, which was not all a dream" (l. 1) offered another rebuttal
to Shelley's hopes: Ianthe's prophetically inspiring "Light, life and
rapture" (*Queen Mab* IX.211) were reversed by the cosmic despair of
frenzy, death and Darkness—"She was the Universe" (l. 82).[25]

This universal darkness which Byron envisioned in July had its
psychological or microcosmic equivalent in *The Prisoner of Chillon*,
written in June when Byron and Shelley visited the Castle of Chillon.
Jerome McGann and Robert Gleckner have recently corrected the
traditional misconceptions surrounding this poem: not thematically
integral with the *Sonnet on Chillon* ("composed after the narrative and
under very different circumstances"), *The Prisoner of Chillon*,
according to McGann, does *not* celebrate "man's ability to preserve
his spiritual freedom despite the worst privations," but rather "drama-
tizes the theme of the crippled life"; similarly, for Gleckner, the poem
is *not* "a tribute to the unconquerable nature of the human mind" but
a "chronicle of the slow decay of the human mind in the dungeon of
its being."[26] The correlative to this restricting clay in this poem is the
dungeon in which Bonnivard delivers his monologue after the death of
his brothers. When "the carol of a bird" restores Bonnivard's ability
"to feel and think" (ll. 252, 278), we expect that he will experience a
Wordsworthian restoration. But Nature charms him to no avail: he
sometimes deems the bird to be his "brother's soul," believes "the
whole earth would henceforth be/A wider prison," compares through
the window the perspective of a "small green isle" to his "dungeon
floor," and is "troubled" by the joys of Nature which can no longer
restore him whether he be "Fettered or fetterless" (ll. 288, 322-23,
344-45, 357, 373). He eventually "Regained [his] freedom with a
sigh" (l. 392), a dismal end which confirmed the reality of his earlier
"scarce conscious" dream:

> For all was blank, and bleak, and grey;
> It was not night—it was not day;
> It was not even the dungeon-light,
> So hateful to my heavy sight,
> But vacancy absorbing space,

And fixedness—without a place;
There were no stars—no earth—no time—
No check—no change—no good—no crime—
But silence, and a stirless breath
Which neither was of life nor death;
A sea of stagnant idleness,
Blind, boundless, mute, and motionless!          (ll. 239-50)

These "dreams" of a physical fall from Edenic love in *The Dream*
and of the cosmic and psychological fall from light and life in *Darkness*
and *The Prisoner of Chillon* qualify the metaphysical ascents in *Childe
Harold* III and thus demonstrate that Byron in Geneva was testing
rather than affirming the Wordsworthian and Shelleyan ideals with
which he had been dosed. After leaving Shelley and Geneva behind, he
would discard his tentative faith in a benevolent Nature and a
metaphysical Love, and judge that such ideals could not survive the
inevitable breaking of the heart into a "shattered guise . . . still,
and cold,/And bloodless" (*Childe Harold* III.xxxiii, significantly Byron's
last addition to this third canto). Nevertheless, Byron in Geneva had
strengthened his conviction that man's mind provided the only refuge
in a fallen world, a conviction that finds its fullest expression in his
next major poems: though "chained and tortured," man's reason was
a "Faculty divine," the "last and only place/Of refuge" (*Childe
Harold* IV.cxxvii); though "cooped in clay," man's mind contained the
"Promethean spark" (*Manfred* I.i.157, 154). By means of this powerfully self-sustained mind, Manfred and the narrator of *Childe Harold*
IV would deny the validity of Wordsworthian and Shelleyan
metaphysics; and the substance of this denial may be found in Byron's
*Prometheus* (written in July at Diodati), a poem ironically influenced
by Shelley.

Shelley's indirect influence on Byron's *Prometheus* is, I believe,
indisputable, particularly since Byron acknowledged this influence to
Thomas Medwin: " 'Shelley, when I was in Switzerland, translated the
"Prometheus" to me before I wrote my ode.' "[27] Although Medwin
was partial to Shelley, there is no reason to doubt the authenticity of
this statement. According to Mary's reading list, Shelley did read
Aeschylus' *Prometheus Bound* in 1816 (probably in Geneva before
Mary conceived *Frankenstein*: "The Modern Prometheus"), and he had
used the Promethean myth to justify his vegetable diet in 1812.[28]
Granted, Byron had read Aeschylus' drama while at Harrow, had
included a sixteen-line translation of it in his *Fugitive Pieces,* and
had likened Napoleon to Prometheus in his *Ode to Napoleon Buona-
parte* (1814). But Shelley's translation of *Prometheus Bound* for Byron

probably renewed his interest in the myth in 1816.[29] Byron, however, interpreted the myth in a manner contrary to Shelley's later *Prometheus Unbound.* Unlike Shelley's hero, Byron's Prometheus symbolizes man's inability to perfect himself in a fallen world. Although man, through Prometheus' gift of mind, could defy the limitations occasioned by the loss of Eden, he still inherited a "funereal destiny," a "wretchedness," and a "sad unallied existence" (ll. 50-52). With neither Demogorgon nor Asia to effect the "hour" of his liberation, Byron's Prometheus could only continue to resist "the inexorable Heaven,/And the deaf tyranny of Fate" (ll. 18-19). Thus Byron's *Prometheus* adumbrates not *Prometheus Unbound,* where Shelley's hero through love is reunited with Asia, but rather *Manfred,* Byron's dramatic embodiment of Promethean defiance and isolation. And by 1818, *Prometheus* and *Manfred* provided Shelley sufficient cause to argue against Byron's fatalism by writing a drama in which Prometheus would be unbound.

Like most of Shelley's influences on Byron during the summer of 1816, his translation of *Prometheus Bound* had complex effects, for Byron's renewed interest in Prometheus undoubtedly determined the "spirit" of his *Sonnet on Chillon,* where Liberty is addressed as the "Eternal Spirit of the chainless Mind" and the unfettered heart. Like Prometheus, Bonnivard was physically bound, but Byron asserted that the spirit of Liberty was "Brightest in dungeons" and gave man hope of his eventual redemption from tyranny. Such a melioristic vision (compare Shelley's 1820 *Ode to Liberty*) is impossible to reconcile with the fatalism of *Prometheus* and *The Prisoner of Chillon,* and the *Sonnet on Chillon* once more reveals the contradictions in Byron's Geneva poetry. If Byron could willy-nilly adopt and reject a Shelleyan faith in redemptive "powers," then perhaps Shelley was not too far from the truth when in July he wrote that Byron was "as mad as the winds." This half-hearted jest to Peacock was to be more earnestly repeated, again to Peacock, after Shelley recognized that the fatalism of *Prometheus, The Prisoner of Chillon, Darkness,* and *The Dream* led to *Childe Harold* IV, which offered "the most wicked & mischievous insanity that ever was given forth."[30]

### III

In her recollections about Geneva, Mary Shelley observed that "perhaps during this summer [Shelley's] genius was checked by association with another poet whose nature was utterly dissimilar to his own, yet who, in the poem [*Childe Harold* III] he wrote at that time, gave tokens that he shared for a period the more abstract and etherialised inspiration of Shelley."[31] Shelley in 1816 did experience feelings of inadequacy in the shadow of Byron and by the winter of

1821/22 he despairingly envied Byron's talents, but I do not believe that his "genius was checked" by his association with the more famous poet. Rather, he appears in 1816 to have used both his time and his "genius" to sustain Byron's faith in the powers of Nature and of Love. To this extent, we can trace the effect of Shelley's association with Byron in *Hymn to Intellectual Beauty* (written during his journey around Lake Geneva with Byron) and *Mont Blanc* (written in the Valley of Chamouni during his tour with Mary and Claire Clairmont).

When Shelley arrived in Geneva in 1816, he was still developing his theories of the imagination, the synthetical action of which would later be figured in the reunification of Prometheus (head) and Asia (heart) in *Prometheus Unbound*. As Shelley noted in a letter to Leigh Hunt in November 1819, the head and the heart, man's understanding and passions, served "the Imagination, who is the master of them both, their God, and the Spirit by which they live and are."[32] In *Queen Mab,* Shelley had anticipated this union, albeit without naming the unifying imagination, when Mab announced that the new man (the unbound Prometheus of 1818) would by the force of Necessity achieve an integrity whereby "Reason and passion [would] cease to combat" (VIII.231). By 1815, when Shelley wrote *Alastor,* the imagination had taken its rightful position not only as the creative faculty but also as a distinct epistemological power "between" the head and the heart. In the terms of Shelley's Preface to *Alastor,* the Poet *"images* to himself the Being whom he loves" by uniting the requisitions of the "intellectual faculties, the *imagination,* the functions of sense" (my italics). Shelley perhaps did not consciously choose to develop a Coleridgean faculty psychology, but by 1815 he considered the imagination as an intuitive power that synthetically embodied "both the warmth of love and the light of reason."[33]

Shelley's faith in the imagination as the power by which man could achieve a psychological unity and thus effect a personal and then social regeneration was, however, far from dogmatic. Having replaced the "blindly-working will" of stern Necessity in *Queen Mab* with a more humanistic reliance on self and imagination in *Alastor,* Shelley doubted his newly found imaginative freedom and objectified these doubts in the Poet of *Alastor.* Yet the frustration and untimely death attending the Poet's search for his idealized mate (what has been called the "epipsyche") did not destroy Shelley's faith in imaginative fulfillment, for in the induction to the poem Shelley cleverly disassociated himself from the Poet-hero and consequently implied that a metaphysical idealism might still be effectual. And Shelley confidently reasserted this faith during the summer of 1816 when he wrote *Hymn to Intellectual Beauty* and *Mont Blanc,* two poems that celebrate man's imaginative ability to transcend empirical phenomena and intuit the existence of an unknown or secret "Power." As many critics have observed, Shelley's response to this Power is determined by the "heart" in *Intellectual Beauty* and by the "head" in *Mont Blanc.* However, this division of purpose somewhat obscures Shelley's intention, for in the first poem the bifocal "Intellectual" Beauty "dost shine upon" and provide "nourishment" to "human thought" (ll. 14, 44) as well as human emotion, and in *Mont Blanc* the "secret Strength of things/Which governs thought" also makes the imaginative man "deeply feel" (ll. 139-40, 83). As Shelley remarked in his *Speculations on Metaphysics* and his *Speculations on Morals,* man "is not a moral, and an intellectual,—but also, and pre-eminently, an imaginative being" and this imagination in its most "comprehensive circumference" is attended by "wisdom and virtue [which] may be said to be inseparable, and criteria of each other."[34] Consequently when Shelley concludes *Mont Blanc* by asserting the capability of the "human mind's *imaginings,*" he celebrates the "wise, and great, and good" man whose imaginative faith in an eternal "Power" provides the strongest motive for ethical action: to "love all human kind" (*Intellectual Beauty,* l. 84) and to "repeal/Large codes of fraud and woe" (*Mont Blanc,* ll. 80-82).

Of these two poems celebrating what Coleridge called the "beautiful and beauty-making power," *Mont Blanc* (written in July when Shelley was absent from Byron) rather than *Intellectual Beauty* (conceived in June and probably written in Byron's presence) reveals to a greater degree the effects of Shelley's association with the elder poet. Having read and praised *Childe Harold* III in MS by 18 July, shortly before he toured the Valley of Chamouni, and having referred to Byron's "Palaces of Nature" (*Childe Harold* III.lxii) at the moment he arrived at Chamouni and viewed Mont Blanc on 22 July,[35] Shelley in *Mont Blanc* (dated 23 July in MS) evidently decided to continue the metaphysical ascent promised by Byron at the end of *Childe Harold* III:

> The clouds above me to the white Alps tend,
> And I must pierce them, and survey whate'er
> May be permitted, as my steps I bend
> To their most great and growing region, where
> The earth to her embrace compels the powers of air.  (cix)

Within the dialectic in *Childe Harold,* Byron had feared that these clouds would "leave vain man below" the Eternity "throned" in the

"Palaces of Nature" (lxii) and had implied that man could not "o'erleap [his] mortal state" (lxxxviii). In *Mont Blanc,* Shelley allayed these fears by following *at first* the course of Byron's mind "which passively/ Now renders and receives fast influencings,/Holding an unremitting interchange/With the clear universe of things around" (ll. 37-40). On the basis of that interchange with sensible things, Byron had hoped that the unseen Alpine summits "reared a throne" for Eternity and Love, "Imperishably pure beyond all things below" (III.civ, lxvii). Similarly, Shelley asserted that Mont Blanc contained the "secret throne" of a "Power [which] dwells apart in its tranquillity,/Remote, serene, and inaccessible" (ll. 17, 96-97).[36] But because these summits were "furled" by the clouds for both poets, Shelley forsook the empirically bound Nature worship of *Childe Harold* III and deepened his metaphysics: the "clear universe of things" for Shelley was not merely objective phenomena which flowed through the mind; it was also thought.[37] In order to analyze this thought, in order to validate his own and Byron's intuition of this eternal Power, Shelley turned the mind in upon itself and sought the source of his metaphysical idealism: descending into "the still cave of the witch Poesy," he sought the source of his mythopoesis by which the mind's intuitions of an unknown Power could be imaged in terms of the Ravine's reception of "Power in likeness of the Arve." Discovering that "nothing exists but as it is perceived" (*On Life*), that the mountain, ravine, and river (as well as their metaphoric equation with the intuitive processes of the mind) had no meaning without the creative imagination ("till the breast/From which they [these intuitions of the Arve's meaning] fled recalls them, thou art there"), Shelley made imaginative thought prior to and greater than empirical thing. With this premise, Shelley could then further lead Byron (and even Wordsworth) to the conclusion that an *unqualified* distinction between the imaginative rendering to and the empirical receiving from Nature (the "unremitting interchange" in *Mont Blanc*), between an imaginative mind fitted to the external world and the external world fitted to an empirical mind ("Prospectus" to *The Excursion*), actually misrepresented the intuitive powers of the mind. Thus Byron's somewhat hesitant and obscuring question in *Childe Harold* III,

> Are not the mountains, waves, and skies, a part
> Of me and of my Soul, as I of them?                  (lxxv)

was countered by Shelley's more confident and clarifying question that emphasized the imagination's power in rendering meaning to Nature:

And what were thou [mountain], and earth, and stars, and sea,
If to the human mind's imaginings
Silence and solitude were vacancy?

Byron, like Wordsworth, had hoped to pierce the clouds of the white
Alps and to "survey whate'er/May be permitted" to an imagination
that was empirically bound to his "mortal state" (III.cix, lxxxviii).
Shelley, like Coleridge in *Dejection: An Ode,* argued that if Byron
"would . . . aught behold, of higher worth,/Than that inanimate
cold world allowed" (compare Byron's "whate'er / May be *permitted*"),
then he should not "hope from outward forms" to gain a knowledge
of a transcendental Power; rather, he should locate the source of
that Power in his own imagination. Shelley, by arguing that "nothing
exists but as it is perceived," was in effect dispersing the empirically
limiting "clouds" attending Byron's epistemology. If Byron could be
reconciled with Nature with this new faith, he could enlarge the circumference of his imagination and intuitively apprehend the Power
manifest even in the nonsensible realities of "Silence and solitude"
(*Mont Blanc,* l. 144). Without that faith, Shelley feared, Byron would
never apprehend the Power awaiting him in that "great and growing
region, where/The earth to her embrace compels the powers of air"
(*Childe Harold* III.cix).

Although *Mont Blanc* was not intended solely to enlarge the
imaginative circumference of Byron's vision in *Childe Harold* III, it
cannot be properly understood without considering the context of the
two poets' interaction in Geneva. My references to Wordsworth and
Coleridge in the discussion of *Mont Blanc* are even warranted by this
interaction, for while Shelley was dosing Byron with Wordsworth,
Byron was at least discussing Coleridge with Shelley. In addition to
reciting *Christabel* (either from memory or from Sara Hutchinson's
transcript of Coleridge's MS) to Shelley on the night of 18 June,[38]
Byron probably described his first and only meeting with Coleridge
in April 1816 as well as his twelve-month correspondence with
Coleridge, who had asked in March 1815 for Byron's assistance in
publishing two volumes of poetry with a "general Preface . . . prefixed" (what eventually became *Sibylline Leaves* and *Biographia
Literaria,* both published in 1817). In October 1815, Coleridge
promised to send Byron a copy of these two volumes prior to publication, but because the printing was delayed it is doubtful that Byron
ever received them before he left England in April 1816. But in
October 1815, Coleridge did send a MS copy of *Christabel,* which,

because of Byron's influence, was published with *Kubla Khan* and *The Pains of Sleep* by John Murray in May 1816.[39]

Byron's recent association with the author of *Christabel* may have renewed Shelley's interest in Coleridge. On 17 July 1816, one week before he toured the Valley of Chamouni, Shelley had asked Peacock about England's "literature, of which when I speak Coleridge is in my thoughts."[40] Two of Coleridge's poems very much in his thoughts at this time were *Hymn Before Sun-rise, in the Vale of Chamouny* and *Kubla Khan,* both of which influenced Shelley's composition of *Mont Blanc* one week later. Shelley's acquaintance with the first of these poems is deducible from his reading of Coleridge's periodical, *The Friend,* the eleventh number of which contained *Hymn Before Sun-rise,* Coleridge's poem about Mont Blanc. I have argued elsewhere that by 1816 "the Shelley circle was acquainted with at least Nos. 1, 5, 13, and 21 of Coleridge's periodical" and that "Shelley had evidently read (and likely possessed) either a collection of the original and separate numbers [1809-10] or the complete *Friend* as reprinted in 1812." Of related interest here is Shelley's indebtedness to No. 5 (14 September 1809) of *The Friend,* in which Coleridge had written, "What an awful Duty, what a Nurse of all other, the fairest Virtues, does not HOPE become." Only a few hours after Shelley returned to England in September, he slightly misquoted this definition of hope in a letter urging Byron to "be persuaded with Coleridge that 'Hope is a most awful duty, the nurse of all other virtues.' "[41] Such a familiarity with *The Friend* suggests that Shelley or Byron carried a copy of the periodical to Geneva and that Shelley read Coleridge's *Hymn Before Sun-rise* immediately before he wrote *Mont Blanc.* This reading would explain the many verbal similarities between the two poems and support Harold Bloom's and Joseph Raben's suggestions that Shelley wrote *Mont Blanc* to reject the submissive orthodoxy in Coleridge's poem.[42]

Shelley apparently was equally indebted to Coleridge's *Kubla Khan* for some of his images in *Mont Blanc,* even though he did not receive his copy of Coleridge's poem (in the *Christabel* volume) until 26 August,[43] one month after he wrote *Mont Blanc.* Shelley may have read a MS transcription of *Kubla Khan* prior to his writing *Alastor* in 1815, as Joseph Raben has argued, but neither Raben nor I can advance sufficient evidence for this assumption. But by June or July 1816, it is more likely that Byron, who heard Coleridge recite *Kubla Khan* in London, acquainted or at least reacquainted Shelley with this dream fragment. On 18 June, while the Geneva circle exchanged ghost stories, Byron repeated from *Christabel* the verses describing

Geraldine's "bosom and half her side." That he also recited portions of
*Kubla Khan* (whether from memory,[44] from a MS transcription of the
poem, or from the May edition of *Christabel, Kubla Khan,* and *The
Pains of Sleep* received by Byron before August) is suggested by the
following comparison which Desmond King-Hele[45] made between
*Kubla Khan* and *Mont Blanc*:

> And *from this chasm, with ceaseless turmoil seething,*
>
> . . . . . . . . . . . . . . . . . . . . . . . .
>
> Through wood and *dale* the sacred *river* ran,
> Then reached the *caverns measureless to man,*
> And sank *in tumult* to a lifeless *ocean.*
>
> (*Kubla Khan,* ll. 17, 26-28, my italics)

>                     *vast caves*
> Shine in the *rushing torrents' restless gleam,*
> Which *from those secret chasms in tumult welling*
> Meet in the *vale,* and one majestic *River,*
> The breath and blood of distant lands, for ever
> Rolls its loud waters to the *ocean waves.*
>
> (*Mont Blanc,* ll. 120-25, my italics)

In my own judgment, these parallels above more conclusively demonstrate Shelley's knowledge of Coleridge's *Kubla Khan* (and perhaps
Byron's indirect influence on *Mont Blanc*) than do those advanced
by Raben from the earlier *Alastor*.

Whether Byron recognized his direct (by *Childe Harold* III) and
indirect (by his discussions with Shelley on Coleridge) effect on *Mont
Blanc* is unknown, but he may have followed Coleridge's and Shelley's
examples and composed his own poem on Mont Blanc. On 22 July,
just before Shelley began *Mont Blanc* in the Valley of Chamouni, he
requested Byron to record his inspiration from the same scene: "We
have this moment arrived at Chamouni. . . . I shall not attempt to
describe to you the scenes through which we have passed. I hope soon
to see in poetry the feelings with which they will inspire you."[46]
Byron first visited Chamouni and Mont Blanc on 30 August 1816 with
his friends Polidori, Hobhouse, and Scrope Davies, and the scenes
perhaps did "inspire" him to write his own poem about the mountain.
During his journey, Byron stopped at several hotels and inns, at one
of which he scratched from a travelers' album Shelley's signature and
designation of himself in Greek as a democrat, philanthropist, and
atheist.[47] At another inn, according to *The Life, Writings, Opinions,*

*and Times of* . . . *Byron* (1825), II, 383-84, Byron apparently wrote his own poem on Mont Blanc:

> The following poetical effusion was written by Lord Byron, in the *"Travellers' Album,"* at the valley of Chamouni, in Switzerland. Some person, possessed of more curiosity than correctness of principle, had torn out the leaf of the book on which it was inscribed; but the lines having been copied by some Englishman, were re-written in the book, at the request of the inn-keeper, and are now exhibited as a precious memento to every traveller, who visits the Glaciers, or *Mer de Glace.*

Shortly before this "poetical effusion" was published by the anonymous author of this biography (the Dedication and Introductory Address being dated June 1825), a separate and slightly different copy of the poem in question was made and prefaced as follows: *"Feb. 14. 1825 Said* to be written by Lord Byron in the Album of the Union Hotel at Chamouni near Geneva." Accompanied by marginal comparisons from *Childe Harold* III, the text of this copy (rather than that in the 1825 biography) is here published through the courtesy of the Humanities Research Center, The University of Texas at Austin.[48] Although it is possible that someone other than Byron wrote "All hail, Mont Blanc" in the hotel album, its parallels with *Childe Harold* III argue for Byron's authorship. Furthermore, the metrical pattern of this spontaneously written poem is the standard iambic tetrameter that Byron had used in the *Stanzas to Augusta* written in England, in *The Prisoner of Chillon,* in *Prometheus,* and in parts of the *Manfred* "Incantation." Moreover, the poem actually condenses Byron's recent reaction to a Wordsworthian ethos: in the first and second stanzas, the persona hopes that a benevolent Nature will make up for his own failures and for other men's deficiencies; in the third and fourth, he concedes that such a restoration is impossible for a man of his unique experiences; and with ironic humility in the final stanza, he takes his anonymous leave from these "transports" which, if they had been incorporated into something like *Childe Harold* III, would have been received by "babbling Fame."

Shelley had hoped that Chamouni and Mont Blanc would confirm Byron's new faith in a metaphysical power both within and without himself. But if "All hail, Mont Blanc" was indeed written by Byron, it does little to fulfill Shelley's expectations. Shelley, of course, did not read this poem, but during his return trip to England he carried and undoubtedly read Claire Clairmont's MS transcription of Byron's

All hail, Mont Blanc! Mont anVert hail!
With thee I can associate still;
And, should all other pleasures fail,
I'll stretch me by the murm'ring rill,
Or into solitude I'll fly,
And commune with the Deity!

Far from the pride and scorn of man
The worthless objects of their care,
The works of nature I can scan,
And sometimes bold, yet fearful, dare
Express those feelings kindly given
By the benevolence of Heaven!

Alone I come! alone I go!
Alike unnoticed and unknown!
Press'd by a weight of lasting woe,
From East to West by tempest blown!
No rest! no peace! until I fly
From time into Eternity!

Yet why—why should I complain?
Are not my other joys my own,
Joys which the multitude disdain,
To duller, happier souls unknown.
Yes, I will bravely dare my lot
Until I die and be forgot!

No need to add my humble name,
Ne'er mentioned but by babbling Fame;
Few will demand to whom belong
These transports of a child of Song.
One who would wish with Poet's fire
And daring hand, to sweep the Lyre!

"But let me quit Man's works, again to read / His Maker's, spread around me" (cix); "But ere these matchless heights I dare to scan" (lxiii); cf. also stanzas lxxi-lxxii.

"I stood and stand alone,— remembered or forgot" (cxii).
"Still must I on; for I am as a weed, / Flung from the rock, on Ocean's foam, to sail / Where'er the surge may sweep, the tempest's breath prevail" (ii).
"rather than forego / Such feelings for the hard and worldly phlegm / Of those whose eyes are only turned below, / Gazing upon the ground, with thoughts which dare not glow" (lxxv).
Cf. "Obscurity and Fame,— / The Glory and the Nothing of a Name" (*Churchill's Grave*, ll. 42-43).

Cf. "Childe" Harold and "a Child of Song" (*Lament of Tasso*, l. 2).

*Childe Harold* III and other poems written in Geneva.[49] In such poems as *The Dream, Darkness, The Prisoner of Chillon,* and *Prometheus,* Shelley discovered that Byron did not sustain the "spirit" of hope in *Childe Harold* III, and immediately upon his arrival in England, he wrote and urged Byron to "be persuaded with Coleridge that 'Hope is a most awful duty, the nurse of all other virtues.' I assure you that it will not depart, if it be not rudely banished, from such a one as you." Byron, however, had had enough and would soon write *Manfred* and *Childe Harold* IV, both of which "rudely banished" the hopes he briefly experienced under the influence of Shelley in 1816.

MORE THINGS ON HEAVEN
AND EARTH: *MANFRED* AND *ALASTOR*

Shelley's return to England gave Byron an opportunity to recon-
sider his Geneva metaphysics and to question whether man's "weight
of lasting woe" could in fact be lifted by Wordsworth's Nature or
Shelley's Love. He would eventually answer these questions in the
negative by writing *Manfred,* the "germs" of which (he later recalled)
could be "found in the Journal . . . sent to Mrs. Leigh"[1]—that is,
the Journal to Augusta (dated 18-29 September 1816), recording his
tour of the Bernese Alps. In this Journal, we find that Byron within
one month of Shelley's departure was undergoing a change. For
example, on 18 September Byron arrived for "the second time . . .
at Clarens, beautiful Clarens"; but without Shelley as his companion,
he did not note this time anything like the "feeling . . . all around
Clarens . . . of the existence of love in its most extended and
sublime capacity, and of our own participation of its good and of its
glory" (Byron's note to *Childe Harold* III.xcix, written while he and
Shelley visited Clarens in June). Wordsworth's Nature was, however,
less fleeting than Shelley's Love, for on the next day Byron could
write:

> The music of the Cows' bells (for their wealth, like the Patriarchs',
> is cattle) in the pastures, (which reach to a height far above any
> mountains in Britain), and the Shepherds' shouting to us from
> crag to crag, and playing on their reeds where the steeps appeared
> almost inaccessible, with the surrounding scenery, realized all
> that I have ever heard or imagined of a pastoral existence. . . .
> *I have lately repeopled my mind with Nature.*

And when Byron transformed this experience into a scene in *Manfred,*

> The natural music of the mountain reed—
> For here the patriarchal days are not
> A pastoral fable—pipes in the liberal air,
> Mixed with the sweet bells of the sauntering herd;
> My soul would drink those echoes. *Oh, that I were*

> *The viewless spirit of a lovely sound,*
> *A living voice, a breathing harmony,*
> *A bodiless enjoyment—born and dying*
> *With the blest tone which made me,*     (I.ii.48-56, my italics)

the additional concluding lines reveal that he still desired an inter-penetration with Nature. Yet such a redeeming experience was denied both to Manfred (the subjunctive, "Oh, that I were," bespeaks futility) and to Byron, even though the latter concluded his Journal to Augusta by claiming that he was still "a lover of Nature and an admirer of Beauty." But Byron also admitted that "the recollections of bitterness, and more especially of recent and more home desolation" prevented Nature from lightening "the weight upon [his] heart," and prevented him from losing his "wretched identity in the majesty, and the power, and the Glory, around, above, and beneath" him during the tour of the Bernese Alps.[2]

Byron's difficulty in retaining the hopes urged on him by Shelley does not mean that he was totally free of Shelley's influence. In fact, while he wrote *Manfred* as "a very wild, metaphysical, and inexplicable kind" and "a sort of mad Drama," he could not quite escape the implications of *Childe Harold* III in which he had been "half mad . . . between metaphysics, mountains, lakes, love unextinguishable, thoughts unutterable, and the nightmare of my own delinquencies." In other words, the Shelleyan "bodiless thought" and the Wordsworthian "Spirit of each spot" from *Childe Harold* III.lxxiv reappeared to populate *Manfred* where "almost all the persons—but two or three—are spirits of the earth and air, or the waters."[3] Indeed, one of these spirits not only celebrated in verse Byron's impressions from the Valley of Chamouni (as Shelley had urged) but spoke with a Shelleyan voice:

> Mont Blanc is the *Monarch of mountains*;
>     They *crowned* him long ago
> *On a throne of rocks*, in a robe of clouds,
>     *With a Diadem of snow.*
> Around his waist are forests braced,
>     *The Avalanche in his hand*;
> But ere it fall, *that thundering ball*
>     Must pause for my command.
> *The Glacier's cold and restless mass*
>     *Moves onward day by day*;
> But I am he who bids it pass,
>     Or with its ice delay.     (I.i.60-71, my italics)

These lines echo parts of Shelley's *Mont Blanc* as well as his 22 July 1816 letter describing to Peacock "the snows on the summit of Mt. Blanc" and its perpetually augmenting glaciers:

> Do you [Peacock] who assert the supremacy of Ahriman imagine him *throned among these desolating snows,* among these palaces of death & frost, sculptured in this their terrible magnificence by the unsparing hand of necessity, & that *he casts around him as the first essays of his final usurpation avalanches,* torrents, *rocks & thunders*—and above all, these *deadly glaciers at once the proofs & the symbols of his reign.*[4]

That Byron should echo some of Shelley's Geneva phrases is not surprising, and these echoes by themselves do not justify Edward Williams' observation that "the idea of the tragedy of 'Manfred'" was Shelley's suggestion.[5] Yet I believe that Williams was essentially correct and that *Manfred* did owe its "idea" to Shelley, particularly to Shelley's *Alastor,* in which the Poet is destroyed by a self-consuming love for his own idealized prototype or second self. Self-destructive love was by no means a new theme for Byron, but prior to Manfred and Astarte, Byron's heroes and heroines did not exhibit a psychological doubling and inseparability to the degree of Shelley's Poet and Veiled Maid in *Alastor.* But after reading Shelley's poem, Byron began explicitly to develop hero and heroine as double representations of a single personality. Such duplication may even be seen in *The Dream* (July 1816) and *The Lament of Tasso* (April 1817), two poems that conveniently enclose the "idea" of *Manfred* as well as the months when it was written. In *The Dream,* the lovers end in madness and misery, but only after the youth had looked upon his maiden's face

> till it could not pass away;
> He had no breath, no being, but in hers;
> She was his voice; he did not speak to her,
> But trembled on her words; she was his sight,
> For his eye followed hers, and saw with hers,
> Which coloured all his objects:—he had ceased
> To live within himself; she was his life,
> The ocean to the river of his thoughts,
> Which terminated all: upon a tone,
> A touch of hers, his blood would ebb and flow.     (ll. 50-59)

Likewise, Tasso's love for Leonora in *The Lament of Tasso* was all the more frustrating because of what he formerly experienced:

> from my very birth
> My soul was drunk with Love,—which did pervade
> And mingle with whate'er I saw on earth:
>
> . . . . . . . . . . . . . . . . . . . .
>
> And with my years my soul began to pant
> With feelings of strange tumult and soft pain;
> And the whole heart exhaled into One Want,
> But undefined and ˙wandering, till the day
> I found the thing I sought—and that was thee;
> And then I lost my being, all to be
> Absorbed in thine;—the world was past away;—
> *Thou* didst annihilate the earth to me! (ll. 149-51, 166-73)

In both of these poems, the Byronic hero, like Shelley's Poet, idealizes his love into a psychological counterpart, a second self without whom he cannot be complete.

When Shelley read *The Dream* and *The Lament of Tasso,* he could not fail to see the effect of *Alastor* on Byron. No written judgment on *The Dream* is extant, but in his letter to Byron in September 1817, Shelley observed that "those lines in which you describe the youthful feelings of Tasso; that indistinct consciousness of its own greatness, which a heart of genius cherishes in solitude, amid neglect and contempt, have a profound and thrilling pathos which I will confess to you, whenever I turn to them, make my head wild with tears."[6] The cause of Shelley's excitement here should be obvious: not only does he echo and invert his conclusion to *Alastor* ("It is a woe 'too deep for tears,'" l. 713), but he also praises the lines quoted above where Byron portrayed in Tasso a sensibility very similar to that of the Poet in *Alastor.*[7] And it was to *Alastor,* which Byron read before he left England[8] and probably reread or at least discussed with Shelley and Mary in the summer of 1816, that the Geneva circle owed such a great debt. It not only influenced parts of *The Dream* and *The Lament of Tasso,* but it also provided the "idea" for three major works begun in Geneva or shortly thereafter: Shelley's own *Revolt of Islam,* Mary's *Frankenstein,* and Byron's *Manfred*—each of which is structured by two characters desiring and representing the unity of a single and complete personality.

Shelley's idea of this psychological and physical doubling was conceived at least by 1811, when he asked Elizabeth Hitchener, "are you not my second self, the stronger shadow of that soul whose dictates I have been accustomed to obey?"[9] By 1815, Shelley had developed this variant of the doppelgänger into the idealized double that man can image to himself by uniting the requisitions of "the intellectual faculties, the imagination, the functions of sense," by uniting "all of wonderful, or wise, or beautiful, which the poet, the philosopher, or the lover could depicture" (Preface to *Alastor*). This imaged double, Shelley explained in *On Love,* could be either a *prototype,* the "soul *within* our soul," the bodiless ideal vainly sought by the Poet of *Alastor;* or the *antitype,* the "soul *out of* my soul," an embodied ideal that Shelley found temporally and temporarily in the Emily of *Epipsychidion* (see l. 238).

Bringing these ideas to Geneva, Shelley evidently dosed Byron and Mary with the theory of the idealized double (or "epipsyche," a word that Shelley apparently never used in this context). Whether or not Byron and Shelley then discussed other varieties of the doppelgänger is unknown; yet their later interest in the artistic use of the double (in January 1822 the two poets discussed the double personalities in Goethe's *Faust* and Calderón's dramas—see Chapter 9 below), their use of doubles, twins, and incest in *The Revolt of Islam, Rosalind and Helen, Epipsychidion, Manfred, Cain,* and *The Deformed Transformed,* Shelley's allusions in *Alastor* to the Narcissus myth (ll. 406-8, 469-74) and to its companion myth of Echo (ll. 590-601), and Byron's reference to Eros and Anteros in *Manfred* (II.ii.92-93) suggest that they did discuss in 1816 instances of sympathetic identification in myth and fiction. Nevertheless, Shelley's consideration of love in *Alastor* provided them with sufficient cause to distinguish between a psychological equivalent (one character completely mirroring the psychology of another) and a psychological complement (one character representing what another needs for psychological completeness). The distinction between equivalent and complement is often difficult to determine, but in either case there is usually a need for the union of the two characters. In Shelley's *Alastor,* the Poet unsuccessfully seeks his equivalent, his ideal prototype in the Veiled Maid; in *Epipsychidion,* the search is for another equivalent, the real antitype in Emilia. However, Shelley's later portraits of Prometheus and Asia, and to some extent Laon and Cythna, emphasize as well the complementary union of head and heart, understanding and affection, reason and love. Whether searching for equivalent or complement, the Shelleyan hero seeks his second self in order to attain that happy and blessed state of the circularly double and primeval man described by Aristophanes in Plato's *Symposium.*

Influenced by these ideas, Mary Shelley and Byron developed their own narratives of the divided self needing or seeking completion in *Frankenstein* and in *Manfred.* In *Frankenstein,* Mary employed enough psychological equivalents and complements to make all of the major characters represent different facets of Frankenstein's personality.[10] Byron, on the other hand, used a simpler form of the doppelgänger by centering his plot on Manfred's relation with "The Lady Astarte, his [physical double and psychological complement]" (III.iii.47), as I interpret and complete Manuel's interrupted discussion of her. That Byron had in mind Shelley's Poet/Veiled Maid relation when he conceived and executed the Manfred/Astarte plot is, I believe, indisputable and a direct effect of his reading of *Alastor* and of his discussions with Shelley in Geneva. Many critics have acknowledged some similarities between *Manfred* and *Alastor,* but by ignoring or forgetting the effect of Shelley's almost daily dialogue with Byron for three months before *Manfred* was written, they have underestimated Shelley's influence on the poem: for example, Samuel C. Chew relegated *Alastor* to a minor position in a list of many works that might have influenced Byron's drama; and Harold Bloom failed to develop his cautiously phrased suggestion that Manfred "calls up the Witch of the Alps, a Shelleyan spirit of amoral natural beauty. To her he speaks an idealized history of the outcast Romantic poet, the figure of the youth as natural quester for what nature has not to give, akin to the idealized portraits of self in Shelley's *Alastor* and Keats's *Endymion*." More recently, however, W. Paul Elledge noted the usefulness of studying *Manfred* in terms of the Preface to *Alastor* and judged that both Poet and Manfred "attempt to objectify an imaginary vision of the ideal that embodies all the wonder of a poet, the wisdom of a philosopher, and the beauty of a lover."[11] But Elledge did not admit that Shelley actually influenced Byron, and by judging Manfred's "extra-personal counterpart" to include not only Astarte but also supra-personal and elemental objects (e.g., the Seven Spirits, Witch of the Alps, Arimanes, eagle, sun), he obscured Byron's particular debt to the Poet/Veiled Maid for the idea of Manfred/Astarte.

By stressing the similarities between *Alastor* and *Manfred,* I do not intend to minimize their considerable differences. Manfred's declamatory rhetoric and heroic defiance place him in the tradition of Faust, Satan, Prometheus, Don Juan, the Wandering Jew, and the Gothic villain (each of which has been studied as the literary antecedent of Byron's hero),[12] and his histrionics sharply contrast with the silent and sometimes pathetic Poet of Shelley's shorter, narrative poem. I do not deny that *Manfred* had numerous literary antecedents, and my purpose is not to preclude other influences on Byron's drama. However, the following demonstration that the stages of the Poet's quest in *Alastor* (solitude and an accompanying sympathy with Nature; an idealistic thirst for occult knowledge followed by a union with a "second self"; a failure to maintain this union and a consequent dissatisfaction with Nature; a vain search for psychological fulfillment which is perhaps denied even in death) not only determine the plot of *Manfred* but also provide a subject heading for Manfred's dialogue with the Witch of the Alps (II.ii) should make evident the extent of Shelley's influence upon Byron's drama.

II

Despite Manfred's lively dialogue with the Witch of the Alps, with the rest of what Peacock termed a "heterogeneous mythological company,"[13] and with the Chamois Hunter and Abbot, Byron's hero, like the Poet of *Alastor,* was a solitary unable to sympathize with humankind; and the description of the Poet, who "lived, he died, he sung, in solitude" (l. 60), aptly characterizes Manfred, who described himself to the Witch of the Alps in this fashion:

> From my youth upwards
> My Spirit walked not with the souls of men,
> Nor looked upon the earth with human eyes;
> The thirst of their ambition was not mine,
> The aim of their existence was not mine;
> My joys—my griefs—my passions—and my powers,
> Made me a stranger; though I wore the form,
> I had no sympathy with breathing flesh. (II.ii.50-57)

With greater disdain, Manfred had rejected the Chamois Hunter: "I am not of thine order" (II.i.38). Manfred, then, was one of those solitaries who "keep aloof from sympathies with their kind, rejoicing neither in human joy nor mourning with human grief" (Preface to *Alastor*).

Although Manfred's self-imposed solitude was more misanthropic than the Poet's, both heroes were redeemed from the "selfish, blind, and torpid . . . unforeseeing multitudes" by their sympathy for Nature—that is, by "loving [something] on this earth"—and by their "sacred thirst of doubtful knowledge" (Preface to *Alastor*). For the Poet, who pursued "Nature's most secret steps" and made "the wild his home" (ll. 81, 99) in lonesome vales,

> Every sight
> And sound from the vast earth and ambient air,
> Sent to his heart its choicest impulses.
> . . . . . . . . the varying roof of heaven
> And the green earth [initially found] in his heart its claims
> To love and wonder. (ll. 68-70, 96-98)

Manfred, whose "joy was in the wilderness" (II.ii.62), had similar "pastimes":

To follow through the night the moving moon,
The stars and their development; or catch
The dazzling lightnings till my eyes grew dim;
Or to look, list'ning, on the scattered leaves,
While Autumn winds were at their evening song.       (II.ii.70-74)

In terms of Shelley's *On Love,* each protagonist found in Nature "a
secret correspondence with [his] heart. There is eloquence in the
tongueless wind, and a melody in the flowing brooks and the rustling
of the reeds beside them, which by their inconceivable relation to
something within the soul, awaken the spirits."[14] With this same
"correspondence," the "Poet's blood,/. . . ever beat in mystic
sympathy/With nature's ebb and flow" (ll. 651-53); and Manfred
judged that man's "inborn spirits have a tint" of the sun, the "Sire of
the seasons! Monarch of the climes" (III.ii.22, 20). And these "inborn
spirits" thirsted after the springs of knowledge: for the Poet,

The fountains of divine philosophy
Fled not his thirsting lips, and all of great,
Or good, or lovely, which the sacred past
In truth or fable consecrates, he felt
And knew;                                              (ll. 71-75)

for Manfred,

Philosophy and science, and the springs
Of Wonder, and the wisdom of the World,
I have essayed.                                        (I.i.13-15)

Manfred further described his scientific method to the Witch of the
Alps:

And then I dived
In my lone wanderings, to the caves of Death,
Searching its cause in its effect; and drew
From withered bones, and skulls, and heaped up dust,
Conclusions most forbidden.                            (II.ii.79-83)

These lines directly reflect not only the narrator's mysterious methods
in the induction to *Alastor,*

I have made my bed
In charnels and on coffins, where black death
Keeps record of the trophies won from thee,
Hoping to still these obstinate questionings
Of thee and thine, by forcing some lone ghost
Thy messenger, to render up the tale
Of what we are;                                        (ll. 23-29)

but they also parallel the Poet's steps over the "awful ruins of the days of old" (l. 108) in order to draw inspiration from the obelisks, tombs, sphinxes, and relics of the dead. And the two heroes achieved identical success in their dedication to those "sciences untaught, / Save in the old-time" (II.ii.84-85): Manfred made his "eyes familiar with Eternity" (II.ii.90); similarly (since Plato has told us that time was created or born as a "moving image of eternity") the Poet saw the "thrilling secrets of the birth of time" (l. 128).

Having intuitively transcended the bourne of time, the Poet and Manfred soon realized that the Tree of Knowledge was not the Tree of Life, for they became aware of their own psychological inadequacy. When external objects "cease[d] to suffice," both protagonists looked within and experienced the need to love. In so doing, the Poet, "Beside a sparkling rivulet" (l. 148), "images to himself the Being whom he loves" (Preface to *Alastor*). The sequence of events in Manfred's history (as addressed to the Witch of the Alps) betrays a similar cause and effect, for his pursuit of knowledge climaxed in a union with his "second self." Like the philosopher Jamblicus, who raised "from out their fountain-dwellings . . ./Eros and Anteros" (II.ii.92-93),[15] Manfred experienced Love and Love's Contrary in his speculative pursuits:

> and with my knowledge grew
> The thirst of knowledge, and the power and joy
> Of this most bright intelligence, until—           (II.ii.94-96)

All this, of course, is dramatic exposition, and in contrast to Shelley's third-person narrative, the climactic events between Manfred and Astarte are not represented. Yet Byron modeled Astarte on Shelley's Veiled Maid, who, as the Poet's psychological equivalent, mirrored his intellectual, imaginative, and sensitive natures:

> Her voice was like the voice of his own soul
> Heard in the calm of thought; its music long,
> Like woven sounds of streams and breezes, held
> His inmost sense suspended in its web
> Of many-coloured woof and shifting hues.
> Knowledge and truth and virtue were her theme,
> And lofty hopes of divine liberty,
> Thoughts the most dear to him, and poesy,
> Himself a poet.                                    (ll. 153-61)

The doubling in *Manfred* is slightly different, for Astarte not only mirrored Manfred by possessing equivalent powers of intellect, but she also (with "gentler powers") complemented Manfred's Faustian pursuit of knowledge:

She was like me in lineaments—her eyes—
Her hair—her features—all, to the very tone
Even of her voice, they said were like to mine;
But softened all, and tempered into beauty:
She had the same lone thoughts and wanderings,
The quest of hidden knowledge, and a mind
To comprehend the Universe: nor these
Alone, but with them gentler powers than mine,
Pity, and smiles, and tears—which I had not;
And tenderness—but that I had for her;
Humility—and that I never had.
Her faults were mine—her virtues were her own.     (II.ii.105-16)

Manfred's pre-play development at this point does not exactly duplicate
the Poet's history in *Alastor,* because the Veiled Maid was a prototype,
an idealized and unbodied soul *within* the Poet's soul, whereas Astarte
was an antitype, a real and physical double (presumably a sister) in
whom Manfred saw his likeness. However, because of Astarte's death
and her "spiritualized" reappearances in the form of the Seventh
Spirit and at the bidding of Nemesis, she becomes as unbodied and
unattainable as the Veiled Maid.

Having provided Manfred an idealized double in the form of
Astarte, Byron also modeled their union on Shelley's narrative in
*Alastor* where the Poet, after imagining a sexual union with the Veiled
Maid, was separated from her when "blackness veiled his dizzy eyes,
and night/Involved and swallowed up the vision" (ll. 188-89). In a
starker fashion, Manfred and Astarte "loved each other as [they] should
not love" and in so doing Manfred "loved her, and destroyed her"
(II.i.27; ii.117). Even closer to the Poet's futile dream vision is
Manfred's initial encounter with Astarte as an idealized presence. In
Act I, the Seventh Spirit appears *"in the shape of a beautiful female
figure"*—and Manfred's reaction,

> Oh God! if it be thus, and *thou*
> Art not a madness and a mockery,
> I yet might be most happy. I will clasp thee,
> And we again will be——,                    (i.188-91)

betrays the power of Astarte over his aspiring soul. Falling senseless
(compare the Poet's trance after the Veiled Maid's embrace), Manfred
hears the "Incantation," which curses with the voice of the "evil
genius" or "κακοδαίμων" that Peacock insisted was so central to
*Alastor.*[16] Byron, apparently believing that a curse motif operated in
*Alastor,* employed the "Incantation" to develop Shelley's suggestion

that passion, "Like the fierce fiend of a distempered dream" (l. 225), gave the Poet no rest. In point of fact, Byron's drama more than *Alastor* conforms to Shelley's oft-debated statement in the Preface that the "Poet's self-centred seclusion was avenged by the furies of an irresistible passion pursuing him to speedy ruin." Echoing this statement, Manfred spoke of the "strong curse" (I.i.47) upon his soul and informed the Witch of the Alps that since the destruction of Astarte, his "solitude is solitude no more,/But peopled with the Furies" (II.ii.130-31).

Notwithstanding the suggestion of an external curse in *Alastor* and *Manfred,* each hero was self-cursed. By the very nature of his intense quest for self-fulfillment in solitude, with Nature, through knowledge, and finally in his momentary union with a second self, the loss of which demonstrated his psychological incompleteness, each hero was impelled to seek once more and above all else that idealized part of himself. Just as the Poet had been "driven/By the bright shadow of that lovely dream" (ll. 232-33), Manfred, as if haunted by the "shadow" (I.i.219) of Astarte, "wandered o'er the earth,/And never found [her] likeness" (II.iv.143-44). And both quests for a counterpart led to similar frustrations. Immediately after his vision of the Veiled Maid, the Poet fell into a trance and awoke to a Nature that no longer satisfied his thirst:

> Whither have fled
> The hues of heaven that canopied his bower
> Of yesternight? The sounds that soothed his sleep,
> The mystery and the majesty of Earth,
> The joy, the exultation? His wan eyes
> Gaze on the empty scene as vacantly
> As ocean's moon looks on the moon in heaven.      (ll. 196-202)

Similarly, after Manfred's encounter with the apparition of Astarte in Act I, he fell senseless and awoke to acknowledge that his former talents and pleasures could not compensate for Astarte's loss:

> The spirits I have raised abandon me,
> The spells which I have studied baffle me,
> The remedy I recked of tortured me;
> I lean no more on superhuman aid;
> It hath no power upon the past, and for
> The future, till the past be gulfed in darkness,
> It is not of my search.—My Mother Earth!
> And thou fresh-breaking Day, and you, ye Mountains,
> Why are ye beautiful? I cannot love ye.

> And thou, the bright Eye of the Universe,
> That openest over all, and unto all
> Art a delight—thou shin'st not on my heart. (I.ii.1-12)

Yet Manfred, as well as the Poet, exhibited a paradoxical relation
with Nature, for each continued to appreciate his natural surroundings:
Manfred could still exclaim, "How beautiful is all this visible world"
(I.ii.37); and the Poet could still commune with the Spirit of Nature
clothed in "undulating woods, and silent well,/And leaping rivulet"
(ll. 484-85). However, Nature no longer provided its former pleasures
and comforts: Manfred sensed that with a "mixed essence" man made
a "conflict of [the visible world's] elements" (I.ii.41-42); and the
Poet, "Obedient to the light/That shone within his soul" (ll. 492-93),
rejected the Spirit of Nature. And with its fulfilling cycle of life
through death, Nature also served as a foil for each protagonist's
"desperate hope" (l. 291) that a self-imposed death would reunite him
with his counterpart.

The death wish for Shelley's Poet resulted from his hope that
death would confirm the promise of sleep:

> Does the dark gate of death
> Conduct to thy mysterious paradise,
> O Sleep? (ll. 211-13)

> For sleep, he knew, kept most relentlessly
> Its precious charge, and silent death exposed,
> Faithless perhaps as sleep, a shadowy lure,
> With doubtful smile mocking its own strange charms.
> (ll. 292-95)

In like manner, Manfred sought death not to forget Astarte but to
regain her forgiveness, her love, and her presence. Protesting too much
for "self-oblivion" and "Forgetfulness" (I.i.144, 136), Manfred really
sought self-integration; as Elledge astutely remarked, Manfred's "quest
throughout the drama is for a reconstruction of the fragmented unity
precipitated by Astarte's death."[17] This quest underlies Manfred's
desire to die; yet as in *Alastor,* death offered Manfred only a hope,
not a certainty. The mind, incomplete even "When stripped of this
mortality," would be "Born from the knowledge of its own *desert*"
and "absorbed in sufferance *or* in joy" (III.iv.133-36, my italics).
Whether "sufferance" be read as "misery" or "endurance," the implication is that Manfred, like the Poet, sensed that death might be "faithless," might not grant the joy of a new life with Astarte. And Byron,
following Shelley's example, accentuated this uncertainty in the pursuit
of death by contrasting Manfred's skeptical hope for a greater life in

death with the emblems of Nature faithfully renewing itself. In *Alastor*, a swan strangely appears when the Poet chooses suicide as a means to his desire (ll. 275-90), and the moon disappears when the Poet dies (ll. 645-62). In like manner, an eagle appears just before Manfred's first suicide attempt on the Jungfrau (I.ii.29-36), and when the sun sets, Manfred follows to death (III.ii.20-30). In contrast to both the Poet and Manfred, the birds have their counterparts (the swan with a "home" and a "sweet mate"; the eagle with "eaglets") and for them death is fearless and fruitful (the swan has the sweetness of its "dying notes"; the eagle could "gorge [its] eaglets" with prey). Again in contrast to both, the moon and the sun could be "reborn" into a new life; as Manfred exclaimed to the sun, "thou dost rise,/And shine, and set in glory." The problem for the Poet and Manfred was whether or not they too would "set in glory."[18]

### III

That Byron's first drama resulted from Shelley's influence is apparent, I believe, from the foregoing evidence of the Alastorian quest in *Manfred*. However, the many similarities between the forms of the two poems do not mean that they share a common "spirit." Quite the contrary, Byron patterned his drama on *Alastor* not to adopt Shelley's theme but to provide Shelley an alternative to the "pale despair and cold tranquillity" (l. 718) that concluded the Poet's apparently futile quest. After the Poet's death, Shelley as narrator had hoped that the immortality of the Wandering Jew would have preserved the Poet (ll. 675-81). In *Manfred*, however, Byron gave the lie to this useless wish by exposing that earthly immortality (Manfred had been for a time cursed "Nor to slumber, nor to die," I.i.254) created even more frustration than the Poet experienced, for only death offered the hope of attaining a prototype or idealized counterpart. Even though death was perhaps faithless, Byron at least offered Shelley and his Poet a more respectable fate—one in which the hero's self, divided though it was, could heroically withstand the possible failure of his quest, even in death. Manfred would emulate the strength of the eagle, that "cloud-cleaving minister," not the fragile beauty of a dying swan; his emblem would be the sun, the "Monarch of the climes" which "set in glory," not the horned moon which with "two lessening points of light" mocked the "two eyes,/Two starry eyes" (ll. 654, 489-90) that beckoned the Poet to his death. And Manfred would defiantly proclaim the immortality of his mind that could look through death and transcend its own "desert."

What finally distinguishes *Manfred* from *Alastor* is the posture with which each hero engaged his quest and met his death, and what evidently violated Byron's sense of decorum was the Poet's passive and futile death and the narrator's failure to question the idealistic premise of the Poet's quest. Having read the *Alastor* volume, Byron probably recognized the restatement of the *Alastor* theme in the accompanying *Mutability*, in which Shelley summarized the narrative action ("We rest.—A dream has power to poison sleep;/We rise.—One wandering thought pollutes the day") as well as the conclusion of his longer poem:

> We are as clouds that veil the midnight moon;
>   How restlessly they speed, and gleam, and quiver,
> Streaking the darkness radiantly!—yet soon
>   Night closes round, and they are lost for ever.

Shelley's Poet was not triumphant; he also was "lost for ever." Unable to affirm that the Poet attained the Veiled Maid in death, Shelley instead emphasized the finality of death:

> No sense, no motion, no divinity—
> A fragile lute, on whose harmonious strings
> The breath of heaven did wander—a bright stream
> Once fed with many-voiced waves—a dream
> Of youth, which night and time have quenched for ever,
> Still, dark, and dry, and unremembered now.          (ll. 666-71)

The Poet became the still lute, the dark and dry stream, and the unremembered dream—a bitter harvest for his youthful idealism. Having implicitly denied the efficacy of an idealistic quest, Shelley had two alternatives in *Alastor*: he could condemn the Poet's dependence on a metaphysical ideal and provide another means for self-sufficiency, as Byron was to do in *Manfred*; or he could retain his idealistic hopes by implying that the Alastorian quest might still be fruitful. Shelley chose the latter course by suspending his identification with the Poet. No matter how much Shelley projected his hopes and fears into the Poet, he was not at this time a poet "Who in another's fate now wept his own" (*Adonais* xxxiv). Up to a point, however, Shelley did identify with his hero: in his apostrophe to Nature, "Mother of this unfathomable world" (l. 18), Shelley as narrator wrote—"I have watched/Thy shadow, and the darkness of thy steps" (ll. 20-21); the Poet, Shelley indicated, had an identical concern—"Nature's most secret steps/He like her shadow has pursued" (ll. 81-82). But unlike the Poet, the narrator had not yet discovered the "thrilling secrets of the birth of time" (l. 128) or encountered his prototype:

> and, though ne'er yet
> Thou hast unveil'd thy inmost sanctuary;

Enough from incommunicable dream,
And twilight phantasms, and deep noonday thought,
Has shone within me, that serenely now
And moveless, as a long-forgotten lyre
Suspended in the solitary dome
Of some mysterious and deserted fane,
I wait thy breath, Great Parent, that my strain
May modulate with murmurs of the air.    (ll. 37-46, my italics)

Nature or the "Great Parent" granted poetic inspiration, but life and death were still "unfathomable" and "veil'd." Unable to "still these obstinate questionings" (l. 26), Shelley provided no answers in *Alastor* and in effect hoped to achieve at another time all of the "wonderful, or wise, or beautiful, which the poet, the philosopher, or the lover could depicture."

In answer to Shelley's "obstinate questionings" about life and death, Byron in *Manfred* asserted the Promethean power of the "Mind which is immortal" (III.iv.129). By means of this immortal mind, Manfred, even though he was separated from his "gentler" self, yielded to nothing external to himself, disavowed the need for metaphysical idealism, and heroically endured his self-divided nature. Frustrated like the Poet in seeking for his counterpart, Manfred nevertheless asserted his independence. His words to the Seven Spirits, which his power had raised,

Slaves, scoff not at my will!
The Mind—the Spirit—the Promethean spark,
The lightning of my being, is as bright,
Pervading, and far darting as your own,
And shall not yield to yours, though cooped in clay,    (I.i.153-57)

are echoed in his self-sustaining encounters with the Chamois Hunter, Witch of the Alps, Arimanes, the Abbot, and the Spirit that comes for his soul in the last scene. And his final words to the Abbot ("Old man! 'tis not so difficult to die") display a confidence in the immortality of his mind, a confidence lacked by Shelley's Poet.

When Manfred's final words to the Abbot were omitted from the first edition, Byron objected that John Murray had "destroyed the whole effect and moral of the poem"[19] and thus emphasized the paradox in his drama—that the mind, by which Manfred had initially pursued knowledge and precipitated the fatal Alastorian quest, provided the only means to endure the death resulting from that quest. This paradox Ward Pafford has termed "the tragic dilemma of mind aspiring to complete independence but constrained by its fleshy condition

within a deterministic universe."[20] Mind might be immortal, but the
human applications of mind were limited by the human condition.
Through knowledge, philosophy, and metaphysics, man could not
attain his ideal counterpart as Shelley had implied but refused to admit
in *Alastor*. According to Manfred,

> *Sorrow is Knowledge*: they who know the most
> Must mourn the deepest o'er the fatal truth,
> *The Tree of Knowledge is not that of Life.*
> *Philosophy and science*, and the springs
> Of Wonder, and the wisdom of the World,
> *I have essayed, and in my mind there is*
> *A power to make these subject to itself—*
> *But they avail not.*                    (I.i.10-17, my italics)

The First Destiny similarly denied the efficacy of metaphysical idealism:

>                     his aspirations
> Have been beyond the dwellers of the earth,
> And they have only taught him what we know—
> That knowledge is not happiness, and science
> But an exchange of ignorance for that
> Which is another kind of ignorance.          (II.iv.58-63)

By declaring that the "Tree of Knowledge is not that of Life," by
repudiating a metaphysical philosophy that would promise all but
"avail not," and yet by asserting the inherent strength of his unyielding
immortal mind, Manfred ("though cooped in [the same] clay" as the
Poet) displayed a Promethean independence antithetical to the Poet's
dependence on a futile and idealistic hope in *Alastor*. Even if Manfred
could not reunite with Astarte in death, he could still give form to the
"mighty lesson we inherit" from Prometheus:

> Like thee, Man is in part divine,
>     A troubled stream from a pure source;
> And Man in portions can foresee
> His own funereal destiny;
> His wretchedness, and his resistance,
> And his sad unallied existence:
> To which his Spirit may oppose
> Itself—an equal to all woes—
>     And a firm will, and a deep sense,
> Which even in torture can descry
>     Its own concentered recompense,

> Triumphant where it dares defy,
> And making Death a Victory.  (*Prometheus*, ll. 47-59)

Manfred taught this same lesson of victory in death to the Spirit that came for his soul:

> What I have done is done; I bear within
> A torture which could nothing gain from thine:
> The Mind which is immortal makes itself
> Requital for its good or evil thoughts,—
> Is its own origin of ill and end—
> And its own place and time: its innate sense,
> When stripped of this mortality, derives
> No colour from the fleeting things without,
> But is absorbed in sufferance or in joy,
> Born from the knowledge of its own desert.
> *Thou* didst not tempt me, and thou couldst not tempt me;
> I have not been thy dupe, nor am thy prey—
> But was my own destroyer, and will be
> My own hereafter.  (III.iv.127-40)

Manfred's Promethean heritage is doubly important here, for it demonstrates not only Byron's indebtedness once more to Shelley's translation of *Prometheus Bound* in 1816, but also the motives behind Byron's adaptation of the Alastorian quest. For Byron, Prometheus offered an emblem of the mind that was enchained in the body, and the conflict between "fire" and "clay" had long figured in Byron's narratives. And in Shelley's use of the double or counterpart, Byron found a useful artistic means to represent the internal conflict of man, "Half dust, half deity" (I.ii.40). Thus Astarte was less of a psychological equivalent to Manfred in mirroring his mind, and more of a psychological complement, for as the "sole companion of his wanderings/And watchings" (III.iii.43-44), she represented Manfred's heart and mortal nature—both of which were in conflict with his immortally aspiring mind. Manfred himself confessed to the Chamois Hunter that he and Astarte formerly possessed "one heart" (II.i.26), but he told the Abbot that this heart was now "withered, or . . . broken" (III.i.145). Because Astarte, representing Manfred's heart, had died, the zealous Abbot sensed the futility of appealing to the half-destroyed Manfred: "my humble zeal . . . May light upon your head—could I say *heart*— / Could I touch *that,* with words or prayers, I should/Recall a noble spirit" (III.iv.47, 50-52). Even the Chamois Hunter unwittingly recognized this noble spirit's divided nature when he cautioned Manfred: "Thy mind and body are alike unfit/To trust each other"

(II.i.2-3); and when he prayed for Manfred: "Heaven give thee rest! /
And Penitence restore *thee* to *thyself*" (II.i.87-88, my italics). In other
words, the "thee" (Manfred's heart or mortality as represented by
Astarte) had been severed from the "thyself" (Manfred's mind with its
immortal aspirations). Having destroyed his own heart, his gentler self
in the person of Astarte, Manfred indeed was "self-condemned" and his
"own destroyer" (III.i.77; iv.139).

By defying his "sad unallied existence" unto death, Manfred in
effect instructed Shelley with two "mighty lessons": first, whether
"absorbed in sufferance or in joy,/Born from the knowledge of its
own desert" (i.e., whether or not the divided self was reunited with
its counterpart in death), the immortal mind could still make "Death
a Victory"; second, the mind only deluded itself by depending on a
metaphysical idealism that promised fulfillment in life or death. In
*Manfred,* then, Byron rejected not only the futility in *Alastor* but also
Shelley's hope in Geneva that man, with an imaginative "faith so mild,"
could be "with nature reconciled" (*Mont Blanc,* ll. 77, 79) by confidently dedicating himself to the "shadow" of Intellectual Beauty:

> Thus let thy power, which like the truth
> Of nature on my passive youth
> Descended, to my onward life supply
> Its *calm,* to one who worships thee,
> And every form containing thee.
> (*Hymn to Intellectual Beauty,* ll. 78-82, my italics)

Having already demonstrated in *Manfred* the futility of philosophy and
science which "avail not," Byron in the person of Manfred also exposed
the folly of Shelley's hope for a metaphysically induced "calm":

> There is a *calm* upon me—
> Inexplicable stillness! which till now
> Did not belong to what I knew of life.
> *If that I did not know Philosophy*
> *To be of all our vanities the motliest,*
> The merest word that ever fooled the ear
> From out the schoolman's jargon, I should deem
> The golden secret, the sought "Kalon," found,
> And seated in my soul. *It will not last,*
> *But it is well to have known it, though but once:*
> It hath enlarged my thoughts with a new sense,
> And I within my tablets would note down
> That there is such a feeling. (III.i.6-18, my italics)

Here, in the person of Manfred, Byron condensed his Geneva summer into but one moment of his hero's experience. The "sought 'Kalon,'" what Shelley had called Intellectual Beauty and what Byron had called "Love" in the Clarens stanzas of *Childe Harold* III, was not to be found. In terms of *Childe Harold* IV, the ideal was a "false creation," "the unreached Paradise of [man's] despair" (cxxii). And like *Childe Harold* IV, *Manfred* (even though Byron called it a "metaphysical" drama) was used to repudiate the Shelleyan metaphysics that had informed *Childe Harold* III. In effect, Byron confessed his own self-delusion in pursuing the Shelleyan ideal, for philosophy was merely the vain exercise of a "mind diseased." Having experienced the effects of philosophy "though but once" (i.e., in Geneva) and having noted the consequent "feeling" in the "tablets" of *Childe Harold* III, Byron now acknowledged to Shelley that both the despair of the Poet in *Alastor* and the self-confident hope of the persona in *Hymn to Intellectual Beauty, Mont Blanc,* and even *Childe Harold* III were products of a mind that misunderstood the human condition.

Shelley, of course, would disagree with Byron's estimate of the human condition in *Manfred*: in 1817, he judged that Byron's drama made him "dreadfully melancholy" and asked Byron why he indulged "this despondency";[21] and in 1818, he "argued against [this same] despondency" in *Julian and Maddalo* (l. 48), a poem that explicitly expresses Shelley's philosophical differences with Byron. These differences were apparent to both poets as early as 1816, and on the basis of the similar "forms" and dissimilar "spirits" of *Manfred* and *Alastor,* I contend that Byron used his drama to reject the idealism with which Shelley had "dosed" him for three months in Geneva. Whatever else *Manfred* may be, it at least is an anti-Shelleyan tract (which Shelley, in turn, would answer in both *Julian and Maddalo* and *Prometheus Unbound*). And Byron, although he may not have openly "'puffed the Snake [Shelley],'"[22] did cryptically acknowledge Shelley's influence on his drama: "it was the *Staubach* and the *Jungfrau,* and something else, much more than Faustus, that made me write *Manfred.*"[23] Suffice it to say that this famous "something else" was not Byron's incestuous relations with Augusta Leigh (as has often been argued), but rather his exposure to *Alastor* and Shelley's ideas. And in order to discover what "made [Byron] write *Manfred,*" we need but alter one word in his epigraph to the drama: "'There are more things in heaven and earth, SHELLEY,/Than are dreamt of in your philosophy.'"[24]

PREPARATIONS FOR A "COLOSSAL"
ARGUMENT BETWEEN THE SNAKE AND THE EAGLE:
*THE REVOLT OF ISLAM* AND *CHILDE HAROLD* IV

When Shelley read *Manfred* in the summer of 1817, he disapproved of its "despondency" but he was to some extent prepared for Byron's denial of the "hopes which will not deceive,/And Virtues which are merciful" (*Childe Harold* III.cxiv). As early as September 1816, Shelley had read *Darkness, Prometheus,* and *The Prisoner of Chillon,* and he had recognized that if Byron was to sustain the faith expressed in *Childe Harold* III he would need frequent "doses" of hope and virtue. No longer able to talk with Byron about such ideals, Shelley upon his return to England wrote three letters asking for "the most minute details" of his friend's experiences and urging him to "be persuaded . . . that 'Hope is . . . the nurse of all other virtues.' . . . it will not depart, if it be not rudely banished, from such a one as you." At the same time, Shelley recommended "the master theme of the epoch in which we live—the French Revolution," and implied that Byron should politicize his newly found hopes in a narrative poem that would inspire hope in others. In his letter of 29 September 1816, Shelley more clearly explained his designs on the spirit of Byron's poetry:

> You contemplate objects that elevate, inspire, tranquillise. You communicate the feelings, which arise out of that contemplation, to mankind; perhaps to the men of distant ages. Is there nothing in the hope of being the parent of greatness, and of goodness, which is destined, perhaps, to expand indefinitely? Is there nothing in making yourself a fountain from which the thoughts of other men shall draw strength and beauty, to excite the ambition of a mind that can despise all other ambition?

But because Shelley himself at this time was apparently planning to become a "parent of greatness" by writing his own epic poem on the "master theme" of the French Revolution, he did not want Byron to "immediately apply [himself] to the composition of an Epic Poem." Instead, he desired that Byron naturally progress until the Shelleyan

" 'truth of things' " impelled him to communicate "some greater enter-prise of thought," and he apologized for not being "qualified to say" what Byron's subject should be:

> In a more presumptuous mood, I recommended the Revolution of France as a theme involving pictures of all that is best qualified to interest and to instruct mankind. But it is inconsistent with the spirit in which you ought to devote yourself to so great a destiny, that you should make use of any understanding but your own— much less mine.[1]

Shelley's self-demeaning presumption above reveals a conflict in his attitudes toward Byron in the fall of 1816: he wanted to transform Byron into a Shelleyan philanthropist, but he did not want thereby to condemn his own poetry into further oblivion. Believing at first that he could profit both Byron and himself by their new association, Shelley on 11 September took the MSS of Byron's Geneva poems to the offices of John Murray and fully expected that he would be allowed to revise the proofs before publication. But when Murray two months later chose William Gifford to perform this service, Shelley experienced "some degree of awkwardness" in this matter, felt rejected by the inner sanctum of Byron's friends, and believed that he had perhaps presumed too much on his new association with Byron, espe-cially since the latter was not returning letters full of "the most minute details" of his experiences on the continent.[2] And on 17 January 1817 after announcing the birth of Allegra (Byron and Claire's daughter) and after giving "an imperfect account" of his recent misfortunes (the suicides of Fanny Godwin and Harriet, his first wife, as well as the Chancery suit which threatened to take his children from him), Shelley concluded a letter to Byron by openly confessing his feelings of in-feriority as a poet:

> I have no other news to tell you, my dear Lord Byron, unless you think this is news: that I often talk, and oftener think, of you; and that, though I have not seen you for six months, I still feel the burden of my own insignificance and impotence.[3]

Shelley had not completely despaired of rivaling Byron as a poet (although he would do so in 1821/22), but he could not help compar-ing himself unfavorably to Byron. For example, in his Preface to the *History of a Six Weeks' Tour* (published in 1817), he indicated that "a great Poet [Byron in *Childe Harold* III] has clothed with the fresh-ness of a *diviner* nature" the same scenes that Mary and Shelley himself had described in their journal and letters. And in the Preface he wrote for *Frankenstein* during the summer of 1817, Shelley mentioned that in Geneva "two other friends . . . agreed to write" ghost stories, "a tale from the pen of one of whom [Byron] would be far more acceptable to the public than any thing I can ever hope to produce."[4]

Because Shelley had advised Byron in 1816 to write an epic on the "master theme" of the French Revolution, he feared that *Laon and Cythna,* his own epic on "the *beau ideal* as it were of the French Revolution,"[5] would be made less "acceptable to the public" by the epic Byron might eventually write. Consequently, he explained in his Preface to *Laon and Cythna* (written during the summer of 1817, published in December, and then revised and reissued as *The Revolt of Islam* in January 1818) that he did not wish "to enter into competition with our greatest contemporary Poets [especially Byron]" in this "first serious" attempt "to awaken public hope and to enlighten and improve mankind." This hope for enlightenment and improvement had been rejected by Byron in the person of Manfred,

> I have had those early visions,
> And noble aspirations in my youth,
> To make my own the mind of other men,
> The enlightener of nations; and to rise
> I knew not whither—it might be to fall;
> . . . . . . . . . . But this is past,
> My thoughts mistook themselves,  (III.i.104-8, 114-15)

but Shelley, even after reading *Manfred,* believed that Byron might still write an epic of hope and thereby condemn *Laon and Cythna* to obscurity. Shelley, however, had little to worry about in connection with Byron, for the latter in *Childe Harold* IV again banished his former hopes, particularly when he explained that the "crutch-like rod" of Circumstance "turns Hope to dust,—the dust we all have trod" (cxxv). After Shelley discovered this "most wicked & mischievous insanity" in Byron's fourth canto, he "remonstrated with [Byron] in vain on the tone of mind from which such a view of things alone arises,"[6] but he nevertheless believed that Byron was "capable, if he would direct his [poetical] energies to such an end, of becoming the redeemer of his degraded country" (Preface to *Julian and Maddalo*).

By 24 September, Shelley had completed *Laon and Cythna* (hereafter called *The Revolt of Islam*) and in a letter to Byron he offered a brief and vague description of his new epic:

> I have been engaged this summer, heart and soul, in one pursuit.
> I have completed a poem which, when it is finished, though I do
> not tax your patience to read it, I will send you. It is in the
> style and for the same object as 'Queen Mab', but interwoven

with a story of human passion, and composed with more attention to the refinement and accuracy of language, and the connexion of its parts.[7]

Shelley was not very specific about *The Revolt of Islam* because he felt "presumptuous" both in writing the epic that he had formerly urged on Byron and in imitating the style of *Childe Harold* III, judged in this same letter to be the "finest specimen" of Byron's powers. Even though he had "conversed with living men of genius" (notably Byron), Shelley insisted in his Preface to *The Revolt* that he "sought to avoid the imitation of any style of language or versification peculiar to the original minds of which it is the character" and that he did "not presume to enter into competition" with his contemporaries. But Shelley was competing with Byron, and he adopted the Spenserian stanza not, as he said, "because . . . there is no shelter for mediocrity" in it but because he had witnessed Byron's successful use of the form in *Childe Harold* III. Shelley actually acknowledged Byron's influence in this respect when he asked himself in a notebook containing drafts for the first two cantos of *The Revolt*: "Is this an imitation of Ld. Byrons poem? It is certainly written in the same metre—Coleridge & Wordsworth to be considered."[8]

Shelley was right to question rather than affirm his "imitation of Ld. Byrons" *Childe Harold* III, even though he did adopt its "metre." If and when he "imitated" Byron's idealization of Love in the Clarens stanzas (xcix-civ) or belief in the "hopes which will not deceive" (cxiv), he merely appropriated from Byron the sentiments that Byron had already taken from Shelley himself. Thus in the manner of *Mont Blanc, The Revolt of Islam* offers a further education to the Byron of *Childe Harold* III. Byron's hero,

> Like the Chaldean, . . . could watch the stars,
>   Till he had peopled them with beings bright
>   As their own beams; and earth, and earth-born jars,
>   And human frailties, were forgotten quite.          (xiv).

Even though Harold could not keep "his spirit to that flight," Byron as narrator (with Shelleyan confidence) could "remount at last/With a fresh pinion . . ./Spurning the clay-cold bonds which round our being cling" (lxxiii). But neither *forgetting* nor *spurning* human frailties was enough for Shelley's Laon, who selflessly sought to improve the social condition of man:

> For, before Cythna loved it, had *my song*
> *Peopled with thoughts the boundless universe,*
> A mighty congregation, which were strong

Where'er they trod the darkness to disperse
The cloud of that unutterable curse
Which clings upon mankind:—all things became
Slaves to my holy and heroic verse,
Earth, sea and sky, the planets, life, and fame
And fate, or whate'er else binds the world's wondrous frame.

(II.xxx, my italics)

Perhaps intentionally echoing Byron's frequent but vain "peopling" in his third canto,[9] Shelley here emphasizes the selfless ideal by which Laon could "disperse / The cloud" of mortality which Byron had hoped to "pierce" in *Childe Harold* III (cix) and which Manfred could not escape in life.

Shelley did not discover the cloud or clay of mortality in *Manfred* until June or early July 1817, that is, after he had written perhaps one half of his epic on the adventures of Laon and Cythna.[10] If Shelley had read *Manfred* before beginning *The Revolt of Islam,* I am convinced that his epic, like the later *Prometheus Unbound* and *Julian and Maddalo,* would have explicitly countered Byron's latest denial of Shelleyan hopes and aspirations. As it is, Shelley's *Revolt of Islam* calls in question the premises of Byron's *Manfred.* Notwithstanding Laon and Cythna's failure to liberate the Golden City, their thoughts did not mistake themselves when they made their own the minds of other men, the enlighteners of nations (see *Manfred* III.i.104-15). Schooled in virtue as well as knowledge, Laon and Cythna engaged a complementary union of "Wisdom and Love" through which they served "divine Equality."[11] Like Astarte, the "sole companion of [Manfred's] wanderings" (III.iii.43), Cythna was Laon's "sole associate, and her willing feet/Wandered with [his] where earth and ocean meet" (II.xxv); however, unlike Astarte, Cythna was united with Laon in both time and eternity, and consequently Shelley's heroes achieved the fulfillment denied to Astarte and Manfred. And that personal fulfillment had social and political consequences:

"Our many thoughts and deeds, our life and love,
Our happiness, and all that we have been,
Immortally must live, and burn, and move,
When we shall be no more;—the world has seen
A type of peace." (IX.xxx)

Furthermore, Shelley's two heroes did not share Manfred's uncertainty at the moment of death, although that moment was inscrutable for all three; as Shelley explained it, " 'Reason cannot know/What sense can neither feel, nor thought conceive' " (IX.xxxiii). Nevertheless, unlike Manfred, who was uncertain whether his mind would be "absorbed in sufferance *or* in joy" after his death (III.iv.135, my italics), Laon and Cythna (identified as " 'the prophetess of love' " in Canto IX.xx) possessed the light of Love by which they could *joyfully* look through death. For Cythna,

> "Yes, Love when wisdom fails, makes Cythna wise;
> Darkness and death, if death be true, must be
> Dearer than life and hope, if unenjoyed with thee";
>
> (IX.xxxiv)

and for Laon at the moment of death,

> the mighty veil
> Which doth divide the living and the dead
> Was almost rent, the world grew dim and pale,—
> All light in Heaven or Earth beside our love did fail.—
>
> (XII.xv)

With this faith in the power of Love, Laon could indeed "set in glory" without Manfred's Promethean defiance. Selflessly sacrificing himself for Cythna and ultimately attaining with her the eternal "Temple of the Spirit" (XII.xli) from which he narrates his tale, Laon also had no need for Manfred's final protestation, "Old man! 'tis not so difficult to die." This important line was not included in the first edition of *Manfred* which Shelley read by 9 July 1817, but he nevertheless recognized that Byron intended Manfred's death to be heroic and fearless. But the possibility of "sufferance" rather than "joy" awaiting Manfred after death appears to have disturbed Shelley, for as he explained in his epigraph to the dedicatory stanzas of *The Revolt of Islam*, "There is no danger to a Man, that knows/What life and death is. . . ." That is, no "danger," no "difficulty," and especially none of Manfred's possible "sufferance" instead of "joy" awaited Laon and Cythna in death. Shelley believed that Byron as well as the tragic Manfred needed this instruction in life and death, and he appears to have chosen his epigraph with ironic intent, because it is taken from Chapman's *The Conspiracy and Tragedy of . . . Byron.*[12]

Because Shelley read *Manfred* while writing the last cantos of *The Revolt,* he surely contrasted Byron's misanthropic Manfred with his own philanthropic Laon. And in *Prince Athanase,* begun after *The Revolt* was finished, Shelley explicitly distinguished the Shelleyan from the Byronic hero. Prince Athanase, like Laon and the redeemed Prometheus, would be neither a Manfred: "Not his the load of any secret crime,/For nought of ill his heart could understand,/But pity and wild sorrow for the same" (ll. 6-8); nor a Conrad/Lara: "Not his the thirst for glory or command,/Baffled with blast of hope-consuming shame" (ll. 9-10). Shelley had similarly distinguished the "spirit" of his poetry from Byron's in a manuscript note he intended to use as a footnote to *The Revolt of Islam* XI.xiv: "This somewhat resembles an incident in [Byron's] 'the Corsair.' The catastrophe & tendency of this involuntary imitation of it is widely different *& an allusion to it might justly be considered as presumptuous.*"[13] Feeling "presumptuous" once again in the shadow of Byron, Shelley did not publish this note, even without the italicized words which he had canceled in the MS. Had he done so, he would have acknowledged his indebtedness to the "form" of *The Corsair* but at the same time emphasized that the "spirit" of his scene was "widely different" from Byron's.

The scene in question is Laon's disguised appearance "Before the Tyrant's throne" in Canto XI of *The Revolt of Islam.* Willing to sacrifice himself if Cythna would be spared and sent to America, Laon accepts Othman's promise, throws back his concealing vest, and reveals that he is Laon. This scene parallels in some respects the actions in Canto II of *The Corsair* in which the pirate Conrad, disguised as a Dervise, enters the Moslems' hall to confront Seyd, the Pacha. When the attack begins, Conrad throws off his concealing vest and leads his troops to a temporary victory. Conrad's actions are, however, "widely different" from Laon's, for the Christ-like Laon sought not to kill and plunder, but to die for Cythna and the cause of selfless virtues. And Laon sustained these virtues even when Othman and the Iberian Priest violated their promise and condemned Cythna to death. On the contrary, Conrad had "cursed [his] virtues as the cause of ill,/And not the traitors who betrayed him still" (I.xi.257-58). Although these lines suggest that Byron's hero was morally wrong or at least culpably ignorant, still Conrad's casuistical defense of his life as a pirate, his respect for women, and his heroic dedication to his crew blur the moral issues that Shelley wished to represent more precisely in the actions of Laon.

It is possible that Shelley did not publish his footnote distinguishing his hero from Conrad because he feared that one reference to *The Corsair* might prompt reviewers to search for other parallels which do, in fact, exist between the two poems. The pirates' attack in *The Corsair,* for example, may have provided the idea for the battle scene in Canto VI of *The Revolt,* for in both encounters the Moslem forces are at first repulsed but upon realizing their superior numbers finally turn and defeat Conrad and Laon. Similar to Conrad who was the only survivor to be captured, Laon was the only survivor of his battle with Othman. And finally, both heroes were rescued by women: Gulnare helped Conrad escape from the Pacha's tower; and on a "black Tartarian horse" (VI.xix), anticipating Byron's *Mazeppa,*[14] Cythna rescued

Laon before he could be captured. But here again, the differences between the two scenes are more important than the similarities: Conrad attacked the Pacha, but Laon was being attacked; Conrad vowed to kill the Pacha, but Laon had formerly preserved Othman's life (V.xxxi-xxxvi); Gulnare did kill Seyd, "That hated tyrant" (III. viii.1487), but Cythna, although she also had been subject to a "cold tyrant's cruel lust" (VII.iv), preached forgiveness, not revenge. And it is Cythna's benevolent presence that ultimately distinguishes Shelley's philanthropic narrative from Byron's tale of passion and piracy. As if to answer Conrad's misanthropic words to Medora, " 'I cease to love thee when I love Mankind' " (I.xiv.405), Cythna envisions a philanthropic brotherhood resulting from her union with Laon, unless " 'as ourselves we cease to love our kind' " (V.xlix).

Shelley's hope for a world ruled by the light of Love was intended to counteract the "gloom and misanthropy" that had "tainted the literature of the age with the hopelessness of the minds from which it flows" (Preface to The Revolt). Because Shelley had experienced this gloom and misanthropy in Byron's works, even in Manfred after he had urged on Byron the "beau ideal" and the awful duty of " 'Hope,' " we may assume that Shelley's remarks in his Preface were directed, at least in part, to Byron.[15] As we have seen, Shelley admitted in 1817 that he did "often talk, and oftener think" of Lord Byron. And his deferential acknowledgments of Byron's genius in 1816 and 1817, his "imitations" of Childe Harold and The Corsair in The Revolt, and the verbal echoes between The Revolt and Byron's Geneva poems (particularly The Prisoner of Chillon)[16] confirm Byron's presence in Shelley's thoughts at this time. Consequently, we may also assume that when Shelley first represented Laon and Cythna as brother and sister in the original version of his epic, he at least recalled what he had earlier termed the "only important calumny that ever was advanced against" Byron,[17] namely the rumors of incest between Byron and Augusta Leigh. Even though Shelley apparently disbelieved these allegations, he must have been surprised by the provocative suggestion of incest in Manfred, which was labeled Byron's personal confession by the reviewers within a week after it was published.[18] Because Shelley did not wish the reviewers of Laon and Cythna to revive the rumors about his and Byron's scandalous conduct in Geneva, he concluded the original Preface to his epic with a plea that "charity and toleration" be exercised for incest and other "crimes of convention," and he insisted in a footnote that the "circumstance" of incest had "no personal reference to the Writer" (as quoted in Julian, I, 247n.). Apparently, Shelley did not at first recognize the dangers of this disclaimer: by protesting so much, he could have forced the reviewers to condemn both *Manfred* and *Laon and Cythna* as casuistical defenses of a "league of Incest." Fortunately for Shelley, only the *Quarterly Review* received and condemned Shelley's original *Laon and Cythna,* and the reviewer did not compare it to Byron's *Manfred.*

Notwithstanding Shelley's probable judgment that the incest in *Manfred* exceeded propriety, his conviction that its "despondency" made him "dreadfully melancholy," and his preference for *Childe Harold* III ("the finest specimen of [Byron's] powers"), he admittedly read *Manfred* "with the greatest admiration" and judged that its praise in the *Edinburgh Review* was "far less than it deserves."[19] These ostensibly contradictory opinions actually resulted from Shelley's critical discrimination between the "form" and the "spirit" of Byron's poetry, in this case *Manfred*: Shelley could simultaneously praise Byron's ability as a poet and assert his own ideas to the contrary. Thus for Shelley at this time, as for John Wilson, who reviewed *Manfred* in *Blackwood's Edinburgh Magazine,* Byron in no great attempt had ever failed: "soon as he begins his flight, we feel that he is to soar upon unflagging wings;—that when he has reached the black and tempestuous elevation of his favourite atmosphere, he will, eagle-like, sail on undisturbed through the heart of clouds, storms, and darkness."[20] Wilson's judgments not only anticipate Shelley's later descriptions of Byron as an "eagle spirit" in *Julian and Maddalo* and as a "tempest-cleaving swan" in the *Euganean Hills,* but they also parallel what may have been Shelley's first attempt in 1817 to record in poetry his opinion of Byron:

> Mighty Eagle, thou that soarest
> Oer the misty mountain forest
> And amid the light of morning
> Like a cloud of glory liest
> And when night descends defiest
> The embattled tempests warning[21]

II

Shelley's later descriptions of Byron as an "Eagle" and Byron's of Shelley as a "Snake" call to mind Canto I of *The Revolt of Islam* where Shelley portrayed the Spirits of Good and Evil as "The Snake and Eagle" (xxxiii) and described them "wreathed in [a ceaseless] fight" (viii). It is more than possible that Shelley created this metaphor without even thinking of Byron, but he could not have failed to apply it to his debate with Byron after writing *Julian and Maddalo* in 1818/19. Even in 1817, Shelley disapproved of *Manfred* and rejected the "gloom and misanthropy" infecting Byron's works; and by January 1818, he eagerly requested Charles Ollier to send Byron's *Childe Harold* IV "the moment" it was published,[22] apparently because he wished to see if the "Mighty Mind" (Shelley's phrase for Byron in an 1818 fragment) could reexperience the deep thinking and the deep feeling manifest in the last half of *Childe Harold* III. Although Byron had promised therein to pierce the clouds in his search for the "hopes which will not deceive" and although Shelley had urged Byron to pursue these same hopes, Shelley was destined for further disappointment. On 20 July 1817 and with the fourth canto "completed" in 126 stanzas (60 more were added before publication in April 1818), Byron explained to Murray that his new poem "treats more of works of art than of Nature"; and on 7 August, that "there are no metaphysics in it."[23] With the Geneva experience behind him, with *Manfred* intervening, and with Hobhouse as a substitute for Shelley, Byron in *Childe Harold* IV judged the Shelleyan metaphysical ideal to be a "false creation" of a "mind diseased" (cxxii). When Shelley realized what Byron had done in this fourth canto, he promptly rejected his fellow poet's "expressions of contempt & desperation."[24]

Shelley, however, was not totally dissatisfied with *Childe Harold* IV, for he admired its concluding address to the Ocean (clxxix-clxxxiv) and was pleased to find in at least two stanzas ideas consistent with his own *Revolt of Islam*. In a manner similar to Cythna's faith in the seasonal cycle and to Shelley's later metaphor in *Ode to the West Wind*, Byron addressed Freedom with revolutionary zeal:

> Yet, Freedom! yet thy banner, torn, but flying,
>  Streams like the thunder-storm *against* the wind;
>  Thy trumpet voice, though broken now and dying,
>  The loudest still the Tempest leaves behind;
>  Thy tree hath lost its blossoms, and the rind,
>  Chopped by the axe, looks rough and little worth,
>  But the sap lasts,—and still the seed we find
>  Sown deep, even in the bosom of the North;
> So shall a better spring less bitter fruit bring forth.     (IV.xcviii)

Shelley admired this stanza enough to use its first two lines as an epigraph to his *Ode to Liberty* (1820), and when he read it in 1818 he certainly recalled his similar prophecy in *The Revolt*:

> "Lo, Winter comes!—the grief of many graves,
>  The frost of death, the tempest of the sword,
>  The flood of tyranny, whose sanguine waves
>  Stagnate like ice at Faith, the inchanter's word,
>  And bind all human hearts in its repose abhorred.

"The seeds are sleeping in the soil: meanwhile
The tyrant peoples dungeons with his prey;
. . . . . . . . . . . . . . . . . . . .
"This is the Winter of the world;—and here
We die, even as the winds of Autumn fade,
Expiring in the frore and foggy air,—
Behold! Spring comes, tho' we must pass, who made
The promise of its birth."                        (IX.xxiii-xxv)

The renovating life of Spring promised in these lines is also evident in
Cythna's earlier remarks in Canto II:

                    "I remember now,
How once, a slave in tortures doomed to die,
Was saved, because in accents sweet and low
He sung a song his Judge loved long ago,
As he was led to death.—All shall relent
Who hear me—tears as mine have flowed, shall flow,
Hearts beat as mine now beats, with such intent
As renovates the world; a will omnipotent!"       (xli)

In *Childe Harold* IV, Byron also referred to this redemptive action
described by Plutarch in his *Life of Nicius*:

When Athens' armies fell at Syracuse,
    And fettered thousands bore the yoke of war,
    Redemption rose up in the Attic Muse,
    Her voice their only ransom from afar:
    See! as they chant the tragic hymn, the car
    Of the o'ermastered Victor stops—the reins
    Fall from his hands—his idle scimitar
    Starts from its belt—he rends his captive's chains,
And bids him thank the Bard for Freedom and his strains.  (xvi)

On the basis of these two parallels, it might seem that Shelley
misinterpreted Byron's expressions of "contempt & desperation" in
*Childe Harold* IV. Yet these expressions of hope are the exception,
not the rule, in this poem, and Byron fails to sustain the Shelleyan
belief that the world might be redeemed. In fact, the exemplum of the
slave's freedom through Art does not apply to the modern world in the
succeeding apostrophe to Venice: "Thy choral memory of the Bard
divine,/Thy love of Tasso, should have cut the knot/Which ties thee
to thy tyrants" (xvii), but it has not. And within this exemplum lies
the paradox of *Childe Harold* IV: man as poet, as creative mind, can
transcend the ruins precipitated by time and fate; yet this aesthetic
experience, even if attainable by all men individually, cannot redeem

man's political and social condition. "The Beings of the Mind" may not be "of clay" (v), but men are; poets may be "Spirits which soar from ruin" (lv), but man's soul is ultimately a "ruin amidst ruins" (xxv); the Byronic mind may, "from the floating wreck which Ruin leaves behind," create "a little bark of hope," but for the body "There woos no home, nor hope, nor life, save what is here" (civ-cv); thus Art can "multiply in us a brighter ray/And more beloved existence," but the artist as man is still within a "state/Of mortal bondage" and creates only as a refuge from frustrating "Hope" and fruitless "Vacancy" (v-vi).

According to Byron in *Childe Harold* IV, Art could idealize and immortalize human existence, thereby providing man a "refuge," but at the same time Art made man even more aware of his mortal limitations. Man's "brightest" moments were those during which he was "Chained to the chariot of triumphal Art," moments to be destroyed, however, when "the weight/Of earth recoils upon us" (l, lii). Such a "recoil" is particularly and painfully evident in Byron's juxtaposition of the stanzas on the "Caritas Romana" (cxlviii-cli) with those on Princess Charlotte's death (clxvii-clxxii). In the former, a Roman daughter nourished her aged and imprisoned father by milk from her own breast, and Byron explained that "sacred Nature triumphs . . . in this/Reverse of her decree" of birth and death. This reversal, however, offered no hope for man, and Byron clearly labeled the "Caritas Romana" a fair fiction. In the introductory stanzas to his fourth canto, he had specifically separated Art's "strange constellations" with its "brighter ray/And more beloved existence" from "that which Fate/Prohibits to dull life in this our state/Of mortal bondage" (v-vi). With identical phrasing, Byron described the "Caritas Romana" as a "constellation of a sweeter ray," purer even than the "starry fable of the Milky Way" (cli). But a fable was not life, and this "brighter" or "sweeter ray" could not penetrate the "storm and darkness" occasioned by the human drama of Princess Charlotte's death in childbirth in November 1817. And when Byron added to the fourth canto his stanzas on her death, he ironically undercut the fiction of the "Caritas Romana": "with maternal grief" Princess Charlotte "clasps a babe [a son who also died], to whom her breast yields no relief" (clxvii). In effect, Byron acknowledged that any real reversal of Nature's decree of birth and death only increased human misery.

Although Shelley labeled Byron's judgments on Art and life as "desperate," Byron believed that he had achieved a Promethean triumph in his aesthetic: like Prometheus, the artist knew "His wretchedness, and his resistance,/And his sad unallied existence"; yet to these frustrations, "his [creative] Spirit may oppose/Itself—an equal to all woes—/. . . making [Art] a Victory" (*Prometheus*, ll. 51-54, 59).

The development of this aesthetic victory in the fourth canto has been fully analyzed by McGann in *Fiery Dust,* but I disagree with his judgment that the "purely 'aesthetic' aspects of the theme of regeneration are related to social [and political] conditions." McGann himself later concedes that "the climactic statement of human creative capabilities set forth at St. Peter's and the Vatican Gallery [cliii-clxiii] is totally without political references." Shelley, to the contrary, believed that Art could regenerate mankind: the Greek bards provided "a light to save," Laon's song could "disperse/The cloud of that unutterable curse/Which clings upon mankind," Cythna's song could "renovate the world," and *The Revolt* itself would "awaken public hope and . . . enlighten and improve mankind" (*The Revolt* I.xxxii; II.xxx, xli; and Preface); consequently, Shelley could not accept Byron's assumption that poets were not the legislators of the world. Byron had learned from Shelley's *Mont Blanc* the reality of "What Mind can make, when Nature's self would fail" (*Childe Harold* IV.xlix), but he had rejected Shelley's evaluation of the mind's intellectual beauty, that "awful LOVELINESS" which "wouldst free/This world from its dark slavery" (*Hymn to Intellectual Beauty,* ll. 69-71). And without the renovating power of Love, the mind's creations merely mocked man with "the unreached Paradise of our despair" (IV.cxxii). No wonder then that Shelley, whose Cythna asserted that poets' conceptions " 'leave/All hope, or love, or truth, or liberty,/. . ./To be a rule and law to ages that survive' " (IX.xxviii), recoiled when he discovered in *Childe Harold* IV that Circumstance "turns Hope to dust" (cxxv), that love is a "phantasy" of a "mind diseased" (cxxi-cxxii), that truth, "a gem which loves the deep," is obscured by "Custom's falsest scale" and by "Opinion an Omnipotence" (xciii), and that Byron's "revolutionary poem" which prophesied liberty "should be so lacking in visions of a transformed political order in Italy (or anywhere else)."[25]

What most disturbed Shelley in *Childe Harold* IV as well as in *Manfred* was Byron's rejection of metaphysical ideals. At the conclusion of *Childe Harold* III, Byron had hesitatingly believed that "there may be/Words which are things" (cxiv), that such words as goodness, virtue, truth, and love signified meaningful ideals for man; but in the fourth canto, he judged that these ideals, these "things whose strong reality/Outshines our fairy-land" of Art, "came like Truth [in Geneva?]—and disappeared like dreams;/And whatsoe'er they were— are now but so" (vi-vii). Byron of course could not escape metaphysical speculation,

> still teems
> My mind with many a form which aptly seems
> Such as I sought for, and at moments found;

but these many ideal forms springing from the creative mind were delusory and ineffectual:

> Let these too go—for waking Reason deems
> Such over-weening phantasies unsound,
> And other voices speak, and other sights surround.[26]          (vii)

Waking Reason's most destructive act occurred in Byron's five-stanza addition (cxx-cxxiv) to the Egeria stanzas in *Childe Harold* IV. His mind teeming with the form of Love in the person of Egeria, Byron attempted to purge this "over-weening phantasy" from both the present and the past cantos of *Childe Harold*. He had formerly noted with Shelleyan reverence in Canto III that Love "is the great principle of the universe, which is there [Clarens] more condensed, but not less manifested; and of which, though knowing ourselves a part, we lose our individuality, and mingle in the beauty of the whole" (Byron's note to stanza xcix). In the fourth canto, however, Shelley's "awful LOVELINESS" was repudiated:

> Oh, Love! no habitant of earth thou art—
> An unseen Seraph, we believe in thee,—
> A faith whose martyrs are the broken heart,—
> But never yet hath seen, nor e'er shall see
> The naked eye, thy form, as it should be;
> The mind hath made thee, as it peopled Heaven,
> Even with its own desiring phantasy,
>
> . . . . . . . . . . . . . . . . . . . .
>
> Of its own beauty is the mind diseased,
> And fevers into false creation:—where,
> Where are the forms the sculptor's soul hath seized?
> In him alone. Can Nature show so fair?
> Where are the charms and virtues which we dare
> Conceive in boyhood and pursue as men,
> The unreached Paradise of our despair,
>
> . . . . . . . . . . . . . . . . . . . .
>
> Who loves, raves—'tis youth's frenzy.          (cxxi-cxxiii)

Byron might agree with Shelley that "Love is . . . the sole law which *should* govern the moral world" (Preface to *The Revolt*, my italics), but Love *could* never be realized: "Nor Worth nor Beauty dwells from out the mind's/Ideal shape of such" (IV.cxxiii). In order that this judgment be properly distinguished from Shelley's similar statement in *Julian and Maddalo* ("'Where is the love, beauty and truth

73

we seek,/But in our mind?'" [ll. 174-75]), we must remember that for Shelley these ideals, once created by the mind, were not the "unreached Paradise of our despair," but rather "'a rule and law to ages that survive'" (*The Revolt* IX.xxviii)—a guide for the attainable progression of the human spirit.

Byron, however, in his fourth canto believed that the ages which survive will merely rehearse the past: "the moral of all human tales" is a fall from freedom and glory to tyranny and barbarism (cviii). And even though Circumstance might rekindle man's hope in freedom by providing another Washington (xcvi), it could just as easily destroy man's hopes through the "immedicable wound" of Princess Charlotte's death (clxvii-clxxii);[27] hence "Circumstance," that "Miscreator" (cxxv), could not effectively minister to "the immedicable soul" (cxxvi) of man, that "barren being" with "senses narrow" and "reason frail" (xciii). With this skeptical distrust of sense and reason, Byron could not share Shelley's hope for man's social and political progression, but he would not resign man's right of thought: though "cabined, cribbed, confined,/And bred in darkness," reason offered man his "only place/ Of refuge" (cxxvii) from which he could consider alternatives to his "heart-aches ever new" (cxxvi). These alternatives—the creation of Art, absorption into Nature, and Promethean endurance—however, only served to highlight the vacancy of the heart and the isolation of the Byronic mind or spirit.

With Art and Nature being both praised and dispraised in *Childe Harold* IV, Byron was reluctant to set upon either his hopes for any fulfillment, yet he did see in St. Peter's and the Vatican a triumph of the artistic spirit: a man's spirit could dilate to contemplate the vast design of St. Peter's, "be enlightened," and share in the glory of the Laocoön and especially the Apollo Belvedere in whose

> delicate form—a dream of Love,
> Shaped by some solitary Nymph, whose breast
> Longed for a deathless lover from above,
> And maddened in that vision—are exprest
> All that ideal Beauty ever blessed
> The mind with in its most unearthly mood,
> When each Conception was a heavenly Guest—
> A ray of Immortality—and stood,
> Starlike, around, until they gathered to a God.          (clxii)

What might be construed above as an artist's successful participation "in the eternal, the infinite, and the one" (Shelley, *Defence of Poetry*) is really little more than another source of frustration for the Byronic artist. Notwithstanding the rhetoric of "heavenly Guest," each conception of ideal beauty that "the sculptor's soul hath seized" is ultimately self-generated and to be judged a "false creation" of a fevered mind (cxxii): just as the vision of Egeria resulted from the "nympholepsy of some fond despair" (cxv) and was succeeded by an acknowledgment that "our young affections run to waste,/Or water but the desert" (cxx), so also the "maddened . . . . vision" of the Apollo Belvedere was "a dream of Love,/Shaped by some solitary Nymph, whose breast/Longed for a deathless lover from above" (clxii) and was succeeded by an acknowledgment that Art eventually "fades away into Destruction's mass,"

> Which gathers shadow—substance—life, and all
> That we inherit in its mortal shroud—
> And spreads the dim and universal pall
> Through which all things grow phantoms; and the cloud
> Between us sinks and all which ever glowed,
> Till Glory's self is twilight, and displays
> A melancholy halo scarce allowed
> To hover on the verge of darkness—rays
> Sadder than saddest night.                    (clxv)

In a manner similar to the narrator-poet's earlier desire to entwine his "thoughts with Nature rather in the fields,/Than Art in galleries" (lxi), the "weary Bard" (clxxiv) at the end of the fourth canto, having achieved no victory through Art, turned to the Ocean and Nature for his spirit's homage:

> Yet not in vain our mortal race hath run—
> We have had our reward—and it is here,—
> That we can yet feel gladdened by the Sun,
> And reap from Earth—Sea—joy almost as dear
> As if there were no Man to trouble what is clear.     (clxxvi)

In the fair copy of Byron's fourth canto, this stanza on the joy to be reaped from "Earth" and "Sea" was immediately followed and to some extent contradicted by the six Ocean stanzas, wherein Byron implied that the conflict between Ocean ("The image of Eternity") and Earth paralleled the destructive conflict between man's spirit and clay. Apparently sensing this possible contradiction, Byron interjected an idealistic hope for joy on "Earth" in two additional stanzas:

> Oh! that the Desert were my dwelling-place,
> With one fair Spirit for my minister,
> That I might all forget the human race,
> And, hating no one, love but only her!

Ye elements!—in whose ennobling stir
I feel myself exalted—Can ye not
Accord me such a Being? Do I err
In deeming such inhabit many a spot?
Though with them to converse can rarely be our lot.

There is a pleasure in the pathless woods,
   There is a rapture on the lonely shore,
   There is society, where none intrudes,
   By the deep Sea, and Music in its roar:
I love not Man the less, but Nature more,
From these our interviews, in which I steal
From all I may be, or have been before,
To mingle with the Universe, and feel
What I can ne'er express—yet can not all conceal. (clxxvii-clxxviii)

Added in March 1818, these stanzas are somewhat unusual in their
context, for they recall Byron's initial and somewhat hesitant reaction
to Nature in *Childe Harold* III (compare stanzas lxxii-lxxiv) and hence
reintroduce the "over-weening phantasies" (IV.vii) denounced at the
beginning of the fourth canto. Notwithstanding the suggestion of a
psychological redemption in these lines, Byron's earlier statements on
Nature necessarily temper his final pursuit of joy. Just as Art was a
"refuge" from "Hope" and "Vacancy" (vi), so also was Nature "a
refuge from . . . hopes decayed" (xxxii); and in relation to the
desirable forms with which the mind teems, "Nature's self would fail"
(xlix). Thus the desire at the end of Canto IV to "forget the human
race," to love "one fair Spirit," and to "mingle with the Universe"
would be unfulfilled. At best, Nature offered isolated man only a
brief respite from his past and future frustration.

    Because neither Art nor Nature could redeem man from his fallen
state, the only viable alternative in *Childe Harold* IV was Promethean
pride: like the Tannen trees, individual minds could still "Endure and
shrink not" from their alien environment and their "bare and desolated
bosoms" (xxi). And even though "All suffering doth destroy, or is
destroyed,/Even by the sufferer—and, in each event,/Ends" (xxii),
"fresh bitterness" will succeed and strike "the electric chain wherewith
we are darkly bound" (xxiii).[28] This interminable Promethean agony
may even be found in Byron's discourse on Art, where the "Immortal's
patience" and the "Immortal's vengeance" were respectively figured in
"Laocoön's torture dignifying pain" (clx) and in Apollo Belvedere's
"beautiful Disdain" (clxi). And this endurance and defiance receive
their fullest expression in Byron's Promethean curse wrought with the
aid of Nemesis in the ruins of the Coliseum:

And if my voice break forth, 'tis not that now
  I shrink from what is suffered: let him speak
Who hath beheld decline upon my brow,
  Or seen my mind's convulsion leave it weak;
But in this page a record will I seek.
  Not in the air shall these my words disperse,
  Though I be ashes; a far hour shall wreak
The deep prophetic fulness of this verse,
And pile on human heads the mountain of my curse!

That curse shall be Forgiveness.—Have I not—
  Hear me, my mother Earth! behold it, Heaven!—
Have I not had to wrestle with my lot?
  Have I not suffered things to be forgiven?
Have I not had my brain seared, my heart riven,
  Hopes sapped, name blighted, Life's life lied away?
And only not to desperation driven,
  Because not altogether of such clay
As rots into the souls of those whom I survey.

                                        (cxxxiv-cxxxv)

Because Shelley's Prometheus would forgive with the sympathetic
resolution for "no living thing to suffer pain" (*Prometheus Unbound*
I.305), Shelley could not accept Byron's self-posturing curse of forgiveness which, as even McGann conceded, "borders dangerously upon an
act of vendetta."[29] And Shelley was quick to condemn Byron's "most
wicked & mischievous insanity" in these "expressions of contempt &
desperation" in his letter to Peacock in December 1818. And at the
same time he not only labeled Byron's Promethean curse the "terror"
of "a mighty thunder-fit" (*Lines Written Among the Euganean Hills*,
ll. 182-83), but also provided Byron an alternative in *Julian and
Maddalo,* where the Maniac's forgiveness of his tormentor impelled him
to "cast away /. . . all revenge, all pride" (ll. 501-2).
  Although Shelley in his December letter to Peacock explained
that he had "remonstrated with [Byron] in vain on the tone of mind"
which prompted these expressions of Promethean defiance and endurance in *Childe Harold* IV, Shelley was not giving up the argument. In
the next two chapters we will see that he wrote *Prometheus Unbound*
as well as *Julian and Maddalo* and the *Euganean Hills* in an attempt to
correct the distorted mirror of Byron's thoughts. The extent of
Shelley's displeasure with Byron is further confirmed by his "Notes on
Sculptures in Rome and Florence" and "The Coliseum," the latter
begun in Rome on 25 November 1818.[30] In the "Notes on Sculptures,"
Shelley directly addresses the author of *Childe Harold* IV:

Byron thinks that Laocoön's anguish is absorbed in that of his children, that a mortal's agony is blending with an immortal's patience. Not so. Intense physical suffering, against which he pleads with an upraised countenance of despair, and appeals with a sense of its injustice, seems the predominant and overwhelming emotion, and yet there is a nobleness in the expression, and a majesty that dignifies torture.

Opposing Byron's view of "Laocoön's torture dignifying pain" (*Childe Harold* IV.clx; cf. "And making Death a Victory" at the conclusion of Byron's *Prometheus*), Shelley believed that it was the "majesty" of the sculpture which "dignifies torture." In effect, Shelley was going beyond the immediate subject ("a disagreeable one" to him) and overlooking Byron's interpretation of the Laocoön as a symbol for Promethean endurance (the "Immortal's patience") in a hostile and inescapable environment:

> —Vain
> The struggle—vain, against the coiling strain
> And gripe, and deepening of the dragon's grasp,
> The Old Man's clench; the long envenomed chain
> Rivets the living links.               (IV.clx)

To Byron, these "links" of the chain were reminders of man's Promethean inheritance: "His wretchedness, and his resistance,/And his sad unallied existence" (*Prometheus*, ll. 51-52). To Shelley, however, Byron's Promethean interpretation of the Laocoön was a painful reminder of a mind that had circumscribed its imagination and that desperately needed to be liberated.

Shelley at this time was already arguing against Byron and for the imagination's liberation in *Julian and Maddalo* and *Prometheus Unbound*, both of which attack the premises of Byron's Prometheanism. But *Childe Harold* IV, especially Byron's Promethean curse within the Coliseum, so angered Shelley that he began in November 1818 a narrative entitled "The Coliseum" in which he could offer a different interpretation of what Byron had called the "long-explored but still exhaustless mine/Of Contemplation" (IV.cxxviii). As in *Manfred* (III.iv.9-42), Byron in *Childe Harold* IV pictured the Coliseum as a "vast and wondrous monument" full of "glory," "power," and "magic" (cxxix); but because he also stressed that "Rome and her Ruin [were] past Redemption's skill" (cxlv) and because he chose this Ruin as the scene for his unredemptive Promethean curse (cxxxii-cxxxvii), Byron primarily used the Coliseum as "the focusing image of man's folly of self-destruction."[31] For Shelley, however, the Coliseum's heritage of superstition, murder, and slavery was overshadowed by its "broad and everlasting character of human strength and genius, that pledge of all that is to be admirable and lovely in ages yet to come." Once again, Shelley took the circumstances of Byron's poetry and reversed the conclusion: the Coliseum did promise "Redemption." And in his letter describing the beauty of the Coliseum to Peacock in December 1818, Shelley judged that the *focusing image* of man's "selfwilled folly" in this world was *not* the Coliseum, but rather *Childe Harold* IV! In this fourth canto, Shelley argued, Byron was "contemplating in the distorted mirror of his own thoughts, the nature & the destiny of man," and in the process he mistakenly chose the ruins of the Coliseum as the place for "expressions of contempt & desperation."

In sharp contrast to the Coliseum sequence in *Childe Harold* IV (but perhaps inspired by Byron's version of the "Caritas Romana" in stanzas cxlviii-cli), Shelley's "The Coliseum" presents a blind father urging hope on his daughter and an accompanying stranger who, like Byron, is in need of such encouragement. If we, the father argues with a Shelleyan intensity, if we can "'enter into the meditations, designs and destinies of something beyond ourselves'" without being constrained by the distortions of Byronic thoughts, then "'the contemplation of the ruins of human power excites an elevating sense of awfulness and beauty,'" not a sense of contempt and despair. To support his point, Shelley's protagonist explains that "'the internal nature of each being is surrounded by a circle, not to be surmounted by his fellows; and it is this repulsion which constitutes the misfortune of the [Byronic] condition of life.'" This "'repulsion,'" Shelley seems to be saying, is evident in Byron's Coliseum sequence where the narrator curses with egotistical and self-alienating assurance. But, according to the father in Shelley's narrative, there is within man another "'circle which comprehends, as well as one which mutually excludes, all things which feel'"; and by "'diminishing the circumference which includes those resembling himself, until they become one with him, and he with them,'" man can increase "'his public and his private happiness.'"

Because of man's capacity for regeneration through the sympathetic imagination, Shelley's protagonist neither called upon the "repulsive" Nemesis nor invoked a self-posturing curse of forgiveness in response to Promethean agony. Instead, in order to reject the self-willed ill of *Childe Harold* IV and to embrace the formula of *Prometheus Unbound,* he comforted his daughter and the stranger by invoking the "comprehensive" power of Love still manifest amid the Ruins of the Coliseum:

"O Power!" cried the old man, lifting his sightless eyes towards the undazzling sun, "thou which interpenetratest all things, and

without which this glorious world were a blind and formless
chaos, Love, Author of Good, God, King, Father! Friend of these
thy worshippers! Two solitary hearts invoke thee, may they be
divided never! If the contentions of mankind have been their
misery; if to give and seek that happiness which thou art, has
been their choice and destiny; if, in the contemplation of these
majestic records of the power of their kind, they see the shadow
and the prophecy of that which thou mayst have decreed that he
should become; if the justice, the liberty, the loveliness, the truth,
which are thy footsteps, have been sought by them, divide them
not! It is thine to unite, to eternize; to make outlive the limits
of the grave those who have left among the living, memorials of
thee."

Byron's narrator, it should be recalled, concluded his curse in the
Coliseum with the expectation that it should "tire/Torture and Time,
and breathe when I expire." But the two Coliseum speeches promised
different results: for Byron's narrator, when the "frame [will] perish"
the curse will breed a vindictive "remorse of Love" (cxxxvii) in his
former associates; for Shelley's protagonist, "when this frame shall be
senseless dust, . . . the hopes, and the desires, and the delights
which animate it now,[will] never be extinguished in my child."

　　Shelley's choice of the Coliseum as the scene for his anti-Byronic
narrative cannot be coincidental. Writing his prose fragment between
reading *Childe Harold* IV in Venice and criticizing it in his December
letter to Peacock, Shelley attempted in this narrative to counter Byron's
"expressions of contempt & desperation" by interpreting the Coliseum
as a symbol of man's progressive spirit. In order to dramatize his
hopes that Byron might still be convinced of the Shelleyan " 'truth of
things,' " Shelley even had the rude stranger (who had interrupted the
father and daughter's conversation) embrace the spirit of redemptive
Love amidst the ruins after the father's invocation. However, neither
Maddalo nor Byron, Shelley later admitted, would so readily undergo
a Shelleyan conversion during the two poets' argument on another
"ruin," the Maniac in Shelley's *Julian and Maddalo.*

## 5 TANGLED BOUGHS OF HEAVEN AND OCEAN: TWO GENII AND A MANIAC

Byron and Shelley had been separated for two years when they met for the second time in Venice on 23 August 1818. One reason for their reunion was Allegra, Byron and Claire Clairmont's young daughter who had accompanied the Shelley party to Milan at the beginning of April and who at the end of April was sent, with her Swiss nurse Elise, to join Byron in Venice. Thereafter, Shelley, Mary, and Claire moved from Milan, through Pisa, to Leghorn, and finally to Bagni di Lucca until Claire persuaded Shelley to escort her to Venice so that she might see Allegra. On Sunday morning, 23 August, Shelley and Claire arrived at the home of Richard Hoppner (the British consul in Venice) and his wife, with whom Allegra had been living for most of August. That afternoon, Shelley proceeded alone to meet Byron in order to discuss Claire's future plans for her daughter. Shelley's motives for this visit were not, however, entirely selfless, for he welcomed the opportunity to share his ideas once more with the poet he had influenced in Geneva. And Byron, according to Shelley, was equally delighted to renew their acquaintance, even though he had already rejected Shelley's former influence. Both poets, we have seen, had already defined their differences with each other in *Manfred* and *The Revolt of Islam*. And shortly after their second meeting in Venice, Shelley would begin not only *Prometheus Unbound* in order to question Byron's enslaving Prometheanism in *Manfred* and *Childe Harold IV*, but also *Julian and Maddalo* in order to have a Shelleyan meliorist and a Byronic fatalist debate the nature of man's Promethean inheritance.

Disregarding for a moment the biographical fact that two poets met for the second time in Venice in 1818, we might envision not only the first meeting between Julian and Maddalo but also between Laon and Manfred, for neither poet could disassociate himself from his own protagonist's judgments; consequently, in Shelley's eyes at least, the forthcoming debate would be equally a product of the philosophical antagonism between Shelley and Byron as well as between Laon and Manfred. Desiring to descant once more "Concerning God, freewill, and destiny./Of all that Earth has been, or yet may be" (*Julian and Maddalo*, ll. 42-43), each poet apparently sensed in the other not only a worthy antagonist but also a personification of his own opposite hopes and fears. The Poet and the narrator of *Alastor*, it will be recalled, had expressed even graver doubts about life after death than had Manfred; and Shelley in *Adonais*, like Manfred and like Wordsworth of the *Elegiac Stanzas*, would reject the "fond illusion" of his hopes for temporal improvement. Conversely, Byron even in *Childe Harold* IV had upstaged Shelley's prophetic hope for political freedom; and the poet of "the isles of Greece," dreaming "that Greece might still be free," would dash down the symbolically enslaving "cup of Samian wine" (*Don Juan*, Canto III). In another vein, Manfred had at one time entertained Laon's high hopes and even Laon experienced with Manfred the same *temporal* reversals of fate and fortune. Nevertheless, even though Maddalo confessed that he shared some opinions with Julian, both characters, like their prototypes, chose to intensify rather than resolve their fundamental antagonism.

Although *Julian and Maddalo* may have had its genesis in Shelley's conversations with Byron during their ride along the Adriatic shore during the afternoon and early evening of 23 August, it also embodies the debate that they had waged during the past two years and that they continued during their occasional meetings in Venice from 23 August until the end of October. Nevertheless, Shelley's description of that first conversation in his letter of 23-24 August to Mary, who had remained behind at Bagni di Lucca, introduces several subjects that later found their way into *Julian and Maddalo*. According to Shelley, he and Byron dispelled some of the confusion surrounding Allegra, and then Byron

> took me in his gondola—much against my will for I wanted to return to Clare at Mrs. Hoppners who was anxiously waiting for me—across the laguna to a long sandy island which defends Venise from the Adriatic. When we disembarked, we found his horses waiting for us, & we rode along the sands of the sea talking. Our conversation consisted in histories of his wounded feelings, & questions as to my affairs, & great professions of friendship & regard for me. He said that if he had been in England at the time of the Chancery affair, he would have moved Heaven & Earth to have prevented such a decision. We talked of literary matters, his fourth Canto which he says is very good, & indeed repeated some stanzas of great energy to me, & Foliage which he quizzes immoderately. When we returned to his palace— which [*the top half of p. 5 (leaf 3) is missing*][1]

One of the "literary matters" discussed in this or a subsequent conversation was certainly the dramatic character of Torquato Tasso. Shelley had already communicated to Byron his great admiration for portions of *The Lament of Tasso,* and four months before their second meeting he had decided to devote "this summer & indeed the next year to the composition of a tragedy on the subject of Tasso's madness."[2] Shelley never completed this tragedy, and by August he probably had written only a fifty-line "Scene from Tasso," a twenty-six-line "Song for Tasso," and a few suggestions for additional scenes.[3] The importance of Shelley's interest in Tasso's madness has already been documented, particularly in Carlos Baker's and G. M. Matthews' analyses of the Maniac in *Julian and Maddalo,*[4] but equally important here, for the debate in *Julian and Maddalo,* is the difference between Shelley's and Byron's portraits of Tasso's life. If Shelley's interest in Tasso can deepen our understanding of *Julian and Maddalo,* then that poem can in turn highlight Shelley's intentions in his fragmentary scenes and songs for a Tasso drama.

The key to this interpoetical problem lies in Byron's and Shelley's Promethean myths of the enslaved man. By having Maddalo allude to Byron's 1816 *Prometheus* (Maddalo cites the madhouse with its belfry tower as the symbol of " 'our mortality;/. . . the emblem and the sign/Of what should be eternal and divine' " [ll. 120-22] just as Byron had addressed Prometheus as a "symbol and a sign/To Mortals of their fate and force;/. . . in part divine,/A troubled stream from a pure source" [ll. 45-48]), Shelley was tracing Byron's 1818 fatalism back to his mythological portrait of man as an enslaved and bound Prometheus. And the poetry Byron wrote between his ode on the enchained Prometheus and Shelley's narrative of the imprisoned Maniac confirms the appropriateness of Maddalo's Promethean " 'emblem and . . . sign' ": *Manfred* and *Childe Harold* IV detail the frustrating limitations on man's intellectual and creative powers; and *The Prisoner of Chillon* and *The Lament of Tasso* literalize and humanize the metaphor and the myth of Prometheus bound. Shelley, of course, would not countenance this enthrallment of man's spirit. Not long after the two poets' second meeting and Shelley's continuing exposure to Byron's ideas, Shelley's Prometheus offered a formula for self-liberation, and Julian/Shelley confronted Maddalo/Byron with the following hope:

> "it is our will
> That thus enchains us to permitted ill—
> We might be otherwise—we might be all
> We dream of happy, high, majestical.
> . . . . . . . . and those who try may find

How strong the chains are which our spirit bind:
Brittle perchance as straw." (ll. 170-73, 180-82)

If Shelley had completed his drama on Tasso's madness at this
time, I am convinced that he would have depicted Tasso's condition
with Julian's faith in the ultimate nobility of the human spirit. For
both Byron and Shelley, prisons and chains were metaphors for much
of the human condition; but for Shelley, like Blake, these were "mind-
forg'd manacles" which could be broken, not merely endured or defied
in the manner of Byron's *Lament of Tasso*. Granted, Byron in that
poem may not have universalized Tasso's complaint into the condition
of all men, but Shelley nevertheless disliked Byron's fatalistic portraits
of enchained men. And in this case, he probably thought that Byron
intended *The Lament of Tasso* to reproduce, on a human level, the
mythic dimensions of *Prometheus* and *Manfred*. At any rate, seven
months after he read Byron's *Lament*, Shelley in April 1818 decided
to devote his whole summer to a drama on Tasso, and he intended, I
believe, to respond to the fatalistic implications of Byron's *Lament*.
Previously, Shelley had used only select portions of Byron's poetry in
order to prove to himself that an opposite meaning could be extracted
from them, e.g., in *The Revolt of Islam* where the incidents borrowed
from *The Corsair* were "widely different" in the Shelleyan adaptation.
But in 1818, Shelley thought that he could more emphatically distinguish his ideas from Byron's by choosing Byron's subject, Tasso's
imprisonment and madness, and writing a drama that would be "widely
different" from *The Lament of Tasso*.

Shelley's dissatisfaction with the Promethean chains in *The
Lament of Tasso* is not easily demonstrable, especially since he wrote
to Byron in September 1817, that "those lines in which you describe
the youthful feelings of Tasso; that indistinct consciousness of its own
greatness, which a heart of genius cherishes in solitude, amid neglect
and contempt, have a profound and thrilling pathos which I will confess
to you, whenever I turn to them, make my head wild with tears."[5]
Shelley here authenticates Pope's warning in the *Essay on Criticism*,

Some, valuing those of their own side or mind,
Still make themselves the measure of mankind:
Fondly we think we honour merit then,
When we but praise ourselves in other men,

for he admired only the Shelleyan background to the Byronic hero.
And in contradistinction to his other comments on Byron's works, he
here admired the "spirit" of the poetry but judged that the "form"
was not "so perfect and sustained a composition." But even Shelley's

praise of the "spirit" of *The Lament* must be qualified, for he isolated only those lines (149-73) describing Tasso's youthful idealism. Shelley may also have admired Tasso's enduring love for Leonora, but he was certainly disappointed to find that this love did not free Tasso, at least spiritually, from his confinement. Instead, he found that Tasso's love and imagination were circumscribed by the weakness of the human spirit ("From long infection of a den like this,/. . . the mind rots congenial with the abyss," ll. 234-35); by pride (Tasso was "too proud to be vindictive," l. 104); and by a *curse* of forgiveness for his tormentors (anticipating the curse in *Childe Harold* IV, which Shelley did not read until September 1818). Because of these defects, Shelley must have judged that the Byronic and Promethean strengths that Byron obviously celebrates in Tasso were actually weaknesses resulting from " 'a want of that true theory, still,/Which seeks a "soul of goodness" in things ill,/Or in himself or others' " (*Julian and Maddalo*, ll. 203-5). In other words, Tasso's imprisonment, like the Maniac's in *Julian and Maddalo*, did not result from " 'destiny' " (as Byron/Maddalo would have Shelley/Julian believe), but rather from his " 'own wilful ill' " (ll. 210-11). Because Tasso need not have been portrayed in such a manner as to suggest that man's fate is beyond his control, Shelley decided to write a drama to show both Tasso and Byron that " 'it is our will/That thus enchains us to permitted ill' " (*Julian and Maddalo*, ll. 170-71).

The little that remains of Shelley's Tasso drama confirms these conclusions, for Shelley it appears would have portrayed a Tasso whose fallen state revealed not only the quality of his former greatness but also the reason (his " 'own wilful ill' ") for that fall. Admiring Byron's lines describing Tasso's youthful idealism, Shelley would have similarly portrayed Tasso with, according to G. M. Matthews, a "physical as well as spiritual idealization." Matthews, who transcribed and analyzed Shelley's fragmentary scene, judged that Shelley's Tasso would have been "unmistakably beautiful" and "divinely inspired." In fact, by depicting what Shelley himself called Tasso's "delicate moral sensibility"[6] *before* his Santa Anna confinement, he would emphasize the tragic nature of Tasso's fall to madness (and not merely an "Imputed madness" as Byron would have it in *The Lament*). Tasso's flaw was to be a lack of that " 'true theory, still,/Which seeks a "soul of goodness" in things ill,/Or in himself or others,' " and this flaw is evident in Shelley's "Song for Tasso":

I loved—alas! our life is love;
But when we cease to breathe and move,
I do suppose love ceases too.

I *thought,* but not as now I do,
Keen thoughts and bright of linked lore,
Of all that men had thought before,
And all that Nature shows, and more.

And still I love, and still I think,
But strangely, for my heart can drink
The dregs of such despair, and live,
And love;
And if I think, my thoughts come fast;
I mix the present with the past,
And each seems uglier than the last.

The youth whose "soul was drunk with Love" in Byron's *Lament*
(l. 150) is here portrayed as having lost that imaginative faith in eternal
love, a loss Shelley intended both to pity and to condemn. But as
Shelley observed in November 1818 after reading Tasso's unprincipled
and flattering sonnets to Alfonso,

> there is much more to pity than to condemn in these entreaties
> and praises of [by] Tasso. It is as a Christian prays to {and}
> praises his God whom he knows to [be] the most remorseless
> capricious & inflexible of tyrants, but whom he knows also to be
> omnipotent.[7]

Because Shelley's reaction to the misguided Tasso is almost identical
to Julian's disdain for the maniacs, who had " 'As much skill as need
to pray/In thanks or hope for their dark lot . . ./To their stern
maker' " (*Julian and Maddalo,* ll. 111-13), we may safely assume that
Shelley's Tasso, like Julian's Maniac, would have been criticized for
his own " 'wilful ill.' " And the "admirably dramatic & poetical"
strength of Tasso's life would lie in the paradox of such an unfortunate
fall from youthful idealism, a paradox that Shelley had confirmed at
least by 7 November 1818 when he interpreted Tasso's handwriting as
"the symbol of an *intense & earnest mind exceeding at times its own
depth,* and admonished to return by the chillness of the waters of
oblivion striking upon its adventurous feet."[8]

   If the foregoing approximates Shelley's intent to use the life of
Tasso as a means to counter *The Lament of Tasso* and consequently
show the moral and intellectual error in Byron's attempt to make Tasso
a blameless hero, then why did he abandon his drama on Tasso? Even
the coadunating imagination of Coleridge could not cope with the
morally complex idea in *Christabel,* and Shelley may have similarly
undertaken too complex a task. But Shelley's November letter to
Peacock reveals another reason. Having examined the handwriting of

*Gerusalemme Liberata,* questioned the self-seeking sonnets to Alfonso, and likened Tasso's lamenting entreaties to the Christian's homage before a tyrannical God, Shelley then observed that

> Tasso's situation was widely different from that of any persecuted being of the present day, for from the depth of dungeons public opinion might now at length be awakened to an echo that would startle the oppressor. But then there was no hope. There is something irresistibly pathetic to me in the sight of Tasso's own hand writing moulding expressions of adulation & entreaty to a deaf & stupid tyrant in an age when the most heroic virtue would have exposed its possessor to hopeless persecution, and—such is the alliance between virtue & genius—which unoffending genius could not escape.

If Shelley was to take Byron to task for his universalized portraits of man in chains from 1816 to 1818, then he must choose an imprisoned madman less pathetic and less particular, with a "situation [*less*] widely different from that of any persecuted being of the present day." In other words, he must choose a madman whose "story, told at length, might be like many other stories of the same kind: the unconnected exclamations of his agony will perhaps be found a sufficient comment for the text of every heart" (Preface to *Julian and Maddalo*). Thus when Tasso's life would no longer serve one of Shelley's purposes, that being to engage Byron once more in an intellectual debate about " 'How strong the chains are which our spirit bind' " (*Julian and Maddalo,* l. 181), then Shelley exchanged the particular Tasso for the universal Maniac in *Julian and Maddalo* where he could confront Byron on the question of all men's Promethean heritage.[9]

## II

At best, Shelley's Tasso drama would have offered a very indirect challenge to a relatively minor poem among Byron's recent works, and by the fall of 1818 Shelley believed that Byron's other "expressions of contempt & desperation" also needed to be challenged. Depressed by the "despondency" in *Manfred* and angered by the "insanity" of *Childe Harold* IV, Shelley decided to write *Julian and Maddalo* and force a Byronic fatalist to contend with a Shelleyan meliorist. At the same time, within this philosophical debate, Shelley could introduce a Prometheus bound in the person of a Maniac who would not resolve but would at least clarify the two poets' different estimates of the human condition.

The characters of Julian and Maddalo were indeed clever devices for Shelley's purpose. The poem opens with the two protagonists on

a friendly ride "Upon the bank of land which breaks the flow/Of
Adria towards Venice" (ll. 2-3), and although Shelley and Byron
took a similar ride on 23 August we should not assume literal fidelity
to their experience. Certainly, Maddalo mirrors Byron, but he also
reproduces traits of the Byronic hero that Shelley had discovered in
*Manfred* and *Childe Harold* IV. These dual sources of Byron the man
and the Byronic hero are suggested by Shelley's Preface:

> Count Maddalo is a Venetian nobleman of ancient family and
> of great fortune, who, without mixing much in the society of his
> countrymen, resides chiefly at his magnificent palace in that city.
> He is a person of the most consummate genius, and capable, if he
> would direct his energies to such an end, of becoming the re-
> deemer of his degraded country. But it is his weakness to be
> proud: he derives, from a comparison of his own extraordinary
> mind with the dwarfish intellects that surround him, an intense
> apprehension of the nothingness of human life. His passions and
> his powers are incomparably greater than those of other men; and,
> instead of the latter having been employed in curbing the former,
> they have mutually lent each other strength. His ambition preys
> upon itself, for want of objects which it can consider worthy of
> exertion. I say that Maddalo is proud, because I can find no other
> word to express the concentered and impatient feelings which
> consume him; but it is on his own hopes and affections only that
> he seems to trample, for in social life no human being can be
> more gentle, patient, and unassuming than Maddalo. He is cheer-
> ful, frank, and witty. His more serious conversation is a sort of
> intoxication; men are held by it as by a spell. He has travelled
> much; and there is an inexpressible charm in his relation of
> his adventures in different countries.

In many respects, the Byronic hero predominates in this capsule
portrait: Maddalo's pride, his Promethean intelligence, and his "intense
apprehension of the nothingness of human life" not only look backward to Manfred and the narrator of *Childe Harold* but forward to
Cain and the narrator of *Don Juan*, these latter two also apprehending
the "Nothingness of life" (see *Cain* II.ii.418-22; *Don Juan* VII.6). And
because Manfred had repudiated "those early visions,/And noble
aspirations in my youth,/To make my own the mind of other men,/
The enlightener of nations" (III.i.104-7), it was only fitting that
Shelley's Maddalo be *capable* but *unwilling* to "direct his energies to
such an end, of becoming the redeemer of his degraded country."

In contrast to Maddalo is the poem's narrator, Julian, a somewhat
passive Laon-figure who believed with Shelley in the "power of man

over his own mind, and the immense improvements of which, by the extinction of certain moral superstitions, human society may be yet susceptible" (Preface). In a manner similar to Byron's "Desert," "pathless woods," and "Ocean" stanzas in *Childe Harold* IV.clxxvii-clxxxiv, Julian loved

>                                        all waste
> And solitary places; where we taste
> The pleasure of believing what we see
> Is boundless, as we wish our souls to be:
> And such was this wide ocean, and this shore
> More barren than its billows.

But unlike the Byronic hero's need for isolation in this environment, Shelley's Julian continues,

>                                 and yet more
> Than all, with a remembered friend I love
> To ride as then I rode.                        (ll. 14-21)

Returning from this cheerful ride, the two friends "grew somewhat serious" and discoursed

> Concerning God, freewill, and destiny.
> Of all that Earth has been, or yet may be;
> All that vain men imagine or believe,
> Or hope can paint or suffering may achieve,
> We descanted; and I (for ever still
> Is it not wise to make the best of ill?)
> Argued against despondency, but pride
> Made my companion take the darker side.
> The sense that he was greater than his kind
> Had struck, methinks, his eagle spirit blind[10]
> By gazing on its own exceeding light.        (ll. 42-52)

This descanting, according to Shelley, was not just the subject of one evening but rather of two years of poetry with Laon and Manfred providing prototypes for Julian and Maddalo. As if to relieve the gloom and despondency suggested by the "darker side" of Byron's poetry, the "sun paused ere it should alight/Over the horizon of the mountains" (ll. 53-54), and Julian reflected on the beauty of Italy and Venice, with its "temples and its palaces . . ./Like fabrics of enchantment piled to Heaven" (ll. 91-92). But with his "darker side" and blinded spirit, Maddalo interposed a madhouse with its belfry tower to obscure the sun and present a Byronic and cynical emblem:

"And such," he cried, "is our mortality;
And this must be the emblem and the sign
Of what should be eternal and divine.—
And like that black and dreary bell, the soul
Hung in a heaven-illumined tower, must toll
Our thoughts and our desires to meet below
Round the rent heart, and pray—as madmen do
For what? they know not, till the night of death,
As sunset that strange vision, severeth
Our memory from itself, and us from all
We sought, and yet were baffled!"          (ll. 120-30)

With these words which echo Byron's 1816/18 poetry, Shelley condensed in Maddalo the themes and imagery of Byron's *Darkness,
Prometheus, Manfred, Childe Harold* IV, and *The Lament of Tasso.*

Although the next morning yielded to this darkness by being
"rainy, cold, and dim," Julian visited Maddalo and discovered an
emblematic light in the natural sweetness of Maddalo's daughter (patterned on Allegra), whose eyes seemed "Twin mirrors of Italian
Heaven" (l. 148). And to oppose Maddalo's dark views on man's frustrated mortality, Julian stressed that man's thoughts and desires
promised more than a "rent heart" and "baffled" expectations; because
man had created his own maniacal prison, he also could liberate himself:

"it is our will
That thus enchains us to permitted ill—
We might be otherwise—we might be all
We dream of happy, high, majestical.
Where is the love, beauty and truth we seek,
But in our mind? and if we were not weak,
Should we be less in deed than in desire?"          (ll. 170-76)

Byron himself had similar desires for man's liberation, but experience
had taught him that man was fated to endure and suffer his mortality.
For Julian and Shelley, however, " 'Much may be *conquered* [as well
as] endured' " because man can " '*do* / [as well as] suffer' " and because
the chains which " 'our spirit bind' " are " 'Brittle perchance as straw' "
(ll. 181-86, my italics). Unable to accept Shelleyan doctrine, Maddalo
proposed to expose the weaknesses in this utopianism and the vanity
of " 'such aspiring theories' " by taking Julian to a Maniac who also
had held such theories. But with indomitable Shelleyan optimism,
Julian concluded the first section of the poem by promising to show
that a lack of " 'true theory' " was the cause of the Maniac's madness:

"I hope to prove the induction otherwise,
And that a want of that true theory, still,
Which seeks a 'soul of goodness' in things ill,
Or in himself or others, has thus bowed
His being—there are some by nature proud,
Who patient in all else, demand but this—
To love and be beloved with gentleness;
And being scorned, what wonder if they die
Some living death? This is not destiny,
But man's own wilful ill."                    (ll. 202-11)

Although Julian stated his position sufficiently well here, Shelley in the first draft of *Julian and Maddalo* further developed Julian's distinction between destiny and will:

this is not destiny—
At least, tho all the past cd not have been
Other than as it was—yet things foreseen
Reason and Love may force beneath their yoke
Warned by a fate foregone—as [?thus] I spoke
A man announced the gondola[11]

These lines, omitted from the received text, succinctly contradict Byron's deterministic judgment in the *Ode on Venice* (which Shelley read before beginning or while writing *Julian and Maddalo*)[12] that the future was "The everlasting *to be* which *hath been*" (l. 59). For Shelley, the contrary was true: "things foreseen/Reason and Love may force beneath their yoke/Warned by a fate foregone." Once more we meet Shelleyan Reason and Love in a productive union, where "Our thoughts and our desires" can recombine the heaven-illumined tower of the soul with the medicable heart. These twin faculties, Shelley certainly remembered, had already been threatened by *Childe Harold* IV where Byron judged reason to be chained (cxxvii) and love to be a form of madness (cxxiii). With the faculties of Byronic man thus enchained and enfeebled, no wonder then that Shelley had Maddalo provide an imprisoned maniac as his emblem, an emblem in perfect accord with Byron's recent poetry. In effect, then, Byron as Maddalo was telling Shelley as Julian to read his poetry wherein man was maniacally enchained. In other words, the Maniac was to be a Byronic hero who, having once shared Shelley's idealism (as the narrator of *Childe Harold* IV had), would argue (as Manfred had done) that the Geneva philosophy was ineffectual in a world of flesh and blood. And Shelley, as he had partially attempted in *Laon and Cythna*, would take this maniacal poetry or poetical maniac and argue that it or he failed to seek " 'a "soul of goodness" in things ill,/Or in himself or others.' "

That the Maniac in *Julian and Maddalo* is an extension of Byron should be self-evident from the logic of the poem: Maddalo, modeled on Byron, presents Byronic proof or empirical evidence to substantiate his case. In this evidence (i.e., the Maniac, a composite portrait of the Byronic hero or Byronic "spirit" of things), we find the same "spirit . . . insane" that Shelley by December 1818 had discovered in *Childe Harold* IV:

> I entirely agree with what you [Peacock] say about Childe Harold. The spirit in which it is written is, *if insane, the most wicked & mischievous insanity that ever was given forth.* It is a kind of *obstinate & selfwilled folly* in which he hardens himself. *I remonstrated with him in vain on the tone of mind from which such a view of things alone arises.* For its real root is very different from its apparent one, & nothing can be less sublime than the true source of these *expressions of contempt & desperation.* The fact is, that first, the Italian women are perhaps the most contemptible of all who exist under the moon; the most ignorant the most disgusting, the most bigotted, the most filthy. Countesses smell so of garlick that an ordinary Englishman cannot approach them. Well, L[ord] B[yron] is familiar with the lowest sort of these women, the people his gondolieri pick up in the streets. He allows fathers & mothers to bargain with him for their daughters, & though this is common enough in Italy, yet for an Englishman to encourage such sickening vice is a melancholy thing. He associates with wretches who seem almost to have lost the gait & phisiognomy of man, & who do not scruple to avow practices which are not only not named but I believe seldom even conceived in England. He says he disapproves, but he endures. He is not yet an Italian & *is heartily & deeply discontented with himself, & contemplating in the distorted mirror of his own thoughts, the nature & the destiny of man, what can he behold but objects of contempt & despair? But that he is a great poet, I think the address to Ocean proves* [in *Childe Harold* IV]. And he has a certain degree of candour while you talk to him but unfortunately it does not outlast your departure. You may think how unwillingly *I* have left my little favourite [Allegra *cancelled*] Alba in a situation where she might fall again under his authority. But I have employed arguments entreaties every thing in vain, & when these fail you know I have no longer any right. No, I do not doubt, & for his sake I ought to hope that his present career must end

up soon by some violent circumstance which must reduce our situation with respect to Alba into its antient tie.—[13]

In this letter to Peacock, Shelley not only distinguishes once more between the "spirit" and the "form" of Byron's poetry but also reveals his knowledge that Byron had denied the Geneva metaphysics in the fourth canto. Wanting to "remonstrate" once again with the poet he had influenced in 1816, Shelley transformed Byron's "obstinate & selfwilled folly" and his "expressions of contempt & desperation" into the Maniac's " 'wilful ill' " and monologue of "despair." And if Maddalo's emblematic Maniac would exhibit " 'a *want* of that true theory, still,/Which seeks a "soul of goodness" in things ill,' " then Julian could victoriously claim that man's " 'wilful ill' " was responsible for the Maniac's insanity; and Shelley could simultaneously claim that Byron's poetry during the last two years was a product of "selfwilled folly."

Shelley's separate portrayal of Byron and of the Byronic hero or "spirit" in the forms of Maddalo and of his emblematic Maniac is consistent with Shelley's other bifocal judgments on Byron. Even in the Preface to *Julian and Maddalo,* Shelley distinguishes between the cordial friend and the philosophical antagonist in the person of Maddalo. This complex separation is further suggested by Maddalo's invitation to visit the Maniac:

> "I knew one like you,
> Who to this city came some months ago,
> With whom I argued in this sort, and he
> Is now gone mad,—and so he answered me,—
> Poor fellow! But if you would like to go,
> We'll visit him, and his wild talk will shew
> How vain are such aspiring theories."  (ll. 195-201)

Although Maddalo insists that his Maniac will prove that Shelleyan theories lead to madness, Shelley has ironically manipulated this invitation to make the Byronic Maddalo introduce a Byronic Maniac. This irony is more apparent in the first draft of the poem where Maddalo had first stated, "I knew one, like you/Who to this city came *two years* ago,"[14] because Byron himself had come to Venice two years ago (November 1816), at which time, "like" Julian, he had been subject to Shelley's " 'aspiring theories' " and his protagonists' minds still teemed with many an idealized form. And in the intervening two years, Shelley had encountered a maniacal psychomachia in three of Byron's poems: Manfred had performed good, had experienced an idealized love with his counterpart, and had attained momentarily the calmness of Shelleyan philosophy, but still destroyed himself; the narrator of *Childe Harold* had expressed in the third canto a Shelleyan faith in attaining ideals, but in the fourth canto he claimed that these ideals were a product of a diseased mind; and Byron's Tasso, at one time a youthful advocate of Shelleyan love, ended in "Long years of outrage—calumny—and wrong;/Imputed madness, prisoned solitude" (ll. 3-4). Thus Shelley saw potential in Byron's recent protagonists (collectively they possessed Shelleyan theories and were then "like" Julian), but he lamented that they showed " 'How vain are such aspiring theories' " (l. 201).

This identification of the Maniac with the Byronic hero (once a Shelleyan idealist) and with the "spirit" of Byron's poetry (including *The Lament of Tasso*) in effect synthesizes the previous and separate identifications of the Maniac as Shelley himself, then as Tasso, and finally as Byron. More recently, two critics of *Julian and Maddalo*, G. M. Matthews and Earl Wasserman, have come closer to the Shelleyan truth of things by seeing, albeit for different reasons than I offer, the Maniac as a composite figure. For Wasserman, the Maniac is "both a utopian theorist like Julian and an impatient idealist like Maddalo. . . . Aspects of Byron's and Shelley's experiences unquestionably are drawn on, and no doubt Shelley's study of Tasso's life and madness left its mark; but it is only in this composite sense that the Maniac, like Julian and Maddalo, 'is also in some degree a painting from nature, but, with respect to time & place, ideal,' as Shelley informed Hunt." With a different viewpoint from Wasserman, who argues that the Maniac's composite character results from Shelley's skeptical incertitude and his consequent desire to present in the ambiguous Maniac a "type representative of what any of the world's inconstancies does to the aspiring mind,"[15] I believe that this composite has its foundation in the Byronic hero and that Maddalo's introduction of the Maniac is an elaborate metaphor for Byron's urging Shelley to read his poems as "representative" of the human condition. Consequently, I can agree in part with Carlos Baker, who has argued that Byron's *Lament of Tasso* determined much of the Maniac's lament; with Matthews, who cautiously agreed that "Tasso's madness is the basis of actuality in *Julian and Maddalo*" but added that the Maniac's portrait was so depersonalized and despecified as to "draw on the personal experience of Byron and Shelley, perhaps of others"; and with G. Wilson Knight and J. E. Saveson, who, in arguing that Byron was the Maniac, incidentally saw the Byronic hero figured in the Maniac's ravings.[16]

Shelley's insistence in his Preface and in his letter to Hunt (15 August 1819) that the Maniac was an idealized rather than a particularized portrait argues in itself for the composite theory and recalls the reasons for his giving up the drama on Tasso, whose situation was too particularized, too "widely different" from that of other physically and mentally enchained individuals. And noticeably lacking from the Maniac's history is an Alfonso who had imprisoned Tasso and hence prompted Tasso's pathetic "expressions of adulation & entreaty to a deaf & stupid tyrant."[17] On the contrary, Shelley's Maniac, with " 'wilful ill,' " would be self-imprisoned and consequently more in keeping with Shelley's view of the Byronic hero. But Byron's *Lament of Tasso*, which Shelley had intended to answer in his own drama, still determined portions of the Maniac's history, and with an eye to Byron's less particularized enchained men, such as Prometheus, Manfred, and the narrator of *Childe Harold*, Shelley created a Maniac who, when compared to Byron's Tasso, even out-Byron's Byron. Compare, for example, the openings of these two dramatic monologues: Byron was content to introduce the "Long years!—It tries the thrilling frame to bear / And eagle-spirit of a Child of Song— / Long years of outrage—calumny—and wrong; / Imputed madness, prisoned solitude" (ll. 1-4); but Shelley, with a more characteristic Byronic flourish, symbolically enlarged this particular prison into the enchainment of life: " 'Month after month,' he cried, 'to bear this load / . . . / To drag life on—which like a heavy chain / Lengthens behind with many a link of pain' " (ll. 300-3). With similar enlargements from Byron's other works, the Byronic Tasso was transformed into the Maniac.

In spite of this transformation, Shelley's Maniac can still be seen as a derivative of Byron's Tasso. Even before Julian meets the Maniac, the scene is set in a manner similar to Byron's *Lament of Tasso*:

> The clap of tortured hands,
> Fierce yells and howlings and lamentings keen,
> And laughter where complaint had merrier been,
> Moans, shrieks, and curses, and blaspheming prayers
> Accosted us.                                    (*Julian and Maddalo*, ll. 215-19)

> Above me, hark! the long and maniac cry
> Of minds and bodies in captivity.
> And hark! the lash and the increasing howl,
> And the half-inarticulate blasphemy.
>                                    (*The Lament of Tasso*, ll. 65-68)

And in broad outline, the fates as well as the prisons of Tasso and the Maniac are identical: each had been a young idealist (the Maniac, a " 'love-devoted youth' " who " 'loved and pitied all things' " [ll. 373, 444]; and Tasso, a youth "drunk with Love,—which did pervade / And

mingle with whate'er [he] saw on earth" [ll. 150-51]); each was disappointed in love with an idealized counterpart (the Maniac's "'spirit's
mate'"; and Tasso's Leonora, his heart's "One Want" which "didst
annihilate the earth" to him [ll. 168, 173]); and each, imprisoned in a
madhouse, sought to escape his painful memories. But neither could
forget, as witnessed by each monologue being addressed to the lady in
question, and neither could find any viable alternative to his grief.
Revenge and vindictiveness were rejected by both Tasso:

> Yes, Sister of my Sovereign! for thy sake
> I weed all bitterness from out my breast,
> It hath no business where *thou* art a guest:
> Thy brother hates—but I cannot detest;
> Thou pitiest not—but I cannot forsake;          (ll. 106-10)

and, with similar expressions, by the Maniac:

> "Then, when thou speakest of me, never say
> 'He could forgive not.' Here I cast away
> All human passions, all revenge, all pride;
> I think, speak, act no ill."          (ll. 500-3)

Suicide was also rejected, albeit for different reasons,[18] even though
death promised respite to the heart's misery and did eventually and
ironically reunite each pair of lovers, "entwined for ever—but too late!"
And finally, while they waited for death, each protagonist judged his
enchainment to be a product of "'destiny,'" but destiny perhaps
directed by his own "'wilful ill'": the Maniac questioned the "'Power
[which] delights to torture us? I know/That to myself I do not
wholly owe/What now I suffer, tho' in part I may'" (ll. 320-22); and
Tasso similarly had questioned his "sad fatality" even though it might
have been "Presumptuous thus to love without design" (ll. 140-41).

The Maniac's and Tasso's similar circumstances should not obscure
their many differences, perhaps the main one being their degrees of
madness: Byron's Tasso claimed that his madness, "not of the mind,"
was merely "Imputed," although he did "feel at times [his] mind
decline" (ll. 52, 4, 189); but in spite of the Maniac's ostensibly
similar claim to be wearing a "'mask of falsehood'" (l. 308), he was
*not* "in his right senses" (Preface)—Maddalo judged "'he grew wild'"
(l. 249) before his imprisonment, Julian referred to his "dark estate"
(l. 574), and the Maniac's disjointed monologue confirms his mental
derangement. At one time "a very cultivated and amiable person"
(Preface), the Maniac had experienced "some deadly change in love/
Of one vowed deeply" (ll. 527-28). The nature of this "deadly change"
in the "lady [who] came with him from France, and [then]/. . . left

him" (ll. 246-47), is obscured by and indeed the cause of the Maniac's
various forms of address to this woman: his " 'spirit's mate' " (l. 337),
" 'Death's dedicated bride' " (l. 384), the Scornful Lady (ll. 398 ff.),
and even " 'child' " (l. 484).[19] As is quite apparent here, I do not
accept the elaborate theories that have isolated three and sometimes
four separate women in the Maniac's monologue; rather, arguing from
Julian and Maddalo's judgment that the Maniac suffered from "some
dreadful ill/Wrought on him boldly, yet unspeakable,/*By a dear friend*"
(ll. 525-27, my italics), from the return of this lady who had "left
him" (l. 247 and l. 599), and from Shelley's Preface, which cautions
readers to expect "unconnected exclamations," I judge that the
Maniac's madness is reason enough for the different forms of address
to a single Lady. Shelley, in fact, through Julian's introduction to the
Maniac's monologue (see especially ll. 286-94), suggests to the reader
that the monologue will have three distinct stages. In the first stage
(ll. 300-43), when the Maniac speaks "sometimes as one who wrote,
and thought/His words might move some heart that heeded not,/If
sent to distant lands" (ll. 286-88)—the Lady in question, it should be
noted, had already left him—he addresses his " 'spirit's mate' " who,
*he claims,* is still " 'compassionate' " and " 'gentle' " (ll. 337-39). In
the second stage of his monologue (ll. 344-82), when the Maniac
speaks "then as one/Reproaching deeds never to be undone/With
wondering self-compassion" (ll. 288-90), he addresses no woman but
advises a " 'few' " past friends that " 'Love sometimes leads astray to
misery' " (l. 349). And in the third and longest stage (ll. 382-510), the
Maniac's "speech/Was lost in grief" with "cold" words made uniform
only by "despair" (ll. 290-94), and he apparently addresses both
" 'Death's dedicated bride' " (l. 384) and the scornful Lady. This
enigmatic bride of Death is not a second and dead lady (frequently
interpreted as Harriet Shelley by critics who see the Maniac as Shelley),
but rather the " 'spirit's mate' " transformed by the Maniac's over-
wrought fancy into a phantasm representing the inconstancy of her
love for him.[20] The Maniac had protested that his spirit's mate still
loved and pitied him, but when he removes " 'A veil from [his] pent
mind' " (l. 383), he finally acknowledges that she was inconstant and
thus tears aside that mask or blot of " 'falsehood' " (l. 308 and l. 530)
by which he had convinced others and to some extent himself that
he was still loved. His epiphany is, however, as incapacitating as his
former delusion, for he sees his spirit's mate in the form of " 'Death's
dedicated bride,' " a phantasmal " 'mockery' " sitting by his side:

> "at the grave's call
> I haste, invited to thy wedding-ball

To greet the ghastly paramour, for whom
Thou hast deserted me . . . and made the tomb
Thy bridal bed . . . But I beside your feet
Will lie and watch ye from my winding-sheet—
Thus . . . wide awake tho' dead . . . Yet stay, O stay!
Go not so soon—I know not what I say—
Hear but my reasons . . . I am mad, I fear,
My fancy is o'erwrought . . . thou art not here . . .
Pale art thou, 'tis most true . . . but thou art gone,—
Thy work is finished . . . I am left alone!—"

(ll. 386-97, Shelley's ellipses)

This exaggeration of the spirit's mate's desertion (her death being a metaphor for her inconstancy) cleverly introduces the reader to her real nature as the serpent-like scornful Lady whom the Maniac " 'loved even to [his] overthrow' " (l. 405): she had returned " 'scorn' " and " 'hate' " for his " 'tears' " and " 'love' " (l. 496), had cursed him, and finally deserted him.

These remarks on the spirit's mate turned scornful Lady in the Maniac's monologue serve four important ends here: they should dispel some of the needless and frequently confusing accounts of three or four separate women in the Maniac's life; they clarify the nature of the Maniac's frequently misinterpreted or ignored " 'mask of false-hood,' " that mask being his self-willed delusion or " 'wilful ill' "; they suggest that the Maniac's history fulfills some of Shelley's original intentions to dramatize Tasso's madness in his love for Leonora;[21] and finally, for the purposes of this study, they prepare for further analysis of the Maniac's function as a composite Byronic hero. The Maniac's complex and painful love for his spirit's mate/scornful Lady perhaps exceeds the Tasso/Leonora formula which Shelley partially copied from Byron's *Lament of Tasso*, but the differences here may be adduced to Shelley's conscious imitation of Byron's *Manfred*, which for Shelley was a more disturbing portrait of man's enslavement after a fall from the Shelleyan "visions,/And noble aspirations" (III.i.104-5).

Shelley's imitation of *Manfred* in *Julian and Maddalo* should not be surprising: when Julian "Argued against despondency" (l. 48) in Maddalo's dark view of human enslavement, he was reenacting Shelley's aversion to the "despondency" in *Manfred* which had made him "dreadfully melancholy."[22] And because Byron had used his drama to show Shelley the weaknesses of his idealistic hopes, it was only fitting that Maddalo attempt to " 'shew/How vain are [Julian's] aspiring theories' " (ll. 200-1) by presenting a Maniac whose monologue would once more contain the lessons of *Manfred*. These lessons, Maddalo would argue, are to be found in the destructive conflict between the

Maniac and his spirit's mate/scornful Lady, a relationship repeating
the essentials of Manfred's fateful love for Astarte, his psychic complement. Astarte, it will be recalled, was Manfred's blood relative, probably
his sister, and she possessed "softened" features, a "quest of hidden
knowledge," "tenderness" (II.ii.108, 110, 114). With striking similarity,
the Maniac's spirit's mate was described in Shelley's first draft as

> Sister, my beloved mate
> And yokefellow of youth *mild* [canceled] tender & wise
> *With* [canceled] Veil that soft spirit watching in thine eyes[23]

Unlike Astarte, however, the spirit's mate did not die, but the Maniac
did imagine her as " 'Death's dedicated bride' " in a vision quite
similar to Manfred's first visionary encounter with Astarte:

> Oh God! if it be thus, and *thou*
> Art not a madness and a mockery,
> I yet might be most happy. I will clasp thee,
> And we again will be—— [*The figure vanishes.*
> My heart is crushed!
> [MANFRED *falls senseless.*
> (I.i.188-91)

With an equally dramatic flourish, the Maniac removed a veil from his
mind and saw a " 'mockery' " whom he urged to " 'stay, O stay' ";
but because she also vanished, he (fearing to be " 'mad' ") was destined
to be " 'left alone' " (ll. 382-97). This loneliness was oppressive for
both the Maniac and Manfred because they could not escape their
thoughts of their departed women: Manfred had sought "Oblivion—
self-oblivion" (I.i.144) and "Forgetfulness" (I.i.136; II.ii.145); and the
Maniac who could " 'forget not' " also sought " 'Oblivion [to] hide
this grief'" (ll. 434, 508). Because the Maniac's continuing love for
his spirit's mate only increased his grief, that is, provided the " 'fuel/
Of the mind's hell' " and condemned him to a " 'living death of
agonies' " (ll. 440-41, 415), he was like Manfred who had been com-
pelled by his love to be his own "proper Hell" and condemned "Nor
to slumber, nor to die" (I.i.251, 254). Both protagonists were thus
cursed (in fact, self-cursed to the extent that each precipitated his
own fate), and in one of the Maniac's unconnected exclamations,
he repeats those curses that his spirit's mate/scornful Lady had
imprecated on him:

> "That you had never seen me—never heard
> My voice, and more than all had ne'er endured
> The deep pollution of my loathed embrace—

That your eyes ne'er had lied love in my face—
That, like some maniac monk, I had torn out
The nerves of manhood by their bleeding root
With mine own quivering fingers, so that ne'er
Our hearts had for a moment mingled there
To disunite in horror—these were not
With thee, like some suppressed and hideous thought
Which flits athwart our musings, but can find
No rest within a pure and gentle mind . . .
Thou sealedst them with many a bare broad word,
And ceredst my memory o'er them,—for I heard
And can forget not . . . they were ministered
One after one, those curses. Mix them up
Like self-destroying poisons in one cup,
And they will make one blessing which thou ne'er
Didst imprecate for, on me,—death."                    (ll. 420-38)

Because Shelley had first conceived of the spirit's mate as the Maniac's sister, these lines recall Manfred's incestuous and fatal "embrace" and "deadliest sin" with Astarte, whom he implored to "loath'st me not" (II.i.87; iv.123-24). Furthermore, the Byronic energy and diction of these lines echo the "Incantation" curse in *Manfred* (the voice therein that of Astarte) and in effect supply the verbal "wrath" (II.iv. 147) that Manfred had expected from the Phantom of Astarte in the Hall of Arimanes. Thus Shelley once again embellished his derivative Byronic hero.

Because the Maniac was a composite colored by Shelley's own conception of what a Byronic hero should be, his character cannot be traced solely to one source, and neither the Tasso/Leonora nor the Manfred/Astarte relation is identical to that between the Maniac and his Lady, their characters being in some particulars quite different from Byron's lovers. Some of these differences can be explained by reference to *Childe Harold,* where, for example, the narrator's "Fame" and "fortunes" were of "hasty growth and blight" (IV.ix), just as the Maniac's " 'fame/Said he was wealthy, or he had been so' " (ll. 233-34);[24] or to *Don Juan,* where the narrator's mockery parallels the Maniac's being " 'a humourist in his way' " (l. 244).[25] But even then, all facets of the composite Maniac cannot be traced, mainly because he is to some degree a caricature. That is to say, Shelley provided Maddalo with an argumentative emblem where the fall from Shelleyan idealism to Byronic enslavement was even more catastrophic than in the case of Manfred or Tasso. In fact, no Byronic hero had been initially so full of love and compassion as the Maniac,

"whose heart a stranger's tear might wear
As water-drops the sandy fountain-stone;
Who loved and pitied all things, and could moan
For woes which others hear not, and could see
The absent with the glance of phantasy,
And with the poor and trampled sit and weep,
Following the captive to his dungeon deep;
    . . . as a nerve o'er which do creep
The else unfelt oppressions of this earth,"          (ll. 442-50)

although we can see here a composite of Prometheus' kindness to all
men, Tasso's love, Manfred's tenderness (II.ii.114), and in *Childe
Harold* the narrator's sympathy for imprisoned man and oppressed
society. Similarly, no Byronic hero had forsaken love and fallen to
such a dejected state as the Maniac, for whom

                    "quick and dark
The grave is yawning:—as its roof shall cover
My limbs with dust and worms under and over,
So let Oblivion hide this grief . . . the air
Closes upon my accents, as despair
Upon my heart—let death upon despair!"          (ll. 505-10)

although we can see here Shelley's implicit judgment that the Byronic
hero, notwithstanding his Promethean desire to make "Death a Victory"
actually did find it "difficult to die." Shelley's Maniac might claim, as
his Byronic prototypes did, that he was "ever still the same / In creed
as in resolve, and what may tame / My heart, must leave the understanding free" (ll. 358-60),[26] but his monologue and his catastrophe belie
that claim and reveal instead that his mind was as tamed and enslaved
as his body.

The Maniac's fate, then, is unquestionably Byronic, albeit exaggerated in places. And by allowing Maddalo to confront Julian with
the Maniac's history, Shelley was once more seeking to confront the
fatalistic arguments in Byron's 1816/18 poetry. But what is most
surprising about this elaborate and metaphoric confrontation is that
Shelley does not proclaim Julian (and thus himself) victorious in his
debate with the Byronic spirit of things. Instead of concluding this
argument about man's enslavement after witnessing the emblematic
Maniac, Julian and Maddalo "Wept without shame" and their "argument was quite forgot" (ll. 516, 520). Nevertheless, had they resumed
their debate, Julian could have claimed victory, for nowhere in the
Maniac's history is there a cause and effect relation to substantiate
Maddalo's contention that Shelleyan idealism, betrayed by destiny,
leads to a " 'rent heart,' " frustrated " 'thoughts and . . . desires' "

(ll. 125-26), and madness (these being Byron's conclusions in *Childe Harold* IV: "Who loves, raves"; and who idealizes, creates an "unreached Paradise of our despair" [cxxii-cxxiii]). To the contrary, Julian could argue that the Maniac's aspirations (as well as Byron's) wanted a " 'true theory' " (l. 203) which demanded not only justice and love, but also patience and hope of the kind that sustained Laon and Prometheus during their imprisonments and that eventually led to their unbinding. Unlike Shelley's Prometheus, who could "hope till Hope creates / From its own wreck the thing it contemplates" (IV. 573-74), the Maniac could not seek " 'a "soul of goodness" in things ill, / [Either] in himself or others.' " Thus he precipitously " 'bowed / His being' " (ll. 204-6) after his one disastrous experience with his spirit's mate:

> "there are some by nature proud,
> Who patient in all else, demand but this—
> To love and be beloved with gentleness;
> And being scorned, what wonder if they die
> Some living death? This is not destiny,
> But man's own wilful ill." (ll. 206-11)

Lacking any hope or patience, the Maniac despaired and intensified his grief by his own " 'wilful ill,' " for he incapacitated his mind by attempting to disguise the failure of his love:

> "And not to speak my grief—O, not to dare
> To give a human voice to my despair,
> But live and move, and wretched thing! smile on
> As if I never went aside to groan,
> And wear this mask of falsehood even to those
> Who are most dear—not for my own repose—
> Alas, no scorn or pain or hate could be
> So heavy as that falsehood is to me." (ll. 304-11)

Even though the Maniac regretted that falsehood, he evidently began to believe his own lie, for he addressed his spirit's mate as if she would " 'weep tears bitter as blood to know / Thy lost friend's incommunicable woe' " (ll. 342-43). Because Julian had already noted that the Maniac in this section only "*thought* / His words *might* move some heart that *heeded not*" (ll. 286-87, my italics), the Maniac's self-delusion is readily apparent. Even Maddalo recognized this delusion, for he "agreed" with Julian that the Maniac suffered

> some dreadful ill
> Wrought on him boldly, yet unspeakable,
> By a dear friend; some deadly change in love

Of one vowed deeply which he dreamed not of;
For whose sake he, *it seemed, had fixed a blot*
*Of falsehood on his mind,* which flourished not
But in the light of all-beholding truth.

(ll. 525-31, my italics)

By agreeing with Julian that the Maniac himself was at least in part
responsible for his madness, Maddalo in effect conceded defeat in this
philosophical debate, but Julian, who had been so eager to prove his
theory, strangely ignored this concession and even qualified it with an
"it seemed." Julian's reactions at the end of the poem are indeed
peculiar, and when he quotes Maddalo's final judgment on the Maniac,

"Most wretched men
Are cradled into poetry by wrong,
They learn in suffering what they teach in song,"     (ll. 544-46)

he seems to be preserving the integrity of Maddalo's anti-Julian argument. Because these lines echo Byron's "Of such materials wretched
men were made" in *The Lament of Tasso* (l. 159) and because these
materials of wretchedness were Tasso's youthful ideals (ll. 149-57),
Maddalo seems to be judging once more that the Maniac's " 'wrong' "
and cause of wretchedness were Julian's vain aspiring theories.

This anticlimactic and ambiguous conclusion to the debate in
*Julian and Maddalo* has puzzled many readers, but Shelley apparently
judged that the irony of Maddalo's introduction of a Byronic hero as
a madman offered sufficient public commentary on the "insanity" of
Byron's poetry and ideas, and that any further judgment on Byron's
errors would have been "presumptuous" and unwise at this time.
Shelley no longer felt inadequate in the shadow of Byron, but if he had
triumphantly proclaimed Maddalo's defeat, he might have alienated the
poet whose friendship he desired for many reasons, one being to
protect Allegra, who now was subject to Byron's influence.[27] Furthermore, the conclusion in which relatively little is concluded is consistent
with Shelley's view of his two-year debate with Byron's obdurate
spirit: because Shelley had "remonstrated with [Byron] *in vain*" on the
"wicked & mischievous *insanity*" of *Childe Harold* IV,[28] Julian chose
to heed Maddalo's warning that his " 'judgment [would] not bend' "
even though Julian could make his " 'system refutation-tight' " (ll. 192,
194). Thus *Julian and Maddalo* in no way concludes Byron and
Shelley's debate; rather it merely clarifies their arguments with respect
to each other's position; it reveals through irony Shelley's judgment
about the insanity and error of the Byronic hero; and it prepares for
*Prometheus Unbound,* where Shelley was once more addressing Byron's
"blind" spirit with Julian's ultimate hope for the Maniac—to "find/An

entrance to the caverns of his mind,/[And] reclaim him from his dark estate" (ll. 572-74).

III

The "caverns" of Byron's mind especially interested Shelley between October 1818 (when he finished Act I of *Prometheus Unbound*) and March 1819 (when he began Act II). During that time, he wrote not only "The Coliseum" (discussed in the previous chapter), his December letter to Peacock, and *Julian and Maddalo*, but also *Lines Written Among the Euganean Hills* into which he interpolated, probably in December, the following thirty-nine-line portrait of Byron:

> Perish! let there only be
> Floating o'er thy [Venice's] hearthless sea,
> As the garment of thy sky
> Clothes the world immortally,
> One remembrance, more sublime
> Than the tattered pall of time,
> Which scarce hides thy visage wan;
> That a tempest-cleaving swan
> Of the songs of Albion,
> Driven from his ancestral streams,
> By the might of evil dreams,
> Found a nest in thee; and Ocean
> Welcomed him with such emotion
> That its joy grew his, and sprung
> From his lips like music flung
> O'er a mighty thunder-fit,
> Chastening terror: what though yet
> Poesy's unfailing river,
> Which thro' Albion winds for ever,
> Lashing with melodious wave
> Many a sacred poet's grave,
> Mourn its latest nursling fled!
> What though thou with all thy dead
> Scarce can for this fame repay
> Aught thine own,—oh, rather say,
> Though thy sins and slaveries foul
> Overcloud a sunlike soul!
> As the ghost of Homer clings
> Round Scamander's wasting springs;
> As divinest Shakespeare's might
> Fills Avon and the world with light

Like omniscient power, which he
Imaged 'mid mortality;
As the love from Petrarch's urn,
Yet amid yon hills doth burn,
A quenchless lamp, by which the heart
Sees things unearthly; so thou art,
Mighty spirit: so shall be
The city that did refuge thee.                    (ll. 167-205)

By this flattering comparison of Byron to Homer, Shakespeare, and Petrarch, Shelley acknowledged that he had recently discovered in *Childe Harold* IV Byron's "hopes of being remembered in my line/ With my land's language" (ix).[29] By encouraging these hopes, however, Shelley was not contradicting his December letter to Peacock in which he privately condemned Byron's fourth canto. Rather, he merely inverted for his public audience (including Byron) the emphasis accorded his distinction between the "spirit" and the "form" of Byron's poetry: in the letter, he condemned the "wicked & mischievous insanity" of the fourth canto and only briefly admitted that Byron "is a great poet, [as] the address to Ocean proves"; but here in the *Euganean Hills,* the form of the "address to Ocean" is seen as redeeming the "insanity" of the anti-Shelleyan spirit in the fourth canto. With regard to these lines in question, "and Ocean/Welcomed him with such emotion/That its joy grew his, and sprung/From his lips like music flung/O'er a mighty thunder-fit,/Chastening terror" (ll. 178-83), G. Wilson Knight first discovered Shelley's veiled reference to *Childe Harold* IV: " 'Music' refers to the great invocation to Ocean . . . succeeding the 'thunder-fit' of the [curse in the] Promethean stanzas [cxxxii-cxxxvii]."[30] With a similar shift of emphasis, Shelley's private condemnation of Byron's familiarity "with the lowest sort of [Venetian] women" and his association "with wretches who seem almost to have lost the gait & phisiognomy of man" becomes in the *Euganean Hills* a public condemnation of Venice whose "sins and slaveries foul/Overcloud a sunlike soul" (ll. 192-93). Though Byron's "sun" be overclouded, as it were, the opprobrium in this public statement belongs to the city and not to the man and thus implies that Shelley still believed Byron's "insanity" and "blindness" capable of cure (compare Julian's stubborn and final hope in Venice that he "might reclaim [the Maniac] from his dark estate," l. 574).

Shelley's disguise of his private judgments in these public half-truths is understandable, for he obviously wished to flatter Byron, to repair any damage that *Julian and Maddalo* might do to Byron's ego, to preserve his friendship with the father of Allegra, and to leave open the question of Byron's reformation. But because Shelley could have as easily written a sonnet to Byron (as he did later) to accomplish these same ends, why did he interpolate these particular lines into the *Euganean Hills,* a poem that ostensibly has little to do with his philosophical antagonist? The answer here is that the *Euganean Hills,* even without the portrait of Byron, is to a considerable extent a product of *Childe Harold* and thus another document in Shelley's continuing debate with Byron. A key to Shelley's purpose here may be found in "To Byron," a fragment he wrote probably between October 1818 and March or April 1819:

> O Mighty Mind, in whose deep stream this age
> Shakes like a reed in the unheeding storm
> Why dost thou rule not thine own sacred rage
> And clothe thy powers in some eternal form
> From thine eternal depths which might wage
> Upon the giddy chasm[31]

Shelley in *Euganean Hills* describes Byron as the poet whose "Ocean" stanzas "chastened" the "thunder-fit" of the Promethean curse; here, in identical fashion, he asks Byron to use his "eternal depths" to "rule" or subdue his frequently expressed "sacred rage." In effect, Shelley was placing the poet of *Childe Harold* IV among "The polluting multitude;/[whose] *rage would be subdued*/By that clime divine and calm" of the "healing paradise" described at the end of *Euganean Hills* (ll. 355-58, my italics). Thus in the manner of the debate in *Julian and Maddalo,* Shelley in *Euganean Hills* was promising Byron an escape from life's mania if he would only accept what Shelley in 1816 described as the " 'most awful duty' " of hope, in this case a hope that "Many a green isle needs must be/In the deep wide sea of misery" (ll. 1-2). By promising that Byron could escape these desolating waters, Shelley was ironically inverting the symbolism of *Childe Harold* IV: the Ocean which for Byron had been "boundless, endless, and sublime—/The image of Eternity" (clxxxiii) and the source of rapturous "joy" (clxxvi) was for Shelley the source of "misery," redeemed only by "flowering islands . . ./In the waters of wide Agony" (ll. 2, 66-67). Such moments of redemption were symbolized not by Ocean but by the sun which at its noontime zenith enabled Shelley to achieve a "boundless, endless, and sublime" interpenetration with all of reality.[32]

Shelley must have consciously chosen to invert Byron's symbolism, for the very presence of the ingratiating thirty-nine-line portrait and the many derivative echoes of the fourth canto in the *Euganean Hills*[33] suggest that his poem was a carefully articulated response to Byron's vision of a devastating Ocean which

> send'st [man], shivering in thy playful spray
> And howling, to his Gods, where haply lies
> His petty hope in some near port or bay,
> And dashest him again to Earth:—there let him lay.
>
> (IV.clxxx)

The Byronic hero, once more upon the waters, might work with Promethean diligence until he

> had bodied forth the heated mind
> Forms from the floating wreck which Ruin leaves behind:

And from the planks, far shattered o'er the rocks,
> Built me a little bark of hope, once more
> To battle with the Ocean and the shocks
> Of the loud breakers, and the ceaseless roar
> Which rushes on the solitary shore
> Where all lies foundered that was ever dear;

but Byronic hope lacked the patience and the conviction of Shelleyan hope, for this hero, even though he could

> gather from the wave-worn store [*sic*]
> Enough for my rude boat, where should I steer?
> There woos no home, nor hope, nor life, save what is here.
>
> (civ-cv)

To the contrary, Shelley could escape from his sea of misery by finding a flowering isle "Mid the mountains Euganean" and by experiencing under the light of the sun a timeless and boundless exhilaration wherein the plains, leaves, vines, grass, flower, line of the Apennine, Alps, every living thing, and his own spirit "Interpenetrated lie/By the glory of the sky" (ll. 313-14). Shelley's faith in the reality of this experience was unswerving even though he could not unequivocally explain its cause:

> Be it love, light, harmony,
> Odour, or the soul of all
> Which from heaven like dew doth fall,
> Or the mind which feeds this verse
> Peopling the lone universe.  (ll. 315-19)

Significant in this equivocation (and a *from* is syntactically demanded in the first and fourth lines above: "Be it [from] love" or be it "[from]

the mind") is a lesson to Byron: if Shelleyan love or its synonymous
idealized forms (denied objective existence in *Childe Harold* IV) did
not explain this "Interpenetration," then the Byronic mind itself
(which in the fourth canto could "people" and "repeople" [see iv, vi,
xix, xlix] at will) was sufficient cause for this experience. In other
words Byron, whose "sunlike soul" associated him with the enlighten-
ing sun and hence identified him as a poet of Apollo and not merely
of Ocean, was being educated in the redemptive functions of his own
creative imagination.

The unifying progression of the sun and light as a symbol for
imaginative regeneration in the *Euganean Hills* takes on additional
meaning when studied in relation to *Childe Harold* IV where Byron
recalled the times when Venice and other kingdoms, cities, and nations
had attained "Power's high pinnacle, when they . . . felt/The
sunshine for a while," but were fated to "melt" and "downward go/
Like Lauwine loosened from the mountain's belt" (xii). And although
St. Mark's steeds still had "gilded collars glittering in the sun," they
were "bridled":

> Venice, lost and won,
> Her thirteen hundred years of freedom done,
> Sinks, like a sea-weed, unto whence she rose!        (xiii)

Shelley could agree with Byron that there was "a desolate cloud o'er
Venice' lovely walls" (xv) and that Venice's desolation was therefore
"shameful to the nations,—most of all,/Albion! to thee: the Ocean
queen should not/Abandon Ocean's children" (xvii). In fact, Byron's
descriptions of Venice are even echoed in Shelley's apostrophe to that
city:

> Sun-girt City! thou hast been
> Ocean's child, and then his queen;
> Now is come a darker day,
> And thou soon must be his prey,
> If the power that raised thee here
> Hallow so thy watery bier.[34]        (ll. 115-20)

But for Shelley, the glittering sunlight on Venice (l. 143) symbolically
expressed a hope that

> if Freedom should awake
> In her omnipotence, and shake
> From the Celtic Anarch's hold
> All the keys of dungeons cold,
> Where a hundred cities lie
> Chained like thee, ingloriously,

> Thou and all thy sister band
> Might adorn this sunny land,
> Twining memories of old time
> With new virtues more sublime.          (ll. 150-59)

Fearing, however, that this hope was unfounded and that Venice might "perish" (l. 160) as Byron had predicted in *Childe Harold* IV (xiii), Shelley (in order to distinguish himself from the poet of "Ocean") took Byron's metaphor of the "desolate cloud" *over* Venice (xv), appropriately changed it to the desolate "Clouds" that would be formed *by* Venice after it sank into the Ocean, and promised "Ocean's child" that even these "Clouds" formed by its own death would eventually be dispersed by the sun of freedom and liberty:

> Clouds which stain truth's rising day
> By her sun consumed away,
> Earth can spare ye: while like flowers,
> In the waste of years and hours,
> From your dust new nations spring
> With more kindly blossoming.          (ll. 161-66)

Byron himself in *Childe Harold* IV had prophesied that the tree of freedom would be sustained by its seed—"So shall a better spring less bitter fruit bring forth" (xcviii). And Shelley, in order to reinstruct Byron in this patient hope and remind him of his responsibility as a poetically inspired legislator and redeemer (see Preface to *Julian and Maddalo*), described the poet of Ocean as an overclouded "sunlike soul." This mixed metaphor indeed creates a *tangled* bough of Heaven and Ocean, but it here suggests that Byron could, Apollo-like, rise above his own sea of misery and through similar prophecies of freedom consume away the "desolate cloud" (*Childe Harold* IV.xv) of "sins and slaveries foul" (*Euganean Hills*, l. 192) which had enchained and darkened man's spirit, including Byron's, in Venice.[35] Shelley had seen the effects of this enchainment not only in *Childe Harold* IV but also in *Ode on Venice,* where the concluding paean to freedom in America (ll. 133-60) was drowned in the "tides" of inexorable Byronic fate:

> There is no hope for nations!—Search the page
>   Of many thousand years—the daily scene,
> The flow and ebb of each recurring age,
>   The everlasting *to be* which *hath been.*          (ll. 56-59)

Shelley of course could not accept this fatalistic judgment, so in answer to Byron's lament for Venice,

> Oh! agony—that centuries should reap

No mellower harvest! Thirteen hundred *years*
Of wealth and glory turned to *dust* and tears,
(ll. 14-16, my italics)

Shelley promised in the *Euganean Hills* that

In the waste of *years* and hours,
From [Venice's] *dust* new nations spring
With more kindly blossoming.          (ll. 164-66, my italics)

And in answer to Byron's complaint that "Tyranny . . . tramples
down/The sparkles of our ashes" (ll. 131-33), Shelley first borrowed
Byron's words and agreed that the "spark lies dead . . ./Trampled
out by tyranny" in his description of Padua's former halls of the
"lamp of learning," but then used the extended metaphor of the
Norway woodman to show Byron, as much a poet of Darkness as he
was a poet of Ocean, that there could be "new fires from antique
light" (ll. 256-84). Byron, granted a "sunlike soul" in the *Euganean
Hills,* was being instructed once more in his responsibility as a poet.

It should be clear that Shelley's self-appointed task in the fragment "To Byron," in *Lines Written Among the Euganean Hills,* and
in *Julian and Maddalo*—all three written between October 1818 and
March or April 1819—was to recapture his former influence over the
older poet and thereby provide him an alternative vision to the one
contained in *Manfred, The Lament of Tasso, Childe Harold* IV, and
*Ode on Venice.* But because of Byron's "obstinate & selfwilled folly,"
Shelley conceded the difficulty of his task. Although I have not been
able to determine exactly the order in which these three "Byron"
poems were written, Shelley appears to have first asked the "Mighty
Mind" to calm his "sacred rage" and to seek an "eternal form" from
his own "eternal depths" ("To Byron"), then to have appealed to
the "sunlike soul" of the creative imagination located in these depths
of the poet of Ocean (*Euganean Hills*), and finally to have judged that
Byron's "sunlike soul" was a source not of light to the world, but of
further blindness to the poet who egoistically refused to use his genius
in the cause of Shelleyan truth:

The sense that he was greater than his kind
Had struck, methinks, his eagle spirit blind
By gazing on its own exceeding light.
(*Julian and Maddalo,* ll. 50-52)

This inversion of the power of the eagle to gaze at the sun makes it
clear that Shelley could only employ "arguments entreaties every
thing in vain"[36] against Byron's darkness. And even Julian's symbolic

sun was temporarily obscured by Maddalo's dark display of the mad-house as life's emblem, but Julian, like Shelley, was undaunted by Maddalo/Byron's words which " 'might . . . have cast/A darkness on [his own] spirit' " were it not for his ability to rise above such " 'sick thoughts' " and rejoice in the dream of " 'happy, high, majesti-cal' " men who could effectually realize the " 'love, beauty and truth' " of their minds (ll. 159-75). So even if Byron's "darker side" (l. 49) contradicted this dream, Shelley would persistently argue his case against the enslaving darkness in order that Byron might someday calm his "sacred rage" against the dying of the light. This persistence caused Shelley, in my judgment, to dramatize his differences with Byron in *The Two Spirits: An Allegory*, a poem that Mary Shelley mistakenly dated 1820 but that was definitely written earlier, most probably as an exercise in preparation for or in conclusion to his debate in *Julian and Maddalo*.[37] *The Two Spirits* cannot with certainty be labeled a "Byron" poem, but the first spirit's arguments that "Night is coming" epitomize the poet who in Geneva had identified with the "Storm, and Darkness" of a "Most glorious Night" (*Childe Harold* III.xcii-xciii), who had predicted then that "Darkness" would engulf the Universe, and who since 1816 had many an extinguished lamp and darkened spirit in his poetry. In contrast, the second spirit's insistence that the light and love and calm within would "make night day" perfectly agrees with Shelley's hope at the end of the *Euganean Hills* and with Julian's faith in the powers of the mind whereby he could withstand Maddalo's "darker side" which " 'might well have [but did not] cast/ A darkness on [his] spirit.' " Because Shelley must have recognized the similarity between *The Two Spirits* and his long debate with Byron, its first four stanzas stand as an appropriate epilogue to the two poets' antagonism in 1818.

*Two genii stood before me in a dream*[38]

THE TWO SPIRITS: AN ALLEGORY

*First Spirit*
O Thou who plumed with strong desire
Would float above the Earth—beware!
A shadow tracks thy flight of fire—
　　　Night is coming!
Bright are the regions of the air
And when winds and beams [    ]
It were delight to wander there—
　　　Night is coming!

*Second Spirit*
The deathless stars are bright above;
If I should cross the shade of night
Within my heart is the lamp of love
    And that is day—
And the moon will smile with gentle light
On my golden plumes where'er they move;
The meteors will linger around my flight
    And make night day.

*First Spirit*
But if the whirlwinds of darkness waken
Hail and Lightning and stormy rain—
See, the bounds of the air are shaken,
    Night is coming!
And swift the clouds of the hurricane
Yon declining sun have overtaken,
The clash of the hail sweeps o'er the plain—
    Night is coming!

*Second Spirit*
I see the glare and I hear the sound—
I'll sail on the flood of the tempest dark
With the calm within and light around
    Which make night day;
And thou when the gloom is deep and stark,
Look from thy dull earth slumberbound—
My moonlight flight thou then mayst mark
    On high, far away.

TRANSCENDENCE AND IMMANENCE:
SHELLEY'S *PROMETHEUS UNBOUND*

Shelley once defined metaphysics as an "inquiry concerning those things belonging to, or connected with, the internal nature of man,"[1] and in *Julian and Maddalo* he articulated what might be called a defensive metaphysics—one whereby he could confront Byron's threatening enchainment of man's "internal nature" in *Manfred, The Lament of Tasso,* and *Childe Harold* IV. By defining Julian's metaphysical assumptions in opposition to Maddalo's, Shelley finally succeeded where before he had failed: *The Revolt of Islam* might have called in question the premises of *Manfred,* but Shelley had finished one half of his epic even before he had read Byron's drama; and the drama on Tasso was rejected as a means to "correct" Byron's dramatic monologue, *The Lament of Tasso.* But Shelley's defense of his metaphysics in *Julian and Maddalo* must be seen only as part of his stratagem, for shortly after meeting Byron on 23 August 1818, he began *Prometheus Unbound* in order to liberate Byron from his vision of man's enslavement. In fact, the bound Prometheus provided Shelley what he desired in the character of the imprisoned Tasso: unable to transform Tasso from a Byronic to a Shelleyan character, Shelley began instead to reform the mythic "parent" of Tasso, the enchained Prometheus whom Byron in 1816 had figured as the emblem and the sign of man's inglorious fate. Shelley's task then was to unbind Prometheus and in the process free Byron from his constraining metaphysics, his embodied judgments about man's internal nature. Obviously, Byron was not the sole cause of *Prometheus Unbound,* and Shelley's choice of Prometheus as the hero of his drama depends perhaps less on Byron's 1816 *Prometheus* than it does on Shelley's knowledge of Aeschylus' drama or even his wife's Byronic rejection of modern Prometheanism in *Frankenstein.* But to ignore Byron in Shelley's motives when he began *Prometheus Unbound* in September 1818 is to misread the effect of the two poets' reunion in August, the intent of Shelley's abandoned Tasso drama, and the presence of *Julian and Maddalo*—all of which point to Shelley's need to define his metaphysics in response to Byron, his need to "'find/How strong the chains are which our spirit bind:/Brittle perchance as straw'" (*Julian and Maddalo,* ll. 180-82).

Shelley never publicly acknowledged his intent to use *Prometheus Unbound* in his debate with Byron, but in his Preface to the drama, he did concede that certain

> contemporary writings may have tinged my composition, for such has been a topic of censure with regard to poems far more popular, and indeed more deservedly popular, than mine. It is impossible that any one who inhabits the same age with such writers as those who stand in the foremost ranks of our own, can conscientiously assure himself that his language and tone of thought may not have been modified by the study of the productions of those extraordinary intellects. It is true, that, not the spirit of their genius, but the forms in which it has manifested itself, are due less to the peculiarities of their own minds than to the peculiarity of the moral and intellectual condition of the minds among which they have been produced. Thus a number of writers possess the form, whilst they want the spirit of those whom, it is alleged, they imitate; because the former is the endowment of the age in which they live, and the latter must be the uncommunicated lightning of their own mind.[2]

Shelley's distinction between the "spirit" of his own drama and the "form" of his contemporaries' works is in one respect merely an appeal to his own integrity; but in a draft of these lines he acknowledged that his language and tone of thought had been modified by "*L. B. & Words. & Coleridge.*"[3] By canceling this specific reference, Shelley probably wished to forestall any charges that he had plagiarized even though he admitted in this same Preface that

> one great poet is a masterpiece of nature which another not only ought to study but must study. He might as wisely and as easily determine that his mind should no longer be the mirror of all that is lovely in the visible universe, as exclude from his contemplation the beautiful which exists in the writings of a great contemporary.

Shelley's "great contemporary" in 1818/19 was Lord Byron, and I submit that the "forms" which "modified" *Prometheus Unbound* were Byron's *Prometheus* and *Manfred*. But true to his distinction between "spirit" and "form" and to his previous ironic uses of Byron's poetry, Shelley borrowed from Byron's Promethean poems only to subvert their metaphysics and simultaneously assert the superiority of his own judgments about man's internal nature.[4]

When Shelley in August 1816 carried Byron's ode on Prometheus back to England to be published in *The Prisoner of Chillon* volume, he had not yet planned to write *Prometheus Unbound*. But exactly two years later he did see in Prometheus a fit emblem and sign of man's "fate and force" and he began his own drama on Prometheus not only to reproduce mythopoeically the moral lessons of *The Revolt of Islam* but also to question the premises of Byron's Prometheanism. In the words of Shelley's Preface to the drama, both poets believed that the "moral interest of the fable, which is so powerfully sustained by the sufferings and endurance of Prometheus, would be annihilated if we could conceive of him as unsaying his high language and quailing before his successful and perfidious adversary." But what distinguishes Byron's Prometheus from Shelley's is that the former has no other alternative than continuing "sufferings and endurance" and defiance of the "perfidious adversary" who is named in the ode as "the inexorable Heaven,/And the deaf tyranny of Fate,/The ruling principle of Hate" (ll. 18-20). By this defiance, Prometheus provided at least a heroic example to an enchained and wretched mankind:

> Thou art a symbol and a sign
> To Mortals of their fate and force;
> Like thee, Man is in part divine,
> A troubled stream from a pure source;
> And Man in portions can foresee
> His own funereal destiny;
> His wretchedness, and his resistance,
> And his sad unallied existence:
> To which his Spirit may oppose
> Itself—an equal to all woes—
> And a firm will, and a deep sense,
> Which even in torture can descry
> Its own concentered recompense,
> Triumphant where it dares defy,
> And making Death a Victory. (ll. 45-59)

Shelley, however, judged that this type of defiance was ultimately ineffectual; and in *Childe Harold* III so did Byron when he deplored man's "wretched interchange of wrong for wrong" and recommended that man remove himself from the "contentious world" and "be alone,/And love Earth only for its earthly sake" (lxx-lxxi). Shelley, however, believed that such isolation violated man's social nature, and he offered his Prometheus a different alternative: to withdraw the curse on Jupiter and thereby replace the Byronic triumvirate of Heaven, Fate, and Hate with the principle of divine and liberating Love for other men. Thus despite his initial suffering, endurance, and even defiance, Shelley's Prometheus eventually learns that "all hope was vain but love" (I.824) and then through that love effects a change in himself and accordingly in man's internal nature for which he is a "symbol and a sign." Because of that change, Demogorgon in Act IV can address both Prometheus and man and even Byron with a mighty lesson:

> To suffer woes which Hope thinks infinite;
> To forgive wrongs darker than death or night;
>   To defy Power, which seems omnipotent;
> To love, and bear; to hope till Hope creates
> From its own wreck the thing it contemplates:
>   Neither to change, nor falter, nor repent;
> This, like thy glory, Titan! is to be
> Good, great and joyous, beautiful and free;
> This is alone Life, Joy, Empire, and Victory!          (IV.570-78)

"To defy Power, which seems omnipotent" and "This is alone Life, Joy, Empire, and Victory" directly echo Byron's conclusion to his ode, "Triumphant where it dares defy,/And making Death a Victory," but noticeably Shelleyan "Life" has replaced Byronic "Death." Moreover, Shelley's imperative, "to hope till Hope creates/From its own wreck the thing it contemplates," not only repeats his former request in 1816 that Byron fulfill the "'most awful duty'" of hope but also, with practically the same diction and syntax, contradicts Byron's description in *Prometheus* of the "ruling principle of Hate,/Which for its pleasure doth create/The things it may annihilate" (ll. 20-22). By twice echoing Byron's ode in Demogorgon's concluding speech, Shelley made evident that victory lay in creative "Life" and not in annihilating "Death." And in order to emphasize this mighty lesson for Byron, whose Prometheus was locked in the "wretched interchange," whose Manfred had rejected the youthful and philanthropic aspirations to "make [his] own the mind of other men,/The enlightener of nations" (III.i.106-7), and who as Maddalo refused to become "the redeemer of his degraded country," Shelley's Prometheus proclaimed his function as both enlightener and redeemer:

>                     I would fain
> Be what it is my destiny to be,
> The saviour and the strength of suffering man.          (I.815-17)

Because Prometheus' fate symbolically expressed for each poet his judgment about man's "internal nature," the differences between Byron's and Shelley's Promethean poems are metaphysical. Shelley could agree with Byron that man was "in part divine," but for him the "divinity in Man"[5] was equivalent to the imagination, a liberating and integrating power of the mind, whereas for Byron the "Faculty divine" was the reason, "chained and tortured" by the body (*Childe Harold* IV.cxxvii). Byron embodied this traditional dualism in his ode on the eternally chained Prometheus, but Shelley rejected this ode as an archaic expression of a still popular philosophy of mind and matter and instead embodied in his liberated Prometheus an intellectual philosophy, the first principle of which was a unified consciousness teleologically destined to perfect itself. This unity was possible, Shelley believed, because man was not merely "a moral, *and* an intellectual" being; he was "also, and pre-eminently, an *imaginative being*."[6] And through the imagination, man could perfect himself: as Shelley explained in *Speculations on Morals*, "Imagination or mind employed in prophetically [imaging forth] its objects is that faculty of human nature on which every gradation of its progress, nay, every, the minutest change depends."[7] These two judgments about the imagination illuminate Shelley's intent in *Prometheus Unbound*, for Prometheus himself, as "the type of the *highest perfection of moral and intellectual nature*, impelled by the purest and the truest motives to the best and noblest ends" (Preface, my italics), is a symbol for the imagination. Because Prometheus as the imagination (or an imaginatively combined "moral and intellectual nature") acts in conjunction with Asia or love ("the great secret of morals"),[8] Shelley in effect validates Wordsworth's definition of the imagination as "intellectual Love" or "feeling intellect" (*The Prelude* XIV.207, 226). That Shelley had partly in mind a faculty psychology whereby the intellectual and moral goals of wisdom and virtue were combined through the action of the imagination is further suggested by his emphasis on the imagination as the instrument of moral enlightenment (or enlightened morality): "the only distinction between the selfish man, and the virtuous man, is that the imagination of the former is confined within a narrow limit, whilst that of the latter embraces a comprehensive circumference. In this sense, *wisdom and virtue may be said to be inseparable, and criteria of each other*."[9] With intellectual wisdom and moral virtue so essential in a man of comprehensive imagination, Shelley was tempted to allegorize the "understanding" and the "passions" as the servants of "the Imagination, who is the master of them both, their God, and the Spirit by which they live and are."[10]

Shelley, however, usually resisted the temptation to allegorize his faculty psychology, apparently believing with Coleridge that allegory was a limited poetical form, providing only "empty echoes" because it "is but a translation of abstract notions into a picture-language which is itself nothing but an abstraction from objects of the senses; the principal being more worthless even than its phantom proxy, both alike unsubstantial, and the former shapeless to boot."[11] In *Queen Mab*, for example, he was content to have Mab didactically proclaim

*117*

the glorious duty and privilege of inseparable "virtue and . . . wisdom" (II.54) and prophesy the time when "Reason and passion [would] cease to combat" after Falsehood no longer fettered "passion's fearless wing" nor seared "reason with the brand of God" (VIII.231; IX.47-48). Similar expressions abound in the less didactic *Revolt of Islam* where, for example, "new love had stirred/Deep thoughts" and where "Love when wisdom fails, makes Cythna wise" (VII.xli; IX.xxxiv). Yet at times in this epic Shelley did tend to equate Laon with Wisdom and Cythna with Love and to see in their union both the enlightenment and purification of their fellow men.[12] In this same fashion in *Prometheus Unbound*, although Prometheus himself is the type of moral *and* intellectual perfection, Shelley linked Prometheus with Wisdom and Asia with Love and in so doing gave each an allegorical status whereby their union in Act III produces or enlarges the imagination through a union of head and heart, wisdom and virtue. And because this imagination is the source of man's progress and because Demogorgon and not Prometheus dethrones the selfish tyranny of Jupiter after the union of Prometheus and Asia, it is possible to equate Demogorgon with the faculty of the liberating imagination. But to distinguish allegorically the faculties of the mind in this mental drama and make Prometheus into Reason, Asia into Love, and Demogorgon into Imagination is to misrepresent the inseparability of these faculties and to obscure Prometheus' function as the redeemer of mankind. One escape from this allegorical dilemma is to regard Prometheus and Demogorgon as two modal representations of the perfection to which human nature might aspire by means of the imagination. Prometheus, as the immortal Titan and as the mortal son of Earth (see I.113, 152-53, 209), was so constituted in order to represent both the abstract perfection or divinity of the Imagination and the incarnate faculty that makes man divine. In the words of Shelley's Preface to *The Cenci*, "Imagination is as the immortal God which should assume flesh for the redemption of mortal passion."[13] Yet in spite of Shelley's many references to the imagination as a divine power, he did not mean to equate the imagination with God who, Shelley frequently asserted, differed "both from man and from the mind of man."[14]

In his *Essay on Christianity*, Shelley distinguished between God and man's divine faculty and in so doing he indicated the difference between Demogorgon and Prometheus in *Prometheus Unbound*. Demogorgon, the "one pervading," "the Eternal, the Immortal," the "mighty darkness/Filling the seat of power," a "living Spirit" with "neither limb,/Nor form, nor outline" (II.iii.79, 95; iv.2-7) is the same figure Shelley in the *Essay on Christianity* called "God": not the personal and transcendent deity of Christianity, but rather "the interfused and overruling Spirit of all the energy and wisdom included within the circle of existing things"; "something mysteriously and illimitably pervading the frame of things."[15] Like Demogorgon, this "God" is indefinitely described because Shelley believed that "where indefiniteness ends idolatry and anthropomorphism begin." And in attempting to explain the relation between this "mysterious principle" of God and the mind of man, Shelley disregarded for the moment that the deep truth is imageless and in effect explained Demogorgon's relation to Prometheus, and both of their relations to man:

We live and move and think, but we are not the creators of our own origin and existence, we are not the arbiters of every motion of our own complicated nature; we are not the masters of our own imaginations and moods of mental being. There is a Power by which we are surrounded, like the atmosphere in which some motionless lyre is suspended, which visits with its breath our silent chords, at will. Our most imperial and stupendous qualities—those on which the majesty and the power of humanity is erected—are, relatively to the inferior portion of its mechanism, indeed active and imperial; but they are passive slaves of some higher and more omnipresent Power. This Power is God.[16]

Thus relative to man, the imagination is an active and imperial power whereby all progress is accomplished; but relative to God, the imagination is a passive instrument. An identical distinction is made in *Prometheus Unbound*: relative to man, the liberated Prometheus is an imperial agent who in the abstract represents man's imagination and accomplishes man's perfection; but relative to Demogorgon, the agent who actually dethrones Jupiter's selfish tyranny which enchains imaginative action, Prometheus is a passive instrument. But relative to man, both Prometheus and Demogorgon are active powers and their combined actions, that is, the simultaneous creations by the human imagination (abstractly considered) and by the benignant principle of the universe, result in man's perfection. In other words, as Shelley explained himself in his *Essay on Christianity*, "the perfection of the human and the divine character is thus asserted to be the same: man by resembling God fulfils most accurately the tendencies of his nature, and God comprehends within itself all that constitutes human perfection. Thus God is a model thro which the excellence of man is to be estimated, whilst the *abstract* perfection [the liberated Prometheus] of the human character is the type of the *actual* perfection [Demogorgon] of the divine."[17] This last statement illuminates Shelley's conception of Prometheus as the "*type* of the highest perfection of moral and intellectual nature, impelled by the purest and the truest motives to the best and noblest ends" (Preface, my italics). Prometheus, who is usually judged in the abstract as a type of potential human perfection, is also intended by Shelley to be "the type of the *actual* perfection of the divine." We see, then, that Prometheus or the imagination is the mediator between Demogorgon (or God) and man, and that he is consequently not an allegorical but rather a symbolic figure. In fact, Prometheus is developed as the perfect exemplum of Coleridge's definition of a symbol as "the translucence of the Eternal through and in the Temporal. It always partakes of the Reality which it renders intelligible; and while it enunciates the whole, abides itself as a living part in that Unity, of which it is the representative." As a symbolic mediator, Prometheus paradoxically makes man aware of his own divinity and yet preserves the distinction between man and God. Thus in his liberated state, Prometheus or the imagination tears aside the painted veil of life and reveals a man who is

> Sceptreless, free, uncircumscribed,—but man:
> Equal, unclassed, tribeless and nationless,
> Exempt from awe, worship, degree, the King
> Over himself; just, gentle, wise,—but man:
> Passionless? no: yet free from guilt or pain,
> Which were, for his will made, or suffered them,
> Nor yet exempt, tho' ruling them like slaves,
> From chance, and death, and mutability,
> The clogs of that which else might oversoar
> The loftiest star of unascended heaven,
> Pinnacled dim in the intense inane.          (III.iv.194-204)

Only Demogorgon can oversoar the intense inane; man, though perfected, is still a man subject to chance, death, and mutability; and Prometheus as the typal mediator of both perfections can with Asia "sit and talk of time and change,/As the world ebbs and flows, [themselves] unchanged" (III.iii.23-24).

In order to become the type of the highest perfection to which man can aspire, Prometheus had to reverse two actions by which his intellectual and moral nature had been corrupted, both actions having taken place prior to the opening of the drama and to Prometheus' desire to reclaim his role as the "saviour and the strength of suffering man" (I.817). When Prometheus first attempted to save men by giving them

> The birthright of their being, knowledge, power,
> The skill which wields the elements, the thought
> Which pierces this dim universe like light,
> Self-empire, and the majesty of love,          (II.iv.39-42)

*120*

his good intentions were perverted to an evil effect because of his own intellectual error: he instituted "the all-miscreative brain of Jove" (I. 448) by giving *only* "wisdom, which is strength, to Jupiter" (II.iv.44) rather than *both* wisdom and love to *man*. Prometheus' twofold error here was evil, evil being defined by Shelley as an action that "produces an overbalance of . . . pain to sentient beings," for Jupiter, in effect Prometheus' creation, knew "nor faith, nor love, nor law" and rained down "famine, and then toil, and then disease,/Strife, wounds, and ghastly death" upon man (II.iv.47, 50-51). In an attempt to remedy this evil, Prometheus became incarnate, arising from his maternal Earth "like a cloud/Of glory . . . a spirit of keen joy" (I.157-58) in order to give directly to "man speech, and speech created thought," and in order to bring Asia or "Love . . . to bind/The disunited tendrils of that vine/Which bears the wine of life, the human heart" (II.iv.72; 63-65). This combined intellectual and moral action was obviously good, one that produced "an overbalance of pleasure . . . to sentient beings,"[18] but the separately enthroned principle of wisdom, miscreative through the absence of Love, continued to persecute man and even Prometheus, despite his wandering over the earth "With Asia, drinking life from her loved eyes" (I.123). Thus the paradise that Prometheus and Asia created and that Asia described to Demogorgon in Act II (iv.59-99) was destined to fall, for Prometheus failed to dethrone the miscreative principle and hence Jupiter continued to rain down

> Evil, the immedicable plague, which, while
> Man looks on his creation like a God
> And sees that it is glorious, drives him on
> The wreck of his own will, the scorn of earth,
> The outcast, the abandoned, the alone.    (II.iv.101-5)

Like man whom he represented, Prometheus was also the "wreck of his own will" in that he claimed that his "own will" was free of Jupiter's "power" (see I.273-74) but nevertheless submitted to that power. In effect enchaining himself, Prometheus confirmed his fallen nature by defying and cursing Jupiter and thus acting in accord with the immoral "interchange of wrong for wrong." By yielding up Love to tyrannous Hate, Prometheus, like Jupiter, separated himself from Asia or Love, "the great secret of morals"; consequently, Prometheus or the imagination, "the great instrument of moral good,"[19] violated his own "destiny to be,/The saviour and the strength of suffering man" (I.816-17). Prometheus therefore fell to the state described by Byron in his ode, with neither a benignant principle (Demogorgon) nor a benignant power (Asia) to comfort his miseries. By selfishly directing his attention to Jupiter rather than to man, Prometheus did indeed grow like what he contemplated (I.450), for by his evil curse he increased the misery and the pain of man:

> Be thy [Jupiter's] swift mischiefs sent
>   To blast mankind, from yon ethereal tower
> Let thy malignant spirit move
> In darkness over those I love:
> On me and mine I imprecate
> The utmost torture of thy hate. (I.274-79)

When Prometheus heard his own words repeated by the Phantasm of Jupiter, he recognized that he had grown like the selfish and proud Jupiter or, in other words, that his own intellectual and moral errors were externalized by Jupiter's existence and tyranny—as Prometheus remarked to Mercury, "Evil minds/Change good to their own nature. I gave all/He [Jupiter] has" (I.380-82).[20] In order to correct his errors and reclaim his sovereignty, Prometheus began to reverse the evil that he himself had occasioned:

> It doth repent me: words are quick and vain;
> Grief for awhile is blind, and so was mine.
> I wish no living thing to suffer pain. (I.303-5)

Prometheus then successfully proved his moral and intellectual superiority by withstanding Mercury's temptation and the Furies' persecution, and after being comforted by the spirits from "the dim caves of human thought" who bore "the prophecy/Which begins and ends in thee" (I.659; 690-91), he reasserted the primacy of love (I.808, 824) and called on Asia (see II.i.89-91), who in Act II would proceed to the realm of Demogorgon in order to confirm the "prophecy" of Prometheus: that the "imagination or mind employed in prophetically [imaging forth] its objects is that faculty of human nature on which every gradation of its progress, nay, every, the minutest change depends."[21]

This prophecy, that man through his imagination is his own liberator, is the lesson of Asia's expository dialogue with Demogorgon in Act II, although the lesson is taught inversely: that man, through a misuse of his imagination, is his own tyrant and enslaver. When Asia first asks "Who made the living world" and "all/That it contains? thought, passion, reason, will,/Imagination?" (II.iv.9-11), Demogorgon answers "God: Almighty God." But God or the overruling power of the universe, she discovers, is not the creator of "terror, madness, crime, remorse" (II.iv.19), those human failings psychologically manifested in

> Abandoned hope, and love that turns to hate;

And self-contempt, bitterer to drink than blood;
Pain, whose unheeded and familiar speech
Is howling, and keen shrieks, day after day;
And Hell, or the sharp fear of Hell.  (II.iv.24-28)

In answer to Asia's question about the creator of these intellectual and
moral disorders, Demogorgon cryptically replies, "He reigns" (II.iv.28,
31), although he clearly implies that these disorders result from man's
miscreative imagination and his own willful ill. Asia, however, not fully
comprehending man's responsibility, asks again, "Who reigns"; then,
after recounting man's genesis and history up to Prometheus' enslavement, she repeats her question once more:

                    but who rains down
Evil, the immedicable plague, which, while
Man looks on his creation like a God
And sees that it is glorious, drives him on
The wreck of his own will, the scorn of earth,
The outcast, the abandoned, the alone?[22]  (II.iv.100-5)

Although Asia knows that Jupiter has "reigned" (II.iv.49) and has
rained down evil, she begins to recognize that he is not the tyrant
responsible for man's psychological disorders and she answers her own
question thusly:

Not Jove: while yet his frown shook heaven, aye when
His adversary from adamantine chains
Cursed him, he trembled like a slave. Declare
Who is his master? Is he too a slave?  (II.iv.106-9)

Demogorgon once again offers a cryptic answer, "All spirits are enslaved which serve things evil" (II.iv.110), but from it we can deduce
that Jupiter, who served evil ways, was enslaved; that Prometheus,
Jupiter's creator, was "his master"; that as "his master," Prometheus
was "too a slave" for he also served things evil; and finally, because
Prometheus abstractly represents the imagination, that the imagination
itself, which can increase its comprehensive circumference through
virtuous action or confine itself within a narrow limit by selfishness
(i.e., Jupiter), is responsible for man's liberation or enslavement.
    A corollary of this deduction is that for Shelley there is no onto-
logical reality intervening or mediating between God (the benignant
principle of the universe) and man (who either enlarges or circumscribes
his imagination by good or evil actions).[23] Thus there is no objectively
existing Jupiter whose purpose is to thwart man and his desires; for
Shelley, only the vulgar would posit a malevolent ontological principle
which, like Byron's "ruling principle of Hate" (*Prometheus*) or Ari-

manes (*Manfred*), was constructed as a casuistical excuse for man's own imaginative failures. Shelley's denial of an ontological principle of evil may seem inconsistent with his judgment that "the Manichæan philosophy respecting the origin and government of the world . . . is at least an hypothesis conformable to the experience of actual facts," but he suggests within this quotation from *On the Devil, and Devils* that this hypothesis was probably "not true" and he never dogmatically asserted that the world was governed by two eternal and antithetical principles. Instead, he saw the two Manichaean principles as "simply a personification of the struggle which we experience within ourselves, and which we perceive in the operations of external things as they affect us, between good and evil." Only the "vulgar" elevate these personifications into the "familiar notions of God and the Devil" or the Manichaean principles of Good and Evil.[24] And in spite of Shelley's belief that "according to the indisputable facts of the case, some evil Spirit has dominion in this imperfect world,"[25] that spirit was a personification, like Jupiter in *Prometheus Unbound*, of man's own willful ill. Thus Asia's question about the source of evil can be answered in the words of her own question: man is the source of evil by which he

> drives him[self] on
> The wreck of his own will, the scorn of earth,
> The outcast, the abandoned, the alone. (II.iv.103-5)

Shelley's arguments in *Prometheus Unbound* that man is his own enslaver and liberator serve to explain Julian's judgment in *Julian and Maddalo* that

> "it is our will
> That thus enchains us to permitted ill—
> We might be otherwise—we might be all
> We dream of happy, high, majestical"; (ll. 170-73)

and his conviction that the Maniac's enslavement resulted not from "'destiny,/But [his] own wilful ill'" (ll. 210-11). In *Julian and Maddalo* as in *Prometheus Unbound*, Shelley attempted to make Byron see that man's fight with destiny was merely misunderstood psychomachia which had been occasioned by man's own selfish and unimaginative actions. Byron had used Prometheus' eternal war with Jupiter (whom Byron had partially depersonalized into the "inexorable Heaven,/And the deaf tyranny of Fate,/The ruling principle of Hate") as the symbol of man's enthrallment by a "funereal destiny." Shelley probably admired the mythopoeic structure of Byron's *Prometheus* but he undoubtedly, at least by 1818, rejected the metaphysics therein. Indeed, Byron had neither the metaphysics nor the motive in the summer of 1816 to introduce into his ode a Demogorgon or an Asia, whose dialogue in the later *Prometheus Unbound* gave Shelley an opportunity to argue that Jupiter or Byron's triune Heaven/Fate/Hate was merely a product of man's miscreative brain rather than a malevolent principle responsible for man's "sad unallied existence." And in some ways, Asia and Demogorgon were Shelley's responses to Byron's metaphysically deficient *Prometheus*, where Love and God were not even figured. But more specifically, Asia and Demogorgon embodied Shelley's direct answer to Byron's Promethean and "metaphysical"[26] drama, *Manfred*, wherein Love and God were figured in the characters of Astarte and the "overruling Infinite" (II.iv.47) but were, from Shelley's viewpoint, sadly deficient in their dramatic and thematic importance.

II

"In many ways, both in form and theme," Wasserman has written, *"Prometheus Unbound* is a reply to *Manfred,"* but he did not pursue the specific replies that Shelley intended. However, he did suggest that in response to "'There are more things in heaven and earth, Horatio,/ Than are dreamt of in your philosophy'"—Byron's epigraph to *Manfred* —"that Shelley, rejecting all theologies, jotted in one of his notebooks his corrective version:

There is more on earth than we
Dream of in our philosophy."[27]

Shelley probably did have Byron in mind when he "reformed" Hamlet's judgment in this fashion, but as the foregoing analysis of *Prometheus Unbound* reveals, I don't believe that Shelley rejected all theologies. Furthermore, believing that Shelley and Byron debated with each other by means of their epigraphs,[28] I judge that Wasserman overlooks the obvious in his otherwise excellent treatment of the epigraph to *Prometheus Unbound: "Audisne haec, Amphiarae, sub terram abdite?"* —which he translates as "Do you hear this, Amphiaraus, hidden away under the earth?" This quotation from Aeschylus' lost drama, *Epigoni*, has been preserved in Cicero's *Tusculan Disputations*, wherein Cleanthes the Stoic uses it to indict Dionysius the Epicurean, an apostate who had abandoned the principles of Zeno's Stoicism. As Cicero explains the circumstances, Cleanthes (addressing Amphiaraus but "meaning Zeno") was "grieving that Dionysius was false to [Zeno's] teaching."[29] But Shelley, according to Wasserman, had a different "meaning" in mind:

Shelley, a latter-day Cleanthes, is similarly lamenting that the stoically resisting Prometheus of Aeschylus' *Prometheus Bound* was to become, in his terms, the weak, hedonistic apostate of the

lost sequel who could not tolerate pain for the sake of his principles and submitted at last to tyrannical Jupiter. At the same
time, instead of asking Stoic Zeno to hear of Epicurean Dionysius,
the epigraph addresses the ghost of Aeschylus, who had allowed
his Prometheus to recant, and in effect asks it to hear Shelley's
entire reorganization of the myth, in which the patiently suffering Titan will resist tyranny by never weakening.[30]

If Wasserman is correct, as I think he is, Shelley consciously inverted
the equivalents in Cicero's account and used this epigraph to announce
that his *Prometheus Unbound* would indict Aeschylus (addressed as
"Amphiaraus") for becoming an apostate like Dionysius. But if Shelley
believed himself to be "a latter-day Cleanthes," he also believed that
Byron was a *latter-day Dionysius*: that is, Byron had recanted the
Shelleyan metaphysics in his Promethean drama, *Manfred*. Thus the
address to Aeschylus/Dionysius under the name of Amphiaraus is also
and perhaps even more so an address to Byron/Dionysius. Byron knew
the story of Dionysius' apostasy and had already likened himself to
Dionysius under different circumstances,[31] and Shelley used this epigraph in order to announce to the author of *Manfred* that his renegade
philosophy was being challenged by *Prometheus Unbound*. Thus the
ironic relationship between Shelley's *Prometheus Unbound* and
Aeschylus' *Prometheus Bound* (according to Wasserman, Shelley's
"procedure is to draw heavily on Aeschylus' play but to reassign the
'borrowings' and re-establish them in a contrary ethical and theological
context so as to transform their meanings radically"[32]) also exists
between *Prometheus Unbound* and *Manfred*: Shelley borrowed from
the "form" of Byron's drama but only insofar as he could use these
"borrowings" to assert his own "spirit" and simultaneously denounce
Byron's apostasy.

What Shelley wanted Byron to "hear" in *Prometheus Unbound*
was a metaphysics that could take the formal circumstances of a Manfred, preserve the "Promethean spark" (I.i.154) of Byron's hero, but
give him an alternative of victory through Life rather than through
Death. Consciously imitating the pattern of Byron's Promethean drama,
Shelley created a Prometheus who, like Manfred, had the "visions"
and "noble aspirations" to make his "own the mind of other men,/
The enlightener of nations" (III.i.104-7), and who also clouded his
vision by an intellectual and moral error, destroyed his love, separated
himself from his psychic complement, and caused his own pain and
isolation. With Manfred's "knowledge grew/The thirst of knowledge,
and the power and joy/Of this most bright intelligence, until—"
(II.ii.94-96)—until he inordinately destroyed his love or heart in the
person of Astarte; similarly, with Prometheus' knowledge and power

(i.e., "wisdom" and "strength"—II.iv.44) given to Jupiter, Shelley's hero began a chain of events that led to hate and to the destruction of love (represented by Asia's separation from Prometheus). These similar pre-play circumstances determined each protagonist in the first scene to seek liberation from his enslavement by calling upon the Spirits of Nature. But in his version of this appeal, Shelley made an important distinction between his hero and Byron's, a distinction he also made in Julian and Maddalo's argument about free will and destiny: whereas Manfred had learned from the Seventh Spirit that he was cursed by destiny (I.i.110-31), Prometheus learned, as I have already demonstrated, that he determined his own destiny; whereas Manfred, a "Son of Earth" (II.ii.28-29, 32; see also II.iv.35), had vainly (i.e., with pride and without success) demanded that the Spirits of "Earth—ocean—air—night—mountains—winds—[his] Star" (I.i.132) help him forget the sin by which he fulfilled his destiny, Prometheus, also a son of Earth (I.152-58), more moderately called upon the Spirits of the Mountains, Springs, Air, and Whirlwinds (I.59-66) in order both to remember and to reverse the action by which he had enchained himself.

Neither Byron's nor Shelley's protagonist was satisfied by the Spirits of Nature, but Prometheus' subsequent "recall" of the curse by means of the Phantasm of Jupiter suggests that Prometheus' more moderate or humble request was a sign that he had greater *strength* than Manfred. This difference in "spirit" between the first scenes of these dramas further suggests that Shelley was offering Manfred a different course of action: because it was Promethean man's "weakness to be proud" (Preface to *Julian and Maddalo*)—witness the intellectual disdain with which Manfred treats the Spirits of Nature—Manfred could have found strength, as Shelley's Prometheus did, in a knowledge tempered by returning humility and love:

> I speak in *grief*,
> Not exultation, for I hate no more,
> As then *ere misery made me wise*. The curse
> Once breathed on thee I would recall.      (I.56-59, my italics)

These lines, which Prometheus spoke just before he called upon the Spirits of Nature, directly repudiate Manfred's judgment that "*Grief* should be the *Instructor of the wise*" (I.i.9, my italics), a phrase that at first seems identical to Shelley's "ere misery made me wise." But there is considerable difference in the intent of each phrase, for Manfred's "wisdom" gained through "grief" was unavailing in Byron's vision of a fallen world unredeemed by love:

> Sorrow is Knowledge: they who know the most

Must mourn the deepest o'er the fatal truth,
The Tree of Knowledge is not that of Life.     (I.i.10-12)

Prometheus' "misery," on the other hand, led to a "grief" that embodied both wisdom and love: he recognized the nature of his own
willful ill, withdrew the hateful curse, and by the end of Act I rediscovered the value of Asia and the hope to be found in love. This hope
opposes the despair of Manfred, who, by the end of his first act,
attempted to achieve forgetfulness and to escape his grief in suicide.
In effect, then, Shelley took the circumstances of Manfred's life and
rewrote them according to his own theories about man's internal
nature. Thus Shelley's intent in *Prometheus Unbound* was identical to
Julian's in *Julian and Maddalo*: Julian wanted to take the circumstances
of the Byronic Maniac (another Promethean sufferer) and

"prove the induction otherwise,
And that a want of that true theory, still,
Which seeks a 'soul of goodness' in things ill,
Or in himself or others, has thus bowed
His being—*there are some by nature proud,
Who patient in all else, demand but this—
To love and be beloved with gentleness;
And being scorned, what wonder if they die
Some living death?* This is not destiny,
But man's own wilful ill."          (ll. 202-11, my italics)

These lines precisely convey Shelley's judgment about Manfred, who
had rejected the Shelleyan "true theory" and who chose death because
of his intellectual pride and his impatience in love. According to
Shelley's *Prometheus Unbound*, what Manfred needed was a faith in
Demogorgon and a corresponding assurance that "*Love*, from its awful
throne of *patient* power/In the *wise heart*" could fold "over the world
its healing wings" (IV.557-58, 561, my italics).

Without the healing wings of Love, man and his society, as
described by both Byron and Shelley, were in a chaotic state. Although
Manfred acknowledged that the world was beautiful, this beauty was
blighted by man's internal conflicts:

But we, who name ourselves its sovereigns, we,
Half dust, half deity, alike unfit
To sink or soar, with our mixed essence make
A conflict of its elements, and breathe
The breath of degradation and of pride,
Contending with low wants and lofty will.     (I.ii.39-44)

The Furies in *Prometheus Unbound* similarly described the state of man:

The good want power, but to weep barren tears.
The powerful goodness want: worse need for them.
The wise want love; and those who love want wisdom;
And all best things are thus confused to ill.          (I.625-28)

The difference between these two judgments is that in Shelley's drama
Prometheus, or man, could reconcile his contradictions by joining his
wisdom and power (which he had mistakenly given without love to
Jupiter) to the love and goodness of Asia. But Byron had no such hope
for man or for Manfred, each predestined to be

an awful chaos—Light and Darkness—
And mind and dust—and passions and pure thoughts
Mixed, and contending without end or order,—
All dormant or destructive.          (III.i.164-67)

Having rejected his 1816 Shelleyan metaphysics, Byron could no longer
believe that Love would fold "over the world its healing wings." Instead, as Byron made explicit in *Childe Harold* IV what was implicit in
*Manfred*, Love or Astarte was "no habitant of earth" and Manfred's
attempt to give in "thought such shape and image" to her created a
phantasm that "haunts the unquenched soul—parched—wearied—wrung
—and riven" (IV.cxxi). With Astarte dead, Manfred saw no hope for a
reintegration of his personality, and Byron might have objected to
Shelley's somewhat facile reunification of Asia and Prometheus in Act
III of his drama. But Shelley would have welcomed such an objection,
for he would have argued (as he may have in fact done after Byron
read *Prometheus Unbound*) that in symbolic terms Astarte provided
Manfred the same moral focus Asia provided for Prometheus. In other
words, Asia, like Prometheus, was nothing more than a symbolic abstraction, and as such she symbolized man's metaphysical power of Love.
In Byron's drama, Astarte essentially represents this same power, but
since Astarte or Love was "no habitant of earth," she became the
unreachable Paradise of Manfred's despair. In contrast, Shelley made
Asia, like Prometheus, incarnate, and by reuniting her with Prometheus after 3,000 years of separation, he stressed the undying nature
of Love as a metaphysical (i.e., internal; or in terms of the myth,
incarnate) power that could liberate the mind of man.

   Shelley's ironic adaptation of *Manfred* in *Prometheus Unbound*
and consequently his continuing debate with Lord Byron do not end
merely with the parallels between Prometheus/Asia and Manfred/
Astarte. And in order to direct the reader as I have myself been
directed, I quote from H. W. Piper's summary of the formal relations
between these two dramas:

Byron's spirits of nature, the Destinies, Arimanes and the 'over-ruling infinite' (the last barely mentioned in *Manfred*) became Shelley's spirits of nature, spirits of human thought, Jove and Demogorgon. The first and second spirits of human thought, who come from the battle-trumpet blast of freedom and the sigh of the drowning seaman who gave his plank to an enemy, are point-by-point answers to Byron's two destinies who raise the Usurper for a nation's destruction and save a pirate from the shipwreck, while his spirits who come from the dreams of the sage and the lips of the poet are less direct answers to the destiny who sows plague and panic in human societies.

Piper did not elaborate on most of these borrowings, perhaps because he also judged that "in the main, *Prometheus Unbound* ignores the details of *Manfred*, and answers Byron by affirming Shelley's own faith."[33] But Shelley did not always ignore the details when he used the form of *Manfred* to articulate, ironically, his own ideas. I have already cited Manfred's and then Prometheus' appeals to the Spirits of Nature, the first demanding forgetfulness of his cursed destiny and the other seeking to "recall" his curse of Jupiter. Neither group of Spirits fulfilled what each protagonist desired: the Seven Spirits informed Manfred that death would not provide forgetfulness to his immortal mind; and the four Spirits did not repeat the curse that Prometheus wanted to remember. But because Prometheus' request, unlike Manfred's, was at least satisfied in this scene when Earth advised him to call up the Phantasm of Jupiter, Shelley seems to be saying that Manfred's appeal for forgetfulness in death was a violation of his own nature. In fact, Manfred ignored the lesson from the Seven Spirits and consciously chose death as a means to escape the conse-quences of his intellectual and moral error. In other words, Manfred, desiring to still his Promethean sufferings of mind and body, chose to make "Death a Victory" in the manner of Byron's Prometheus. And in spite of his many difficulties, as he explained to the Witch of the Alps,

> My solitude is solitude no more,
> But *peopled with the Furies*;—I have gnashed
> My teeth in darkness till returning morn,
> Then cursed myself till sunset;—I have prayed
> For madness as a blessing—'tis denied me.
> I have affronted Death—but in the war
> Of elements the waters shrunk from me,
> And fatal things passed harmless; the cold hand
> Of an all-pitiless Demon held me back,

> . . . . . . . . . *I dwell in my despair—*
> *And live—and live for ever,* (II.ii.130-50, my italics)

Manfred finally succeeded in becoming his "own destroyer" (III.iv.139). Shelley transformed Manfred's sufferings, "peopled with the Furies," into Prometheus' long encounter with the Furies in Act I.326-634; and even though Prometheus experienced equally intense pain, he made explicit his and Shelley's distaste for Manfred's choice of death:

> Alas! pain, *pain ever*, for ever!
> I close my tearless eyes, but see more clear
> Thy works within my woe-illumined mind,
> Thou subtle tyrant! *Peace is in the grave.*
> The grave hides all things beautiful and good:
> *I am a God and cannot find it there,*
> *Nor would I seek it*: for, though dread revenge,
> *This is defeat, fierce king, not victory.*
>
> (I.635-42, my italics)

Because Manfred by virtue of his immortal mind was also "a God," Prometheus is here preaching to his Byronic predecessor that the grave or death, even in defiance, was defeat, and that the only victory lay in preserving the integrity of the mind by means of synthetic Love, the "Life of Life" (II.v.48). Prometheus, therefore, could very appropriately be the speaker of the epigraph: "Do you hear this, [Manfred], hidden away under the earth?"

Following Prometheus' repudiation of death and the grave as a solution to his long years of suffering, he is comforted by the fair Spirits from the "dim caves of human thought" (I.659), and Shelley's purpose here was to use these Spirits as a reply not only to his own Furies but also to their dramatized equivalent in *Manfred*, the Destinies. And in the songs of these fair Spirits lies Shelley's most ingenious rebuke to Byron; as Piper observed, "the first and second spirits of human thought, who come from the battle-trumpet blast of freedom and the sigh of the drowning seaman who gave his plank to an enemy, are point-by-point answers to Byron's two destinies who raise the Usurper for a nation's destruction and save a pirate from the ship-wreck." The importance of Piper's discoveries demands quotation of these point-by-point answers:

| | |
|---|---|
| The Captive Usurper, | On a battle-trumpet's blast |
|   Hurled down from the throne, | I fled hither, fast, fast, fast, |
| Lay buried in torpor, | 'Mid the darkness upward cast. |
|   Forgotten and lone; | From the dust of creeds outworn, |
| I broke through his slumbers, | From the tyrant's banner torn, |

I shivered his chain,
I leagued him with numbers—
He's Tyrant again!
With the blood of a million
he'll answer my care,
With a Nation's destruction—
his flight and despair!
(*Manfred* II.iii.16-25)

Gathering 'round me, onward borne,
There was mingled many a cry—
Freedom! Hope! Death! Victory!
Till they faded thro' the sky;
And one sound, above, around,
One sound beneath, around, above,
Was moving; 'twas the soul of love;
'Twas the hope, the prophecy,
Which begins and ends in thee.
(*Prometheus Unbound* I.694-707)

The Ship sailed on, the Ship
sailed fast,
But I left not a sail, and I
left not a mast;
There is not a plank of the
hull or the deck,
And there is not a wretch to
lament o'er his wreck;
Save one, whom I held, as he
swam, by the hair,
And he was a subject well
worthy my care;
A traitor on land, and a pirate
at sea—
But I saved him to wreak
further havoc for me!
(*Manfred* II.iii.26-33)

A rainbow's arch stood on the sea,
Which rocked beneath, immovably;
And the triumphant storm did flee,
Like a conqueror, swift and proud,
Between, with many a captive cloud,
A shapeless, dark and rapid crowd,
Each by lightning riven in half:
I heard the thunder hoarsely laugh:
Mighty fleets were strewn like chaff
And spread beneath a hell of death
O'er the white waters. I alit
On a great ship lightning-split,
And speeded hither on the sigh
Of one who gave an enemy
His plank, then plunged aside to die.[34]
(*Prometheus Unbound* I.708-22)

The tyrannical and piratical enslavements that Byron in his two songs
had attributed to destiny, Shelley judged to be the product of man
whose "will made, or suffered" these self-imprisonments (III.iv.199).
All of these mind-forged manacles could be broken, Shelley argued, if
Byronic man would liberate his mind by the power of Love—the power
he celebrated in the above prophecies from the "dim caves of human
thought." And the "soul of love," celebrated in the collective rejection
of the church and the state ("the dust of creeds" and "the tyrant's
banner") and in the personal act of giving "an enemy/His plank," was
the metaphysical power he wanted Byron to acknowledge—metaphysical
in the sense that it was man's internal power rather than an unrealizable
ideal. Love for Shelley was very much a "habitant of earth" which
could free man from the enslavement of Byronic destiny.

The Destinies in *Manfred* were a mythopoeic extension of what
Byron called "the deaf tyranny of Fate" in his 1816 ode; in the same

manner, Arimanes, whom the Destinies served, was the mythic equivalent of the "ruling principle of Hate" (*Prometheus*, ll. 19-20). In his turn, Shelley transformed Arimanes into Jupiter, and the similarities between Manfred's and Prometheus' antagonists are the result of Shelley's imitation: just as Arimanes had been a supreme tyrant, such that "Life is his,/With all its Infinite of agonies—/And his the Spirit of whatever is" (II.iv.14-16), the tyrannical Jupiter was "the supreme of living things" (II.iv.113); just as the Destinies had ordered Manfred to "Bow down and worship," to "kneel" before Arimanes (II.iv.30-36), Mercury demanded that Prometheus be "suppliant," and "Let [his] will kneel" before Jupiter (I.377-78). The difference between these two tyrants, however, is more important than their similarity, for Shelley withdrew the ontological independence of Byron's Arimanes and reduced him to a "phantasm" that was merely a product of man's miscreative mind. (Implicitly in *Manfred* and explicitly in *Childe Harold* IV, Byron had denied the immanence of Shelleyan Love; Shelley reciprocated in *Prometheus Unbound* by denying the transcendence of Byronic Hate.) Furthermore, Shelley's philosophical system posited a supreme Power that, determined or set in motion by man's imaginative and moral regeneration, would dethrone the tyrannical principle. In terms of the drama, Demogorgon, as a result of Prometheus' regeneration, dethroned Jupiter and thus externalized the internal metaphysics that Shelley wanted Byron to "hear."

Shelley introduced Demogorgon into *Prometheus Unbound* in order to clarify his own intellectual philosophy and at the same time to provide Byron a solution to the problems experienced by Manfred. Just as Shelley enlarged Astarte's narrative and thematic functions in the character of Asia, so also he took Byron's "overruling Infinite" and transformed him into Demogorgon. Byron, it will be recalled, had once referred to a divinity in his drama, when Manfred bid Arimanes to

> bow down to that which is above him,
> The overruling Infinite—the Maker
> Who made him not for worship.         (II.iv.46-48)

In these lines, Shelley found the potential solution to Manfred's Promethean complaint, and by turning this creative "Maker" into Demogorgon he infused into his drama a teleological purpose which Byron had denied with respect to Manfred. And Demogorgon's function was not merely to intervene fortuitously as the redeemer of Prometheus and mankind—an action that Shelley as well as Byron would have rejected as unbefitting both the human and the divine nature. According to Shelley, God or the supreme Power or Demogorgon, differing from the mind of man, had no will[35] and therefore did not will the events that imprisoned or liberated man. For this reason, Demogorgon acted only in accord with man's will; that is, he dethroned Jupiter only to externalize what had already occurred metaphysically within Prometheus. God's "will" is therefore determined by Prometheus' (i.e., man's) willful actions—these being the only efficient causes of his enslavement or freedom. In *Manfred*, however, the "overruling Infinite" had no effect on human action—neither as a god who would freely intervene on man's behalf nor as a benignant Power teleologically directed by man's benevolent action. Byron never attained the metaphysical assurance for such a view of God, and instead, as he confessed in his 1821 "Detached Thoughts," "always believed that all things depend upon Fortune, and nothing upon ourselves."[36] Aware of "the existence of so much pure and unmixed evil in the world . . . which he could not reconcile to the idea of a benevolent Creator," Byron told Dr. James Kennedy in 1823 that life was "'a predestination of events, and that that predestination depends on the will of God.'"[37] He similarly told Lady Blessington a few months earlier that "'to live and to suffer are . . . synonymous.'"[38] These later judgments about man's predestined and suffering life merely confirm the fatalism apparent in *Manfred*, a fatalism that gave Byron, according to Shelley, "an intense apprehension of the nothingness of human life" (Preface to *Julian and Maddalo*). In terms of Shelley's *On Life*, then, Byron was one of those who "in living . . . lose the apprehension of life" and consequently deny "the character of all life and being," namely "a spirit within [man] at enmity with nothingness and dissolution."[39] Shelley specifically witnessed Byron's denial of this "spirit" in *Manfred*, wherein death and oblivion were sought to escape a predestined suffering. But Shelley claimed that destiny was merely a creation of man's enfeebled imagination and an excuse for his willful ill; and he responded to Byron's misapprehension of life by writing *Julian and Maddalo* and *Prometheus Unbound*. In both, but particularly in the latter, he proclaimed his intellectual philosophy and celebrated man's metaphysical "spirit . . . at enmity with [Byronic] nothingness and dissolution," the "spirit" that, according to Demogorgon, "is alone Life, Joy, Empire, and Victory" (IV.578).

III

The importance of *Manfred* in the philosophical dialogue between Byron and Shelley is perhaps unequaled, for it provided Byron an answer to Shelley's *Alastor* and it was in return answered by *Julian and Maddalo* and *Prometheus Unbound*. But the "spirit" of *Manfred* was also embodied in Byron's *Childe Harold* IV, which Shelley read while writing Act I of his lyrical drama and which he condemned in December 1818 for its "obstinate & selfwilled folly."[40] Not having read this fourth canto in time to structure a fully developed answer to it in *Prometheus Unbound*, Shelley was for the most part content merely to reassert what Byron had denied in *Childe Harold* IV: that Love (Asia) was an incarnate habitant of earth. But in at least one place, the song of the Fourth Spirit from the caves of human thought (the first two of these Spirits had provided "point-by-point answers" to the Destinies in *Manfred*), Shelley did respond explicitly to Byron's fourth canto. This Fourth Spirit's description of a poet who can watch the "lake-reflected sun illume/The yellow bees in the ivy-bloom" and then "from these create . . ./Forms more real than living man,/Nurslings of immortality" (I.744-49), directly echoes Byron's lines in *Childe Harold* IV:

> The Beings of the Mind are not of clay:
> Essentially immortal, they create
> And multiply in us a brighter ray
> And more beloved existence.[41]                    (v)

Although these parallel expressions embody what appears to be an identical aesthetic, Byron observed in his next lines that these beings of the mind are phantasies "which Fate/Prohibits to dull life in this our state/Of mortal bondage." In other words, poetry's ideal forms can provide temporary mental escape, but they cannot redeem man from his moral and intellectual failures. To the contrary in Shelley's drama, one of the poet's ideal forms awakened the Fourth Spirit of human thought who then "sped to succour" Prometheus with the "prophecy" of the imagination liberated. The relation between the poet, the Fourth Spirit, and Prometheus sounds complex, but it reveals Shelley's faith in the redemptive function of poetry: a poet's creation will awaken human thought, and this thought will then strengthen the imagination. Shelley *precisely* repeated this message of the Fourth Spirit in his *Defence of Poetry*: "*Poetry* enlarges the circumference of the *imagination* by replenishing it with *thoughts* of ever new delight."[42]

The hope that Shelley placed in poetry in Act I he repeated more confidently in Act III when the reunited Prometheus (imagination) and Asia (love) expect to be visited from the "human world" (III.iii.44) by *verbal* "echoes" of human love and *visual* "apparitions" of imaginative beauty: these voices and shadows, these sounds and shapes, according to Prometheus,

> Shall visit us, the progeny immortal
> Of Painting, Sculpture, and rapt Poesy,
> And arts, tho' unimagined, yet to be.

The wandering voices and the shadows these
Of all that man becomes, the mediators
Of that best worship love, by him [man] and us
Given and returned; swift shapes and sounds, which grow
More fair and soft as man grows wise and kind,
And veil by veil, evil and error fall.                    (III.iii.54-62)

Once more we are made aware of what Coleridge called the trans-
lucent symbol that "partakes of the Reality which it renders intelligible": between "him" (man liberated by imagination and love) and
"us" (Prometheus and Asia, the symbols of that imagination and love),
the "swift" and "wandering" creations of the imagination are given
and returned. This circular reciprocity of man's imagination giving to
and receiving from his own imagination is partially glossed by Shelley's
judgment in *A Defence of Poetry* that "poetry administers to the
effect by acting upon the cause."[43] That is, only through the self-
circling energies of man's imagination will Prometheus (the symbol for
that imagination) continue to reign over the fallen Jupiter; only
through imagination's reign, continually strengthened by its own poetry,
its own self-sustaining power, will "veil by veil, evil and error fall."

    Within a world transformed by such a poetically self-vitalizing
imagination, all men will eventually acknowledge what Prometheus
has taught them: "To love, and bear; to hope till Hope creates/From
its own wreck the thing it contemplates" (IV.573-74). According to
the Spirit of the Hour, there will be

    None, with firm *sneer*, [who] *trod out* in his own *heart*
    The sparks of *love* and *hope* till there remained
    Those bitter ashes, a soul *self-consumed*,
    And the wretch crept a vampire among men,
    Infecting all with his own hideous ill.

                                        (III.iv.144-48, my italics)

With these lines, Shelley in effect prophesies the death of the Byronic
vision. In fact, these lines must have been directly addressed to the
proud Byron whom Shelley similarly described in his Preface to *Julian
and Maddalo*: "I say that Maddalo is *proud*, because I can find no
other word to express the concentered and impatient feelings which
*consume* him; but it is on his own *hopes* and *affections* only that he
seems to *trample*" (my italics). In terms of Shelley's perception of his
fellow poet, Byron was an apostate: in the summer of 1816 Byron
had celebrated the immanence of Love in Clarens (*Childe Harold* III.
xcix-civ) and had entertained "hopes which will not deceive" (III.cxiv);
in September of 1816 Shelley wanted Byron to "be persuaded with
Coleridge that 'Hope is a most awful duty, the nurse of all other vir-

tues.' I assure you that it will not depart, if it be not rudely banished, from such a one as you";[44] but in his poetry since 1816 Byron had "rudely banished" both Hope and Love, especially in *Childe Harold* IV, where destiny or "Circumstance, that unspiritual God/And Miscreator . . ./. . . turns Hope to dust" (cxxv) and where "Love [is] no habitant of earth" (cxxi). And in *Prometheus Unbound* Shelley lamented that nothing remained of Byron's "sparks of love and hope" but the "bitter ashes" of his apostasy: *"Audisne haec, Amphiarae, sub terram abdite?"*

## 7

SOME PENETRABLE STUFF: SHELLEY
AND BYRON DIFFERING MORE THAN EVER ON
POLITICS, DRAMA, MORALITY, AND KEATS

Although Shelley and Byron did not meet with each other from
the fall of 1818 until August 1821, both were similarly engaged during
this time in "the very *poetry* of politics," a phrase Byron used to
express his hopes for the "grand object" of "a free Italy."[1] Encouraged
by the revolutionary movements in Spain and Greece as well as in Italy,
the two poets were at the same time disappointed by the political events
in England during 1819/20, especially the Peterloo Massacre, the Cato
Street Conspiracy, and Queen Caroline's divorce trial for which Shelley
mistakenly believed that Byron had returned to England in August
1820.[2] When Shelley, who had lived in Pisa since February 1820, finally
visited Byron in Ravenna for a two-week period in August 1821, he
was pleased to discover that his fellow poet was still deeply "immersed
in politics & literature." And four days after his arrival on 6 August,
he wrote to Mary in Pisa and explained that the interest Byron "took
in the politics of Italy, & the actions he performed in consequence of
it, are subjects not fit to be *written*, but are such as will delight &
surprise you."[3] Shelley could not write openly of these subjects because
of Byron's involvement with the Italian Carbonari, a secret revolutionary society he had joined because of his association with his mistress
Teresa Guiccioli and her family, the Gambas. Shelley was equally
interested in the cause of Italian freedom and during the Neapolitan
revolution had written *Ode to Naples* (August 1820) to express his
belief that "Hope, and Truth, and Justice can avail." Byron, however,
was more practically committed to the same cause and apparently
offered both his money and his services to the new constitutional
government in Naples.[4] When this government quickly surrendered to
the Austrians in 1821, Shelley wrote to Byron that despite there being
"no strong personal reasons to interest me, my disappointment on
public grounds has been excessive. But I cling to moral and political
hope, like a drowner to a plank." Byron also continued to hope, but
felt "taken in" by the Neapolitans and "more ashamed of them than
they are of themselves."[5]

Byron had already expressed his shame for the Italians in his *Prophecy of Dante* (written in 1819), in which he pleaded that they unite and throw off their Austrian tyrants. Believing to some extent with Shelley that poetry and politics were interrelated, he also wrote in 1820/21 three historical dramas (*Marino Faliero, The Two Foscari, and Sardanapalus*) in which he embodied his ideas on political freedom in England and Italy. Shelley's concern for reform is equally apparent in his works at this time: in the *Prometheus Unbound* volume (1820) are *An Ode, Written October 1819, Before the Spaniards Had Recovered Their Liberty, Ode to the West Wind*, and *Ode to Liberty*, the last recording an "idealized history" of liberty from its birth in Greece to its struggles in England and Europe in 1820. Appealing to the popular audience that read Byron's works, Shelley also wrote a number of poems specifically directed to the political sentiments of the oppressed in England, e.g., *The Masque of Anarchy, Song to the Men of England, and Sonnet: England in 1819*. Complementing these political poems is the "readable" *A Philosophical View of Reform*, "a kind of standard book for the philosophical reformers politically considered."[6] As in *The Masque of Anarchy*, Shelley argued in this volume that in the face of another Peterloo Massacre the true patriot would exhort the men of England "peaceably to risque the danger, and to expect without resistance the onset of the cavalry, and wait with folded arms the event of the fire of the artillery and receive with unshrinking bosoms the bayonets of the charging battalions." Fearing that civil war in England, "waged from whatever motive," would extinguish "the sentiment of reason and justice in the mind," Shelley believed in "accommodating [his] theories to immediate practice," but he insisted upon moral action based upon the principles of the imagination.[7]

Shelley's concern for moral action was also apparent in his altering judgments about Byron in August 1821, for he found that his fellow poet was "greatly improved . . . in moral views" because of Teresa Guiccioli's influence. He reported to Mary that Byron was "becoming what he should be, a virtuous man"; and to Peacock, that he had "got rid of all those melancholy and degrading habits which he indulged at Venice." And despite Shelley's serious reservations about Byron's *Marino Faliero* (to be discussed in this chapter), he was very impressed when Byron read to him the fifth canto of *Don Juan*, in which there was "not a word which the most rigid assertor of the dignity of human nature could desire to be cancelled." Because of these improvements in Byron, Shelley felt even more insignificant in the shadow of the poet he had recently characterized as the "Pilgrim of Eternity," and he informed Mary, "I despair of rivalling Lord Byron, as well I may: and there is no other with whom it is worth contending."[8]

Between 1818 and 1821, Shelley had in fact contended with Lord Byron by adopting what he called "a *sermo pedestris* way of treating human nature quite opposed to the idealism"[9] of *Prometheus Unbound.* This more realistic approach is visible not only in *Julian and Maddalo* but also *The Cenci*, the political poems of 1819/20, and *Letter to Maria Gisborne.* Shelley even borrowed Byron's *ottava rima* for two of his more fanciful poems in 1820, *The Witch of Atlas* and the translation of Homer's *Hymn to Mercury.* The Byronic tone and manner of *Beppo* and *Don Juan* are especially evident in the introductory stanzas to *The Witch of Atlas*:

> Wordsworth informs us he was nineteen years
>  Considering and retouching Peter Bell;
> Watering his laurels with the killing tears
>  Of slow, dull care, so that their roots to hell
> Might pierce, and their wide branches blot the spheres
>  Of heaven, with dewy leaves and flowers; this well
> May be, for Heaven and Earth conspire to foil
> The over-busy gardener's blundering toil.

> My Witch indeed is not so sweet a creature
>  As Ruth or Lucy, whom his graceful praise
> Clothes for our grandsons—but she matches Peter,
>  Though he took nineteen years, and she three days
> In dressing. Light the vest of flowing metre
>  She wears; he, proud as dandy with his stays,
> Has hung upon his wiry limbs a dress
> Like King Lear's "looped and windowed raggedness."[10]

> (ll. 25-40)

Such wit on Shelley's part is also apparent in the ironies abounding in his delightful *On the Devil, and Devils*, which he concluded by observing that after the fall of Adam and Eve,

> God . . . it is said, assigned a punishment to the Serpent, that its motion should be as it now is along the ground upon its belly. We are given to suppose, that before this misconduct it hopped along upon its tail; a mode of progression which, if I were a Serpent, I should think the severer punishment of the two.[11]

Byron may have even borrowed this anecdote from Shelley when he wrote Thomas Moore from Pisa and explained why he called Shelley "the Serpent" and "the Snake":

> Shelley's allusion to his "fellow-serpent" [in a note on the auto-da-fé in December 1821], is a buffoonery of mine. Goethe's

Mephistofilus calls the serpent who tempted Eve "my aunt, the renowned snake;" and I always insist that Shelley is nothing but one of her nephews, walking about on the tip of his tail.[12]

Contending with Byron, Shelley also wrote two satires during this period, *Peter Bell the Third* (1819) and *Oedipus Tyrannus; or, Swellfoot the Tyrant* (1820). Inspired by Wordsworth's publication of *Peter Bell* and Queen Caroline's divorce trial, these two works attacked literary dullness, political apostasy, and tyranny in a manner anticipating but not equalling Byron's more controlled *Vision of Judgment.* Shelley never possessed Byron's talent for satire, and when Byron read to him by 10 August the fifth canto of *Don Juan,* he was probably surprised to find that his own somewhat labored satire in *Oedipus Tyrannus* had its dramatic effect reproduced by Byron in a single stanza. Displaying a reserved sympathy for the English Queen while describing Queen Semiramis, Byron wrote:

> That injured Queen, by Chroniclers so coarse
> Has been accused (I doubt not by conspiracy)
> Of an improper friendship for her horse
> (Love, like religion, sometimes runs to heresy):
> This monstrous tale had probably its source
> (For such exaggerations here and there I see)
> In writing "Courser" by mistake for "Courier":
> I wish the case could come before a jury here.[13]      (V.61)

Shelley's surprise and "despair of rivalling Lord Byron" as a satirist at this time was undoubtedly increased if the two poets compared their satires on Wordsworth's *Peter Bell* in addition to those on the Queen's trial. With a more experienced and trenchant wit than Shelley had demonstrated in *Peter Bell the Third,* Byron ridiculed Wordsworth's "ultra-legitimate dulness" quite effectively in only four stanzas (written March 1820):

> There's something in a stupid ass,
> And something in a heavy dunce;
> But never since I went to school
> I heard or saw so damned a fool
> As William Wordsworth is for once.
>
> And now I've seen so great a fool
> As William Wordsworth is for once;
> I really wish that Peter Bell
> And he who wrote it were in hell,
> For writing nonsense for the nonce.

It saw the "light in ninety-eight,"
  Sweet babe of one and twenty years!
And then he gives it to the nation
  And deems himself of Shakespeare's peers!

He gives the perfect work to light!
  Will Wordsworth, if I might advise,
Content you with the praise you get
  From Sir George Beaumont, Baronet,
And with your place in the Excise![14]

The similarities between Shelley's and Byron's literary enterprises at this time should not make us confuse the distinctions between the two writers, both of whom were recording different aesthetic principles in an argumentative fashion, Shelley responding to Peacock's *Four Ages of Poetry* by means of *A Defence of Poetry* (1821) and Byron entering the Bowles/Pope controversy by means of his first and second *Letter to John Murray* (1821). In other words, we should not go so far as the reviewer who in 1839 treated

> "Peter Bell the Third" as Shelley's, because his widow, no doubt, possesses ample proof of the fact. But, judging by internal evidence, we should have suspected Byron's participation, not merely in suggesting but executing. Shelley is represented to have entertained great admiration of Wordsworth: Byron missed no opportunity of ridiculing the poet or attacking the man. Shelley, as his widow observes, was "ideal," and often mystical: "Peter Bell the Third," though not devoid of mysticism, is often real, satirical, and with a worldly knowledge, in which we conceive Shelley to have been deficient. If, however, it is entirely his own composition, there seems little doubt as to the source of the inspiration.[15]

Notwithstanding Shelley's source of inspiration, he did not wholly appropriate the negative tone by which Byron had formerly denounced Wordsworth. As Carlos Baker has argued, "Shelley was both punishing and praising Wordsworth in *Peter Bell the Third*,"[16] and his tempered criticism resulted from a conviction, as expressed in the 1820 fragment, "A Satire on Satire," that "Satire's scourge" was not the most effective way to reform mankind. Paralleling satire to the instruments of political and religious persecution, Shelley judged that

> If Satire's [scourge] could awake the slumbering hounds
> Of Conscience, or erase with deeper wounds,
> The leprous scars of callous infamy;
> If it could make the present not to be,
> Or charm the dark past never to have been,

Or turn regret to hope; who that has seen
What Southey is and was, would not exclaim,
"Lash on!" and be the keen verse dipped in flame.     (ll. 17-24)

But because Shelley argued that satire could not accomplish these goals
and that it instead compounded man's folly ("This cannot be, it ought
not . . . evil still—/Suffering makes suffering—ill must follow ill./Harsh
words beget hard thoughts"), he believed that Southey would be better
served by a friend who softened "harsh truths with friendship's gentle
tone" than by a satirist who made "innocent ink/With stagnant truisms
of trite Satire stink" (ll. 35-37, 46, 49-50). Shelley believed that Byron
was far from a "trite" satirist, and in 1821 he was especially pleased
to discover in the latest canto of Don Juan "a moral to each error
tacked" (V.2), but he had formerly objected to Byron's animadversions
against Southey in the "Dedication" to Don Juan, calling them "more
like a mixture of wormwood & verdigrease than satire. The poor wretch
will writhe under the lash." And even though Shelley shared Byron's
dislike for Southey, he was pleased that the "personal" attack on
Southey had been omitted when Don Juan was published in 1819.[17]

Shelley's attitude toward vituperative satire is consistent with his
ideas on reform at this time, for personal attack whether by poetical
invective or political revolution could extinguish "the sentiment of
reason and justice in the mind." According to the Preface of The
Cenci, the "fit return to make to the most enormous injuries is kindness and forbearance, and a resolution to convert the injurer from his
dark passions by peace and love. Revenge, retaliation, atonement, are
pernicious mistakes." That Shelley recognized the political implications
of his drama on Beatrice Cenci's revenge is suggested by his letter to
Charles Ollier in which he considered the recent Peterloo Massacre in
terms of his drama:

> The same day that your letter came, came the news of the Man-
> chester work, & the torrent of my indignation has not yet done
> boiling in my veins. I wait anxiously [to] hear how the Country
> will express its sense of this bloody murderous oppression of its
> destroyers. 'Something must be done . . . What yet I know not'
> [The Cenci III.i.86-87].[18]

Both Byron and Shelley agreed that something had to be done during
this time of revolution and reform, and they used their works to "legislate" their political and poetical judgments. But these judgments frequently had different moral and aesthetic premises, as witnessed by
Shelley's own remark after spending but one day with Byron: "we
talked a great deal of poetry & such matters last night: & as usual

differed & I think more than ever." One of these differences, to be discussed in the last section of this chapter, arose from the two poets' conflicting judgments about contemporary poets, particularly John Keats, whom Shelley in *Adonais* had praised over Byron's objections. A less obvious but equally important difference resulted from the two poets' recent dramatic efforts, *Marino Faliero* being criticized by Shelley, and *The Cenci* censured by Byron. Shelley expressed the difference quite succinctly to Leigh Hunt on 26 August: "if 'Marino Faliero' is a drama, the 'Cenci' is not."[19]

Shelley's judgment that these two dramas are to be considered as mutually exclusive is somewhat surprising, especially since both are historical dramas about tyranny and slavery. After both protagonists are sexually violated, they lawlessly seek revenge on their violators, justify their vengeance to themselves, and are finally executed after a long trial scene where merciless justice and tyrannical order are re-established. More specifically, after Beatrice Cenci is raped by her father, she successfully plots her father's death; is apprehended, and is sentenced to death by a papal court in Rome. After the wife of Marino Faliero, the Doge of Venice, is sexually slandered by Michel Steno and after the Venetian Forty give Steno a slight sentence and fail to satisfy Faliero's desire for vindication, he unsuccessfully plots the death of Steno and the Venetian Senators, is apprehended, and is executed following his trial by the Council of Ten. These dramatic parallels between *Marino Faliero* and *The Cenci* are for the most part coincidental, for Shelley wrote his drama in the summer of 1819 and Byron wrote his in the summer of 1820, apparently without having read *The Cenci*.[20] More important, however, than the similarities between these two dramas are their differences which demonstrate the two poets' continuing antagonism in 1819/20 and explain Shelley's judgment in 1821 that he and Byron "differed . . . more than ever."

II

Shelley's disappointment with *Marino Faliero* resulted from a number of circumstances, not the least being Byron's critical letter to the author of *The Cenci* on 26 April 1821:

> I read *Cenci*—but, besides that I think the *subject* essentially *un*dramatic, I am not an admirer of our old dramatists *as models*. I deny that the English have hitherto had a drama at all. Your *Cenci*, however, was a work of power, and poetry. As to *my* drama, pray revenge yourself upon it, by being as free as I have been with yours.[21]

Shelley reciprocated by being "as free" with *Marino Faliero* four months later when he described to Mary Shelley why he differed so much with Byron:

> He affects to patronize a system of criticism fit only for the pro-
> duction of mediocrity, & although all his fine poems & passages
> have been produced in defiance of this system: yet I recognize
> the pernicious effects of it in the 'Doge of Venice', & it will
> cramp & limit his future efforts however great they may be
> unless he gets rid of it. I have read only parts of it, or rather he
> himself read them to me & gave me the plan of the whole.

Shelley's complaint about the "pernicious effects" of Byron's system in *Marino Faliero* and his later judgment that "if 'Marino Faliero' is a drama, the 'Cenci' is not"[22] are not, however, merely the reactions of his wounded pride. Rather, Shelley's disappointment is attributable to at least two other reasons: since 1818 when he had heard the plans for *Marino Faliero*, Shelley had looked to Byron "for substituting something worthy of the English stage, for the miserable trash which, from Milman to Barry Cornwall, has been intruded on it since the demand for tragical representation";[23] furthermore, he had attempted his own reform of the English stage by writing *The Cenci* (1819) as well as criticism on the drama in *A Defence of Poetry* (1821). But when Shelley read *Marino Faliero*, he discovered that Byron's dramatic principles and practices were very unlike his own. A study of the two poets' differences in this respect is made somewhat difficult by a number of contradictions: for example, Byron preferred to imitate the Greeks rather than Shakespeare, yet at the same time extensively echoed Shakespeare; Shelley preferred to imitate Shakespearean models, yet had an "approach . . . more Greek than Elizabethan"; and Byron denied that he wrote his historical dramas for the stage, yet hoped that *Marino Faliero* would be staged.[24] In spite of these problems, the reasons for Byron's and Shelley's dislike for each other's dramas can, with reasonable certitude, be established.

In Byron's April 1821 letter to Shelley, he judged that *The Cenci*, despite its being a "work of . . . poetry," too closely followed the old English dramas and was consequently not "a drama at all"; what he meant was that *The Cenci* failed to meet his relatively strict standards of the dramatic unities of time and place. As he explained in his Pref-ace to *Sardanapalus*, "with any very distant departure from them [unities of time and place] , there may be poetry, but can be no drama." Byron frequently differentiated between the poetry of drama and its form, and his description of his historical dramas in a 14 July 1821 letter to John Murray is typical:

My object has been to dramatize, like the Greeks (a *modest* phrase!), striking passages of history, as they did of history and mythology. You will find all this very *unlike* Shakespeare; and so much the better in one sense, for I look upon him to be the *worst* of models, though the most extraordinary of writers. It has been my object to be as simple and severe as Alfieri.[25]

Byron had already informed Murray in February that his dramas would be "simple and severe,"[26] qualities Byron surely judged to be lacking in *The Cenci* where, as in Shakespearean drama, dramatic action was extended to considerably more than twenty-four hours and occupied more than one place. With this freedom which Byron opposed, Shelley was able to represent, albeit offstage, the precipitating cause of Beatrice Cenci's revenge, that being the climactic rape of Beatrice by her father between Acts II and III; and he could more thoroughly dramatize the conflict between Beatrice and her tyrannical father, who in the first scene of Act I implies his incestuous design when speaking to Cardinal Camillo. This conflict builds that same evening in the Banquet scene where Count Cenci gleefully announces the death of his two sons and tells Beatrice that "a charm shall make [her] meek and tame" (I.iii.167). The next morning (II.i), Beatrice refuses to acknowledge her father's design while she speaks with her stepmother, Lucretia, and in the following scene (II.ii) the conflict is broadened when Cardinal Camillo listens to the complaints of Giacomo, Beatrice's brother who had been financially ruined by Count Cenci. At the conclusion of Act II, Giacomo is tempted to kill his father by Orsino, an Iago-like schemer who lusts for Beatrice despite his priestly vows. The climax of this developing conflict occurs in the first scene of Act III, at a period at least two days[27] after the first scene of the drama, when Beatrice reveals that she has been violated by her father and plots his death with the aid of Orsino and Giacomo. The Cenci party then departs the next day, Wednesday, for Petrella Castle, where Cenci is murdered at midnight on Thursday; the conspirators return on Friday to Rome for Act V, the long trial scene concluded by Beatrice's preparation for her execution.

The main difference between the plot of *The Cenci*, briefly described above, and that of *Marino Faliero* is that in the latter Byron's "desire of preserving . . . a nearer approach to unity than the irregularity, which is the reproach of the English theatrical compositions, permits" (Preface to *Marino Faliero*) caused him to sacrifice what Shelley had gained in structuring the conflict between slave and tyrant. In *The Cenci*, Shelley used almost three full acts (with a dramatic time exceeding forty-eight hours) in order to dramatize Beatrice's conflict with her father, the incestuous rape, and her plotting of revenge and parricide. In contrast, Byron reduced his dramatic time to twenty-four hours, did not introduce Faliero's antagonists until Act V, and used expository speeches to suggest rather than represent Faliero's conflict with the Venetian patricians. Accordingly, by the conclusion of Act I, Byron has already presented Michel Steno's pre-play sexual slander, the Venetian Forty's sentence of house arrest which Faliero judges inadequate for Steno's offense, the Doge's desire for revenge, and his discovery of the means for revenge when the conspirator, Israel Bertuccio, brings him knowledge of the forthcoming revolution. Such a first act, according to Shelley, was full of "severe and unharmonising traits," and he believed that dramatic interest would have been better served if Byron had represented on stage the Doge's developing conflict with Steno and the patricians.[28] Instead, Byron used most of his dramatic time for exposition: for example, in Act II, scene i, Angiolina records the nature and history of her love for Faliero; and in scene ii, the plebeian conspirators led by Israel Bertuccio and Philip Calendaro reveal their grievances against the Venetian state and their desire for revenge. In Act III the Doge accompanies Israel to the conspirators' house and after more exposition assumes command of the rebellion which he schedules for sunrise. In the interim, Bertram betrays his fellow conspirators by warning his benefactor, Patrician Lioni (IV.i); at sunrise, the Doge and the conspirators are apprehended (IV.ii), all are convicted of treason (V.i), and the Doge is executed (V.iv).

The differences between Byron's and Shelley's dramatic techniques as implied in the above summaries are more apparent when we contrast their trial scenes in Act V. Because Byron chose to be "simple and severe," his final act offers, relative to Shelley's complex portrayal of Beatrice, little if any alteration in the character of the Doge. In the first scene, the conflict between freedom (sought by conspirators) and law (as applied by the Venetian Senators) is for the first time dramatically represented when the Council of Ten confronts and condemns Israel Bertuccio and Philip Calendaro. This conflict is further represented by the confrontation between Faliero and the Council, by Angiolina's vain plea that Venetian justice be tempered with mercy, and by her rebuke of Michel Steno for the exciting action that precipitated the Doge's fall. The second scene of Act V is used for more exposition, the Doge explaining that he had been cursed for his youthful rashness and that his fall was the "work of Fate" (V.ii.66). In the following scene (iii), the Doge himself utters a prophetic curse on Venice and is led to his death, a decapitation that the Venetian plebeians struggle to witness because of their sympathy for the Doge's heroic efforts: "Then they have murdered him who would have freed us" (V.iv.21). Byron's portrayal of Faliero's unaltering character here

*147*

emphasizes the fundamental irony of a Doge who must destroy the
Venetian state in order to save it. In spite of Byron's intent, however,
Shelley would have judged that the dramatic action here was "stagnant"
and that the four scenes were "stationary, episodical, useless,"[29] at
least when compared to his own final act in *The Cenci*, where dramatic
tension is sustained by a number of new developments in the action.
In the first scene, the dissembling Orsino betrays Giacomo to the papal
guards in order that the former might escape from Rome. In the next
scene, Marzio confesses that Giacomo, Orsino, Beatrice, and Lucretia
had planned the murder he committed, but when confronted by
Beatrice who protests her innocence, he declares that Beatrice is not a
parricide (V.ii.156-65). The following scene further complicates the
action, for Lucretia and Giacomo confess their guilt, but Beatrice still
claims her innocence. In the final scene, both Cardinal Camillo and
Bernardo, Beatrice's younger brother, fail to dissuade the Pope from
executing Beatrice, and she continues to protest her innocence and
holiness (V.iv.110, 149) while preparing for death.

Beatrice's complicating claim for innocence in Act V, while
serving Shelley's dramatic intent, must have been especially displeasing
to Byron, whose dramatic principles in *Marino Faliero* precluded such
complication. Byron never specifically criticized Beatrice, but we can
construct his probable reaction to her by examining "Byron and Shelley
on the Character of Hamlet," an article, probably written by Mary
Shelley, which appeared in the *New Monthly Magazine and Literary
Journal* in 1830.[30] Purporting to be an eyewitness account of a lengthy
debate between Byron and Shelley, this article records judgments consistent with the two poets' different estimates of Shakespeare: Byron
complains that *Hamlet* is full of "poetry" but deficient in dramatic
"art"; and Shelley, arguing for both poetry and art, concludes in a
prepared essay that *Hamlet* " 'is, in itself, a complete and reasonable
whole, composed in an harmonious proportion of difference and
similitude, into one expressive unity.' " Because Byron made similar
complaints about the "*un*dramatic" *Cenci* and because Shelley would
have judged his own drama an "expressive unity," it is possible, despite the undistributed middle of my logic, to use this debate on
*Hamlet* in order to elucidate the poets' different estimates of *The
Cenci*. Thus Byron's complaint that Hamlet is a "most lame and
impotent hero" who fails to do "any thing like a man" in a play that
is "a colossal enigma" suggests Byron's reaction to Beatrice Cenci.
Byron, like many subsequent critics of Shelley's drama, did not understand the enigmatic Beatrice who, in Act V, protests her innocence
even though she was a parricide. Furthermore, Byron's judgment on
Ophelia—"how gross are the scenes of her madness! She, too, seems as

inconsistent and as false a character as her faithless lover"—must reflect
Byron's reaction to Beatrice's mad scenes (III.i; V.iv) and to her "incon-
sistency." Byron could praise the poetry and genius of both *Hamlet*
and *The Cenci*, but for him the complexity of action and of character
in these two plays was "essentially *un*dramatic," that is to say too far
distant from the "severe" structure of *Marino Faliero* and from the
relatively "simple" development of the Doge's character after Act I,
scene i. Because Byron denied that Shakespeare, the older English
dramatists, and the imitative Shelley were able to write drama, any
defense that Shelley would make of his *Cenci* in 1821 would probably
have been met with the same critical indifference that Byron exhibited
in 1822 with respect to *Hamlet*: when Shelley finished his oral defense
of Shakespeare's play, he "looked up, and found Lord Byron fast
asleep."

### III

In spite of Shelley's dislike for the "form" of *Marino Faliero*,
which, unlike *Manfred*, did not exhibit "freedom from common rules,"[31]
it might be argued that he admired the "spirit" of Byron's drama, the
same spirit of political liberalism having informed much of Shelley's
own poetry in 1819 and 1820. That Byron embodied his own political
hopes in *Marino Faliero* is beyond question: G. Wilson Knight has
astutely observed that in this drama "Byron has a theme corresponding
to his own political discontents as a revolutionary aristocrat"; David
Erdman concluded that *Marino Faliero* was "the immediate literary
consequence" of the Cato Street conspirators who had plotted to
assassinate the cabinet ministers in England in 1820; and Edward Dudley
Hume Johnson in "A Political Interpretation of Byron's *Marino Faliero*"
argued that Byron wrote his drama "in a mood of high hope for the
emancipation of the Italians from the tyrannical government which
was oppressing them" and at the same time recorded his judgments
about political revolution in England. According to Johnson, Marino
Faliero was an "imaginative projection of the author into circumstances
like those which make up the plot of the tragedy."[32] By directing and
yet disdaining the plebeian conspirators, Marino Faliero embodies
Byron's judgment to Murray on 21 February 1820: "if we must have
a tyrant, let him at least be a gentleman who has been bred to the
business, and let us fall by the axe and not by the butcher's cleaver."
In spite of Byron's later protestations to Murray that *Marino Faliero*
"is not a political play, though it may look like it," he more frankly
acknowledged to Kinnaird that his drama was "full of republicanism
[and] so will find no favour" with Murray.[33]

Shelley himself was not above propagandist poetry in 1819 and

1820, for he wrote many poems calling for political freedom and justice. Because his epigraph to the 1820 *Ode to Liberty* was taken from Byron's *Childe Harold* IV ("Yet! Freedom, yet thy banner, torn, but flying,/Streams like the thunder-storm *against* the wind"), he apparently still believed that Byron, despite his fatalistic "system," might serve the spirit of reform and become "the redeemer of his degraded country" (Preface to *Julian and Maddalo*). Moreover, Shelley in *A Philosophical Review of Reform*, written in 1819/20, included Byron as one of the liberal reformers whose poetry offered

> an intense and impassioned power of communicating intense and impassioned impressions respecting man and nature. The persons in whom this power takes its abode may often, as far as regards many portions of their nature, have little tendency [to] the spirit of good of which it is the minister. But although they may deny and abjure, they are yet compelled to serve that which is seated on the throne of their own soul. And whatever systems they may [have] professed by support, they actually advance the interests of Liberty. It is impossible to read the productions of our most celebrated writers, whatever may be their system relating to thought or expression, without being startled by the electric life which there is in their words. They measure the circumference or sound the depths of human nature with a comprehensive and all-penetrating spirit at which they are themselves perhaps most sincerely astonished, for it [is] less their own spirit than the spirit of their age.[34]

Shelley here is undoubtedly describing many of his contemporaries, but he is at the same time specifically describing Byron, who did "deny and abjure" the spirit of the Shelleyan system but nevertheless continued to "serve that which is seated on the throne of [his] own soul," that "sunlike soul" described in the *Euganean Hills*. "Whatever may be [Byron's] system relating to thought or expression," his words had an "electric life," a phrase recalling Shelley's frequent references to the "lightning" in Byron's poetry. Furthermore, Shelley's description of the poets who inadvertently serve "the interests of Liberty" details the same paradox that Shelley in 1820 ascribed to Byron and his poetry: with respect to "the general system of his character, . . . the wit & poetry which surround, hide with their light the darkness of the thing itself. They contradict it even; they prove that the strength & beauty of human nature can survive & conquer all that appears most inconsistent with it."[35] With reasonings such as these, Shelley was intentionally bringing Byron into the fold of "the unacknowledged legislators of the world" in spite of Byron's "system" of poetry.[36]

Because Shelley was more than interested in Byron's political poetry, he might be expected to have admired the reform-oriented *Marino Faliero*. But he did not, and his first reaction to Byron's drama suggests the reasons for his displeasure. He wrote to Mary from Ravenna that Byron "affects to patronize a system of criticism fit only for the production of mediocrity, & although all his fine poems & passages have been produced in defiance of this system: yet I recognize the *pernicious* effects of it in the 'Doge of Venice', & it will cramp & limit his future efforts however great they may be unless he gets rid of it" (my italics). I requote Shelley's strictures here in order to contrast them with his different judgments in 1820 that Byron's poetical "form" frequently redeemed the fatalistic "spirit" of his poetry; and in order to emphasize the word "pernicious," one that Shelley need not have used if he objected merely to the form of *Marino Faliero*. "Pernicious," for Shelley, usually denoted a moral defect (see the "pernicious" mistakes of Beatrice and Satan in the Prefaces to *The Cenci* and *Prometheus Unbound*), and by citing the "pernicious effects" of Byron's system, he in effect condemned the moral as well as the dramatic principles of Byron's political drama. As Shelley wrote in *A Defence of Poetry* a few months before he read *Marino Faliero*, moral and dramatic principles mutually define each other: "the drama at Athens, or wheresoever else it may have approached to its perfection, coexisted with the moral and intellectual greatness of the age," but "in periods of the decay of social life, the drama sympathises with that decay." Shelley then proceeded to explain the relations between decaying moral and dramatic systems, and in so doing he exactly prefigured his reaction to *Marino Faliero* a few months later:

> Tragedy becomes a cold imitation of the form of the great master-pieces of antiquity, divested of all harmonious accompaniment of the kindred arts; and often the very form misunderstood, or a weak attempt to teach certain doctrines, which the writer considers as moral truths; and which are usually no more than specious flatteries of some gross vice or weakness, with which the author, in common with his auditors, are infected. Hence what has been called the classical and domestic drama. Addison's "Cato" is a specimen of the [former].[37]

Had Shelley read *Marino Faliero* prior to writing this, I am certain he would have considered using Byron's political drama rather than Addison's *Cato* not only as an example of "a cold imitation" of classical drama "divested of all harmonious accompaniment" (cf. Shelley's strictures on the "severe and unharmonising traits" of Byron's drama), but also as an example of an attempt in drama "to teach certain [political] doctrines" which were reducible to "specious flatteries of some gross vice or weakness." Shelley did not object to Byron's republicanism, but he did object to Byron's explicitly embodying his doctrines in *Marino Faliero*, for "drama is no fit place for the enforcement of [such doctrines or dogmas]" (Preface to *The Cenci*). Moreover, Shelley rejected the casuistry with which the Doge justified his revolutionary principles, a casuistry that he judged reflected Byron's own failure to discriminate virtue from the exigencies of revolutionary action.

Shelley's judgment that tragedy should be "pure," that is, free from the kind of authorial presence that damaged *Marino Faliero*, is best understood in light of *The Cenci* where he purposefully avoided introducing the "dogma" and even the "beautiful idealisms" of *Prometheus Unbound* in order to emphasize Beatrice's immoral casuistry. Because Shelley wrote his tragedy "without any of the peculiar feelings & opinions which characterize" his other works and because he attended "simply to the impartial development" of the characters therein,[38] many readers have been unable to decide whether *The Cenci* complements or contradicts the premises of *Prometheus Unbound*. That Shelley judged Beatrice morally wrong for her revenge and morally reprehensible for her protested innocence of parricide in Act V is, I believe, beyond question. Shelley himself wrote to Leigh Hunt in May 1820 that he had in *The Cenci* sacrificed his "own peculiar notions *in a certain sort* by treating of any subject *the basis of which is moral error.*"[39] Since moral error was the subject of his drama, *The Cenci* differs from *Prometheus Unbound* not because Shelley altered his moral principles of good and evil, but only because he chose this time to present moral evil unredeemed by good. The Preface to *The Cenci* makes clear Shelley's moral judgment about Beatrice's choice of revenge in response to her father's tyranny: "Undoubtedly no person can be truly dishonoured by the act of another; and the fit return to make to the most enormous injuries is kindness and forbearance, and a resolution to convert the injurer from his dark passions by peace and love. Revenge, retaliation, atonement, are pernicious mistakes." Critics who believe that Beatrice escapes Shelley's strictures against revenge have been forced to see the Preface to *The Cenci* and the drama itself as irreconcilable. For example, Stuart Curran believes that Shelley in the above quote is "referring to the Beatrice of history; his premises are inadequate to encompass the character whom he created. She murders her father not out of revenge, but imperative self-defense; not because he raped her body, but because he ravaged her spirit, 'poisoning/The subtle, pure, and inmost spirit of life' (III.i.22-23), turning her 'good into evil.'"[40] Curran's point, however, reveals the same casuistry that afflicts Beatrice, for "no person can be truly dishonoured by the act of another": neither her body nor her mind had been ravaged to the extent she *mistakenly considered* them to be. Shelley makes this important distinction in his Preface by observing that "this daughter [considered historically *and* dramatically], after long and vain attempts to escape from what she *considered* a perpetual contamination both of *body and mind,* at length plotted with her mother-in-law and brother to murder their common tyrant." Shelley then observed that Beatrice "was urged to this tremendous deed by an *impulse which overpowered its horror*" and described her as "a most gentle and amiable being, a creature formed to adorn and be admired, and thus *violenty thwarted from her nature by the necessity of circumstance and opinion*" (Preface, my italics). The rape was obviously beyond Beatrice's control; but "circumstance and opinion" were "necessary" only insofar as they resulted from the conditions of her religious environment, and Shelley believed that Beatrice had both the obligation and the ability to escape these conditions which caused her to "consider" that she was perpetually contaminated both in body and mind. What all of this means, as the following remarks will demonstrate, is that, for Shelley, Beatrice both killed her father and casuistically protested her innocence because she was an Italian Catholic.

By avoiding "the error of making [his characters] actuated by [his] own conceptions of right or wrong, false or true" (Preface), Shelley created a drama that is uniquely self-contained—its dramatic action and speeches are constructed in terms of the Italian Catholic ethos rather than Shelley's own ethics. In the Preface, the reader is forewarned that he will find in both Count Cenci and his daughter a startling "combination of an undoubting persuasion of the truth of the popular religion with a cool and determined perseverance [of moral innocence] in enormous guilt." Religion for the Italian Catholics, Shelley argues,

> is adoration, faith, submission, penitence, *blind* admiration; *not a rule for moral conduct.* It has no necessary connexion with any one virtue. The most atrocious villain may be rigidly devout, and, without any shock to established faith, confess himself to be so. Religion . . . is . . . a passion, a persuasion, *an excuse, a refuge; never a check* [my italics].

Here lies the key to Beatrice's casuistry, for she, like her father, is a "villain" who by adherence to her religious faith lacks "a rule for moral conduct" and in fact uses religion as an "excuse" for her revenge and parricide, which she terms "a high and holy deed" (IV.ii.35). Accordingly, she tells Marzio the murderer that he was "a weapon in

*153*

the hand of God/To a just use" (IV.iii.54-55), repeats that he was a "sword in the right hand of justest God" (iv.126), and claims that Cenci's death proves God to be "wise and just" (iv.134). Using God's vengeance in her defense, Beatrice claims that she is "more innocent of parricide/Than is a child born fatherless" (iv.112-13), and in Act V she explains to Marzio her special circumstances with her earthly and heavenly fathers: even though she had once "lifted up to God, the father of all,/Passionate prayers" (I.iii.118-19) for her father, she reasons after the rape that her

> hate
> Became the only worship I could lift
> To our great father, who in pity and love,
> Armed thee, as thou dost say, to cut him off;
> And thus his wrong becomes my accusation;
> And art thou the accuser? If thou hopest
> Mercy in heaven, show justice upon earth:
> Worse than a bloody hand is a hard heart. (V.ii.126-33)

Marzio, being another "atrocious villain" who finds in religion an "excuse," then concedes that on the basis of this "higher truth" that Beatrice is "most innocent" (ii.164-65). Unfortunately, some critics have failed to heed Shelley's warning that his conceptions of right and wrong are *not* expressed in the drama and have been misled into believing that this "higher truth" was Shelley's. Categorically, it is not. Thus, Beatrice's "convincing" claims for her own innocence in Act V do not reflect Shelley's judgments; rather, Shelley merely exaggerated these claims in order to make the audience aware of her casuistical reasoning based on the Old Testament notion of God's vengeance. Instead of needing a justification by such a perverse moral doctrine, Beatrice, according to Shelley, should have followed Christ's admonitions and Prometheus' example that man forgive those who inflict pain, for "undoubtedly no person can be truly dishonoured by the act of another; and the fit return to make to the most enormous injuries is kindness and forbearance, and a resolution to convert the injurer from his dark passions by peace and love" (Preface).

It might be argued that none of these noble sentiments would have made Beatrice's pain easier to bear, but Shelley would not accept that argument. In Act V, Beatrice summarizes her life as follows:

> I, alas!
> Have lived but on this earth a few sad years
> And so my lot was ordered, that a father
> First turned the moments of awakening life
> To drops, each poisoning youth's sweet hope; and then

> Stabbed with one blow my everlasting soul;
> And my untainted fame; and even that peace
> Which sleeps within the core of the heart's heart.     (ii.118-25)

Because she later repeats that her "pangs are of the mind, and of the heart,/And of the soul" (iii.65-66), it is clear, as Shelley stated in the Preface, that Beatrice "considered" the rape a "perpetual contamination both of body and mind," and her error lies in this "consideration" which only aggravated her misery. In effect, she believed in the same patriarchal and tyrannical Christianity that prompted her father to believe she could be contaminated by incest: according to the Count, Beatrice would become

> to her own conscious self
> All she appears to others; and when dead,
> As she shall die unshrived and unforgiven,
> A rebel to her father and her God,
> Her corpse shall be abandoned to the hounds;
> Her name shall be the terror of the earth;
> Her spirit shall approach the throne of God
> Plague-spotted with my curses. I will make
> Body and soul a monstrous lump of ruin.     (IV.i.87-95)

Shelley and any reasonable Christian would judge as patently absurd that Beatrice's rape damns her soul. But because Beatrice believes that her body and soul have been perpetually contaminated, she is to be pitied and condemned for the same errors that motivate her father— pitied because she considers the effects of the rape more painful than they actually are; condemned because she assumes her father's casuistry in order to justify her revenge. As Terry Otten recently demonstrated, "Beatrice battles to maintain her innocence—only to reenact her father's guilt," for she "exonerates her act of murder on the grounds of carrying out God's will, just as Cenci lays claim to Heaven's favor in the improbable deaths of his sons."[41]

Beatrice's moral degeneration may be described as a Shelleyan tragedy, defined by Harold Bloom as the "fall of the imagination, or rather the falling away from imaginative conduct on the part of a heroically imaginative individual."[42] Such a tragic action controls *The Cenci*, for Beatrice is first portrayed as a patient heroine in accord with the concluding description of the imaginative man in *Prometheus Unbound*: she has selflessly suffered woes, forgiven wrongs, defied the power of her father, loved him, borne his malevolence, and hoped for his reformation; but after the rape, she changes and falters—she is transformed from a Prometheus directed by love into a Jupiter motivated by hate. With such an imagination circumscribed by her religious beliefs, she discovers only an "ill world where none are true," and contributes to the false and wretched interchange between the "oppressor and the oppressed" (V.iii.68, 75). For Beatrice, the noblest virtue of hope becomes "Worse than despair" (V.iv.97), and despite her apparent rejection of "harsh despair" in her last speech to Bernardo and her recommendation that he have "mild, pitying thoughts," she still protests that she "Lived ever holy and unstained" (V.iv.149). Beatrice's ambivalence here precludes a complete recognition of her evil, but Shelley's explicit rejection of "what is vulgarly termed a moral purpose" appears to be responsible for this ambivalence; rather than resolving the tragedy with a traditional anagnorisis by which he could dogmatically point to Beatrice's error, he aimed to teach "the human heart, through its sympathies and antipathies, the knowledge of itself" (Preface).

Having written *The Cenci* with a dramatic purpose as outlined above, Shelley had many reasons for rejecting the "pernicious effects" of Byron's *Marino Faliero*. He had attempted to teach the human heart to know itself and accordingly had neither condemned nor exonerated Beatrice in the play and thereby forced his audience to participate in her moral dilemma: "it is in the restless and anatomising casuistry with which men seek the justification of Beatrice, yet feel that she has done what needs justification; it is in the superstitious horror with which they contemplate alike her wrongs and their revenge, that the dramatic character of what she did and suffered, consists" (Preface). Byron's *Marino Faliero* similarly depicts a casuistical justification for revenge, but unlike Beatrice who convinces herself of her innocence, Byron's Doge is fully aware of his guilt. This self-awareness on the Doge's part is not dramatically suspect, but Shelley feared that Byron portrayed Faliero too sympathetically and that an audience might condone or at least willingly imitate his revenge. Shelley's fear was not unfounded, for even Byron acknowledged to Murray in January 1821 that Faliero's "passion . . . is so natural, that I am convinced that I should have done precisely what the Doge did on those provocations."[43]

Faliero's self-justification occasionally sounds like that employed in *The Cenci*: in his dialogue with Angiolina he cites the "law of Heaven [of] blood for blood" (II.i.244); and in response to his wife's Christ-like recommendation that we "forgive our enemies," he asks "Doth Heaven forgive her own? Is there not Hell/For wrath eternal?" (II.i.260-62). And he later parallels his revenge to God's wrath in the form of "the sheeted fire from Heaven" which blasted "Without distinction . . ./Where the Dead Sea hath quenched two Cities' ashes" (III.ii.420-23). It might be argued here that Byron employed the same subtlety found in *The Cenci* where Italian Catholicism is "a refuge; never a check" for revenge. But this is not so, for Byron made it apparent that Faliero, despite his appeal to the higher law of Old Testament morality, recognizes the baseness of his actions. He calls himself and the plebeians "traitors" (III.i.78) and acknowledges that

> the very means I am *forced*
> By these fell tyrants to adopt is such,
> That I abhor them doubly for the deeds
> Which I must do to pay them back for theirs.
>
> (III.i.114-17, my italics)

The Doge frequently judges the immorality of his vengeance, and in this sense he is morally or at least intellectually superior to Beatrice Cenci. But to Shelley, the Doge was a more dangerous casuist, one who admits that his means were evil but were justified by the ends: to Israel Bertuccio, he argues that his revenge's "consequence will sanctify the deed" (III.i.73); to Bertram, that "we'll wash away/All stains in Freedom's fountain" (III.ii.80-81); to his nephew, that "there are things/Which make revenge a virtue by reflection" and that "injured souls/Oft do a public right with private wrong,/And justify their deeds unto themselves" (IV.ii.102-7); and to himself, that the "noble end must justify" the means when he "must work by crime to punish crime" (IV.ii.161, 168). Important in these ethical pronouncements is the Doge's categorical imperative: he *must* work by crime; he is *forced* to adopt immoral means. With these statements, Byron implied that fate determined the actions of the Doge, who after the failure of the conspiracy admits to his nephew that it was "vain to war with Fortune" and then repeats the lesson of Byron's 1816 *Prometheus*: they would meet their enchainment "As men whose triumph is not in success,/But who can make their own minds all in all,/Equal to every fortune" (IV.ii.272, 277-79).

The fatalism in *Marino Faliero* is made more explicit in Act V when the Doge recalls his youthful rashness:

> the sluggish Bishop who
> Conveyed the Host aroused my rash young anger,
> By strange delay, and arrogant reply
> To my reproof: I raised my hand and smote him,
> Until he reeled beneath his holy burthen.      (ii.20-24)

In response, the bishop had cursed the Doge, prophesying that "'The Hour will come/When he thou hast o'erthrown shall overthrow thee'" and that he would be crowned a Doge only to die "'headless'" (V.ii.

28-29, 37). Nor could Faliero forget the omen at his own crowning when the dense mist so misled his pilot that the Doge was mistakenly disembarked "Between the Pillars of Saint Mark's, where 'tis/The custom of the state to put to death/Its criminals" (V.ii.59-61). But after being apprehended as a criminal against the state, the Doge finds

> a comfort in
> The thought, that these things are the work of Fate;
> For I would rather yield to Gods than men,
> Or cling to any creed of destiny,
> Rather than deem these mortals, most of whom
> I know to be as worthless as the dust,
> And weak as worthless, more than instruments
> Of an o'er-ruling Power.             (V.ii.65-72)

This "o'er-ruling Power" is the same malevolent spirit of the universe that all of Byron's heroes have had to face, and its presence here explains the Doge's perplexing speech about free will in his earlier dialogue with Israel Bertuccio. Faliero, appalled by his grave decision to kill the patricians, many of whom had been his friends, argued that *"This will I—must I—have I sworn to do,/Nor aught can turn me from my destiny"* (III.ii.496-97, Byron's italics). When Israel suggested that the Doge chose to lead the conspirators through his own free will, Faliero redefined his fatalism:

> And thou dost well to answer that it was
> "My own free will and act," and yet you err,
> For I *will* do this! Doubt not—fear not; I
> Will be your most unmerciful accomplice!
> And yet I act no more on my free will,
> Nor my own feelings—both compel me back;
> But there is *Hell* within me and around,
> And like the Demon who believes and trembles
> Must I abhor and do.        (III.ii.513-21, Byron's italics)

By having the Doge fatalistically argue that his will was not free (*"will* do" equals "Must . . . do"), Byron implied that the Doge was not morally responsible for his actions. And Shelley, whose Beatrice offered no fatalistic excuse for her revenge, feared that Byron was sacrificing his principles to political expediency, to moral casuistry, and to predestined action. In particular, Shelley feared that not only the Doge but also Byron believed that "our private wrongs have sprung from public vices"; and that the desire to "renew the times of Truth and Justice,/Condensing in a fair free commonwealth/Not rash equality but equal rights" (III.ii.154, 168-70) justified a crime-for-crime morality. For Shelley, however, private wrongs were the source of both public and private vices; and the only redemption of the state lay not in any inescapable crime for crime but rather in the moral regeneration of each individual. Contrasting Beatrice's moral weakness when she argued that "ill must come of ill" (I.iii.151), Shelley stated his own opinion in another 1819 poem, *The Masque of Anarchy*: "'Blood for blood— and wrong for wrong—/Do not thus when ye are strong'" (xlviii). Thus the revenge, retaliation, and atonement operative in *The Cenci, Marino Faliero*, and contemporary politics were pernicious mistakes and they resulted, in Shelley's opinion, not from "'destiny/But man's own wilful ill'" (*Julian and Maddalo*, ll. 210-11). Thus in spite of Marino Faliero's (IV.ii.56) and Beatrice Cenci's (V.iv.109) similar judgments that man is by instinct and by deeds a "Cain" who atones for the pain he suffers, only Byron believed that man was destined to such a fate. What Shelley attempted to do in both *Prometheus Unbound* and *The Cenci* was to show that man's vengeance resulted from his moral and therefore imaginative deficiencies. Without imaginative enlightenment, man would continue to enslave himself by his own actions; as Shelley had argued in another poem directed to Byron,

> Men must reap the things they sow,
> Force from force must ever flow,
> Or worse; but 'tis a bitter woe
> That love or reason cannot change
> The despot's rage, the slave's revenge.
>
> (*Euganean Hills*, ll. 231-35)

Neither love nor reason alone, as demonstrated by Prometheus and Asia's ineffectuality when separated, would release man from his self-perpetuated enslavement.

When Shelley heard Byron read parts of *Marino Faliero* to him in August 1821, he judged that its "pernicious effects" resulted from Byron's impoverished imagination: the drama was no place for the enforcement of dogmas, especially when these dogmas might justify an immoral revolutionary ethic. Shelley believed that Byron's drama might even further circumscribe the imaginations of the audience who desired a justification of violent revolutions. Poetry and politics were inextricably mixed and Shelley had already judged in *A Philosophical View of Reform* that "the French were what their literature is . . . with little imagination" and had indicted their revolutionary desire "to wreak revenge, . . . in itself a mistake, a crime, a calamity."[44] Before Shelley read *Marino Faliero*, he had placed its author among the "unacknowledged legislators" who might elevate the audience's imagination, but when he found that this drama's "legislative" principles could lead to anarchy, he judged in his 7 August 1821 letter to Mary that he and Byron "differed . . . more than ever." Byron had merely confirmed Shelley's fear which had been expressed a year earlier in his *Ode to Liberty*: "O vain endeavour!/If on his own high will a willing slave,/[Man] has enthroned the oppression and the oppressor" (xvii). If the world's literature was to be darkened by the casuistical justification of the slave's revenge on the tyrant in *Marino Faliero*, then the unimaginative slaves would merely produce tyranny in another form. This fear, in part confirmed by Byron's dramatic and moral principles which even sanctioned the Doge's concluding "curse" on Venice and her "serpent seed" (V.iii.44-101), made Shelley conclude his letter to Mary on 10 August 1821 with a bitter prediction: "We [Shelley and Byron] have good rumours of the Greeks here & [of] a Russian war. I hardly wish the Russians to take any part in it—My maxim is with AEschylus το δυσσεβὲς—μετα μεν πλειονα τικτει, σφετερα δ' εικοτα γεννα—There is a Greek exercise for you.— How should slaves produce any thing but tyranny—even as the seed produces the plant."[45] Even though this "sad reality" was represented in both *The Cenci* and *Marino Faliero*, Shelley hoped that his drama would teach the human heart the cause of moral error, but feared that Byron's would vindicate the ways of slave to tyrant.

IV

Because Shelley disapproved of the casuistry in *Marino Faliero*, he was probably amused when he read in August 1821 the *Letter to [John Murray], Esqre, on the Rev. W. L. Bowles's Strictures on the Life and Writings of Pope* (February 1821), wherein Byron defended Pope by arguing that "the highest of all poetry is ethical poetry, as the highest of all earthly objects must be moral truth. . . . are we to be told that ethical poetry, or didactic poetry, or by whatever name you term it, whose object is to make men better and wiser, is not the *very first order* of poetry?" Although Byron further argued that didactic poetry "is the highest of all poetry, because it does that in *verse*, which the greatest of men have wished to accomplish in prose,"[46] he used most of his *Letter* to reply specifically to Bowles's attack on Pope and therefore did not explain what or how moral principles should be infused into poetry. But his few judgments on didactic poetry directly contradict Shelley's opinions in the Preface to *Prometheus Unbound*: "Didactic poetry is my abhorrence; nothing can be equally well expressed in prose that is not tedious and supererogatory in verse." And at the same time Byron argued for didactic poetry, Shelley was writing in *A Defence of Poetry* that a poet "would do ill to embody his own conceptions of right and wrong . . . in his poetical creations. . . .

[Poets] have frequently affected a moral aim, and the effect of their poetry is diminished in exact proportion to the degree in which they compel us to advert to this purpose." As we have seen in the extreme case of *The Cenci*, Shelley's practice conformed to his theory that the highest poetry should avoid dogmatic ethical pronouncements. Moral goodness, he argued in his *Defence*, was a condition of men who imagined "intensely and comprehensively," rather than learned "admirable doctrines" of ethical science. Because "the great instrument of moral good is the imagination," he wrote poetry to awaken and enlarge "the mind itself by rendering it the receptacle of a thousand unapprehended combinations of thought."[47]

Byron, however, never shared Shelley's beliefs in the imagination, and in his first *Letter* to John Murray called "'imagination' and 'invention,' the two commonest of qualities: an Irish peasant with a little whisky in his head will imagine and invent more than would furnish forth a modern poem." In effect, Byron was criticizing his own imaginative inventiveness, for in the same *Letter* he classified himself among the "moderns" who had corrupted the taste established by Pope: "I *have* been amongst the builders of this Babel, attended by a confusion of tongues, but *never* amongst the envious destroyers of the classic temple of our predecessor [Pope]." In the words of his letter to Francis Hodgson two months earlier, he was not like "Southey and Wordsworth and such renegado rascals with their systems" which led to "the scoundrels of scribblers . . . trying to run down *Pope*."[48]

Byron had attacked some of these scoundrels in March 1820 when he defended Pope in the last half of "Some Observations upon an Article in *Blackwood's Magazine*." Disliking his contemporaries who had formed or were formed into "schools of poetry," he declared that it was "the age of the decline of English poetry" and criticized "three personages, Southey, Wordsworth, and Coleridge" for their "very natural antipathy to Pope." These three "Lakers" had been ridiculed before in *English Bards* and most recently in *Don Juan* (I.205), but this time he discovered a new opponent in John Keats, "a tadpole of the Lakes, a young disciple of the six or seven new schools," who had decried Pope in *Sleep and Poetry*.[49] This disciple came to Byron's attention again in October 1820 when he received from Murray a volume of "Johnny Keats's *p-ss a bed* poetry." After he read a favorable review of Keats's 1820 volume in the *Edinburgh Review*, he more contemptuously characterized this "Jack Keats or Ketch, or whatever his names are" in his November letters to Murray: he was a "miserable Self-polluter of the human mind" in his "Onanism of Poetry"; his writing was "a sort of mental masturbation" with "a Bedlam vision produced by raw pork and opium"; and he was a "little dirty blackguard."[50] When Byron wrote his first *Letter* (7-10 February 1821) on the Bowles/Pope controversy, he again criticized "the declining age of English poetry" because of its "depreciation of Pope,"[51] but he did not discuss Keats in terms of this decline. But by 12 March 1821, Byron sent to Murray "*addenda to the Letter on Bowles*" in which he once more criticized Southey, Wordsworth, and Coleridge as Lakers and identified Leigh Hunt as another "system-maker" with a ragamuffin proselyte, "a Mr. John Ketch," whose vulgar and "'shabby-genteel'" poetry debased contemporary literature.[52]

When Byron sent to Murray these remarks on John Ketch, he did not know that Keats had died on 23 February and was not informed until he received Shelley's letter of 16 April. In his response, on 26 April, Byron praised Shelley's poetry ("because it is of *no* school"), insisted that he disliked Keats as a member "of *that second-hand* school of poetry," and explained his recent critical efforts:

> I have published a pamphlet on the Pope controversy, which you will not like. Had I known that Keats was dead—or that he was alive and so sensitive—I should have omitted some remarks upon his poetry, to which I was provoked by his *attack* upon *Pope*, and my disapprobation of *his own* style of writing.[53]

In the preceding month, Shelley had indirectly praised Keats over Pope in his conclusion to *A Defence of Poetry* by announcing that "in spite of the low-thoughted envy which would undervalue contemporary merit . . . we live among such philosophers and poets as surpass beyond comparison any who have appeared since the last national struggle for civil and religious liberty." But in his reply to Byron on 4 May, he affected neutrality in what may be called the Keats/Pope controversy:

> I did not know that Keats had attacked Pope; I had heard that Bowles had done so, and that you had most severely chastised him therefor. Pope, it seems, has been selected as the pivot of a dispute in taste, on which, until I understand it, I must profess myself neuter. I certainly do not think Pope, or *any* writer, a fit model for any succeeding writer; if he, or they should be determined to be so, it would all come to a question as to under *what forms* mediocrity should perpetually reproduce itself; for true genius vindicates to itself an exemption from all regard to whatever has gone before.[54]

These observations are in the third of a series of five letters in which Shelley and Byron argued Keats's merits, and in these letters we find the genesis of Shelley's *Adonais*. They also serve to explain the reasons behind Shelley's portraits of Byron in *Adonais* and the reasons for

Byron's surprise when he found himself the first in the procession of mourners at the bier of the poet he had formerly labeled a "tadpole of the Lakes."

In the first of these letters, Shelley announced to Byron on 16 April that

> Young Keats, whose 'Hyperion' showed so great a promise, died lately at Rome from the consequences of breaking a blood-vessel, in paroxysms of despair at the contemptuous attack on his book in the *Quarterly Review*.[55]

Not having read *Hyperion*, Byron was unconvinced of Keats's promise and expressed his different opinion in his reply to Shelley on 26 April:

> I am very sorry to hear what you say of Keats—is it *actually* true? I did not think criticism had been so killing. Though I differ from you essentially in your estimate of his performances, I so much abhor all unnecessary pain, that I would rather he had been seated on the highest peak of Parnassus than have perished in such a manner. Poor fellow! though with such inordinate self-love he would probably have not been very happy. I read the review of *Endymion* in the *Quarterly*. It was severe,—but surely not so severe as many reviews in that and other journals upon others.
>
> I recollect the effect on me of the *Edinburgh* on my first poem; it was rage, and resistance, and redress—but not despondency nor despair. I grant that those are not amiable feelings; but, in this world of bustle and broil, and especially in the career of writing, a man should calculate upon his powers of *resistance* before he goes into the arena.[56]

Because he had not yet read any of Byron's formal criticism of Keats, Shelley was both surprised and angered by Byron's apparent insensitivity in this letter. In his reply on 4 May, Shelley defended Keats and argued that Byron's reaction to the review of *Hours of Idleness* should not be used as a standard for judging Keats:

> The account of Keats is, I fear, too true. Hunt tells me that in the first paroxysms of his disappointment he burst a blood-vessel; and thus laid the foundation of a rapid consumption. There can be no doubt but that the irritability which exposed him to this catastrophe was a pledge of future sufferings, had he lived. And yet this argument does not reconcile me to the employment of contemptuous and wounding expressions against a man merely because he has written bad verses; or, as Keats did, some

good verses in a bad taste. Some plants, which require delicacy
in rearing, might bring forth beautiful flowers if ever they should
arrive at maturity. *Your* instance hardly applies. You felt the
strength to soar beyond the arrows; the eagle was soon lost in
the light in which it was nourished, and the eyes of the aimers
were blinded. . . . As to Keats' merits as a poet, I principally
repose them upon the fragment of a poem entitled 'Hyperion',
which you may not, perhaps, have seen, and to which I think
you would not deny high praise. The energy and beauty of his
powers seem to disperse the narrow and wretched taste in which
(most unfortunately for the real beauty which they hide) he has
clothed his writings.[57]

Shelley was apparently taken by his defense of Keats as a flower that
required "delicacy in rearing," for within the next six weeks he wrote
*Adonais*, an elegy on Keats that repeated the metaphor in the sixth
stanza ("Like a pale flower . . . whose petals nipt before they blew/
Died on the promise of the fruit") and in the Preface ("The genius of
the lamented person . . . was not less delicate and fragile than it was
beautiful; and where canker-worms abound, what wonder, if its young
flower was blighted in the bud?").

If it be presumptuous to suggest that Shelley wrote *Adonais* in
order to correct Byron's ill opinion of Keats (that Shelley placed
Byron, an opponent of Keats, first in the procession of mourners at
the bier of Adonais argues for this presumption), the letters he exchanged
with Byron on Keats were at least responsible for some parts of his
elegy, especially two of the stanzas in Urania's apostrophe to Adonais:

"O gentle child, beautiful as thou wert,
Why didst thou leave the trodden paths of men
Too soon, and with weak hands though mighty heart
*Dare the unpastured dragon in his den?*
Defenceless as thou wert, oh! where was then
*Wisdom the mirror'd shield, or scorn the spear?*
Or hadst thou waited the full cycle, when
Thy spirit should have filled its crescent sphere,
The monsters of life's waste had fled from thee like deer.

"The herded wolves, bold only to pursue;
The obscene ravens, clamorous oer the dead;
The vultures, to the conqueror's banner true,
Who feed where Desolation first has fed,
And whose wings rain contagion;—how they fled,
When like Apollo, from his golden bow,
*The Pythian of the age one arrow sped*

And smiled!—The spoilers tempt no second blow,
They fawn on the proud feet that spurn them lying low."

(xxvii-xxviii, my italics)

In the first stanza printed above, Shelley was obviously recalling Byron's warning in his letter of 26 April that "in this world of bustle and broil, and especially in the career of writing, a man should calculate upon his powers of *resistance* before he goes into the arena." Shelley merely transformed Byron's "arena" into the "'den'" of a dragon or reviewer; and Byron's *"resistance"* into "'Wisdom the mirror'd shield, or scorn the spear.'" In this last image, Shelley was specifically alluding to the satiric spear of *English Bards and Scotch Reviewers*, the *"resistance"* Byron had chosen in response to the harsh treatment of *Hours of Idleness* by the *Edinburgh Review*. In his letter to Shelley, Byron had unfavorably compared Keats's "despondency" and "despair" to his own *"resistance,"* and Shelley had responded on 4 May that *"Your* instance hardly applies," because "you felt the strength to soar beyond the arrows; the eagle [Shelley's frequent metaphor for Byron] was soon lost in the light in which it was nourished." Nevertheless, Shelley made use of Byron's "instance" in the stanza about the dragon and the spear; moreover, in the following stanza where Byron is referred to as the "'Pythian of the age'" from whose bow "'one arrow [*English Bards*] sped'" toward the reviewers ("'wolves,'" "'ravens,'" and "'vultures'"), Shelley reversed the image he had used to describe Byron soaring "beyond the arrows."[58]

Byron's reference to his own *"resistance"* in the face of adverse criticism intrigued Shelley enough to reread *English Bards and Scotch Reviewers* during May, probably before he protested on 4 May that Byron's "instance" didn't apply. No record of this rereading exists, but the echoes of *English Bards* in *Adonais*, particularly in the two stanzas quoted above, sufficiently prove Shelley's interest in Byron's satire. For example, what Keats lacked to defend himself, "'Wisdom the mirror'd shield, or scorn the spear,'" echoes Byron's ironic claim in *English Bards* that he could resist with neither "Reason's shield" nor "the arrows of satiric song" (ll. 691, 38). And Shelley's caricature of the reviewers as

"The herded wolves, bold only to pursue;
The obscene ravens, clamorous oer the dead;
The vultures, to the conqueror's banner true,
Who feed where Desolation first has fed,
And whose wings rain contagion;—how they fled,"

was inspired by Byron's earlier description of the reviewers as wolves and harpies:

*165*

Northern Wolves, that still in darkness prowl;
A coward Brood, which mangle as they prey,
By hellish instinct, all that cross their way;
Aged or young, the living or the dead,
No mercy find—these harpies must be fed.
Why do the injured unresisting yield
The calm possession of their native field?
Why tamely thus before their fangs retreat,
Nor hunt the blood-hounds back to Arthur's Seat?     (ll. 429-37)

Byron's concluding description of these reviewers as "men in buckram" who shall "feel they too [like poets] are 'penetrable stuff'" now that he, "so callous grown," can "deride the critic's starch decree" (ll. 1049-50, 1057, 1059), was transformed by Shelley into scorn for those reviewers who "scatter their insults and their slanders without heed as to whether the poisoned shaft lights on a heart made *callous* by many blows, or one, like Keats's composed of more *penetrable stuff*" (Preface to *Adonais*, my italics).[59] Shelley's description of Keats being felled by the critic's "poisoned shaft" contrasts that of Byron as an "eagle" with "the strength to soar beyond the arrows" in his letter of 4 May, and both images seem to be borrowed from Byron's description in *English Bards* of Henry Kirke White's death:

So the struck Eagle, stretched upon the plain,
No more through rolling clouds to soar again,
Viewed his own feather on the fatal dart,
And winged the shaft that quivered in his heart.

(ll. 841-44)

Shelley was probably attracted to these lines because White had been another young poet who had died in his youth, one who contributed to his own death (hence "his own feather on the fatal dart") by "too much exertion in the pursuit of studies" (Byron's note). And Shelley's reading of Byron's elegiac lines,

Unhappy White! while life was in its spring,
And thy young muse just waved her joyous wing,
The Spoiler swept that soaring Lyre away,
Which else had sounded an immortal lay,     (ll. 831-34)

may have had no slight influence on his decision to elegize Keats in *Adonais*.[60]

By using the "instance" of *English Bards and Scotch Reviewers* in *Adonais*, Shelley presumed on his friendship with Byron, but he apparently believed that his more famous friend would both recognize and defend the genius of John Keats after reading *Hyperion*. And he

*166*

sought to enlist Byron in this cause by praising him as the "'Pythian of the age'" from whose "'golden bow'" the reviewers fled and before whose "'proud feet'" they fawned. Shelley continued this praise of Byron's satiric art in another stanza which he intended to use in *Adonais*:

> His life seemed one long Carnival, one merry
> Farewell to flesh, to which all bid farewell
> Before they pass the melancholy ferry.
> He laughed, and as the arrow of laughter fell,
> Wounding with sweet and bitter mirth, it well
> Distilled the balm from its fine point to heal
> The wounds which were inflicted—but the spell
> Bound them like chains of strong and glittering steel
> Which spirits in the fire of mother wit anneal.[61]

Having previously observed that Byron's wit redeemed the "bitter mockery" in his later satires (see note 35), Shelley in this stanza attempted to encompass Byron's "sweet and bitter mirth" in both *Beppo* (where Byron wrote of the Venetian "Carnival, which being/ Interpreted, implies 'farewell to flesh'" [vi]) and *Don Juan* (where Byron ironically discussed his "resolution every spring/Of reformation" [I.119]). But Shelley did not include this stanza in the published *Adonais*, perhaps because he felt that Byron would not welcome an allusion to his Venetian pleasures. Instead, he risked Byron's displeasure by making him the first of the mourners at the bier of Keats:

> The Pilgrim of Eternity, whose fame
> Over his living head like Heaven is bent,
> An early but enduring monument,
> Came, veiling all the lightnings of his song
> In sorrow.           (xxx)

To forestall any resentment that Byron might have to this enforced tribute to Keats, Shelley deferentially praised his friend's greatness as a poet. And, as in *Lines Written Among the Euganean Hills*, he characterized Byron with the latter's own words, the "Pilgrim of Eternity" recalling Childe Harold as one of the "wanderers o'er Eternity," a "Pilgrim of my Song," and "the Pilgrim" (III.lxx; IV.clxiv; clxxxvi).

When Shelley sent Byron a copy of *Adonais* on 16 July, he still felt uncomfortable about presuming upon Byron's opinion of Keats, and he apologized for the poem's excesses:

> Although I feel the truth of what I have alleged about his 'Hyperion,' and I doubt, if you saw that particular poem, whether you would not agree with me; yet I need not be told that I have been

*167*

carried too far by the enthusiasm of the moment; by my piety, and my indignation, in panegyric. But if I have erred, I console myself by reflecting that it is in defence of the weak—not in conjunction with the powerful. And perhaps I have erred from the narrow view of considering Keats rather as he surpassed *me* in particular, then as he was inferior to others: so subtle is the principle of self! . . . As to the Poem I send you, I fear it is worth little. Heaven knows what makes me persevere (after the severe reproof of public neglect) in writing verses; and Heaven alone, whose will I execute so awkwardly, is responsible for my presumption.[62]

This self-effacement is not wholly consistent with Shelley's earlier remark to the Gisbornes that *Adonais* was "perhaps better in point of composition than any thing"[63] he had ever written, but Shelley had written his elegy while laboring under his own sense of inferiority as a poet, particularly in relation to Byron (see below, Chapter 9). Not wanting Byron to be affronted by the homage paid by the "Pilgrim of Eternity," Shelley asked him to read *Hyperion* and to be assured that Keats, even if he "surpassed" the author of *Adonais*, was nevertheless "inferior" to Byron.

Byron read *Adonais* in July but when Shelley visited him in Ravenna in August, he never mentioned the poem. Shelley conjectured that Byron's reticence resulted "from modesty on account of his being mentioned in it,"[64] but Byron had other motives, for he undoubtedly felt embarrassed as a public mourner for a poet whom he had publicly condemned. Accordingly, after Byron read *Adonais*, he instructed John Murray on 30 July to "omit *all* that is said *about him* [Keats] in any *MSS*. of mine, or publication" and acceded to Shelley's judgment that "*Hyperion* is a fine monument." But Byron still could not "approve of Keats's poetry, or principles of poetry, or of his abuse of Pope" and he offered to Murray a less than Shelleyan version of Keats's death:

"Who killed John Keats?["]
  "I," says the Quarterly,
  So savage and Tartarly;
  "'Twas one of my feats."

"Who shot the arrow?"
  "The poet-priest Milman
  (So ready to kill man),
Or Southey or Barrow."

And at the end of this letter, Byron disparagingly observed that "he who would die of an article in a review would probably have died of something else equally trivial. The same thing nearly happened to Kirke White, who afterwards died of a consumption."[65] Byron made many of these same judgments in a letter to Shelley written about the same time, but he wasn't quite so flippant:

> The impression of "Hyperion" upon my mind—was—that it was the best of his works.—Who is to be his editor?—It is strange that Southey who attacks the reviewers so sharply in his Kirke White—calling theirs "the ungentle craft"—should be perhaps the killer of Keats.—Kirke White was nearly extinguished in the same way—by a paragraph or two in "The Monthly."—Such inordinate sense of censure is surely incompatible with great exertion—have not all known writers been the subject thereof?[66]

Byron's reference to Kirke White establishes an ironic refrain around *Adonais*, for Shelley had apparently reread the lines on White in *English Bards* even before he began his elegy on Keats.

Keats's death and Shelley's *Adonais* caused Byron to revise even further his public pronouncements on the author of *Hyperion*. Just before and after Shelley's arrival in Ravenna on 6 August, Byron instructed Murray to omit the ridicule of Keats and the *"Suburban School"* in the *Addenda* which he intended for his first *Letter* on Bowles but which Murray had included in the proofs for the second *Letter*.[67] In September, Byron requested proofs of his "Some Observations upon an Article in *Blackwood's Magazine*," and he evidently wanted to alter therein his criticism on Keats as "a tadpole of the Lakes." He received these proofs in time to have them in Pisa, for on 7 November Edward Williams noted that Byron "lends us a small pamphlet now printing called 'Some Observations,' but upon S[helley]'s recommendation does not intend to publish it. It is well written, but certainly not becoming in him to notice the vulgar attacks of the envious or malicious."[68] But Williams was misinformed, for on 12 November Byron enclosed in a letter to Murray the proofs of "Some Observations" and asked that the article be published in a volume entitled *Miscellanies*. And instead of omitting his criticism of Keats, he added a note on the same day to explain his revised judgment on the author of *Hyperion*:

> Mr. Keats died at Rome about a year after this was written, of a decline produced by his having burst a blood-vessel on reading the article on his *Endymion* in the *Quarterly Review*. I have read the article before and since; and although it is bitter, I do not think that a man should permit himself to be killed by it. But a young

man little dreams what he must inevitably encounter in the course of a life ambitious of public notice. My indignation at Mr. Keats's depreciation of Pope has hardly permitted me to do justice to his own genius, which, malgré all the fantastic fopperies of his style, was undoubtedly of great promise. His fragment of *Hyperion* seems actually inspired by the Titans, and is as sublime as Æschylus. He is a loss to our literature; and the more so, as he himself before his death, is said to have been persuaded that he had not taken the right line, and was reforming his style upon the more classical models of the language.[69]

Byron had conceded, at least publicly, that *Hyperion* was as sublime as Shelley had argued, but he could not forgive Keats for his weakness or for his depreciation of Pope. So despite *Adonais* and Shelley's placing of Byron in the procession of mourners, Byron never fully retracted his ill opinion of Keats's poetry. Medwin reported that in Pisa Byron was " 'always battling with *the Snake* [Shelley] about Keats' "; and even in April 1823, Lady Blessington and Byron "nearly quarrelled . . . because [she] defended poor Keats."[70] By that time, Byron had written Canto XI of *Don Juan* and had offered his own version of Keats's death:

> John Keats, who was killed off by one critique,
>     Just as he really promised something great,
> If not intelligible,—without Greek
>     Contrived to talk about the Gods of late,
> Much as they might have been supposed to speak.
>     Poor fellow! His was an untoward fate:—
> 'Tis strange the mind, that very fiery particle,
> Should let itself be snuffed out by an Article.          (60)

Byron had similarly dismissed Keats as a "Poor fellow" in his letter to Shelley on 26 April 1821, but this time Shelley was not alive to answer Byron; in the words of Byron's next stanza in Canto XI, Shelley had "the long grass grow/Above his burnt-out brain, and sapless cinders" (61).

THE TREES OF KNOWLEDGE
AND OF LIFE: SHELLEY'S RESPONSE TO
*THE PROPHECY OF DANTE, DON JUAN, THE VISION
OF JUDGMENT,* AND *CAIN*

Shelley's visit to Ravenna in August 1821, like his visit to Venice
in 1818, had as one of its purposes the future arrangements to be
made for Allegra, who had been under Byron's direction since 1818.
In May 1820, Shelley had agreed to take Claire to see her daughter,
but the trip was canceled after Byron refused to meet with Claire.
Ten months later, Byron placed Allegra in the convent of Bagnacavallo, and in a letter dated 24 March 1821 Claire asked if she could
remove Allegra from this convent and place her in an English board-
ing school chosen by Byron's own friends, presumably to include the
Hoppners, with whom Allegra had resided for a time in 1818/19.
With this arrangement, Claire hoped to be able to visit Allegra as often
as Byron's friends allowed, but she didn't know that even the Hoppners
had turned against her as a result of her rumored sexual relations with
Shelley. Because Byron also credited these rumors and was therefore
more than ever opposed to Claire's influence upon their daughter, he
rejected her proposal in a letter, now lost, which Shelley received and
answered by 17 April. Attempting to mediate this dispute, Shelley
agreed with Byron that Claire's letter had been "sufficiently provok-
ing" and her "views respecting Allegra . . . unreasonable," and he
offered Mary's and his own help in arranging Allegra's future. Byron
replied to Shelley on 26 April, thanked him for his concern, and
invited him alone (i.e., without Claire) to Ravenna. Such a trip
Shelley thought inconvenient at the time and instead asked Byron
on 4 May to visit him and Mary at Pisa, stressing that Claire would
not be there. Byron did not respond to this invitation, perhaps
because in Claire's letter of 24 March from Florence she had
announced she would return to Pisa, and Shelley eventually journeyed
to Ravenna, arriving there on the evening of 6 August.[1]
Upon his arrival, Shelley learned that Byron considered taking
Teresa Guiccioli and the Gambas to Switzerland, and he convinced
Byron that Allegra should accompany them. At Byron's request,

*171*

however, Shelley helped persuade Teresa to remain in Italy and by 15 August he wrote to Mary that Byron had decided to move with Teresa and the Gambas to Pisa, but he didn't know if Allegra would accompany them there. Because of this uncertainty, Shelley suggested to Mary that they should alter their plans to winter in Florence and instead remain in Pisa, where they could protect Claire's interests. Shelley's frustrations in this controversy are suggested by a marginal note in the manuscript notebook containing his *Essay on Christianity*:

> To Alba, eyes, depth, amicableness, like Albè, better with me [her?] than with him. Infants dont know their father from a stranger. The Mother a mist—a torrent cinctured spot [—] mountain tops [this reading very doubtful] scattered by the storm.[2]

The storm imagery in this note somewhat suggests Shelley's veiled reference to the Byron/Claire conflict in *Epipsychidion*, his "idealized history" written in January/February 1821:

> Thou too, O Comet beautiful and fierce,
> Who drew the heart of this frail Universe
> Towards thine own; till, wreckt in that convulsion,
> Alternating attraction and repulsion,
> Thine went astray and that was rent in twain;
> Oh, float into our azure heaven again!　　　　　(ll. 368-73)

As Kenneth Neill Cameron has observed, the reference to the Comet "must be to Claire Clairmont (who was then at Florence), the 'alternating attraction and repulsion' referring to a previous entanglement of Shelley and Claire, and the 'going astray' and wrecking of the Comet referring to Claire's later affair with Byron."[3]

Whether the "attraction and repulsion" line refers to Shelley and Claire is questionable, but Shelley discovered a more disastrous entanglement on the evening of 6 August when Byron repeated to him the so-called Hoppner scandal—Elise, Allegra's Swiss nurse once employed by the Shelleys, had informed the Hoppners in 1820 that Claire had given birth to Shelley's child, that they had sent the child to a foundling hospital, and that they had abused Mary in this affair. The Hoppners had reported this story to Byron in a letter of 16 September 1820 in order that Allegra be permanently separated from her mother, and Byron had responded on 1 October that he believed the facts of the story despite Elise's untrustworthiness. Shelley was not informed of these false accusations until he joined Byron in Ravenna, and in a letter dated 7 August 1821 he immediately urged Mary to "write to the Hoppners a letter refuting the charge. . . . If you will send the letter to me here, I will forward it to the Hoppners." When Mary's letter arrived on 16 August, he instead gave it to "Lord Byron, who has engaged to send it with his own comments to the Hoppners," comments that would presumably explain why Byron revealed the secret after "the Hoppners had exacted from [him] that these accusations should be concealed" from the Shelleys.[4] Whether or not Byron confessed in August that he had initially believed the Hoppner scandal, the accusations themselves were enough to depress Shelley: in his letter to Mary on 7 August, he wrote, "my patience & my philosophy are put to a severe proof, whilst I refrain from seeking out some obscure hiding place where the countenance of man may never meet me more"; and in spite of his expectations of being joined by Byron in Pisa, he repeated to Mary on 16 August that his

> greatest content would be utterly to desert all human society. I would retire with you & our child to a solitary island in the sea. . . . —I would read no reviews & talk with no authors.—If I dared trust my imagination it would tell me that there were two or three chosen companions beside yourself whom I should desire.— But to this I would not listen.—Where two or three are gathered together the devil is among them, and good far more than evil impulses—love far more than hatred—has been to me, except as you have been it's [*sic*] object, the source of all sort[s] of mischief. So on this plan I would be *alone* & would devote either to oblivion or to future generations the overflowings of a mind which, timely withdrawn from the contagion, should be kept fit for no baser object.

Shelley acknowledged, however, that such a scheme was impractical and that he and Mary should instead form a society in Pisa with their "own class, as much as possible, in intellect or in feelings," but his imagined withdrawal from society bespeaks a dissatisfaction with life that makes his writings in 1821 and 1822 different from his former poems, which melioristically celebrated man's capacity for social reform.

## II

Not long after Shelley's previous reunion with Byron in Venice, he wrote *Lines Written Among the Euganean Hills*, in which he also imagined an escape from the pains of life to an idyllic island, "Where for me, and those I love, / May a windless bower be built, / Far from passion, pain, and guilt" (ll. 343-45). But in 1818, Shelley believed that his happiness there might "even entice / To our healing paradise / The polluting multitude" (including Byron), who would be directed by "the love which heals all strife" until they "would change" and "the earth grow young again" (ll. 354-73). But by 1821, Shelley's 1818/19 faith, as expressed in *Euganean Hills* and *Prometheus Unbound*, had considerably changed, for the multitude (including other "authors" and even "two or three chosen companions") would be excluded from the island he described in his letter to Mary. In effect, by emphasizing a personal rather than a social ideal, Shelley was restricting his former Promethean hopes. And this restriction was not merely a result of the depressing Hoppner scandal, for by February 1821 he had already transformed his social myth into a personal hope in *Epipsychidion*, wherein he and his idealized "lady of the solitude" in the person of Emilia Viviani would remove only themselves to "a lone dwelling" and "an isle under Ionian skies, / Beautiful as a wreck of Paradise" (ll. 514, 484, 422-23). And Shelley further qualified his former meliorism by suggesting that this desire for a perfect temporal union between himself and Emilia would inevitably lead to their mutual destruction.

Shelley's modification in 1821 of his former hopes for man's improvement was, however, far from emphatic, especially in light of his *Defence of Poetry*, which argues that imagination and love are the instrument and secret of man's moral reformation. But in *Epipsychidion*, as well as in *Adonais* and *Hellas*, Shelley began to question his former meliorism and in so doing acted as his own Byronic antagonist. In the Preface to *Epipsychidion*, for example, after depersonalizing the poem into lines written by a man who had since "died at Florence," Shelley claimed that it was the writer's "hope to have realised a scheme of life, suited perhaps to that happier and better world of which he is now an inhabitant, but hardly practicable in this." Shelley's "perhaps" and "hardly" qualify somewhat his rejection of his former hope that man could reclaim some of his prelapsarian inheritance, but it is clear, as Wasserman has argued, that Shelley's "faith in utopia has grown slight and nearly untenable, and his hope . . . is obviously directed toward death." And in the concluding third of *Epipsychidion*, Shelley's vision of a perfect earthly union with his antitype succeeds to a realization that such a union necessarily leads to the destruction of the corporeal self: in Wasserman's terms, "personal millennium turns out to be a future immortality";[5] in Shelley's, his and Emilia's spirits will be like two conjoined "meteors of expanding flame, / . . . / Which point to Heaven" (ll. 576, 583) until there will be but

> One hope within two wills, one will beneath
> Two overshadowing minds, one life, one death,
> One Heaven, one Hell, one immortality,
> And one annihilation. (ll. 584-87)

Not love and life, but love and death become unified in this vision which Shelley cannot find words to complete, and in his final apostrophe to the very poem he is composing, he asks that it and his other poems celebrate love, even though love itself might destroy man's hopes for a temporal paradise:

> "Love's very pain is sweet,
> But its reward is in the world divine,
> Which, if not here, it builds beyond the grave."　　(ll. 596-98)

By qualifying his former hope that love could regenerate man "here" in this world, Shelley was in effect questioning that same "'awful duty'" of hope that he had vainly urged on Byron in September 1816.[6] When Byron rejected this millennial hope in *Manfred* (as well as *Childe Harold* IV), it made Shelley so "dreadfully melancholy" that he wrote *Prometheus Unbound*, *Julian and Maddalo*, and *Lines Written Among the Euganean Hills* in order to refute Byron's darker judgments about life. But in 1821, Shelley acknowledged partial agreement with Byron's judgments in *Manfred* when, in a canceled Preface to *Epipsychidion*, he described his own frustrations (in the person of the fictitious author of the poem) as "additional proof that 'The tree of Knowledge is not that of Life' [*Manfred* I.i.12] ." His error, according to the same Preface, "was, θνητος ὠν μὴ θνητὰ φρονεῖν,"[7] the same error that one of Arimanes' spirits discovered in Manfred: "This is to be a mortal, / And seek the things beyond mortality" (II. iv.157-58). Three weeks before he died, Shelley acknowledged this same "error, and I confess it is not easy for spirits cased in flesh and blood to avoid it," when he judged that love "consists in seeking in a mortal image the likeness of what is perhaps eternal."[8] The Poet of *Alastor* similarly erred by vainly searching in life for the prototype of his conception, but neither he nor the Shelleyan narrator of the poem had much hope for fulfillment in death. By 1821, however, Shelley's uncertainty about a permanent temporal union with his idealized antitype (the embodied prototype described in *On Love* as the "unattainable point to which Love tends") was succeeded by a faith in an immortality "beyond the grave." This same faith may be found in *Adonais*, which, unlike the elegiac mourning for the Poet in *Alastor*, celebrates death as a triumph over life.

In *Adonais*, written four months after *Epipsychidion*, Shelley also questioned his hopes in man's ability to reform society. Because Keats's death bore witness to the wretchedness of a temporal existence, Shelley "in another's fate now wept his own" (xxxiv) and contrasted Keats's newly acquired immortality to his own temporal life, which, "like a dome of many-coloured glass, / Stains the white radiance

of Eternity" (lii). Furthermore, he conceded that his former millennial vision was in error:

Why linger, why turn back, why shrink, my Heart?
*Thy hopes are gone before: from all things here*
*They have departed;* thou shouldst now depart!
A light is past from the revolving year,
And man, and woman; and what still is dear
Attracts to crush, repels to make thee wither.
The soft sky smiles,—the low wind whispers near:
'Tis Adonais calls! oh, hasten thither,
No more let life divide what Death can join together.

(liii, my italics)

Because Shelley no longer espoused the utopian creed of Julian, he no
longer needed to define himself in opposition to a Maddalo. Consequently, he brought the "Pilgrim of Eternity" to the bier of Adonais
not to debate the strength of man's Promethean chains but only to
force Byron to acknowledge the quality of Keats's poetry. Shelley
himself appeared among the mourners as one whose past "thoughts"
about temporal improvement now hounded him, "their father and
their prey" (xxxi). Doubting his own capabilities as a poet (even
Urania, the mother of poets, did not know him),[9] Shelley "Made bare
his branded and ensanguined brow, / Which was like Cain's or Christ's.
—Oh! that it [like Christ's] should be so!" (xxxiv). Shelley never
quite explained why he introduced *"Christ* as an antithesis to *Cain,"*[10]
but by preferring to be like Christ crucified, he hoped to escape the
unredeemed and fallen world that Cain had been condemned to
wander without the benefit of death; he hoped to find shelter "From
the world's bitter wind / . . . in the shadow of the tomb" (li) and to
inherit through death an immortality.

Shelley's denials of his former Promethean hopes did not, however, lessen his reverence for the human spirit. In *Hellas*, written
between his visit to Ravenna in August and Byron's arrival in Pisa in
November, he could still "attach himself to those ideas which exalt
and ennoble humanity" and conjecture "the condition of that futurity
towards which we are all impelled by an inextinguishable thirst for
immortality" (Shelley's note on ll. 197-238 of *Hellas*). This "condition" of futurity seems to be purposefully vague, for Shelley refused
to declare whether the free and "brighter Hellas" (l. 1066) would be
realized in time or eternity:

If Greece must be
A wreck, yet shall its fragments re-assemble,

> And build themselves again impregnably
>   In a diviner clime,
> To Amphionic music on some Cape sublime,
> Which frowns above the idle foam of Time.    (ll. 1002-7)

Although Shelley seems to be saying here that the spirit of Greece's golden years, produced by "thought and its eternity" (l. 699), awaits man after death in "a diviner clime" transcending time, the faint possibility that "the world divine" might be "here" as well as "beyond the grave" (*Epipsychidion*, ll. 597-98) sustains the hope that

> Another Athens shall arise,
>   And to remoter time
> Bequeath, like sunset to the skies,
>   The splendour of its prime;
> And leave, if nought so bright may live,
> All earth can take or heaven can give.    (ll. 1084-89)

But because Shelley indeed feared that "nought so bright may live" in this world of mutability, he concluded his final chorus to *Hellas* by suggesting that man's inextinguishable thirst for a better human life would not be quenched:

> O cease! must hate and death return?
> Cease! must men kill and die?
> Cease! drain not to its dregs the urn
>   Of bitter prophecy.
> The world is weary of the past,
> O might it die or rest at last!

Thus "chance, and death, and mutability," which Shelley formerly believed man could rule "like slaves" (*Prometheus Unbound* III.iv.200-1), were destined, he seems to say in 1821, to tyrannize man until his death.[11]

The change in Shelley's vision has frequently been demonstrated by closer readings of his 1821/22 poetry than I have provided above,[12] but little has been written on Shelley's correspondingly changed relations with Lord Byron. In effect, Shelley had considerably less reason to criticize Byron, for on the one hand he now shared some of Byron's doubts about man's temporal progress, and on the other he discovered that Byron was rid of his former degrading habits and was actively interested in the progress of political freedom in Italy and Greece. Furthermore, Shelley believed that Byron's moral transformation was to some extent reflected in his recent poetry. He could still find fault in Byron (indeed, writing to John Gisborne on 22 October 1821 that

"Lord B. is . . . quite cured of his gross habits—as far as habits—the perverse ideas on which they were founded are not yet eradicated"[13]), but at practically the same time Shelley chose to ignore these "perverse ideas" when he highly praised three of Byron's works: *The Prophecy of Dante, Don Juan* III-V, and *Cain: A Mystery*—the first two of which were written between Shelley's visits to Byron in 1818 and 1821. Each of these poems contains what might be termed Shelleyan ideas and expressions, and Shelley's reaction to them qualifies his judgment in August 1821 that he and Byron differed more than ever. Nevertheless, in each of these works, Byron ultimately denied, as he had done in *Manfred* and *Childe Harold* IV, Shelley's former metaphysical assumptions about the human condition. By ignoring these denials and by refusing to debate Byron once again on the subjects of "God, freewill, and destiny. / Of all that Earth has been, or yet may be" (*Julian and Maddalo*, ll. 42-43), Shelley in effect gave witness that he was no longer the uncompromising meliorist that Byron believed him to be.

III

*The Prophecy of Dante* (written in 1819 but not published until April 1821, when it appeared with *Marino Faliero*) occupies a peculiar place in Byron's and Shelley's intellectual relations, for its differences with *The Lament of Tasso* reflect Shelley's partial influence on Byron in 1818, its argument continues the debate that Shelley recorded in *Julian and Maddalo*, and its theme anticipates many of Shelley's later judgments about poetry and life in 1821. Shelley may have read Byron's *Prophecy* during his visit to Ravenna in August 1821, and certainly had read it by 14 September when on the six hundredth anniversary of Dante's death he wrote to Byron his thoughts on the poem:

> The poetry of [*The Prophecy of Dante*] is indeed sublime; and if it have not general admiration, you ought still to be contented; because the subject, no less than the style, is addressed to the few, and, like some of the highest passages in 'Childe Harold', will only be *fully* appreciated by the select readers of many generations.[14]

Shelley liked both the subject and style of *The Prophecy of Dante* because Byron had superimposed an aesthetic vision and a political prophecy onto the form of the dramatic monologue he had used earlier in *The Lament of Tasso*. Byron was still depicting "Man's frail world" (I.1), but this time he belatedly took Shelley's advice, offered in a letter of 29 September 1816, of benefiting the human race as had

"Homer, or Shakespeare" by becoming "a fountain from which the thoughts of other men shall draw strength and beauty."[15] Byron was not content for long to play Maddalo opposite Shelley's Julian: his *Prophecy* in fact rivals Shelley's hopes for a liberated Italy in *Lines Written Among the Euganean Hills*; and it fulfills Shelley's prophecy therein that the "Mighty spirit" of Byron, once more compared to Homer, Shakespeare, and this time Petrarch, would give fame to the "city that did refuge" him (ll. 194-205).[16]

Byron's "city" in 1818 was Venice and its "sins and slaveries foul" needed to be redeemed by his "sunlike soul" so that at least from the city's "dust new nations [might] spring / With more kindly blossoming" (*Euganean Hills*, ll. 192-93, 165-66). Byron, as it were, took up Shelley's repeated challenge and in his *Prophecy* rent the "veil of coming centuries" (II.35) so that he might, through Dante, instill in the nineteenth-century Italians a Shelleyan hope that their political liberation would be advanced through the influence of art. Despite Italy's "sable web of Sorrow" which persisted from the four-teenth until the nineteenth century, Byron's Dante took "Over the gleams that flash athwart thy gloom / A softer glimpse" (III.36-38) and with images that suggest parts of Shelley's *Two Spirits: An Allegory* and *Euganean Hills*, condensed five centuries of Italy's grandeur:

> some stars shine through thy night,
> And many meteors, and above thy tomb
> Leans sculptured Beauty, which Death cannot blight:
> And from thine ashes boundless Spirits rise
> To give thee honour, and the earth delight.      (III.38-42)

Dante foresees, however, that the honor and fame achieved by such "Spirits" as Petrarch, Ariosto, and Tasso will not liberate Italy, and in effect reproduces Byron's earlier complaint that Venice's "love for Tasso" failed to "cut the knot / Which ties thee to thy tyrants" (*Childe Harold* IV.xvii). Nevertheless, Byron's increasing sympathy for the Italians caused him, through the device of Dante's monologue, to prophesy that

> more than these illustrious far shall be
> The Being—and even yet he may be born—
> The mortal Saviour who shall set thee free,
> And see thy diadem, so changed and worn
> By fresh barbarians, on thy brow replaced;
> And the sweet Sun replenishing thy morn,
> Thy moral morn, too long with clouds defaced,

And noxious vapours from Avernus risen,
Such as all they must breathe who are debased
By Servitude, and have the mind in prison.       (III.52-61)

By such expressions, which again parallel those in *Euganean Hills*,
Byron urged upon the Italians "*one* deed—Unite" (II.145), and
sensing in himself something of a prophet who had anticipated the
Italian revolution, he informed Murray in August 1820 that "the
time for the *Dante* [not yet published] would be good now . . . as
Italy is on the eve of great things."[17]

Byron's hope for the Italians did not, however, blind him to the
political realities in Europe at the time. After hearing in April 1820
that the "Spanish and French affairs have set the Italians in a ferment,"
he conceded nonetheless that the Italians "want Union, and they want
principle; and I doubt their success."[18] Byron had similarly qualified
his hopes in *The Prophecy of Dante* by having Dante doubt that the
Italians would unite under their leaders, especially the poet-prophets
whose "finer thoughts" and "intense / Feeling of that which is, and
fancy of / That which should be" would inevitably lead to frustration.
Asking "shall [the artists'] bright plumage on the rough / Storm be
still scattered," Dante tempers his hopeful vision with a Byronic
judgment that man's clay cannot be redeemed by his fire:

> Yes, and it must be;
> For, formed of far too *penetrable stuff*,
> *These birds of Paradise but long to flee*
> *Back to their native mansion, soon they find*
> *Earth's mist with their pure pinions not agree,*
> *And die or are degraded*; for the mind
> Succumbs to long infection, and despair,
> And vulture Passions flying close behind,
> Await the moment to assail and tear.       (III.161-75, my italics)

Had Shelley read these lines while concluding *Prometheus Unbound*
in 1819, he would have objected to such a bitter prophecy. But
Shelley did not read *The Prophecy of Dante* until two years later,
by which time in *Adonais* he had already rejected his own hopes and
consequently could find little to dislike in Byron's poem, especially
since these lines anticipated his own images in *Adonais* where earth's
"mist" and "the contagion of the world's slow stain" were "out-
soared" (xl) by Keats, who had also been formed of "penetrable
stuff" (Preface). Rather than disliking Byron's lines on the pure
"birds of Paradise," Shelley admired and even imitated them, as seen
in his *Triumph of Life*, where he expands Byron's "vulture Passions

flying close behind" into the chaotic triumphal process that is escaped only by

> the sacred few who could not tame
> Their spirits to the Conqueror, but as soon
> As they had touched the world with living glame
> Fled back like eagles to their native noon.[19]      (ll.128-31)

In *Adonais*, Shelley had similarly desired to flee back to his "native noon" or mansion, to join Keats in death, and to escape his forsaken Promethean hopes which "Pursued, like raging hounds, their father and their prey" (xxxi). But when he read *The Prophecy of Dante*, he discovered a new Prometheanism by which such despair might at least be endured:

> For what is Poesy but to create
> From overfeeling Good or Ill; and aim
> At an external life beyond our fate,
> And be the new Prometheus of new men,
> Bestowing fire from Heaven, and then, too late,
> Finding the pleasure given repaid with pain,
> And vultures to the heart of the bestower,
> Who, having lavished his high gift in vain,
> Lies chained to his lone rock by the sea-shore?
> So be it: we can bear.                    (IV.11-20)

Recalling Byron's 1816 ode *Prometheus*, Dante's pronouncement here contradicts or at least severely qualifies his other prophecy that a "mortal Saviour" might be found to set Italy free. As a unit, then, *The Prophecy of Dante* straddles a philosophical or at least a political fence, for it has too much hope for the fatalist and too much despair for the meliorist. But such ambivalence serves as a paradigm of Byron's position in 1819 (as well as Shelley's in 1821), for both poets had been susceptible to each other's opposing arguments in 1818 and since then both had hoped and despaired over man's condition. Shelley no longer wished to debate with Byron whether " 'destiny' " or man's " 'wilful ill' " prevented human perfectibility, and instead agreed with Byron that their art should at least immortalize man's quest for the immutable, even though a temporal realization of that quest was probably impossible.

Byron had, of course, immortalized that artistic quest in his earlier poetry, particularly in the stanzas of *Childe Harold* IV (cliii-clxiii) describing St. Peter's, the Laocoön, and the Apollo Belvedere. But in 1818, Shelley wished to correct the "expressions of contempt

& desperation" in Byron's poetry and tended to overlook Byron's aesthetic which found a "refuge" in art:

> The Beings of the Mind are not of clay:
> Essentially immortal, they create
> And multiply in us a brighter ray
> And more beloved existence: that which Fate
> Prohibits to dull life in this our state
> Of mortal bondage. *(Childe Harold* IV.v)

But by 1821, Shelley doubted his own metaphysical assumptions about man's temporal perfectibility, and consequently he tended to overlook "the perverse ideas . . . not yet eradicated"[20] from Byron and instead praised Byron's "sublime" aesthetic which was essentially identical to that which he had read in *Childe Harold* IV:

> But thus all they
> Whose Intellect is an o'ermastering Power
> Which still recoils from its encumbering clay
> Or lightens it to spirit, whatsoe'er
> The form which their creations may essay,
> Are bards; the kindled Marble's bust may wear
> More poesy upon its speaking brow
> Than aught less than the Homeric page may bear;
> One noble stroke with a whole life may glow,
> Or deify the canvass till it shine
> With beauty so surpassing all below,
> That they who kneel to Idols so divine
> Break no commandment, for high Heaven is there
> Transfused, transfigured: and the line
> Of Poesy, which peoples but the air
> With Thought and Beings of our thought reflected,
> Can do no more. *(Prophecy of Dante* IV.20-36)

Unlike Shelley, Byron here did not premise his aesthetic on the imagination as a creative and moral power, but he did anticipate Shelley's judgments in *A Defence of Poetry* that "bards" or poets were not only writers but also "the authors of . . . music, of the dance and architecture, and statuary, and painting"; and that all of this "poetry redeems from decay the visitations of the divinity in Man."[21] According to Byron's Dante, when poets do "lend / Their thoughts to meaner beings," then "high Heaven is . . . / Transfused, transfigured" (IV.3-4, 32-33); but even the "Poets who have never penned / Their inspiration" have a "God within them" and after death they will rejoin "the stars" (IV.1-2, 5).

Having similarly used the stars to image the burning fountain to which Keats returned, Shelley was favorably disposed to Byron's conception of poets and poetry when he read *The Prophecy of Dante* in 1821. Moreover, Byron's depiction of Dante as one of "the unacknowledged legislators of the world" (albeit one whose legislation had not freed man from political tyranny in six hundred years) also pleased Shelley, because in *A Defence of Poetry* he had recently termed Dante "the first awakener of entranced Europe" and "the Lucifer of that starry flock which in the thirteenth century shone forth from republican Italy, as from a heaven, into the darkness of the benighted world." Dante's words, Shelley had written, were "instinct with spirit; each is as a spark, a burning atom of inextinguishable thought; and many yet lie covered in the ashes of their birth, and pregnant with a lightning which has yet found no conductor." Shelley had long been impressed by the "lightning" in Byron's own poetry, and now he was even more impressed to find in Byron's dramatic monologue a "conductor" of one of the "episodes to that great poem, which all poets, like the co-operating thoughts of one great mind, have built up since the beginning of the world."[22] Part of that single episode Shelley found in Dante's prophetic vision of Italian art:

> Art shall resume and equal even the sway
> Which with Apelles and old Phidias
> She held in Hellas' unforgotten day.
> Ye shall be taught by Ruin to revive
> The Grecian forms at least from their decay,
> And Roman souls at last again shall live
> In Roman works wrought by Italian hands,
> And temples, loftier than the old temples, give
> New wonders to the World.           (IV.41-49)

Shortly after he read these lines, Shelley himself turned to "Hellas' unforgotten day" and through his *Hellas* contributed to "that great poem" another episode that would "*suggest* the final triumph of the Greek cause as a portion of the cause of civilisation and social improvement" (Preface, my italics). But like Byron, Shelley in 1821 was far from confident that such a triumph could be achieved in a mutable world.

Shelley's praise for *The Prophecy of Dante* does not mean, however, that he accepted all of its judgments, particularly those recommending Promethean endurance. According to Byron and his persona Dante, the artist should "bear" the adverse world if he, "having lavished his high gift in vain, / Lies chained to his lone rock by the sea-shore" (IV.18-20). But Shelley, still believing that such endurance would be futile, preferred in the face of an unredeemable world to let "it die or rest at last" and to seek a final triumph "In a diviner clime" (*Hellas*, ll. 1101, 1005). Otherwise the artist, like Byron's Dante, was destined to be "long and deeply wrecked / On the lone rock of desolate Despair" (I.138-39), and Shelley sensed that Byron once more condoned the immoral effects of that despair. Despite Dante's claim to be free of thoughts of "Vengeance" and "Revenge" (I.100, 113), he suffered from the same circumscribed imagination that afflicted Beatrice Cenci:

> Great God!
> Take these thoughts from me—to thy hands I yield
> My many wrongs, and thine Almighty rod
> Will fall on those who smote me. (*Prophecy* I.118-21)

Dante's hate was directed at the city of his birth and he could not still his need for revenge at the end of his prophecy:

> Florence! when thy harsh sentence razed my roof,
> I loved thee; but the vengeance of my verse,
> The hate of injuries which every year
> Makes greater, and accumulates my curse,
> Shall live, outliving all thou holdest dear—
> Thy pride, thy wealth, thy freedom, and even *that,*
> The most infernal of all evils here,
> The sway of petty tyrants in a state. (IV.111-18)

Such vengeance, even when directed against tyranny, was unacceptable to Shelley, and its presence in *The Prophecy of Dante* caused Shelley to complain in October about "the perverse ideas . . . not yet eradicated" from Byron. And true to his moral principles, Shelley in *Hellas* still believed in the return of "Love for hate, and tears for blood" (l. 737) and perhaps with Byron's *Prophecy* in mind argued that

> Revenge and wrong bring forth their kind,
> The foul cubs like their parents are,
> Their den is in their guilty mind,
> And Conscience feeds them with despair. (ll. 729-32)

But in his letter to Byron on 14 September, Shelley did not object to Dante's "pernicious mistake" which, like that of Marino Faliero, justified personal vengeance, apparently because of his admiration for the "sublime" poetry of *The Prophecy*, which reproduced so many of his own ideas about poetry and life in 1821. Such admiration prompted Shelley to be more tolerant of any remaining deficiencies in Byron's moral system.

## IV

In 1821, Shelley's tolerance even extended to *Don Juan*. He had always admired the "form" of Byron's satire (in a style "infinitely better" than *Beppo*), but after hearing Byron read the first canto by October 1818 he objected to its "spirit," particularly in the "Dedication" which was "more like a mixture of wormwood & verdigrease than satire." [23] By January 1820 Shelley read "in print" *Don Juan* I-II and in spite of the omission of the animadversions against Southey in the "Dedication" and against Sir Samuel Romilly in stanza 15 of Canto I, he still informed Byron that the spirit of his poem was inferior to its form:

> I have read your 'Don Juan' in print, and I observed that the *murrain* has killed some of the finest of the flock, i.e., that your bookseller has omitted certain passages. *The personal ones, however, though I thought them wonderfully strong, I do not regret.* What a strange and terrible storm is that at sea, and the two fathers, how true, yet how strong a contrast! Dante hardly exceeds it. With what flashes of divine beauty have you not illuminated the familiarity of your subject towards the end! The love letter, and the account of its being written, is altogether a masterpiece of portraiture; of human nature laid with the eternal colours of the feelings of humanity. Where did you learn all these secrets? I should like to go to school there. *I cannot say I equally approve of the service to which this letter was appropriated; or that I altogether think the bitter mockery of our common nature, of which this is one of the expressions, quite worthy of your genius.* The power and the beauty and the wit, indeed, redeem all this— chiefly because they belie and refute it. [24]

By criticizing *Don Juan* as one of the "expressions" of Byron's "bitter mockery of our common nature," Shelley repeated his former objections to Byron's ideas: he saw in this satire the same spirit of "contempt & despair" that had marred the poetry of *Childe Harold* IV. Consequently, he questioned whether Byron had indeed satisfied the didactic intent of satire, which traditionally demands that the satirist provide, explicitly or implicitly, a moral imperative by which man can reform himself. Furthermore, Shelley in 1820 was still enough interested in reform to question whether a moral purpose could in fact justify the scourge of satire, for he feared that "Suffering makes suffering—ill must follow ill" ("A Satire on Satire," l. 36).

In Shelley's next three letters on *Don Juan*, all written in 1821, he no longer criticized Byron's "bitter mockery," partly because he himself doubted whether "our common nature" was worthy of his

defense and hopes. Still praising the form ("the poetical parts") of
Byron's satire in April 1821, Shelley, as in his September letter on
*The Prophecy of Dante*, chose not to criticize the objectionable spirit
informing parts of *Don Juan* I-II:

> The last work of yours I have seen is 'Don Juan', in the poetical
> parts of which you seem to have equalled the finest passages in
> your former poems; except the *curse* in 'Manfred', the stanzas
> in Chillon in the 3rd, and the address to Ocean, in the 4th Canto
> of 'Childe Harold'. You have now arrived about at the age at
> which those eternal poets, of whom we have authentic accounts,
> have ever begun their supreme poems; considering all their others,
> however transcendent, as the steps, the scaffolding, the exercise
> which may sustain and conduct them to their great work. If you
> are inferior to these, it is not in genius, but industry and resolu-
> tion. Oh, that you would subdue yourself to the great task of
> building up a poem containing within itself the germs of a perma-
> nent relation to the present, and to all succeeding ages! [25]

By urging Byron to write a great poem or epic for and of his age,
Shelley as in 1816 and 1818 was still trying to influence both the
form and spirit of his friend's poetry. In a letter of 16 July 1821,
Shelley reaffirmed his admiration of the forms of Byron's previous
" 'disjecti membra poetae,' " but urged that his friend "*ought*—and if
there is prophecy in hope, that you *will* write a great and connected
poem, which shall bear the same relation to this age as the 'Iliad', the
'Divina Commedia', and 'Paradise Lost' did to theirs." [26] Three weeks
later, Shelley found that his prophecy and hope were "in a certain
degree" fulfilled by the fifth canto of *Don Juan*:

> He has read to me one of the unpublished cantos [V] of Don
> Juan, which is astonishingly fine.—It sets him not above but far
> above all the poets of the day: every word has the stamp of
> immortality.—I despair of rivalling Lord Byron, as well I may:
> and there is no other with whom it is worth contending. This
> canto is in style, but totally, & sustained with incredible ease &
> power, like the end of the second canto: *there is not a word*
> *which the most rigid assertor of the dignity of human nature*
> *could desire to be cancelled*: it fulfills in a certain degree what
> I have long preached of producing something wholly new & rela-
> tive to the age—and yet surpassingly beautiful. It may be vanity,
> but *I think I see the trace of my earnest exhortations to him to*
> *create something wholly new*.[27]

Shelley had been attempting to urge something "wholly new" on

Byron since 1816, and he was particularly pleased to discover that
Byron's fifth canto virtually lacked the cynical digressions and tone
of the first two cantos and that *Don Juan* might therefore "become
a moral model" (V.2) in the traditional mode of satire. But of equal
importance to the change that Shelley perceived in Byron is the change
in Shelley's own perceptions of the "dignity of human nature." Byron
might claim to be more interested in "instructing than delighting"
(V.2), but the substance of that instruction had not materially changed
since 1818. Consequently, the Shelley of *Julian and Maddalo* would
not have so readily condoned Byron's judgments, through the character of Johnson, that "Men are the sport of circumstances" and that
"time strips our illusions of their hue" (V.17, 21). But the Shelley of
*Adonais* had seen such judgments confirmed and had already denied
his former illusion that perfected man could rule chance, death, and
mutability in a perfected world. Therefore, Shelley could now accept
Bryon's vision of the frailty of human life:

> To try if I could wrench aught out of death
> Which should confirm, or shake, or make a faith;
>
> But it was all a mystery. Here we are,
>     And there we go:—but *where*? five bits of lead,
> Or three, or two, or one, send very far!
>     And is this blood, then, formed but to be shed?
> Can every element our elements mar?
>     And air—earth—water—fire live—and we dead?
> *We*, whose minds comprehend all things? No more;
> But let us to the story as before.          (V.38-39)

Shelley had similarly phrased this same question in the second move-
ment of *Adonais* ("Nought we know, dies. Shall that alone which
knows / Be as a sword consumed before the sheath / By sightless
lightning?" [xx]), only to answer it by affirming that the death of
the elemental body was but a prelude to an immortal existence.
Within the next two months after his visit to Ravenna, Shelley would
discover that Byron had similarly affirmed man's immortality in *The
Prophecy of Dante* as well as in the third canto of *Don Juan*:

> My altars are the mountains and the ocean,
> Earth, air, stars,—all that springs from the great Whole,
> Who hath produced, and will receive the soul.          (III.104)

After Shelley read cantos III-V of *Don Juan* by 21 October 1821,
he more than ever praised both its form and its new spirit, and he was
disappointed that Byron intended to abandon, at least temporarily,
his unique satire:

Many thanks for Don Juan—It is a poem totally of its own species, & my wonder and delight at the grace of the composition no less than the free & grand vigour of the conception of it perpetually increase.—*The few passages which any one might desire to be cancelled in the 1st and 2d Cantos are here reduced almost to nothing.* This poem carries with it at once the stamp of originality and a defiance of imitation. Nothing has ever been written like it in English—nor if I may venture to prophesy, will there be; without carrying upon it the mark of a secondary and borrowed light. —*You unveil & present in its true deformity what is worst in human nature*, & this is what the witlings of the age murmur at, conscious of their want of power to endure the scrutiny of such a light.—*We are damned to the knowledge of good & evil, and it is well for us to know what we should avoid no less than what we should seek.*—The character of Lambro—his return—the merriment of his daughters guests made as it were in celebration of his funeral—the meeting with the lovers—and the death of Haidée,— are circumstances combined & developed in a manner that I seek elsewhere in vain. The fifth canto, which some of your pet Zoili in Albermarle St. said was *dull*, gathers instead of loses, splendour & energy—the language in which the whole is clothed—a sort of c[h] ameleon under the changing sky of the spirit that kindles it— is such as these lisping days could not have expected,—and are, believe me, in spite of the approbation which you wrest from them—little pleased to hear. One can hardly judge from recitation and it was not until I read it in print that I have been able to do it justice.—This sort of writing only on a great plan & perhaps in a more compact form is what I wished you to do when I made my vows for an epic.—But I am content—You are building up a drama, such as England has not yet seen, and the task is sufficiently noble & worthy of you.[28]

Shelley had not yet seen *Cain* when he wrote this letter and was therefore actually not "content" with Byron's decision to write drama instead of satire, for such dramas he feared were not only on "the wrong road" but also merely parts of the "'disjecti membra poetae'" which delayed Byron from expanding the "plan" of *Don Juan* into a great epic. Shelley's concern for Byron's enterprise reflects in part his dissatisfaction with his own epic, *The Revolt of Islam*, for he now shared Byron's belief that the "tree of Knowledge is not that of Life," and consequently recognized that his own epic's "beautiful idealisms of moral excellence" could not significantly reform the human condition. If he revised his epic, he would "*Materially* improve" it: "I have

many corrections to make in it, and one part will be wholly remod-
elled."[29] In any revised version, love would still be "celebrated . . .
as the sole law which should govern the moral world," but because
Shelley now realistically distinguished between what *should* and
*could* be accomplished, he would undoubtedly revise his epic's
"succession of pictures" which embodied his former enthusiastic
belief that love could "awaken public hope and . . . enlighten and
improve mankind" to bring about a "rapid . . . awakening of an
immense nation from their slavery and degradation to a true sense of
moral dignity and freedom" (Preface to *The Revolt of Islam*). Shelley
now doubted whether such social and political salvation could be uni-
versally achieved and instead agreed with his old adversary that "we
are damned to the knowledge of good & evil" and implied that neither
destiny nor free will could replace the tree of bitter knowledge with
the tree of life.

Although Shelley no longer believed that good could triumph
over evil, he still argued that it was "the province of the poet to attach
himself to those ideas which exalt and ennoble humanity" (note to
*Hellas*), and he also believed by 1821 that a poet could serve morality
through the "negative way" of satire. Retracting his former objections
to the scourge of satire, Shelley acknowledged his and what he thought
to be Byron's new morality by observing that "it is well for us to
know what we *should* avoid no less than what we *should* seek" (my
italics). Shelley now found moral imperatives in *Don Juan*, for the
"sad truth" of things which had once prompted Byron's "romantic"
fatalism was now treated in a "burlesque" fashion (IV.3): whereas
Byron had used "cabined, cribbed, confined" to describe the tragic
enslavement of man's reason in *Childe Harold* IV.cxxvii, he used the
identical phrase to describe Juan's comic condition while on Lambro's
ship destined for the slave market of Constantinople (IV.75). Juan's
eventual escape from this enslavement serves as a comic correlative to
the bard who in Canto III sang "The Isles of Greece," an impassioned
appeal that the Greeks "Dash down" their manacles. And Shelley
must have been particularly pleased to note that Byron concluded
this lyric by recalling his hope in *Childe Harold* III that "there may
be / Words which are things,—hopes which will not deceive" (cxiv):

> But words are things, and a small drop of ink,
>   Falling like dew, upon a thought, produces
> That which makes thousands, perhaps millions, think.
>
> (*Don Juan* III.88)

Shelley thus could hope that Byron would no longer dismiss such
"words" as mere creations of "desiring phantasy" in a "mind diseased"

as he had in 1817/18 (see *Childe Harold* IV.vii; cxxi-cxxii). And if Bryon seemed to recall his former "romantic" despair by exclaiming in *Don Juan*, "Oh, Love! what is it in this world of ours / Which makes it fatal to be loved" (III.2), Shelley would have judged that such a fatalism was more than enough belied and refuted by the witty treatment of love and marriage (III.3-11) and by the beautiful description of the love between Juan and Haidée, a love no more "fatal" than what Shelley himself acknowledged in *Epipsychidion*.

Because Shelley approved of Byron's new "spirit" and believed that Byron's epic was superior to his own, *The Revolt of Islam*, he again experienced feelings of insignificance in the shadow of Byron. But he could console himself by seeing at least a "trace" of his influence in *Don Juan*, an influence he evidently mentioned to Trelawny in 1822:

> "Yet, at Venice, I urged Byron to come out of the dismal 'wood of error' into the sun, to write something new and .cheerful. 'Don Juan' is the result. The poetry is superior to 'Childe Harold,' and the plan, or rather want of plan, gives scope to his astonishing natural powers." [30]

Had Shelley read Cantos VI-VII, he might not have so readily claimed that Byron had escaped from the " 'wood of error,' " for his old adversary resumed his cynical assaults on the "dignity of human nature." But by June 1822 (when these two cantos were completed), Shelley had already written his own poem on the *triumph* of life over man's spirit and had approved of Byron's portrayal of "mortal nature's nothingness" in *Cain* (II.ii.422); consequently he might not have been disturbed by Byron's increasing doubts about man's "soul or mind," "*Knowledge*," and even "*ultimate* existence" (VI.22, 63) or by Byron's "holding up the Nothingness of life" (VII.6) once more.

V

In his conversations with Trelawny, Shelley could have more accurately claimed a direct influence on *The Vision of Judgment*, which Byron completed after Shelley visited him in Ravenna. As in Venice in 1818, Byron and Shelley in 1821 discussed their mutual dislike for Robert Southey and his self-righteous opinions in the *Quarterly Review*, and these discussions caused Byron each time to intensify his attacks on the poet laureate. In Venice, however, Shelley neither approved nor requested these attacks; instead, he complained that the "Dedication" to *Don Juan* was "more like a mixture of wormwood & verdigrease than satire." And by 1820 Shelley still disapproved of such invectives, believing that Southey would be better served by "friendship's gentle tone" rather than by the satirist's scourge ("A Satire on Satire"). But by 1821 Shelley had had enough: because he believed that Southey had written or at least sanctioned the savage criticism on Hunt, Keats, and himself during the past four years in the *Quarterly Review*, and because he no longer associated satire with "the dismal 'wood of error,'" he now directed Byron "to attack the Quarterly"[31] in the hopes that Southey would once more feel the scourge of Bryon's satire. In the words of "A Satire on Satire," Shelley still believed that "Suffering makes suffering—ill must follow ill" (l. 36), but he was no longer able to check his desire for revenge:

> who that has seen
> What Southey is and was, would not exclaim,
> "Lash on!" and be the keen verse dipped in flame;
> Follow his flight on wingèd words, and urge
> The strokes of the inexorable scourge.        (ll. 22-26)

Having given similar advice to Byron in August 1821, Shelley must have recognized its effect when he read *The Vision of Judgment* in November.

Shelley's influence on *The Vision of Judgment*, even though the poem was begun before his August visit in Ravenna, recalls his former influence on Byron's public pronouncements against Southey. Prior to Shelley's arrival in Venice on 23 August 1818, Byron had already written portions of the "Dedication" and Canto I of *Don Juan*, the first draft of which was finished by 6 September. But between 6 September and 11 November, that is, during and after Byron and Shelley's occasional visits with each other from August through October at which time they complained about Southey and the *Quarterly Review*, Byron renewed his attack on the poet laureate: to the "Dedication," he added stanza 3 ("You, Bob! are rather insolent, you know,/ . . . And fall, for lack of moisture quite a-dry, Bob!") and stanza 11 (with its alternative couplet, "Would *he* [Milton] subside into a hackney Laureate? / A scribbling self-sold soul-hired scorned Iscariot"); to Canto I, he added stanza 205 (with the "so quaint and mouthey" Southey); and in a prose preface intended for *Don Juan*, he wrote that the apostate Southey had been "reduced to prey upon such Snatches of fame as his contributions to the Quarterly Review . . . can afford him—by the abuse of whosoever may be more consistent—or more successful than himself;—and the provincial gang of scribblers gathered round him."[32] Byron's animadversions here against Southey and his "gang of scribblers" partly resulted from Southey's "abuse" of Shelley ("whosoever may be more consistent"), an abuse that Byron may have found in Southey's essay "Rise and Progress of

Popular Disaffection," appearing in the *Quarterly Review* of January 1817. This essay seems to attack Shelley, the "Hermit of Marlow" who wrote *A Proposal for Putting Reform to the Vote*, but if Byron or even Shelley did not know about this review,[33] they were sufficiently angered by reading the review of Leigh Hunt's *Foliage* in the *Quarterly* for January 1818, wherein Shelley was rebuked in a footnote as the author of *Laon and Cythna*,

> the production of a man of some ability, and possessing itself some beauty; but we are in doubt, whether it would be morally right to lend it notoriety by any comments. We know the author's disgraceful and flagitious history well, and could put down some of the vain boasting of his preface. At Eton we remember him notorious for setting fire to old trees with burning glasses, no unmeet emblem for a man, who perverts his ingenuity and knowledge to the attacking of all that is ancient and venerable in our civil and religious institutions.

Because Southey had once called Shelley "the *blackest of villains*" and had "said, on his return from Switzerland two years ago, that 'Shelley and [Byron] were in a league of Incest,' " the two poets readily concluded that Southey was the "dirty, lying rascal" who had in this review "attacked Shelley in an oblique and shabby manner." [34] And in the spirit of such a conclusion, Byron had more than enough reason to inveigh against Southey in his additions to *Don Juan*.

In 1818 Shelley neither requested nor sanctioned Byron's renewed attack on Southey, but in 1821 he uncharacteristically suspended his moral opposition to revenge and directed Byron to attack their adversary once more. In the interim, Shelley and *The Revolt of Islam* had been condemned in the April 1819 *Quarterly*, and in June 1820 Shelley wrote to ask Southey if he was the "unprincipled hireling" who had slandered him. Southey replied that he was not, but used the opportunity to condemn Shelley's unorthodox life and opinions. In response, Shelley defended his principles in a letter of 17 August, but he was further angered when his own life was likened to that of the Cenci in Southey's second letter:

> You have sought for temptation and courted it; you have reasoned yourself into a state of mind so pernicious that your character, with your domestic arrangements, as you term it, might furnish the subject for the drama more instructive, and scarcely less painful, than the detestable story of the Cenci, and this has proceeded directly from your principles.[35]

Ironically enough, Shelley did adopt the Cenci principle of revenge and began to attack Southey and the *Quarterly* by drafting a letter to its editor, William Gifford. In this letter, which apparently was neither completed nor sent, Shelley condemned first the anonymous "wretch" who had reviewed *The Revolt of Islam* in 1819 and then the anonymous reviewer of Keats's *Endymion* in 1818. Shelley argued that this savage review had so affected Keats that insanity had led to consumption "from which there are now but faint hopes of his recovery."[36] Blaming the *Quarterly* as he did, Shelley intensified his attack after he learned that Keats did not recover: in a letter to Byron on 16 April 1821, he complained that Keats died "from the consequences of breaking a blood-vessel, in paroxysms of despair at the contemptuous attack on his book in the *Quarterly Review*";[37] in *Adonais*, he condemned the "viperous murderer" (xxxvi) who had reviewed *Endymion*; in a canceled Preface to his elegy, he argued that Gifford and "Mr. Southey especially" shared the blame "in permitting to their subordinate associates so great a licence, not of praise which can do little mischief, but of censure which may destroy—and has destroyed one of the noblest specimens of the workmanship of God";[38] and in the received Preface he denounced the *Quarterly* reviewers and labeled Southey, although not by name, "a most base and unprincipled calumniator." In order to keep Byron informed of his reponse to the *Quarterly*, Shelley on 16 July sent him a copy of *Adonais* and explained,

> I have been unwillingly, and in spite of myself, induced to notice the attack of the *Quarterly* upon me; it would have been affectation to have omitted the few words in which I allude to it. I have sought *not* to qualify the contempt from which my silence has hitherto sprung—and at the same time to prevent any paper war, as it regards my case; which, averse as I am from all wars, is the only one which I should unconditionally avoid. I have had some correspondence with Southey on the subject, who denies that he is the author of the article upon the 'Revolt of Islam'; and I learn that it lies between the Rev. Mr. Milman and Mr. Gifford. There for the present it rests.[39]

But Shelley did not let the matter rest; a month later in Ravenna he was not so "averse" to a paper war and he purposefully enlisted Byron to attack the *Quarterly*.

Shelley's request was extremely well timed, for Byron in August discovered that the *Quarterly* was "itching to assail" him, and he had already been angered by the libels against the "Satanic School" in Southey's Preface to *A Vision of Judgment*. Byron had written only a few stanzas of his own *Vision of Judgment* on 7 May 1821 (that

*193*

is, three months before Shelley's visit), but after Shelley left, Byron took up the "attack" as he had promised: on 31 August, he warned Murray that if the *Quarterly* continued its present policies, he would "give Mr. Milman [whom Shelley suspected as the hostile reviewer of *The Revolt of Islam*], and others of the crew, something that shall occupy their dreams"; on 4 September, he sent Murray a note to the Appendix of *The Two Foscari* in which he defended Shelley's poetry against those who were "blinded by baseness and bigotry," rebuked Southey for the calumnies "which he scattered abroad on his return from Switzerland against me and others [including Shelley]," and defended himself and Shelley against Southey's charge that they made up a " 'Satanic School' " which threatened "the religion of the country"; and on approximately 20 September (after finishing and sending *Cain* to Murray), he resumed *The Vision of Judgment*, finished "about sixty stanzas" by 1 October, and sent Murray the finished "106 stanzas" on 4 October.[40] In the Preface to his satire, Byron once more defended Shelley against membership in "a supposed 'Satanic School' " by describing him as one of the writers who, "in their individual capacities, have done more good, in the charities of life, to their fellow-creatures, in any one year, than Mr. Southey has done harm to himself by his absurdities in his whole life."[41]

Byron defended Shelley in this manner but without specifically mentioning him by name, apparently because he respected Shelley's desire to avoid a "paper war" with Southey and the *Quarterly Review*.[42] But after Shelley discovered the veiled references to himself in the Preface to *The Vision of Judgment* (which he read by early November) and in the note in the Appendix to *The Two Foscari* (which he read perhaps in November but no later than January 1822), he feared that his part in Byron's attack on Southey was still too apparent. Having received a warning in September to "expect a fresh stab from Southey whenever he has an opportunity,"[43] Shelley did not wish to provoke Southey and consequently avoided any praise of *The Vision of Judgment* in his correspondence. But his liking for Byron's latest satire is, I believe, sufficiently evident: Shelley read "aloud 'The Vision of Judgment' " on the evening of 9 November 1821, and Edward Williams seems to echo Shelley by judging it "a sublime composition which displays the greatness of his genius above any other of his works; but I am in doubt if it can be published or rather I fear no publisher can be found for it in these times"; in January 1821, Shelley seems to have included Byron's satire on Southey (together with *The Prophecy of Dante, Don Juan,* and *Cain*) among the enviable "late works of this spirit of an angel" which he had discovered in Byron during the last months of 1821; and on 4 July 1822, four days before he died and three months before *The Vision of Judgment* appeared in *The Liberal*, Shelley judged it would be *"more* than enough to set up the Journal"[44] that he, Byron, and Leigh Hunt planned to publish. Shelley, therefore, seemed to condone and enjoy Byron's latest satire: in October 1821, he read *Don Juan* III without objecting to Byron's occasional ridicule of Southey (see stanzas 79, 93-94, 97); and if he had any second thoughts about enjoying this revenge, he could easily justify Byron's "bitter mockery" of Southey by claiming for *The Vision of Judgment*, as he had for *Don Juan* I-II, that "the power and the beauty and the wit, indeed, redeem all this—chiefly because they belie and refute it."[45]

VI

Because Shelley would not openly sanction *The Vision of Judgment* for fear of retaliation from Southey and the *Quarterly Review*, he appears to have compensated Byron by openly praising *Cain: A Mystery*, which he read in manuscript and judged "second to nothing of the kind" by 4 November 1821,[46] three days after Byron arrived in Pisa. *Cain* was published with *Sardanapalus* and *The Two Foscari* on 19 December, and in January 1822 Shelley asked Peacock about Byron's "last volume, & if you before thought him a great Poet what is your opinion now that you have read *Cain*." Shelley hadn't yet read the other two dramas, but his enthusiasm for *Cain* caused him to ask John Gisborne on 12 January,

> What think you of Lord Byron now? Space wondered less at the swift and fair creations of God, when he grew weary of vacancy, than I at the late works of this spirit of an angel in the mortal paradise of a decaying body.

Two weeks later he again remarked to Gisborne that "Cain is apocalyptic—it is a revelation not before communicated to man."[47]

Byron may have discussed his writing of *Cain* while the two poets were together in Ravenna, for a month later Shelley predicted that Byron would "produce something very great; and that familiarity with the dramatic power of human nature, will soon enable him to soften down the severe and unharmonising traits of his 'Marino Faliero.'"[48] And such deficiencies were indeed eliminated in *Cain*: Byron had turned from the historical drama and its "unharmonising" demand for long speeches of exposition to a speculative drama that encouraged frequent and rapid questions and answers; instead of the Doge's "severe" and lengthy descriptions of his conflicts and character, Cain reveals character in dramatic conflict, especially with Lucifer

*195*

and Adah, the two characters who represent Cain's antagonistic desires for knowledge and love. Byron still maintained the dramatic unity of time, but he violated the unity of place in order to dramatize Cain's choice of knowledge over love, that is, his departure from Adah in order to journey through the abyss of space with Lucifer. With that freedom, Byron further explored the contraries of life and death, good and evil, love and knowledge in this second of his "metaphysical" dramas. Like *Manfred, Cain* demonstrated to Shelley that Byron could achieve a "freedom from common rules," [49] the same rules that had restricted Byron's genius in *Marino Faliero.*

Many of Byron's contemporaries judged that the "freedom" in *Cain* was more theological than artistic, and they cited what they believed to be Shelley's atheistical influence on it. His London friends, Byron told Trelawny, thought that *Cain* was "a suggestion of Shelley"; Richard Carlile in *The Republican* declared that " 'Cain, a Mystery,' is an Atheistical poem, the groundwork of which is borrowed from Shelley's Queen Mab"; a "Letter from Paddy" in *Blackwood's Edinburgh Magazine* observed that "since Shelley has been with [Byron], he has written 'Cain' "; and Thomas Moore complained that

> Boldness, and even licence, in politics, does good, . . . but, in religion, it profits neither here nor hereafter; and, for myself, such a horror have I of both extremes on this subject, that I know not *which* I hate most, the bold, damning bigot, or the bold, annihilating infidel. . . . You will easily guess that, in all this, I am thinking not so much of you, as of a friend and, at present, companion of yours, whose influence over your mind . . . I dread and deprecate most earnestly.[50]

Shelley, however, denied any such influence and stressed that he and Byron still differed in their irreligious notions:

> Lord Byron has read me one or two letters of Moore to him, in which Moore speaks with great kindness of me; & of course I cannot but feel flattered by the approbation of a man, my inferiority to whom I am proud to acknowledge.—Amongst other things, however, Moore, after giving Lord B. much good advice about public opinion &c. seems to deprecate *my* influence over his mind on the subject of religion, & to attribute the tone assumed in Cain to my suggestions.—Moore cautions him against my influence on this particular with the most friendly zeal, & it is plain that his motive springs from a desire of benefiting Lord B. without degrading me.—I think you know Moore.—Pray assure him that I have not the smallest influence over Lord Byron in this particular; if I had I certainly should employ it *to eradicate from his great*

*mind the delusions of Christianity*, which in spite of his reason, seem perpetually to recur, & to lay in ambush for the hours of sickness & distress. Cain was *conceived* many years ago, & begun before I saw him last year at Ravenna; how happy should I not be to attribute to myself, however indirectly, any participation in that immortal work.[51]

Byron's friends might have judged *Cain* to be unorthodox because Lucifer identifies God as the source of evil, but Shelley believed that Byron's drama still embodied the traditional "delusions of Christianity," that is, the Christian belief in a personal as well as a vindictive God. "There is no [such] God," Shelley argued in *Queen Mab*; and in *The Revolt of Islam, Prometheus Unbound,* and *The Cenci* he tried to eradicate the anthropomorphic conception of a vengeful deity. But Byron, Shelley concluded, had failed to profit from reading his four major poems.

Byron seems to have anticipated that he would be accused of imitating the atheistic Shelley, for less than a week before he finished *Cain* he sent to Murray a note (to "annex to the *Foscaris*" which would be published with *Cain*) wherein he emphasized that his and Shelley's metaphysics were quite different:

Another charge made, I am told, in the 'Literary Gazette' [19 May 1821, p. 308] is, that I wrote the notes to 'Queen Mab;' a work which I never saw till some time after its publication, and which I recollect showing to Mr. Sotheby as a poem of great power and imagination. I never wrote a line of the notes, nor ever saw them except in their published form. No one knows better than their real author, that his opinions and mine differ materially upon the metaphysical portion of that work; though in common with all who are not blinded by baseness and bigotry, I highly admire the poetry of that and his other publications.[52]

By distinguishing the "spirit" of his own poetry from Shelley's, Byron obviously hoped to forestall any criticism that *Cain*, even though it was written in Ravenna and begun before Shelley's visit, was a product of the "Satanic School" of Pisan poets. But by "highly" praising the "poetry" of Shelley's works, particularly *Queen Mab*, Byron inadvertently gives us reason to suspect that the "form" of Shelley's poetry was responsible for the mythic dimensions of his latest drama. Thomas Medwin suspected part of this influence, concluded that "Byron owes to Shelley the platonic idea of the Hades,—the pre-adamite worlds, and their phantasmal shapes, perhaps suggested by Lucian's Icaro Menippus," and even "taxed" Byron for "having plagiarized his lines in 'Cain' from

Earth's distant orb appeared
The smallest light that twinkles in the heavens;
Whilst round the chariot's way
Innumerable systems rolled,
And countless spheres diffused
An ever varying glory, &c.          [*Queen Mab* I.250-55]."[53]

Medwin, however, didn't go far enough, for he could have easily compared Queen Mab's flight in the "magic car" to educate Ianthe,

This is thine high reward:—the past shall rise;
Thou shalt behold the present; I will teach
The secrets of the future,          (II.65-67)

with Lucifer's education of Cain during their flight through the abyss
of space:

but fly with me o'er the gulf
Of space an equal flight, and I will show
What thou dar'st not deny—the history
Of past and present and of future worlds.          (II.i.22-25)

Despite this and many other parallels between these two poems,
*Cain* verifies Byron's judgment in September 1821 that his and
Shelley's opinions "differ materially upon the metaphysical portion"
of *Queen Mab*.[54] Mab shows Ianthe a "future" in which "Reason and
passion cease to combat" in man, for whom "A garden shall arise, in
loveliness / Surpassing fabled Eden" (VIII.231; IV.88-89). But Lucifer
argues for Byron that reason and passion or knowledge and love are
mutually exclusive (I.420-33) and that future man will inherit only
the bitter fruits of his worst, his second fall:

First-born of the first man,
Thy present state of sin—and thou art evil—
Of sorrow—and thou sufferest—are both Eden
In all its innocence compared to what
*Thou* shortly may'st be; and that state again
In its redoubled wretchedness, a Paradise
To what thy sons' sons' sons, accumulating
In generations like to dust (which they
In fact but add to), shall endure and do.          (II.ii.219-27)

Opposing Shelley's judgment in 1813 that "care and sorrow, impo-
tence and crime, / Languor, disease, and ignorance" (IX.9-10) will be
eliminated from human society, Byron argues through Lucifer that
evil is everlasting: "it must still roll on the same, / A part of all things"
(II.ii.236-37). Such a vision also contradicts Shelley's hope in *Prome-*

*theus Unbound* that man will grow "wise and kind, / And veil by veil, evil and error fall" until "All things . . . put their evil nature off" (III.iii.61-62; iv.77). In effect, Byron's *Cain* invalidates the liberating effects of the human imagination by reproducing only the expository action of *Prometheus Unbound*: wisdom (Prometheus and Cain) is enslaved by its own perversion (Jupiter and Lucifer) and simultaneously separated from redemptive love (Asia and Adah). Whereas such action is reversed in Shelley's drama of imaginative self-liberation, it is confirmed as the "everlasting *to be* which *hath been*" (*Ode on Venice*, l. 59) in Byron's drama of self-enslavement.

What Cain needed, according to the logic of Shelley's *Prometheus Unbound* and *Essay on Christianity*, was a Demogorgon—a divine "model thro which the excellence of man is to be estimated," an excellence achieved by Prometheus' imaginative liberation, dethronement of Jupiter, and reunion with Asia. But Cain had for his divine "model" a mere anthropomorphic representation of his own conflicting tendencies toward good and evil, and thus suffered, albeit anachronistically, from the same "delusions of Christianity, which in spite of his reason, seem perpetually to recur" in Byron. By means of Cain's self-inquiry (his "own / Dissatisfied and curious thoughts" being externalized in the character of Lucifer [I.402-3]), he inductively reasons to and creates "the great double myst'ries, the *two principles*" and concludes that "Evil and good are things in their own essence" and that "good and evil seem / To have no pow'r themselves, save in [God's] will" (II.ii.404; 452; III.274-75). Such conclusions deny Shelley's faith in a unitary Demogorgon and his belief in *Queen Mab* that good and evil are relative and human rather than absolute and divine frames of reference: "there is neither good nor evil in the universe, *otherwise than as the events to which we apply these epithets have relation to our own peculiar mode of being.*" [55] Byron in *Cain*, therefore, may have appropriated Shelley's lines in *The Revolt of Islam* that

> Two Powers o'er mortal things dominion hold,
> Ruling the world with a divided lot,
> Immortal, all-pervading, manifold,
> Twin Genii, equal Gods,                    (I.xxv)

but he did not accept Shelley's qualification that these Manichaean "Powers" of good and evil were created ("they burst the womb of inessential Nought") by man himself ("when life and thought / Sprang forth"). That the conflict between these "equal Gods" in *The Revolt of Islam* is "symbolic of the conflict between the good and evil powers

within man, not between powers anterior to man"[56] is further demonstrated by Shelley's *On the Devil, and Devils*:

> To suppose that the world was created and is superintended by
> two spirits of a balanced power and opposite dispositions, is sim-
> ply a personification of the struggle which we experience within
> ourselves, and which we perceive in the operations of external
> things as they affect us, between good and evil.

When the "vulgar," Shelley continues, give an objective reality to their
personifications, they "arrive at the familiar notions of God and the
Devil."[57] Both Byron and Cain, according to Shelley, shared these
"vulgar" delusions and consequently enslaved themselves in a world
of their own making—a world they erroneously believed to be "created and . . . superintended by" coeternal principles of good and evil.

Shelley did not, however, voice these objections to Byron's
Manichaeism when he praised *Cain* in his letters to Peacock and Gisborne, partly because he believed that the apocalyptic "form" of the
drama belied once again Byron's fatalistic "spirit" and partly because
in 1821 he could more readily accept Byron's fatalism. Shelley still
believed that the "perfection of the human and the divine character"
was identical and that "God is a model thro which the excellence of
man is to be estimated, whilst the *abstract* perfection of the human
character is the type of the *actual* perfection of the divine,"[58] but
he now doubted whether man could realize that perfection in this
world. Thus Shelley in 1821 could simultaneously reject Byron's
Manichaean theology and yet accept the consequences of that theology:
he and Byron might wrangle e'er so long on whether God's malevolence or man's willful ill caused man to fall, but he himself suggested
in the concluding chorus to *Hellas* that man could not escape his fallen
nature:

> O cease! must hate and death return?
> Cease! must men kill and die?
> Cease! drain not to its dregs the urn
>     Of bitter prophecy.                    (ll. 1096-99)

Shelley wrote these lines either soon before or soon after he read
*Cain*:[59] if before, he was prepared, albeit reluctantly, to discover in
Byron's "apocalyptic . . . revelation not before communicated to man"
that the prophetic urn had been drained to its "dregs" and that "hate
and death" were immedicable conditions of man; if after, then he was
urging Byron to "cease" writing such bitter prophecies, for he feared
that Byron's vision of man's inheritance from Cain was all too accurate.
Shelley in one note on *Hellas* also seems to be recommending that in

future poems Byron disregard the "Gordian knot of the origin of evil" ("concerning which all men are equally ignorant") and instead "attach himself to those ideas which exalt and ennoble humanity." Whether or not this note was written after Shelley read *Cain*, it helps to explain his very complex reaction to Byron's drama: *Cain* was in error because it embodied the "delusions of Christianity," especially the

> received hypothesis [that] a Being resembling men in the moral attributes of his nature, having called us out of non-existence, and after inflicting on us the misery of the commission of error, should superadd that of the punishment and the privations consequent upon it.

But Byron's faulty premises did not, according to Shelley, necessarily invalidate the conclusion in *Cain* that man in this world is subject to the inheritance of "hate and death." Shelley would have preferred Byron to "exalt and ennoble humanity" by concluding "that eternity is the inheritance of every thinking being," [60] but he could not refuse his assent to Byron's judgments about man's painful earthly condition.

## VII

By early November 1821, three months after he announced to Mary that he despaired "of rivalling Lord Byron," Shelley had read and praised four of Byron's most recent works, *The Prophecy of Dante, Don Juan* III-V, *The Vision of Judgment*, and *Cain: A Mystery*, all of which made him feel more insignificant in the shadow of Byron. Shelley probably recognized the "trace" of his influence on these works, even though each denied his former Promethean faith that man could be perfected in this world. But because he himself doubted much of what he had formerly affirmed, Shelley neither objected to Byron's portrayal or ridicule of man's imperfections nor planned to engage his old antagonist in a poetical debate about the human condition. Shelley conceded victory to Byron in this debate on the subject of man's inheritance in this world, although he still believed that the "delusions of Christianity" kept Byron from properly considering man's inheritance in eternity. But Shelley confessed that he had "not the smallest influence over Lord Byron in this particular" and consequently gave up attempting "to eradicate from his great mind" these delusions. Instead, he attempted to live unenviously in the shadow of this "great mind" which had confirmed its power and fame in four recent poems. Deferring to Byron's genius, Shelley in Pisa addressed the following sonnet to his famous friend:

> If I esteemed you less, Envy would kill

Pleasure, and leave to wonder and despair
The ministration of the thoughts that fill
My mind, which, like a worm whose life may share
A portion of the Unapproachable,
Marks your creations rise, as fast and fair
As perfect worlds at the Creator's will,
And bows itself before the Godhead there.

But such is my regard, that, nor your fame
Cast on the present by the coming hour
Nor your well-won prosperity and power
Move one regret for his unhonoured name
Who dares these words.—The worm beneath the sod
May lift itself in worship to the God.[61]

Shelley, however, protests a bit too much here, for in 1822 he experienced more than "one regret for his unhonoured name," and his "Envy" for Byron did eventually destroy the "Pleasure" of their friendship.

SERPENTS IN THE DEEP
AND GODS IN THE HEAVEN: THE TRIUMPH
OF LIFE-IN-DEATH

In August 1821, Shelley announced to Mary that his "greatest content would be utterly to desert all human society," but he reluctantly accepted the "other side of the alternative . . . to form for ourselves a society of our own class, as much as possible, in intellect or in feelings."[1] When Byron joined Shelley and Mary in Pisa on 1 November, that society was nearly complete: in addition to Teresa Guiccioli and the Gambas (who had preceded Byron by two months), there were Edward and Jane Williams (who had arrived in Pisa in January) and John Taaffe (who had made Shelley's acquaintance in November 1820); Thomas Medwin had left Pisa in February 1821 but returned on 14 November, Edward Trelawny arrived on 14 January 1822, and Shelley hoped that Leigh Hunt and his family would quickly join this literary society. Byron had not brought Allegra with him, and Shelley was disappointed to learn that she still remained in the convent at Bagnacavallo. And by 11 December, he apparently wished not a little to unsettle Byron, for he invited Claire to join them in Pisa. At the same time, he informed Claire that the "Pisan circle" had not pleased him in its early stages:

> The Exotic as you please to call me droops in this frost—a frost both moral & physical—a solitude of the heart—These late days I have been unable to ride—the cold towards sunset is so excessive & my side reminding me that I am mortal. Medwin rides almost constantly with Lord B[yron] & the party sometimes consists of Gamba, Taaffe Medwin & the Exotic who unfortunately belonging to the order of mimosa thrives ill in so large a society. I cannot endure the company of many persons, & the society of one is either great pleasure or great pain.[2]

The "frost" of Shelley's winter in Pisa is partially adducible to his difficulties in living with Mary ("The cold chaste Moon" who had before occasioned "frost" and "a death of ice" [*Epipsychidion*, ll. 281, 313, 316]), but an equal if not greater cause is to be found in his increasingly strained relationship with Byron, his almost daily companion from 1 November until Shelley himself left Pisa on 27 April.[3] Part of Shelley's aggravation resulted from his invidious office of mediator in the unresolved disputes between Byron and Claire concerning their daughter and also between Byron and Leigh Hunt for the purpose of establishing a journal, eventually published in October 1822 as *The Liberal*. But Shelley's greatest discontent from August 1821 until his death on 8 July 1822 resulted from his "despair of rivalling Lord Byron" and his belief that "there is no other with whom it is worth contending."

Not long after the two poets were together in Pisa, Shelley attempted to give poetic form to his feelings in relation to Byron: as the "worm beneath the sod" (a metaphor embodying "the Snake," Byron's nickname for him), Shelley lifted himself "in worship to the God" and envied not only the "power" of Byron's most recent works but also the "fame" and "prosperity" of his rival (*Sonnet to Byron*). This envy of Byron's fame and money surfaced in August when Shelley tried to explain the reasons for his "despair." Writing to Mary from Ravenna that Byron had "finished his *life* up to the present time & given it to Moore," Shelley emphasized that Moore had sold these memoirs "to Murray for *two thousand pounds*":

> I wish I had been in time to have interceded for a part of it for poor Hunt.—I have spoken to him [Byron] of Hunt, but not with a direct view of demanding a contribution; & though I am sure that if asked it would not be refused—*yet there is something in me, that makes it impossible.*—Lord Byron & I are excellent friends, & were I reduced to poverty, or *were I a writer who had no claims to a higher station than I posess* [sic]—or did I posess a higher than I deserve, we should appear in all things as such, & I would freely ask him any favour. *Such is not now the case—The demon of mistrust & of pride lurks between two persons in our situation. . . . I think the fault is not on my side; nor is it likely, I being the weaker. . . . What is passing in the heart of another rarely escapes the observation of one who is a strict anatomist of his own.*[4]

But Shelley was partly at "fault" and more correctly anatomized his own envy of the *"two thousand pounds"* and "higher station" in a letter he wrote at approximately the same time to Peacock:

> I write nothing, and probably shall write no more. It offends me to see my name classed among those who have no name. If I cannot be something better, I had rather be nothing. . . . My

motive was never the infirm desire of fame; and if I should continue an author, I feel that I should desire it. This cup is justly given to one only of an age [Byron]; indeed, participation would make it worthless: and unfortunate they who seek it and find it not.[5]

Shelley was trapped by his own logic: because he did "continue an author" he did experience "the infirm desire of fame." But ruled by the "demon of . . . pride" and the belief that "participation would make [the cup of fame] worthless," he had second thoughts about joining Byron and Hunt in publishing a journal. After returning to Pisa from Ravenna, he wrote Hunt that Byron "proposes that you should come and go shares with him and me, in a periodical work . . . in which each of the contracting parties should publish all their original compositions, and share the profits"; but, Shelley insisted, "*nothing would induce me to share in the profits, and still less in the borrowed splendour, of such a partnership*," and he repeated that he desired to be "nothing" and confessed that he could not even ask Byron for money to help pay Hunt's travel expenses to Italy.[6] Shelley in effect desired to rival Byron by achieving for himself the fame and money of which he felt unjustly deprived, and he confessed this desire in an infrequently quoted remark one month later. Requesting Ollier to print Mary Shelley's romance, *Castruccio, Prince of Lucca* in half volumes and on thin paper which would be sent to Pisa for corrections, Shelley added:

> Lord Byron has his works sent in this manner; and no person, who has either *fame* to lose or *money* to win, ought to publish in any other manner [my italics].
>
> By-the-bye, how do I stand with regard to these two great objects [fame and money] of human pursuit? I *once* sought something nobler and better than either; but I might as well have reached at the moon, and now, finding that I have grasped the air, I should not be sorry to know what substantial sum, especially of the former, is in your hands on my account.

That Byron's success prompted Shelley's concern for fame and money is beyond question; and that Shelley's envy of Byron was affecting his writing is suggested by a "riddle" Shelley added in the next paragraph of his letter to Ollier:

> *Charles the First* is conceived, but not born. Unless I am sure of making something good, the play will not be written. Pride, that ruined Satan, will kill *Charles the First*, for his midwife would be only *less than him whom thunder has made greater* [*Paradise Lost* I.257-58; see also VI.824-66].[7]

The solution to this riddle is quite simple, particularly when we recall Shelley's fear in Ravenna that the "demon of . . . pride" might destroy his relationship with Byron: Shelley was to Byron as Satan was to God, and his pride dictated that he would write *Charles the First* only if it could help him in his battle for fame against Byron, "*him whom thunder* [of public recognition] *has made greater.*" Thus Shelley's later posturing as the lowly "worm beneath the sod" lifting "itself in worship to the God" of Byron's talents (*Sonnet to Byron*) must be read for its diabolical irony: Shelley's protestations merely masked his Satanic desire to wrest from Byron the "Paradise of fame" ("The False Laurel and the True," l. 5).

By means of his allusions to *Paradise Lost* in this letter and poem (and elsewhere during 1821/22), Shelley in effect called upon Milton to witness his moral transformation from Prometheus into Satan during the past three years. No longer willing to live in the shadow of Byron's fame, Shelley keenly experienced the pride of Satan who questioned, "Know ye not mee?" and who affirmed, "If I must contend, said he, / Best with the best . . . / . . . more glory will be won. / Or less be lost" (*Paradise Lost* IV.828, 851-54). We can be certain that Shelley knew this particular speech: not only did he twice allude to a part of it ("there sitting where ye durst not soar" [IV.829]) in *Adonais* (xxxviii) and in his unfinished letter to William Gifford;[8] but he also had used the "Know ye not mee" speech to reveal Prometheus' pride in Act I of *Prometheus Unbound*:

> Know ye not me,
> The Titan? He who made his agony
> The barrier to your else all-conquering foe?
> . . . . . . . . . . . . . . me alone, who check'd,
> As one who checks a fiend-drawn charioteer,
> The falsehood and the force of him who reigns
> Supreme. (ll. 117-28)

In 1818, however, Shelley gave Satanic pride to Prometheus only to serve as that from which Prometheus was redeemed by recalling the curse; in the words of the Preface, Shelley's hero, in his redeemed state, was "exempt from the taints of ambition, envy, revenge, and a desire for personal aggrandisement, which in the Hero [Satan] of Paradise Lost, interfere with the interest." Shelley in 1818 could identify his personal morality with that of Prometheus; but by 1821, he, unlike Prometheus yet like Satan, was *not* exempt from "ambition, envy, revenge [consider his reaction to the *Quarterly Review*], and a desire for personal aggrandisement," all of which developed because of his association with Lord Byron.

Shelley's conception of himself in relation to Satan, Milton, Byron, and God—a strange company indeed—began to take form while he was writing *Adonais*, wherein he lamented Milton's death (iv), praised Byron as the "Pilgrim of Eternity," and chose Urania, Milton's Muse in *Paradise Lost*, to be the widowed mother of Adonais. When Urania, who is also the mother of Milton, Byron, Moore, and Hunt (see Chapter 8, n. 9), fails to recognize Shelley, we expect the latter to reply, "Know ye not me?" But Shelley in *Adonais* had for the time being reconciled himself to being shut out from what he later called the "Paradise of fame." And by using imagery from *Paradise Lost* for his portraits of himself and Byron, he anticipates his later comparison of himself as *"less than him* [Byron] *whom thunder has made greater"*: Byron came "veiling all the *lightnings* of his song" and Shelley came vanquished "As the last cloud of an expiring storm, / *Whose thunder is its knell"* (xxx-xxxi, my italics). That the writing of *Adonais* caused Shelley to consider himself and Byron in terms of Milton and of *Paradise Lost* is also suggested by three of his letters to Byron at this time: on 16 April 1821, he announced Keats's death immediately after comparing Byron to "those eternal poets [including Milton]" who at a similar age began "their supreme poems [including *Paradise Lost*]"; on 4 May he contrasted Byron's "strength" as a poet to Keats's weaknesses and then explained that he himself would never be able to "write anything worth calling a poem," that *The Cenci* had been "a complete failure," and that *Prometheus Unbound* was "also a very imperfect poem"; and on 16 July he sent *Adonais* to Byron, predicted again that Byron *"will* write a great and connected poem, which shall bear the same relation to this age as the 'Iliad', the 'Divina Commedia', and 'Paradise Lost' did to theirs," and described himself as unworthy of the company of either Milton or Byron:

> As to the Poem [*Adonais*] I send you, I fear it is worth little. Heaven knows what makes me persevere (after the severe reproof of public neglect) in writing verses; and *Heaven alone, whose will I execute so awkwardly, is responsible for my presumption* [my italics].[9]

Shelley's concluding remark demonstrates that by July 1821 he had already conceived a Satanic justification of his own pride and envy of the "Paradise of fame." One month later he would "despair of rivalling Lord Byron"; two months later he would reverse the image of *Adonais* ("Whose thunder is its knell") in order to engage *"him whom thunder has made greater"* in a battle for fame; and in the winter of 1821/22 he would adopt Satan's methods and as the "worm beneath the sod" speciously flatter Byron as the "God" of poets.

That Shelley experienced both inferiority and Satanic "presumption" in his relations to Byron and that he defined these feelings with Milton in mind are further confirmed by three other letters he wrote at this time. To Hunt on 26 August he announced that he was too proud to share in the "profits" and "splendour" of Byron's proposed periodical but hoped that Hunt would respond to Byron's invitation and soon migrate "to these 'regions mild of calm and serene air' [Milton's *Comus*, l. 4]." In a second letter to Hunt on 6 October, Shelley announced that "Lord Byron is expected every day" and conjectured that Hogg would be inconsolable at Hunt's departure from England: "I wish you could bring him with you—he will say that *I am like Lucifer who has seduced the third part of the starry flock* [*Paradise Lost* V.708-10]." And on 26 January 1822, Shelley informed John Gisborne that Byron's "last Volume" (*Sardanapalus, The Two Foscari*, and the "apocalyptic" *Cain*) contained "finer poetry than has appeared in England since the publication of Paradise Regained."[10] Thus by January 1822 (also the terminal date for the *Sonnet to Byron*, prefixed "Jan^y 22-1822" in Mary's fair copy), Shelley's envy for Byron's fame and fortune had resulted in Shelley comparing himself to Milton's Satan and comparing Byron to Milton, to Milton's God, and to the "thunder" of that God. With that conclusion in mind, we turn to three other poems that, I believe, were influenced by these same circumstances and consequently were written between April 1821, when Shelley conceived *Adonais*, and January 1822.

The first and most important of these poems is the fragment known as "The False Laurel and the True," the text of which I take from its unemended printings by Forman and Rogers:

And what art thou presumptuous who profanest
    The wreath to mighty Poets only due
Even whilst, like a forgotten name thou wanest
    Touch not those leaves which for the eternal few
Who wander oer the Paradise of fame
    In sacred dedication ever grew—
One of the crowd thou art,—without a name
    Ah friend 'tis the false laurel which I wear
And though it seem like it is not the same
    As that which bound Milton's immortal hair
Its dew is poison, and the hopes which quicken
    Under its chilling shade, though seeming fair
Are flowers which die almost before they sicken
    And that I walk thus proudly crowned withal

Is that I know it may be thunderstricken
  And this is my distinction, if I fall
I shall not creep out of the vital day
  To common dust nor wear a common pall
But as my hopes were fire, so my decay
  Shall be as ashes covering them. Oh, Earth
Oh friends, if when my          has ebbed away
  One spark be unextinguished of that hearth
Kindled in[11]

Because this poem is written in terza rima, uses the image of the "unextinguished . . . hearth," and is found in the same notebook (Bixby-Huntington I) containing Shelley's rough draft for the first three stanzas of *Ode to the West Wind*, both Forman and Rogers would date this poem 1819. But the notebook in question contains a number of 1821/22 poems, and I judge that the depression in "The False Laurel and the True" is more characteristic of the Shelley who despairingly envied the power of Milton and Byron in 1821/22 than the Shelley who hopefully sought a creative rebirth in the *West Wind*. Although the fragment can be interpreted as Shelley's dialogue with himself in which he recalls his former *West Wind* and asks for at least "One spark" of fame after death, it can be more properly read as Shelley's dramatic creation of a dialogue between himself (a Satanic poet exiled from the "Paradise of fame") and his "friend" Byron who, according to Shelley at this time, possessed the "laurel" of Milton and the poetical power of Milton's God. The resemblances between this fragment and Shelley's previously cited statements in 1821/22 are too startling to ignore: described as "a forgotten name" and "without a name" (cf. Shelley's "classed among those who have no name" in his August letter to Peacock, Urania's failure to recognize Shelley in *Adonais*, and Shelley's "unhonoured name" in *Sonnet to Byron*), and accused of being "presumptuous" (cf. "Heaven alone . . . is responsible for my presumption" and his claim for a "higher station" in his letters of 16 July to Byron and 8-10 August to Mary), Shelley responds that his "false laurel" and "flowers . . . die almost before they sicken" (cf. Shelley's self-portraits in *Adonais* ["On the withering flower / The killing sun smiles brightly"] and in his 11 December letter to Claire [the "mimosa" or "Exotic . . . droops in this frost"]), but that he will "proudly" achieve "distinction" if his laurel is "thunderstricken" (cf. "Whose thunder is its knell" in *Adonais* and "only *less than him* [Byron] *whom thunder has made greater*" in Shelley's letter of 25 September). Even though Shelley could characterize himself as the "worm beneath the sod" (*Sonnet to Byron*), he refused in this frag-

ment to "creep out of the vital day / To common dust" and hoped
that his rivalry with the "thunder" of Lord Byron would insure him
at least "One spark" of immortality among subsequent generations.

The two other poems reflecting Shelley's interest in Milton at
this time are the fragment "Milton's Spirit" and the lyric "To Edward
Williams." The first of these has been included among the poems of
1820 in the *Julian* edition, but if Rogers is correct in assuming that
it was intended for *Adonais*,[12] then it was written during Shelley's
period of extreme self-doubt in 1821/22. Here the characteristic
"thunder" once more appears, but this time Shelley does not specifically contrast his own weakness to the power of Milton's spirit:

> I dreamed that Milton's spirit rose, and took
> From life's green tree his        Uranian lute;
> And from his touch sweet thunder flowed, and shook
> All human things built in contempt of man,—
> And sanguine thrones and impious altars quaked,
> Prisons and citadels . . .

Although Shelley may have written this fragment for *Adonais* and
intended it to be read in the spirit of Wordsworth's "Milton! thou
shouldst be living at this hour," it is equally probable that he wrote
it during his last winter in Pisa (compare the "lute" taken from "life's
green tree" with the "guitar" wrought from a tree in the 1822 poem
"With a Guitar: To Jane") and intended to represent Byron, whom he
judged to rival Milton, as "Milton's spirit" incarnate. If this be the
case, then the "sweet thunder" that "shook" the "sanguine thrones" was
to be found in Byron's recent political dramas and in *The Prophecy of
Dante*; and the "impious altars quaked" as a result of *Cain* and *The
Vision of Judgment*. These works, together with *Don Juan* III-V,
caused Shelley by January 1822 both to envy Byron's God-like and
Miltonic accomplishments and to lament his own Satanic fall.

Shelley's fallen state is reflected in a third poem, "The serpent
is shut out from Paradise," a copy of which he sent to Edward Williams on 26 January.[13] This lyric is not merely a sexual lament, for
Shelley was also shut out from the "Paradise of fame," and he
resented having to act

> a forced part in life's dull scene.
> Of wearing on my brow the idle mask
>    Of author, great or mean,
> In the world's Carnival. I sought
> Peace thus, and . . . I found it not.        (stanza iv)

By this time, Shelley defined himself not only in terms of Milton's

*Paradise Lost* (which is echoed in stanza ii of "The serpent is shut out from Paradise") but also in the terms of Goethe's *Faust*, which he was translating by January 1822. And having been made aware that Faust and Mephisto were *"one* person, represented symbolically, only in a two-fold shape,"[14] Shelley now compared himself to the Satanic Faust: the eight lines of Shelley's sixth stanza (beginning "The crane o'er seas and forests seeks her home") are directly adapted from Faust's speech to Mephisto in the "Wood and Cave" scene (ll. 3345-65). Two scenes earlier (ll. 3179-86) we find Faust in the Garden with Margaret who *"plucks a daisy"* while she repeats "He loves me—loves me not" and joyfully concludes "He loves me."[15] Shelley in the fifth stanza of his lament was not so lucky:

> Full half an hour, to-day, I tried my lot
> With various flowers, and every one still said,
>     "She loves me,—loves me not."—
> And if this meant a Vision long since fled—
> If it meant *Fortune, Fame*, or Peace of thought—
>     If it meant—(but I dread
> To speak what you may know too well)
> Still there was truth in the sad oracle.                    (my italics)

Shelley here catalogues for us his problems in the winter of 1821/22: true, this "sad oracle" *meant* the lack of love from "Mary" (what he dreaded "To speak") and the failure of his Promethean "Vision" of human perfectibility; but it also *meant* his failure to attain what he described on 25 September as those "two great objects of human pursuit," fame and fortune.[16]

Despite Shelley's protestations that he had no "regret for his unhonoured name" (*Sonnet to Byron*), that he was proud of the "hatred," content with the "scorn," and indifferent to the "Indifference" he had received as a poet ("The serpent is shut out from Paradise," stanza ii), and that he valued "neither the fame [the reviews and journals] can give, nor the fame they can take away" (in his letter of 25 January 1822 to Horace Smith),[17] a final look at Shelley's first three months with Byron in Pisa confirms that he was extremely disturbed by an irrefutable logic: without fame, he could not earn money; without money, he was too depressed to write; unable to write, he could never attain fame. Consider, for example, that on 29 November he lamented his "want of popularity"; on 11 December he had "no confidence" and judged that to write in "solitude or put forth thoughts without sympathy is *unprofitable* vanity"; and in January he had "been long idle,—& as far as writing goes, despondent." In this last letter, written to Peacock, Shelley complained that he was finding *Charles the First* "a devil of a nut . . . to crack," that he could not cure the "consumption of [his] purse," and that he had nothing "better to do than furnish this jingling food for the hunger of oblivion, called *verse*." In a letter written to Ollier at the same time, Shelley's fear of oblivion and poverty meant that he "exceedingly desired the immediate publication of 'Hellas' from *public* [i.e., for fame] no less than *private* [i.e., for money] reasons."[18] Fearing that he could no longer write, Shelley hoped that his previous works might solve his problems and consequently on 25 January asked Hunt "if Ollier has published *Hellas* and what effect was produced by Adonais." But he feared the worst: "My faculties are shaken to atoms & torpid. I can write nothing, & if Adonais had no success & excited no interest what incentive can I have to write." Shelley wanted money so that he might finance Hunt's journey to Pisa, but confessed that

> Past circumstances between me & L. B[yron]. render it *impossible* that I should accept any supply from him for my own use, or that I should *ask* it for yours if the contribution could be supposed in any manner to relieve me, or to do what I would otherwise have done. It is true, that I *cannot*—but how is he to be assured of this?—[19]

Among these past circumstances were certainly Shelley's pride and his envy of Byron's "fame," "prosperity," and "power" (*Sonnet to Byron*) during their first three months together in Pisa. Shelley in some ways experienced the same frustration that he was embodying in the character of Charles I, for in a note summarizing the action of the first two acts of his drama, he indicated that part of Act I, scene ii would be devoted to the King's "methods for securing money & power."[20] Shelley also desired to secure "money & power," but he was faced, as was Charles I, with the dilemma of a circular logic: Laud counseled the king that a victory over Scotland "will lend power, and power bring gold"; but Cottington proposed the reverse, to "begin first" with "Gold [which] must give power" (ii.338-40). Like his protagonist, Shelley lacked both.

While Shelley vainly labored to write *Charles the First* in January and feared that *Hellas* would be as ill-received as *The Cenci*, his frustration was increased by reminders of Byron's abilities as a dramatist. He had learned of Byron's interest in "building up a drama, such as England has not yet seen" in Ravenna, and he was sufficiently impressed by the "dramatic" *Prophecy of Dante* in September, *Cain* in November, *Heaven and Earth* by December, and *Sardanapalus, The Two Foscari,* and *Werner* by January.[21] Shelley could not help but compare himself to Byron, for he was frequently forced to read aloud from these latest dramas, to witness Mary copying *Heaven and Earth* and *Werner*, and to judge specimens of Byron's dramatic writing. Medwin, for example, recorded on 20 November that Byron handed "part of his MS. of 'Heaven and Earth'" to Shelley and asked, "'tell me what you think of it.'" Medwin did not supply Shelley's immediate reaction but later quoted Byron as saying, "'Shelley tells me that the choruses in "Heaven and Earth" are deficient.'"[22] Concerning Shelley's reaction to *The Deformed Transformed*, however, Medwin was considerably more graphic:

> Some days after these remarks, on calling on him [Byron] one morning, he produced 'The Deformed Transformed.' Handing it to Shelley, as he was in the habit of doing his daily compositions, he said:
> "Shelley, I have been writing a *Faustish* kind of drama: tell me what you think of it."
> After reading it attentively, Shelley returned it.
> "Well," said Lord Byron, "how do you like it?"
> "Least," replied he, "of any thing I ever saw of yours. It is a bad imitation of 'Faust;' and besides, there are two entire lines of Southey's in it."
> Lord Byron changed colour immediately, and asked hastily what lines? Shelley repeated,
>
> > 'And water shall see thee,
> > And fear thee, and flee thee.'
>
> "They are in 'The Curse of Kehama.'"
> His Lordship, without making a single observation, instantly threw the poem into the fire. . . . Whether it was hatred of Southey, or respect for Shelley's opinions, which made him commit an act that I considered a sort of suicide, was always doubtful to me.[23]

That such a scene actually occurred is confirmed by Trelawny: "I was in the room—*half a sheet* of M.S. of The Deformed Transformed was given Shelley to read—which had been written in the night—& that half which was distroyed [*sic*]."[24] Because Byron did not begin *The Deformed Transformed* until after he completed *Werner* on 20 January, the incident described by Medwin and Trelawny probably occurred in February.[25] Regardless of how much of the drama Shelley read that morning, if he judged it to be an "imitation of 'Faust,'" then he certainly knew that Byron's hero, like Goethe's, would be tempted and then accompanied by a diabolical antagonist; and he probably had read Byron's first scene, in which the

deformed Arnold is tempted and taunted by a Mephistophelean
"Stranger," agrees to a "compact" in order to receive a new body, is
transformed into Achilles, witnesses a second transformation whereby
his rejected and deformed body is assumed by the "Stranger" (who
then calls himself Caesar), and then is unable to escape his deformities
now in the person of the diabolical Caesar, his inescapable "shadow"
or second self. Even if Shelley did not read all of this spectacular first
scene, he knew that Byron, by imitating *Faust*, intended to use the
devil as Arnold's second self or doppelgänger, for in January 1822 he
had discussed with Byron the dramatic possibilities of such character
duplication. Part of this discussion was prompted by *Retsch's Series
of Twenty-Six Outlines, Illustrative of Goethe's Tragedy of Faust*, a
volume that Byron had requested from Murray in December and that
arrived in Pisa by 12 January.[26] What the two poets discovered in it
were not only illustrations and a prose translation (with certain scenes
only summarized), but also a short introduction which argued "that
the easiest clue to the moral part of this didactic action is, to consider
Faust and Mephistopheles as *one* person, represented symbolically,
only in a two-fold shape" (p. 2). Having read and discussed this interpretation with Byron, Shelley quickly discerned a month later that
Arnold and the diabolical Caesar in *The Deformed Transformed* were
also to be considered as *"one* person, represented symbolically, only
in a two-fold shape" and that Byron had made explicit what was
barely suggested in Goethe's drama: in one scene, Mephisto puts on
the gowns of Faust in order to delude one of his young students;[27]
in Byron's first scene, the Mephistophelean "Stranger" puts on the
body of Arnold after the latter adopts the new form of Achilles.

Despite Byron's clever use of a double transformation in *The-
Deformed Transformed*, Shelley apparently disliked it, for he judged
the drama to be a "bad imitation of 'Faust'" and even taunted Byron
for having plagiarized two lines from Southey. But Shelley was not
exactly a disinterested critic of Byron's latest drama; in fact he was
personally humiliated by his rival's ingenious use of the devil as
doppelgänger: having decided to rival Lord Byron as a dramatist yet
finding "Charles the Ist . . . a devil of a nut . . . to crack,"[28] Shelley
discovered by February 1822 that he had inadvertently provided
Byron the dramatic means by which to externalize Arnold's internal
conflict in *The Deformed Transformed*. Byron, of course, had access
to the interpretation that judged Mephisto and Faust as double representations of a single personality, had read other works in which one
character serves as a psychological complement or equivalent to the
protagonist (e.g., Shelley's *Alastor, Revolt of Islam,* and *Epipsychidion*;
Mary's *Frankenstein*; Monk Lewis's *Wood Daemon* and *Bravo of Venice*;

Le Sage's *Le Diable Boiteux*; and Dryden's *Amphitryon*), and had even himself experimented with the doppelgänger in *Manfred* and *Cain*. Nevertheless, Shelley could only judge that he also was responsible for Byron's plot, because in January 1822 he not only translated parts of *Faust* for Byron, discussed with him the suggestion in the *Retsch* volume that Mephisto was Faust's double, explained for him the resemblance between *Faust* and Calderón's *El Magico Prodigioso* (another drama that Shelley was translating and in which the devil acts as doppelgänger), but he also was translating or at least summarizing for Byron a scene from a second Calderón drama, *El Purgatorio de San Patricio*, in which the protagonist (Ludovico Enio) was shadowed by a mantled figure ("un Hombre Embozado") who acted as Enio's skeletal "second self." When Shelley became acquainted with the plot of *The Deformed Transformed*, he immediately recognized that Byron had adapted Enio's encounter with his "second self" in order to structure the conflict between Arnold and his metamorphic doppelgänger.

Medwin witnessed Shelley's reaction to *The Deformed Transformed* and he even knew that Shelley had provided Byron the Calderón plot about a hero shadowed by his doppelgänger, but he never put the proverbial two and two together. In fact, Medwin confused Byron scholarship for nearly one hundred and fifty years by telling Washington Irving about Byron's so-called "Unwritten Drama," a drama that was actually the *unfinished*, not the unwritten *Deformed Transformed*. According to Medwin, Byron in late January or early February 1822, that is, "during a short poetical repose between the burning of the Deformed Transformed and [the completion by 20 January of] Werner," planned to write a doppelgänger drama based on a Calderón plot. For "the outline of the story Lord Byron was indebted to Shelley," and we now know that Shelley outlined a single scene from Calderón's *El Purgatorio de San Patricio*. But Medwin mistakenly described this Enio-"Hombre Embozado" scene as an entire drama (misnamed *"Embozado"*) about a Spanish nobleman (the depraved Alfonzo) pursued by his mantled doppelgänger: in the scene of confrontation as described by Medwin, Alfonzo kills his pursuer "who in falling utters 'are you satisfied!' his mantle drops off and [Alfonzo] discovers—his own image the spectre of himself—his self—He dies with horror!" Even though Medwin heard Byron summarize this plot, explain that the doppelgänger "at every turn . . . intrudes like the demon in Faust," and state that he would adapt this plot "in the genuine spirit of Goethe," he failed to recognize this adaptation in *The Deformed Transformed* and consequently believed Byron intended to write still another drama. That *The Deformed Transformed* was in fact this

"Unwritten Drama" and would have been finished in accord with its Calderón source (that is, with Arnold killing himself by killing Caesar, his diabolical doppelgänger), I have argued elsewhere.[29] Here, however, I wish to restress Shelley's frustration and humiliation when he learned of Byron's doppelgänger drama in February, at which time Medwin even noted that "Byron threatened to make himself as voluminous & prolific an author as Shakespeare." Shelley keenly felt this threat, especially since he could not continue *Charles the First* and at the same time had inadvertently given Byron the idea for a new drama. If Shelley then reflected on his enforced association with Byron in the so-called Satanic School of poetry, he would not have been amused by the ironies: Byron was once more the God who this time had thunderously reduced Satan to dramatic form in *The Deformed Transformed*; but Shelley could only characterize himself as the envious and despairing Satan, once more "thunderstricken" by Byron's talents in drama.

As if Byron's "fame" and "power" as a dramatist were not sufficient insults to Shelley in February 1822, Byron's "prosperity" once again became a source of aggravation. On Christmas, the two poets had agreed "to give a thousand pounds to the other who first came to their estate," and by 15 February they received notice that Lady Noel had died the month before. Shelley therefore reasonably expected to receive this thousand pounds which he could use to help Hunt, but Byron apparently did not honor his wager.[30] Nevertheless, Shelley used the circumstances of Byron's inheritance to secure more money for Hunt: on 15 February he asked Byron for a loan of £250, probably expecting it to be canceled by the £1,000 debt. But Byron only agreed to furnish "with *tolerable willingness* the sum requested"; that is, despite his having become "a rich, a still richer man" and his new debt to Shelley, Byron asked Shelley to return the £250 after the death of Sir Timothy. Because of this requirement, Shelley complained to Hunt on 17 February that "Many circumstances have occurred between myself & Lord B. which make the intercourse painful to me, & this last discussion about money particularly so." Even though Byron expressed "himself *again* warmly about this literary scheme" of *The Liberal*, Shelley stressed that he would "take no more share in this or in any other conjunction than is absolutely necessary" to protect Hunt's interests.[31]

By 2 March, Shelley informed Hunt that Byron was even more willing to begin *The Liberal* and that his *loan* to Hunt might be eventually considered as a *gift*. Despite this "fit of returning generous feeling" on Byron's part, Shelley again complained that particular dispositions in Lord B's character render the close & exclusive intimacy with him in which I find myself, intolerable to me. . . . No feelings of my own however shall injure or interfere with what is ever nearest to them—your interest, & I will take care to preserve the little influence I may have over this Proteus in whom such strange extremes are reconciled until we meet.

Shelley was not being completely honest here, for Byron's "dispositions" were no more aggravating than his success as a poet, particularly since Shelley had

written nothing for this last two months [January and February]. . . . What motives have I to write.—I *had* motives—and I thank the god of my own heart they were totally different from those of the other apes of humanity who make mouths in the glass of the time—but what are *those* motives now? The only inspiration of an ordinary kind I could descend to acknowledge would be the earning £100 for *you*—& that it seems I cannot.

In his next letter to Hunt, however, Shelley more honestly explained his envy of Byron's fame and money:

Certain it is, that Lord Byron has made me bitterly feel the inferiority which the world has presumed to place between us and which subsists nowhere in reality but in our own talents, which are not our own but Nature's—or in our rank, which is not our own but Fortune's.

Shelley confessed that he "did wrong in carrying this jealousy of my Lord Byron into his loan" to Hunt, but he once more considered his jealousy as Satanic in character: "Alas, how am I fallen from the boasted purity in which you knew me once exulting!"[32]

By April 1822, Shelley was apparently satisfied with his mediation between Byron and Hunt, but not with that between Byron and Claire. Claire had even proposed a fantastic scheme to kidnap Allegra, and in order to prevent any such action Shelley urged Byron to remove Allegra from the convent at Bagnacavallo. But this suggestion, according to Mary in a letter of 20 March, "appears in the highest degree to have exasperated" Byron. As Shelley explained it to Claire, "I was endeavouring to induce him to place Allegra in the institute at Lucca, but his jealousy of my regard for *your* interests will, since a conversation I had with him the other day, render him inaccessible to my suggestions." This "conversation" between the two poets is probably the one described by Dowden:

Elizabeth Parker, an orphan girl sent by Mrs. Godwin to live with Lady Mountcashell, a firm and affectionate friend of Claire's, wrote to the unhappy woman, relating what Shelley had told on the preceding evening at Casa Silva respecting his interview with Byron. "I never saw him [Shelley] in a passion before," said Elizabeth; "last night, however, he was downright, positively angry. . . . Mr. Shelley declared to Lady Mountcashell that he could with pleasure have knocked Lord Byron down; for when he mentioned that you were half-distracted with alarm about the child's health, and also that you were yourself in very declining health, he saw a gleam of malicious satisfaction pass over Lord's [*sic*] Byron's countenance. 'I saw his look,' Mr. Shelley said; 'I understood its meaning; I despised him, and I came away.' These were his own epigrammatic words."[33]

Such a scene caused Mary on 20 March to fear a duel between Shelley and Byron, "whose hypocrisy & cruelty rouse one's soul from its depths." And Shelley decided to "take our house *far* from Lord Byron's, although it may be impossible suddenly to put an end to his detested intimacy." In a letter written four days later, Shelley again refused to be drawn into Claire's scheming, partly because he "*could not* refuse Lord Byron's challenge" to a duel if that came to pass.[34] And in another letter written to Claire at this time, he hinted that he might even challenge Byron to a duel:

It is of vital importance both to me and to yourself, to Allegra even, that I should put a period to my intimacy with L[ord] B[yron], and that without *éclat*. No sentiments of honour or justice restrain him (as I strongly suspect) from the basest insinuations, and the only mode in which I could effectually silence him I am reluctant (even if I had proof) to employ during my father's life. But for your immediate feelings I would suddenly and irrevocably leave this country which he inhabits, nor ever enter it but as an enemy to determine our differences *without words*.[35]

Shelley didn't explain what these "basest insinuations" were, but Leslie Marchand conjectured that Byron may have "still believed the story of Shelley's having had a child by Claire."[36] If this was the case, Byron may have revealed that he had not sent Mary's denial of Elise's charges to the Hoppners.

Before Shelley could take Mary, Claire (who had arrived from Florence on 15 April), and the Williamses away from Byron and Pisa, he learned that Allegra had died on 20 April in the convent at Bagnacavallo. Claire was not informed of her daughter's death until 2 May, by which time the Shelley party had moved to the Casa Magni on the Gulf of Spezia. Byron remained behind in Pisa until the middle of May and then moved to a villa in Montenero, near Leghorn, but Shelley could not easily forget the man he had grown to despise, especially when he recalled that he and Claire had urged Byron to remove Allegra from the convent. On 12 May, Shelley was again reminded of his enemy when his new boat arrived with "Don Juan" painted across the mainsail. His "noble friend [was] carrying the joke rather too far," and between these two "friends," Shelley assured Claire at the end of May, there was "a great gulf fixed, which by the nature of things must daily become wider." Despite such a gulf, Shelley still envied Byron's *divine* accomplishments as a poet: "I do not write," he complained to Horace Smith in May, because "I have lived too long near Lord Byron & the sun has extinguished the glow-worm; for I cannot hope with St. John, that '*the light came into the world, & the world knew it not.*'" On 18 June, Shelley hoped that this "mentally capricious" φῶς would not ruin "Hunt's prospects in establishment of the Journal," but vowed he would "see little of Lord Byron. . . . I detest all society—almost all, at least—and Lord Byron is the nucleus of all that is hateful and tiresome in it." Shelley did, however, enjoy the society of Edward and Jane Williams while they sailed along their "delightful bay in the evening wind, under the summer moon, until earth appears another world. Jane brings her guitar, and if the past and the future could be obliterated, the present would content me so well that I could say with Faust to the passing moment, 'Remain, thou, thou art so beautiful.'" But the "passing moment" could not provide Shelley, threatened by Byron's past and future accomplishments, with the same assurance he needed as a poet:

> I write little now. It is impossible to compose except under the strong excitement of an assurance of finding sympathy in what you write. Imagine Demosthenes reciting a Philippic to the waves of the Atlantic! Lord Byron is in this respect fortunate. He touched a chord to which a million hearts responded, and the coarse music which he produced to please them disciplined him to the perfection to which he now approaches. I do not go on with 'Charles the First'. I feel too little certainty of the future, and too little satisfaction with regard to the past, to undertake any subject seriously and deeply. I stand, as it were, upon a precipice, which I have ascended with great, and cannot descend without *greater*, peril, and I am content if the heaven above me is calm for the passing moment.[37]

On this precipice, Shelley could only momentarily escape from his recent anxieties: he might cut out "Don Juan" from his boat's mainsail, but he could not so effectively eliminate his envy and dislike of Lord Byron. Hunt still had not arrived and Shelley feared the forthcoming partnership between "the wren & the eagle," because Hunt and Byron might become "two thunderbolts"[38] whose conjunction would destroy the "calm" of the "heaven above." That such a "calm" or "content" was indeed momentary is suggested by the number of terrifying visions Shelley experienced at the Casa Magni. On 6 May he was troubled enough about Allegra's death to see "a naked child rise from the sea, clap its hands as if in joy and smiling at him."[39] And on 22 June, four days after claiming to be content for the passing moment (even though Mary had recently miscarried), Shelley dreamt that

> Edward & Jane came in to him . . . their bones starting through their skin, the faces pale yet stained with blood . . . Edward said—["] Get up, Shelley, the sea is flooding the house & it is all coming down." S[helley] got up . . . & thought he saw the sea rushing in. Suddenly his vision changed & he saw the figure of himself strangling me [Mary], that had made him rush into my room . . . when my jumping out awoke him, or as he phrased it caused his vision to vanish.

In discussing this vision of his doppelgänger with Mary the next morning, Shelley described *another* recent vision: "he had seen the figure of himself which met him as he walked on the terrace & said to him— 'How long do you mean to be content.'"[40] This important third vision recalls Calderón's scene in which Enio confronts his skeletal second self in *El Purgatorio de San Patricio*, this scene having been provided by Shelley for Byron's use in *The Deformed Transformed*. In Byron's summary of this incident, the hero actually kills himself by killing his mantled doppelgänger "who in falling utters 'are you satisfied!'" Because Shelley's doppelgänger similarly utters, "How long do you mean to be content," we may conclude that Calderón's and Byron's dramas returned to haunt him and that he was subconsciously confronting death in the form of his own suicide.[41]

That Shelley's discontent with life in general and dissatisfaction with Byron in particular caused him to consider his own death is revealed by two more self-destructive expressions taken from the works of Goethe and Milton—two poets, like Calderón, whom Shelley associated with Byron (that is, Byron was imitating Goethe in *The Deformed Transformed* and rivaling Milton with *Cain*). In the letter to John Gisborne on 18 June, Shelley uttered what James Rieger has correctly called a "suicidal formula" when he considered obliterating "the past and the future" and saying "with Faust to the passing moment, 'Remain, thou, thou art so beautiful'"; Faust, Shelley remembered, wished to die ("Dann will ich gern zugrunde gehn!/ Dann mag die Totenglocke schallen") if he ever said "zum Augenblicke . . ./Verweile doch! Du bist so schön!"[42] Shelley repeated his death wish in a letter to Trelawny, also written on 18 June, by paraphrasing Milton's "To lay their just hands" on *Virtue*, "that Golden Key/That opes the Palace of Eternity" (*Comus*, ll. 13-14) when he asked "to hold in my possession" the poisonous *prussic acid*, "that golden key to the chamber of perpetual rest."[43] Shelley had quoted *Comus* (l. 4) nearly a year before when he invited Hunt to join Byron and himself in Italy's "'regions mild of calm and serene air,'" but since then Byron had disrupted these "regions mild" and had driven Shelley "upon a precipice" which he had ascended with great peril and from which he could not "descend without *greater*, peril": that is, only through the greater peril of suicide could he hope to attain a "calm" for more than "the passing moment."


II

Faced with the immediate threat of suicide, however, Shelley was uncertain whether death would lead to "the chamber of perpetual rest," and sometime during the spring of 1822 he recalled Petrarch's *Trionfo della Morte* which he had read in September 1819.[44] After rereading this *Triumph of Death* and probably all six of Petrarch's *Trionfi* (which A. C. Bradley conveniently summarized as "in turn the triumph of Love over man, especially in his youth; the triumph of Chastity over Love; that of Death over all mortality; that of Fame over Death; that of Time over Fame; and that of [Eternity] over Time"), Shelley conceived the idea of *The Triumph of Life*, which, as I argue below, should be more accurately entitled *The Triumph of Life-in-Death*. The nature of Shelley's indebtedness to Petrarch is partially suggested by Bradley's summary of the action in the initial *Triumph of Love*:

> Here Petrarch, lying in early morning on the grass in a solitary place, and wearied with sad thoughts of the past, falls asleep. In his sleep he sees a great light, and within this light four white coursers drawing a car, in which sits Love, like a conqueror in a Roman triumph. Around the car he sees innumerable mortals, dead and alive; and one of them, a friend who recognizes him, points out and describes to him the most famous of the victims. Here we have in outline the main scheme of Shelley's fragment.[45]

But neither Bradley nor any later critic has realized that Shelley wrote *The Triumph of Life* to serve as the seventh and probably final triumphal procession in the series begun by Petrarch. That is, Petrarch concluded his processions with a faith that Eternity would triumph over Time and reward man with Paradise. But Shelley doubted Petrarch's as well as his own former faith in such an Eternity and predicted that Life would triumph even over Eternity. Accordingly, the pains of Life in Shelley's poem pursue practically all men beyond the grave into a state of prolonged if not perpetual purgatory.

For the last two years before his death on 8 July 1822, Shelley had been able to overcome, at least rhetorically, his fears of death: for example, in *Hellas* (note to ll. 197-238), despite the "presumption," he argued that "eternity is the inheritance of every thinking being"; in *Adonais* (liii), despite his reluctance ("Why linger, why turn back, why shrink, my Heart?"), he affirmed that Death was not as faithless as Life ("oh, hasten thither,/No more let life divide what Death can join together"); in *Epipsychidion* (ll. 124-25, 586-87, 598), he feared his audacity ("What have I dared? where am I lifted? how/Shall I descend, and perish not?") but could descend from this precipice and predict that "one annihilation" meant "one immortality" to be attained " 'beyond the grave' "; in *The Witch of Atlas* (lxiii), he was one of the "mariners of that wide lake" of life making a "course unpiloted" to "an unknown goal," but believed that "immortal forms" awaited in "bright bowers . . ./Beneath the weltering of the restless tide"; and in *Una Favola*, he did not finish his narrative about the twin enchantresses of Life and Death, but he stressed Death's promise of " 'Love and Eternity' " in a kingdom that could be called " 'Paradise.' " But all such affirmations did not avail when Shelley began *The Triumph of Life* in the spring of 1822: seriously considering suicide as a means of achieving "the chamber of perpetual rest," he challenged not only Petrarch's but his own former assumptions that the repose of Eternity awaited him in Death.

That Shelley feared Death as much as Life in *The Triumph of Life* is demonstrated by a number of frequently overlooked circumstances. First, he purposefully inverted Faust's desire at sunset to pursue the sun in its westerly course and thus to attain a physical immortality:

Ich eile fort, ihr ewges Licht zu trinken,
*Vor mir den Tag und hinter mir die Nacht,*
*Den Himmel über mir und unter mir die Wellen.*

(ll. 1086-88, my italics)

Shelley took these italicized lines, reversed the time of day from sunset to sunrise, faced the same direction (to the west, with the sun *behind* him), and wrote:

> before me fled
> The night; behind me rose the day; the Deep
> Was at my feet, & Heaven above my head. (ll. 26-8)

By facing the west at sunrise rather than at sunset, Shelley made clear that he was hoping not for physical immortality by drinking "ewges Licht" but for spiritual immortality by drinking eternal Darkness. As all commentators on *The Triumph of Life* have acknowledged, light or Life is a deceitful enchantress that deforms; but as no critic has properly emphasized, light or Life in Shelley's poem pursues man *even into the valley of Death* and should be termed the car of *Life-in-Death* which enthralls man beyond the grave. If Shelley, as he feared, could not escape that light of Life in Death, then he would never be able to achieve the perpetual rest of an eternal Darkness: the "Sun" of Time in Petrarch's *The Triumph of Time* had obscured the "star" of Fame which ruled in *The Triumph of Fame*; in Shelley's *The Triumph of Life*, the "icy cold" light of Life was greater than Petrarch's light of Time, for it "obscured with      light/The Sun as he the stars" (ll. 78-79) and hence was fitter to do battle with the eternal Darkness. Because Shelley feared that this light of Life would in fact penetrate through Death into the eternal Darkness, his *Triumph of Life* must be read as an extension and repudiation not only of Petrarch and Goethe but also of Calderón: in the midst of his translation from Faust is a translation from Calderón's *La vida es sueño*:[46] already agreeing with Calderón that Life was a Dream, he began in *The Triumph of Life* to portray Life-in-Death as a Nightmare.

That the triumphal procession of Life is also one of Life-in-Death and that Shelley feared Death for that reason are also demonstrated by the obvious fact that the dead Rousseau and the elemental or nonspiritual forms of "'The Wise,/The great, the unforgotten'" (including, for example, "'All that is mortal of great Plato'") who did not properly "'know themselves'" or "'repress the mutiny within'" themselves (ll. 208-13, 254) are *still enchained* by the conqueror Life; in other words, Life continues to enthrall the dead even as it pursues the living who flee before the car in the van. Therefore in response to the narrator's final question, "'Then, what is Life?'" the answer is a terrifying enchantress who in most instances ("the sacred few" to be discussed below) apparently cannot be escaped by Death. The dead Rousseau still has not found "perpetual rest," does not know "'Whither the conqueror hurries'" him (l. 304), and asks the narrator

(Shelley acting as "'spectator'") to "'turn/Actor or victim in this wretchedness'" (ll. 305-6) so that he (Rousseau as well as Shelley) may learn whether Life-in-Death can eventually be escaped. With the hope of "Heaven" or "perpetual" *immortality* above him but with the fear of the "Deep" or "perpetual" *mortality* under him, Shelley looks for comfort to the "night" of Death facing him in the west but envisions a state in which the threatening "light" of Life triumphs over the dead as well as the living. Beatrice Cenci's fears that there might "be/No God, no Heaven, no Earth in the void world" and that death might lead to an everlasting embrace in her father's "hellish arms" (V.iv.57-66) were no greater than Shelley's, that Life's pains (including the "hateful" presence of Byron whom he had recently characterized as both "God" and the "sun") awaited him in Death.

A discussion of Byron's influence on Shelley's last poem must await a further consideration of the car of Life-in-Death which has more antecedents than Petrarch's *Trionfi*. The car is first described as "the young moon" bearing

> The ghost of her dead Mother, whose dim form
> Bends in dark ether from her infant's chair,
>
> So came a chariot on the silent storm
> Of its own rushing splendour, and a Shape
> So sate within as one whom years deform
>
> Beneath a dusky hood & double cape
> Crouching within the shadow of a tomb,
> And o'er what seemed the head, a cloud like crape,
>
> Was bent a dun & faint etherial gloom
> Tempering the light.                                    (ll. 84-93)

East and west, light and darkness, Life and Death are fused into this image, and as I. A. Richards and Donald Reiman have argued,[47] Shelley employs Milton's description of Death (*Paradise Lost* II.666-73) to image his chariot of Life—not merely, however, to show that Life is destructive, but instead to show that Life and Death are inseparable and together condemn man to a purgatorial state that is either *perpetual* or at least *prolonged* (Rousseau, Plato, et al. are still enchained). Such an inseparability was not exactly a new idea for Shelley: he had rebuked the Maniac for dying "'Some living death'" in *Julian and Maddalo* (l. 210); in *Epipsychidion* he had described his own purgatorial state of Death-in-Life when he, with the "cold chaste" Mary,

> was nor alive nor dead:—
> For at her silver voice came Death and Life,
> Unmindful each of their accustomed strife,
> Masked like twin babes, a sister and a brother;    (ll. 300-3)

and in *Una Favola*, Life and Death were twin sisters vying for the love of a youth who mistrusted both of them, particularly Life, who "had the fame of a potent enchantress," who "was more false than any Siren," and who in one appearance was *"crowned with a rainbow."*[48]

The rainbow's association with the enchantress Life in *Una Favola* enables us to explain Iris' perplexing and dual function in *The Triumph of Life*. Iris does not appear in the narrator's first vision of Life-in-Death as the "cold glare" and blinding "light" of the chariot in which sat the crouching "Shape/. . . whom years deform/Beneath a dusky hood & double cape" (ll. 77-89). But Iris does serve Life-in-Death when she draws "'her many coloured scarf'" before the "'shape all light'" (ll. 357, 352) who enthralls Rousseau and then offers him the cup of Nepenthe; *and* when she builds with "'vermilion/And green & azure plumes'" the "'moving arch of victory'" (ll. 439-40) over the "'cold bright car'" of "'cold light, whose airs too soon deform'" Rousseau (ll. 434, 468). Iris is thus used by Shelley to equate the enchanting "'fair shape'" (l. 412) of Life (the "'shape all light'") with the deforming foul shape of Death (the "'cold light'"), and the common denominator here, in addition to Iris, is the classical figure of Circe, who is both enchantress *and* deformer. That the beautiful "'shape all light'" is like Circe, described as "The daughter of the Sun" (l. 51) in *Comus* (frequently a source of Shelley's images and ideas in 1822), is suggested by her lineage in *The Triumph of Life*: engendered by "'the bright omnipresence/Of morning'" (ll. 343-44), she stands in relation to her father

> "Amid the sun, as he amid the blaze
>   Of his own glory, on the vibrating
> Floor of the fountain, paved with flashing rays."    (ll. 349-51)

Her lineage, her "'crystal glass/. . . with bright Nepenthe'" (ll. 358-59), and her offering the cup by which Rousseau can "'quench [his] thirst'" but becomes instead like "'a shut lily, stricken by the wand/Of dewy morning's vital alchemy'" (ll. 400-2), all point to the figure of Circe and her enchanting son in Milton's *Comus*.[49] And when this seducing light becomes the deforming light of the chariot, the Circean characteristics of Life-in-Death are retained. The "'cold light'" of the "'car's creative ray'" (ll. 468, 533) soon distorts the human form:

Rousseau is transformed into "an old root which grew/To strange distortion" (ll. 182-83); and the "'Phantoms diffused around'" (l. 487) the chariot's captives are described as eaglets, elves, apes, vultures, falcons, gnats, and flies (ll. 489-508). Shelley had discovered such "foul disfigurement" (*Comus*, l. 74) not only in Petrarch and Dante but also in Milton's as well as Calderón's descriptions of Circe's captives, who had been transformed into either trees or animals.[50]

Circe had not always been such a threatening figure to Shelley, for two years earlier she had appeared in a playful guise in *The Witch of Atlas* to give faith to Shelley, one of

> the weak mariners of that wide lake [of Life]
> Where'er its shores extend or billows roll,
>   Our course unpiloted and starless make
> O'er its wide surface to an unknown goal.                    (lxiii)

Shelley's Witch was another Circean daughter of the Sun and water (ii); a "lovely lady garmented in light" (v); a triumphal figure conveyed by an underwater boat which "some say" was wrought from a car, "the chariot of [Venus'] star" (xxxi); and a "wizard-maiden" who gave to the "most beautiful" a "Strange panacea in a crystal bowl" and to the "less beautiful" such dreams that prompted a king to "dress an ape up in his crown" and to have "a gaudy mock-bird . . . repeat/The chatterings of the monkey" (lxviii-lxxiv). When these characteristics were transferred to the Circean figure of Life-in-Death, Shelley lost the confidence that had been provided by his former Witch who with Petrarchan faith

> in the calm depths her way could take,
> Where in bright bowers immortal forms abide
> Beneath the weltering of the restless tide.                    (lxiii)

No longer confident that such "immortal forms" awaited him in "the calm depths," Shelley in 1822 feared that the "restless tide" of Life extended into a purgatorial state beneath the waters of Death.

Shelley revealed his fears of purgatory as early as January 1821 when he sent *The Witch of Atlas* to Ollier for publication. Disturbed by the critical reception of *The Cenci*, Shelley considered writing another drama but at the same time doubted whether he would "write more. I could be content either with the Hell or the Paradise of poetry; but the torments of its purgatory vex me, without exciting my power sufficiently to put an end to the vexation."[51] That vexation was significantly increased after August 1821 when he unsuccessfully engaged Byron in a rivalry for the "Paradise of fame." Being condemned by the "God" of Byron's talents to the purgatory of neglect

and poverty, Shelley considered escaping that state by suicide until
he realized that he might be exchanging the temporal purgatory of
Life for the eternal purgatory of Life-in-Death. In order to give form
to such a horrifying experience, Shelley turned to the terza rima not
only in Petrarch's *Trionfi* but also in Dante's *Purgatorio* (parts of
which he had translated), and he adopted the procession of suffering
multitudes where he saw fit: for example, the poets Virgil and Statius
(the latter not appearing until the twenty-first canto) were able to
lead Dante up the ascents of purgatory, but Rousseau had no knowledge of the "'opposing steep of that mysterious dell'" (l. 470) within
the purgatorial state of Life-in-Death; Beatrice, preceded by the rainbow (xxix.76-78), "clad . . . with hue of living flame" (xxx.32-33),
and attended by the "triumphal chariot" (xxix.107) of the Church,
awaited at the end of *Purgatorio* to guide Dante through Paradise,
whereas Shelley's Life-in-Death, served by Iris, emanating light, and
transformed from a "'light from Heaven'" into the "'cold bright car'"
(ll. 429, 434), awaited at the beginning of *The Triumph of Life* to
enthrall man in the purgatorial state. Because of these and other
deliberate borrowings from Dante's *Purgatorio*,[52] Shelley's "strange
trance" occurring between "the *Deep* / . . . at [his] feet, & *Heaven*
above [his] head" (ll. 27-29, my italics) can be interpreted only as a
parody of Dante's vision of the purgatory that lies between *Inferno*
and *Paradisio*. Failing to attain "either . . . the Hell or the Paradise
of poetry" during his life, Shelley feared that Life-in-Death would
also condemn him to an inescapable and vexing purgatory.

Goethe's lines about "Heaven" and the "Deep" ("Den Himmel
über mir und unter mir die Wellen") have taken us to Dante by way
of Milton and Calderón, indeed a circuitous route of influence on
*The Triumph of Life*, but one that has been determined by Shelley's
envy of Byron in the spring of 1822. It was Byron, Shelley bitterly
acknowledged to himself, who now indeed rivaled the masters of
western literature, and if Byron could adapt Dante (in *The Prophecy
of Dante*), Milton (in *Cain*), Goethe and Calderón (in *The Deformed
Transformed*), then Shelley reasoned that if he could superadd these
writers to Petrarch, he might finally wrest from Byron some portion
of the "Paradise of fame" before he died. As Donald Reiman has
demonstrated, Shelley also used material from Rousseau in *The
Triumph of Life*,[53] but he no longer considered Rousseau among the
sacred few eternal poets. In July 1816 (shortly after suicidally refusing Byron's aid during a storm on Lake Geneva at the exact spot
where Rousseau's "Julie and her lover were nearly overset, and where
St. Preux was tempted to plunge with her into the lake"), Shelley
had judged that Rousseau was "the greatest man the world has pro-

duced since Milton."[54] But by 1822 Shelley believed that Byron was
the greatest poet since Milton, and hence Rousseau (replaced by Byron
in the "Paradise of fame") was the perfect exemplum for Shelley
(also "extinguished" by the "sun" of Byron's talents) of a poet who
had not yet escaped the purgatorial state of Life-in-Death. According
to Shelley (and Petrarch), one of the accustomed vicissitudes of Life
that extends beyond the grave was the *fame* sought by men of genius:
and Byron's talents obscured those of Rousseau, even as Rousseau's
had obscured those of former artists. Rousseau, therefore, according
to *The Triumph of Life*, was among those captives

> whose fame or infamy must grow
> Till the great winter lay the form & name
> Of their own earth with them forever low.                    (ll. 125-27)

No wonder then that Rousseau didn't know "'Whither the conqueror
[of Life-in-Death] hurries'" him. And if Death would not eliminate
Shelley's purgatorial vexations experienced in a Life that would not
grant him *fame*, no wonder that he had second thoughts about suicide:
the "great winter" of Eternal darkness might never come.

 Shelley's concern for both *fame* and *money* during the last year
of his life necessarily excluded him, he believed, from

> the sacred few who could not tame
> Their spirits to the Conqueror, but as soon
> As they had touched the world with living flame
>
> Fled back like eagles to their native noon,
> Or those who put aside the diadem
> Of earthly thrones or gems.                    (ll. 128-33)

These frequently misunderstood lines have syntactical and exclusive
reference *only* to those who have attained "fame or infamy" (l. 125)
in Life or after Death. If a philosopher or moralist (like Socrates and
Christ, "they of Athens & Jerusalem," l. 134) or if a poet (perhaps
like Keats) could resist the temptation of purposefully seeking fame
or money ("earthly thrones or gems") during his life, then he could
escape the torments of Life-in-Death and as one of "the sacred few"
return to his "native noon." But Shelley in 1822 had envied Byron's
fame and money to such a degree that he no longer was among these
"sacred few." And in order to announce in *The Triumph of Life* that
Byron was the main cause of his purgatorial torments, Shelley in a
"strange trance" turned not only to Dante's vision of *Purgatorio* but
also to Byron's *Prophecy of Dante* and used Byron's own words to
damn himself to the vexations of such a purgatory. In *The Prophecy*

*of Dante*, Shelley discovered that Byron's Dante had also distinguished between "the sacred few":

> But few shall soar upon that Eagle's wing,
> And look in the Sun's face, with Eagle's gaze;   (III.70-71)

and those who are enchained by a desire for fame and money in Life:

> He who once enters in a Tyrant's hall
> As guest is slave—his thoughts become a booty,
> And the first day which sees the chain enthral
> A captive, sees his half of Manhood gone—
> The Soul's emasculation saddens all
> His spirit; thus the Bard too near the throne
> Quails from his inspiration, bound to *please*.   (III.80-86)

Shelley phrased his lines on "the sacred few" who "Fled back like eagles to their native noon" by combining Dante's description of the "few . . . upon . . . Eagle's wing" with Dante's subsequent lament that

> These birds of Paradise but long to flee
> Back to their native mansion, soon they find
> Earth's mist with their pure pinions not agree,
> *And die or are degraded.*   (III.169-72, my italics)

Shelley's indisputable rephrasings of Goethe, Milton, Petrarch, and Dante in *The Triumph of Life* argue for his purposeful imitation of these lines as well. And because of Shelley's esemplastic fears of the purgatorial pains in both Life and Death, neither of which seemed to offer an escape from Byron, he found in *The Prophecy of Dante*, immediately following Byron's lines about the poets who "*die or are degraded*" (my italics), the inspiration for his vision in *The Triumph of Life* of those poets who "die" *and* "are degraded"[55] even in death:

> for the mind
> Succumbs to long infection, and *despair,*
> *And vulture Passions flying close behind,*
> Await the moment to assail and tear;
> And when, at length, the wingéd wanderers stoop,
> Then is the Prey-birds' *triumph*, then they share
> The spoil, *o'erpowered* at length by one fell swoop.
> Yet some have been untouched who learned to bear,
> Some whom no Power could ever force to droop,
> *Who could resist themselves even,* hardest care!
> *And task most hopeless; but some such have been,*
> *And if my name amongst the number were,*
> *That Destiny austere, and yet serene,*

> *Were prouder than more dazzling fame unblessed.*
>
> (III.172-85, my italics)

By patterning his vision of the triumphal figure of Life-in-Death on these lines which resonate throughout *The Triumph of Life* and by developing that vision in terms of the works of Petrarch, Dante, Calderón, Milton, Rousseau, and Goethe (the last five of whom Shelley associated with Byron), Shelley revealed, however obscurely and indirectly, that Byron's "hateful" presence continued to torment him into the last days of his life.

## III

Whether Shelley actually killed himself is an unanswerable question, but his fears of a purgatorial state of Life-in-Death sufficiently argued for remaining in the purgatory of Life, a purgatory, however, that Byron served only to increase during the first week of July 1822. Shelley together with Edward Williams sailed from the Casa Magni to Leghorn on 1 July to meet with Hunt, who had finally arrived to establish *The Liberal* with Byron. But by 2 July Shelley's worst fears about the alliance between "the wren & the eagle" were confirmed: because the Gambas were being exiled, Byron was "on the point of leaving Tuscany" and abandoning Hunt; Byron had rudely ignored Hunt's sick wife upon their arrival in Leghorn and he apparently indicated that "he did not wish his name to be attached" to *The Liberal*; Hunt had spent all of the money advanced to him by Byron and was even 60 crowns in debt; and Shelley, with no money, was forced on 7 July to borrow from Byron £50, part of which he may have given to Hunt.[56] Once more Byron's fame and money (both of which Hunt needed) reminded Shelley of his own deficiencies. But by 8 July, Shelley was able to convince Byron to contribute *The Vision of Judgment*, the translation of *Pulci*, and any yet unpublished prose tracts to *The Liberal*.[57]

Having temporarily at least reconciled Byron and Hunt, Shelley then set sail with Edward Williams to return to the Casa Magni. And in his possession was Jane Williams' letter of 6 July which contained an ironic prophecy about the final separation between Byron and Shelley: "Lord B[yron]'s departure gives me pleasure; for whatever may be the present difficulties and disappointments, they are small, to what you would have suffered had he remained with you. This I say in the true spirit of prophecy so gather consolation from it." Jane here attempted to comfort Shelley, who on 4 July had expressed his fears that he had lost, "perhaps for ever," the few hours of pleasure he had experienced with her in recent months. Jane apparently sensed the gravity of his distress, for she added a postscript to her prophecy of "consolation": "Why do you talk of never enjoying moments like the past, are you going to join your friend Plato or do you expect I shall do so soon?"[58] She apparently did not realize that Shelley had considered suicide but feared Death as much as Life, and she certainly did not know that Byron within the past month had rephrased Plato in such a manner as to provide a fitting epitaph for the author of *The Triumph of Life*. Immediately before perverting Socrates' doctrine to prove "the Nothingness of life," Byron parodied Socrates' last words as reported in Plato's *Apology*:

> We live and die,
> But which is best, you know no more than I.[59]
>
> (*Don Juan* VII.4)

Shelley was equally uncertain about Life and Death, and consequently we will never know whether he welcomed the opportunity of Death on 8 July 1822. To disguise our ignorance, we can only turn to Byron's description a year later of a man who had ascended a "precipice" (*Don Juan* XIV.5) with great peril and who could not descend without the greater peril of suicide:

> 'Tis true, you don't—but, pale and struck with terror,
>    Retire: but look into your past impression!
> And you will find, though shuddering at the mirror
>    Of your own thoughts, in all their self confession,
> The lurking bias, be it truth or error,
>    To the *unknown*; a secret prepossession,
> To plunge with all your fears—but where? You know not,
> And that's the reason why *you do—or do not.*
>
> (XIV.6, my italics)

IV

Despite the fact that Byron in *Don Juan* frequently alluded to Shelley after his death, the above quoted lines on suicide probably were not intended to comment on the tragedy of 8 July 1822. Byron, it seems, did not understand the extent of Shelley's envy and despair in their rivalry, and he most certainly was not aware that this rivalry prompted Shelley to consider suicide. Byron did not even know that Shelley in 1821/22 had substantially altered his metaphysical assumptions about man's destiny, and consequently he continued to criticize his fellow poet for a utopianism that had already been rejected. At this same time, however, Byron began to praise Shelley as a poet and as a man: in the note (September 1821) to the Appendix of *The Two*

*Foscari*, for example, he objected to the "metaphysical portion" of *Queen Mab* but admired "the poetry of that and . . . other publications" by Shelley.[60] Not long after this judgment, in his "Detached Thoughts" begun on 15 October 1821, Byron described his general dissatisfaction with "literary men" but noted "several exceptions": "men of the world, such as Scott, and Moore, etc., or visionaries out of it, such as Shelley, etc." After Moore complained about Shelley's influence on *Cain*, Byron on 4 March 1822 defended Shelley but once more distinguished between the man and the metaphysician:

> As to poor Shelley, who is another bugbear to you and the world, he is, to my knowledge, the *least* selfish and the mildest of men—a man who has made more sacrifices of his fortune and feelings for others than any I ever heard of. With his speculative opinions I have nothing in common, nor desire to have.

And on 22 May, unaware that his own "fortune" was envied by the man who made so many "sacrifices," Byron in a conversation with George Bancroft even vindicated Shelley's "speculative opinions":

> Shelley, he added, was translating "Faust," and this led him to a defense of Shelley.
>
> "You may have heard," said he, "many foolish stories of his being a man of no principle, an atheist, and all that; but he is not." And he explained what appeared in Shelley as atheism was only a subtle metaphysical idealism.

All of these remarks serve to validate Byron's words, according to Medwin, that "'Shelley has more poetry in him than any man living; and if he were not so mystical, and would not write Utopias and set himself up as a Reformer, his right to rank as a poet, and very highly too, could not fail of being acknowledged.'" Byron repeated the substance of this judgment to James Hamilton Browne in 1823:

> [Byron] bore honourable testimony to the extensive learning of poor Shelley, who had aided him to compose, or correct, some of the notes to his works, thereby rendering him essential service. He maintained that Shelley, from the wonderful facility of his versification, and aptitude at metaphor, would, but for his unfortunate predilection for metaphysics in poetry, have ranked in the foremost circle amongst modern bards: asserting, that no one wrote better, when he selected a lucid theme, and allowed the reader fully to understand and appreciate his effusions.

And shortly before Byron himself died in Greece in 1824, he insisted to George Finlay that "'Shelley was really a most extraordinary genius'" although he was "'quite mad with his metaphysics.'"[61]

According to Teresa Guiccioli, Byron did have "'a great affection for Shelley, and a great esteem for his character and talents; but he was not his friend in the most extensive sense of that word.'" After Shelley's death, Byron himself explained that his "propensity" for friendship was limited: "I did not even feel it for Shelley, however much I admired and esteemed him; so that you see not even vanity could bribe me into it, for, of all men, Shelley thought highest of my talents,—and, perhaps, of my disposition."[62] Byron was at least half correct, for Shelley had excessively praised his rival's talents in *Julian and Maddalo, Euganean Hills, Adonais, Hellas,* and *Sonnet to Byron.* But Byron, according to Trelawny, refused to bestow publicly a "friendly word" on Shelley:

> [Byron to Trelawny] "To-day I had another letter warning me against the Snake (Shelley). He, alone, in this age of humbug, dares stem the current, as he did to-day the flooded Arno in his skiff, although I could not observe he made any progress. The attempt is better than being swept along as all the rest are, with the filthy garbage scoured from its banks."
>
> Taking advantage of this panegyric on Shelley, I observed, he might do him a great service at little cost, by a friendly word or two in his next work, such as he had bestowed on authors of less merit.
>
> Assuming a knowing look, he continued,—
>
> "All trades have their mysteries; if we crack up a popular author, he repays us in the same coin, principal and interest. A friend may have repaid money lent—can't say any of mine have; but who ever heard of the interest being added thereto?"
>
> I rejoined,—
>
> "By your own showing you are indebted to Shelley; some of his best verses are to express his admiration of your genius."
>
> "Ay," he said, with a significant look, "who reads them? If we puffed the Snake, it might not turn out a profitable investment. If he cast off the slough of his mystifying metaphysics, he would want no puffing."
>
> Seeing I was not satisfied, he added,—
>
> "If we introduced Shelley to our readers, they might draw comparisons, and they are 'odorous.'"[63]

We should suspect that Trelawny invented at least part of this dialogue, because Byron would have referred to the note affixed to *The Two Foscari* where he did praise Shelley's poetry. Nevertheless, with the exception of this note (where Shelley, the "author" of *Queen Mab,* is not mentioned by name),[64] Byron did not use his poetry to "puff" Shelley. And even in this note, Byron was more interested in disassociating himself from Shelley's metaphysical atheism than in praising his poetry.

Because Byron was disturbed by Shelley's death in July and the "extraordinary effect"[65] of his cremation on 16 August, we might expect to find Shelley's name included in the cantos of Don Juan written around this time. But we look in vain, even in Canto XI (October 1822) among stanzas 56-61 which list the poets dead (Keats) and alive (including Scott, Moore, Wordsworth, Coleridge, and Southey) with whom Byron had contended for fame. But we can discover at least an allusion to Shelley:

> The list grows long of *live and dead pretenders*
>    To that which none will gain—or none will know
> The Conqueror at least; who, ere time renders
>    His last award, *will have the long grass grow*
> *Above his burnt-out brain, and sapless cinders.*
>    If I might augur, I should rate but low
> Their chances.                                    (61, my italics)

The effect of Shelley's "burnt-out brain, and sapless cinders" may be traced in other stanzas of Cantos IX-XI, all written between the middle of August and the middle of October. Pratt and Steffan, for example, conjectured that the "melancholy tone of the opening stanzas of [Canto X] may have some connection with the recent death and burial of Shelley,"[66] but they ignored the more obvious melancholy following the Wellington stanzas which begin Canto IX. There in nine stanzas (11-19) Byron reminds his readers, after Shelley's death and cremation, that "Death laughs" and "its lipless mouth grins without breath," and then asks in a manner recalling the imagery of Hellas (ll. 197-200)[67] and The Triumph of Life (which Byron could hardly have read),

> Why should not Life be equally content,
>    With his Superior, in a smile to trample
> Upon the nothings which are daily spent
>    Like bubbles on an ocean much less ample
> Than the eternal deluge, which devours
> Suns as rays—worlds like atoms—years like hours?    (IX.13)

Invoking Shakespeare ("'To be or not to be! that is the question'"), Horace ("'Oh dura ilia messorum!'"), and Montaigne ("'Que sçais-je?'") in successive stanzas, Byron, like Shelley, was uncertain whether Life or Death offered a better state of *being*, and he concluded his stanzas of doubt by writing another, albeit cynical, memorial to Shelley:

> It is a pleasant voyage perhaps to float,
>   Like Pyrrho, *on a sea of speculation;*
> *But what if carrying sail capsize the boat?*
>   *Your wise men don't know much of navigation;*
> *And swimming long in the abyss of thought*
>   *Is apt to tire*: a calm and shallow station
> Well nigh the shore, where one stoops down and gathers
> Some pretty shell, is best for moderate bathers.
>
> (IX.18, my italics)

In opposition to Shelley, Byron always considered himself as one of the more "moderate bathers" in the "sea of speculation"; and in Shelley's portrait of him as Maddalo, he had already warned Julian, "'if you can't swim,/Beware of Providence'" (ll. 117-18).

Byron could content himself by skeptically rejecting Shelley's allegiance to those "heathenish philosophers" who "Make Love the Main Spring of the Universe" (IX.73),[68] but he nevertheless sought answers to the same questions that Shelley asked of Life and Death. In Canto X, he admitted that "getting nigh grim Dante's 'obscure wood'" of middle age made him reflective, and in attempting to "stave off thought, which . . ./. . . sticks to me through the abyss/ Of this odd labyrinth" of *Don Juan*, he declared, "I *won't* philosophize, and *will* be read" (27-28). Byron's protestation here reflects his belief that metaphysics had ruined Shelley's poetry, especially since Shelley had made (in Trelawny's recollection of Byron's words) no "'progress'" when he "'dare[d] stem the current'" rather than be "'swept along as all the rest are, with the filthy garbage scoured from its banks.'" But not long after Shelley's cremation, Byron in Canto X confessed that he, like Shelley, *immoderately* abandoned the shore at times for "the abyss of [metaphysical] thought" (IX.18):

> In the Wind's Eye I have sailed, and sail; but for
>   The stars, I own my telescope is dim;
> But at the least I have shunned the common shore,
>   And leaving land far out of sight, would skim
> The Ocean of Eternity: the roar
>   Of breakers has not daunted my slight, trim,
> But *still* sea-worthy skiff; and she may float
> Where ships have foundered, as doth many a boat.    (X.4)

Once more Byron's words reflect the recent death of Shelley, who had found it "very puzzling on the brink/Of what is called Eternity, to stare,/And know no more of what is here than there:—" (X.20).

Having a "telescope . . . dim," the more skeptical Byron did not share Shelley's eagerness to pursue the questions of Life and Death.

And when he reflected on his occasional philosophizing in Cantos IX-XI of *Don Juan*, he regretted that he did "grow too metaphysical" (IX.41) and declared that he would "leave off metaphysical/Discussion" (XI.5). But such declarations to return to the immediacy of his plot would not still his questioning: even in Canto XV, his question, "why will I thus entangle/Myself with metaphysics?" was followed by the admission, "And yet, such is my folly, or my fate,/I always knock my head against some angle/About the present, past, or future state" (91). And within eight more stanzas, he again returned to the same metaphysical questions that had disturbed Shelley:

> Between two worlds life hovers like a star,
> 'Twixt night and morn, upon the horizon's verge:
> How little do we know that which we are!
> How less what we may be! The eternal surge
> Of time and tide rolls on, and bears afar
> Our bubbles; as the old burst, new emerge,
> Lash'd from the foam of ages; while the graves
> Of Empires heave but like some passing waves.          (XV.99)

Such images hauntingly recall Shelley's vision with the "night" before him and the "day" behind in *The Triumph of Life*: those destroyed by Life-in-Death were as "foam after the Ocean's wrath"; if "'Figures ever new/Rise on the bubble'" or glass of Life, they "'all like bubbles on an eddying flood/Fell into the same track at last & were/Borne onward'" (ll. 27, 163, 248-49, 458-60) by the chariot of Life-in-Death. Shelley's *Life* and Byron's *Ocean* had both promised certain images of Eternity; neither, each feared in his last unfinished poem, would fulfill its promise.

## EPILOGUE: AN ISLAND PARADISE

The tragic circumstances of Shelley's death not only increased Byron's doubts about man's immortality but also provided an occasion for him to resolve at least some of these doubts by writing an elegy on Shelley. But as previously noted, Byron did not publicly wish to "puff" the Snake, and he appears to have been content with the occasional and obscurely phrased "memorials" to his fellow poet in the last cantos of *Don Juan*.[1] Byron, however, did personally grieve the loss of "the *best* and least selfish man [he] ever knew,"[2] and I believe we can discover his final and public tribute to Shelley (as well as an exoneration of the "Ocean" that destroyed him) in *The Island; or, Christian and His Comrades*, his last complete narrative poem begun in Genoa by January 1823, finished perhaps by February, and sent to England on 29 March.[3] In this poem, which begins with the mutiny on the *Bounty* and ends with the happy days of an island paradise, Byron may also have represented some of his hopes for the liberation of Greece, to which he journeyed in the summer of 1823 and in which he died the following year on 19 April 1824.

Ostensibly, *The Island* has nothing to do with Shelley or for that matter Greece, even though the rebirth metaphor is once used specifically to embody Byron's political hopes:

> Even Greece can boast but one Thermopylæ,
> Till *now*, when she has forged her broken chain
> Back to a sword, and dies and lives again! (III.56-58)

In one half of the poem, however, such optimism is belied by a typically Byronic version of the Promethean struggle: oppressed by the circumstances of Bligh's command, Christian with both success and guilt leads the mutiny against Bligh, returns with his men to the island paradise of Toobonai, and finally dies in his battle for freedom after an English ship arrives to apprehend him and his men. But interwoven with this narrative are the episodes of another mutineer, Torquil, who escapes recapture, symbolically dies into life, and regains the paradise of his desires. Because this narrative action resembles what Byron hoped for Greece, Carl Woodring once suggested that "symbolically, Torquil is Greece."[4] If this be the case, we might even interpret Christian's death (in order to save Torquil) as Byron's wish to die for Greece. Such an argument, however, ignores the dates of *The Island*: Byron's interest in Greece was not actively renewed until after he finished this poem.

In my judgment, Byron's portrait of Torquil looks backward to Shelley more than forward to Greece. That is, Torquil (even though he might have been modeled on the historical George Stewart) is a Shelleyan hero, or at least one embodying Byron's understanding of Shelley and his protagonists. Like Byron himself, Torquil was an able swimmer and an "offspring of the Hebrides" (II.165) who under different circumstances might have become a warrior; but like the Shelley Byron knew, Torquil was a "blue-eyed" and "fair-haired" youth who was "Eager to hope, but not less firm to bear,/Acquainted with all feelings save despair" (II.163, 165, 177-78). He with Christian and the other mutineers shared the same "hope" that Shelley had formerly urged on Byron and that the latter recorded in his *Epistle to Augusta* (1816):

> *The world is all before me*; I but ask
> Of Nature that with which she will comply—
> It is but in her Summer's sun to bask,
> To mingle with the quiet of her sky,
> To see her gentle face without a mask,
> And never gaze on it with apathy.     (xi, my italics)

This same desire to regain the paradise from which Adam and Eve were thrust (see *Paradise Lost* XII.646) is found in *The Island*: "The waters with their world were all before" the mutineers who had "Young hearts, which languished for some sunny isle,/Where summer years and summer women smile" (I.5, 27-28). But eventually reality shattered their dreams when the "vengeance of their country's law" assaulted "their guilt-won Paradise": "Proscribed even in their second country, they/Were lost; in vain the World before them lay" (III.38-39, 43-44). And thus the Byronic hero fails in his paradigmatic journey to attain the "Paradise of [his] despair" (*Childe Harold* IV. cxxii)—that is, except for Torquil, who retains this paradise through the efforts of Neuha, his "bride of Toobonai" (II.211).

Torquil and Neuha are unique in Byron's poetry, for only they survive the "night" of experience to enjoy with each other the "happy days/As only the yet infant world displays" (IV.419-20). All other idyls, for example, those of Conrad and Medora or Juan and Haidée, are destroyed by chance, death, or mutability. But in *The Island*, Byron accepts the "Utopian" vision he had formerly rejected in Shelley's poetry. In fact, he uses circumstances from Shelley's poetry to celebrate love as the means to triumph over death and to redeem the fallen world. For example, Torquil and Neuha's union "in one absorbing soul" which can possibly "merge . . . in the great shore" (II.305, 391) repeats Shelley's hope to become with Emily "The living soul of this Elysian isle,/Conscious, inseparable, one" (*Epipsychidion*, ll. 539-40); their love, which is like that of "the devotee" who "in his ecstasy" uplifts his soul "gloriously to God" and which is described as "the all-absorbing flame/Which, kindled by another, grows the same,/Wrapt in one blaze" (II.370-80), recalls Shelley's judgments that "The spirit of the worm beneath the sod/ In love and worship, blends itself with God" and that his and Emily's love was "like two meteors of expanding flame" which became "the same" (*Epipsychidion*, ll. 128-29, 576-77); Neuha's rescue of Torquil from the attack resembles Cythna's rescue of Laon in Canto VI of *The Revolt of Islam*; the submarine entrance to "'Neuha's Cave'" is like the entrance to Cythna's prison (*Revolt* VII.ix-xii), the cave itself resembling that of Prometheus and Asia (*Prometheus Unbound* III.iii. 10-24) and having a legendary history (IV.192-230) similar to the lone dwelling sought by Shelley and Emily in *Epipsychidion* (ll. 483-512);[5] finally, Torquil and Neuha's resurrection from this cave in the "black rock" and their return to the *"infant world"* of Toobonai (IV.10, 420, my italics) in effect fulfill Shelley's hope in *Lines Written Among the Euganean Hills* that

> Other flowering isles must be
> In the sea of life and agony:
> Other spirits float and flee
> O'er that gulf: even now, perhaps,
> On some rock the wild wave wraps,
> With folding wings they waiting sit
> For my bark, to pilot it
> To some calm and blooming cove,
> Where for me, and those I love,
> May a windless bower be built,
> Far from passion, pain, and guilt,
> . . . . . . . . . . . . . . . . . . . . . . . .
> And the *earth grow young again.*     (ll. 335-45, 373, my italics)

Even if all of these parallels are coincidental, Byron had undoubtedly read each work in question,[6] and in 1816 he believed Shelley to be of the "'tribe of the Otaheite philosophers'";[7] consequently, he must have thought of Shelley when he portrayed Torquil and when he penned what was apparently the real mutineers' cry, "'Huzza! for Otaheite!'"[8]

Most important for our understanding of *The Island* and this last episode in the long and complex history of the relations between Byron and Shelley is Shelley's 1818 poem, *Lines Written Among the Euganean Hills*. Because Shelley therein had envisioned his own death "On the beach of a northern sea" where he "Lies a solitary heap,/One white skull and seven dry bones" with no one to "lament for him" (ll. 45, 48-49, 62), and at the same time eulogized Byron as the poet of "Ocean" (ll. 178-83), I believe that Byron was attracted to reread it before elegizing Shelley in *The Island*. He would have discovered that Shelley's vision of a flowering isle had been fleeting, for the "Pain" of experience returned with "Autumn's evening" (ll. 333, 321). In 1818, however, Shelley hoped within the diurnal metaphor of his poem that the "soft sunshine" of a new morning would herald another and more enduring island in the "sea of life and agony" (ll. 348, 336). Byron seems to have been aware of this controlling rebirth metaphor in the *Euganean Hills*, and after the sea proved indeed agonizing for Shelley on 8 July 1822, he offered to his fellow poet an elegiac memorial that fused the destructiveness of Ocean, the rebirth metaphor of death leading to life, and the enduring island paradise for a Shelleyan character. In the song from Toobonai, flowers are symbolically gathered from the sepulchre (II.7, 21) to introduce the motif of life after death: the sun sets on Toobonai

> as if he left
> The World for ever, earth of light bereft,
> Plunged with red forehead down along the wave,
> As dives a hero headlong to his grave, (II.362-65)

but Torquil and Neuha are sustained by the light of love and innocently ask "if indeed the day were done" (II.369);[9] Greece is described as having "forged her broken chain/Back to a sword, and dies and lives again" (III.57-58); Torquil and Neuha plunge into the Ocean to an apparent death only to be saved in "'Neuha's Cave'" and to be restored to the life of Toobonai; and a "hundred fires . . ./Blazed O'er the general revel of the night" of resurrection, "A night succeeded by such happy days" (IV.415-16, 419). By employing such a metaphor for Torquil's rebirth and attainment of Paradise, Byron extends the metaphoric "sunshine" of the *Euganean Hills* to give, in my judgment, Shelley a final memorial—a flowering *Island* with perpetually "happy days." Ironically, Byron did not know that Shelley by 1821 had forgone practically all such utopian fancies and that by July 1822 he had hoped to escape all such lights in an eternal Darkness. But as Shelley had feared, he was pursued by the "sun" of Byron's talents even into the Valley of Death.

APPENDIX A: SOME LITERARY RELATIONS
BETWEEN BYRON AND SHELLEY FROM 1810
TO 1816

Thomas Jefferson Hogg and Shelley were expelled from Oxford University in March 1811, and soon afterwards they arrived in London where Shelley purchased a volume of Byron's *English Bards and Scotch Reviewers* and read it aloud to Hogg while they walked in the country. Hogg later recalled that Shelley was "greatly delighted" with Byron's satire and added that "such was his first introduction to Byron; such his first acquaintance with his brother poet, for he had never read those early attempts which were the moving cause of the furious onslaught."[1] Such, however, was not exactly the case, for Shelley by the spring of 1810 had read and plagiarized from two poems included in Byron's 1808 edition of *Poems: Original and Translated*, a volume following and differing from Byron's 1807 edition of *Hours of Idleness*. That Shelley read at least part of the 1808 edition is suggested by his plagiarism from Byron's lyric now entitled "I would I were a careless child," and first published in *Poems: Original and Translated*. In this lyric, Byron had asked, "Ah! why do dark'ning shades conceal/The hour when man must cease to be?" (*Poetry*, I, 206). With the identical question, Shelley concluded a ten-stanza poem he sent in a letter to Edward Graham on 22 April 1810 (*PBSL*, I, 7-8):

> Ah why do darkning shades conceal
>   The hour when man must cease to be?
> Why may not human minds unveil
>   The dark shade of futurity?

A few months later in 1810, Shelley included a revised and shorter version of this ten-stanza poem in his novel *St. Irvyne; or, The Rosicrucean* (published by December 1810). In this novel we also find another poem that was plagiarized from Byron's "Lachin y Gair," first published in *Hours of Idleness* and then reprinted in *Poems: Original and Translated*. The nature of Shelley's borrowings are suggested by the following italicized passages from the two poems:

"Lachin y Gair," stanza 3

*"Shades of the dead! have I not*
*heard your voices*
*Rise on the night-rolling breath of*
*the gale?"*
Surely, the soul of the hero rejoices,
And *rides* on the *wind*, o'er his
own Highland *vale!*
Round Loch na Garr, while the
*stormy mist* gathers,
Winter presides in his cold icy car:
Clouds, there, *encircle* the *forms*
of my *Fathers;*
They dwell in the *tempests* of
*dark* Loch na Garr.

(*Poetry*, I, 172)

from *St. Irvyne*

*Ghosts of the dead! have I not*
*heard your yelling*
*Rise on the night-rolling breath of*
*the blast,*
When o'er the *dark* ether the *tem-*
*pest* is swelling,
And on eddying *whirlwind* the thun-
der-peal past?

For oft have I stood on the *dark*
height of Jura,
Which frowns on the *valley* that
opens beneath;
Oft have I braved the chill *night-*
*tempest's* fury,
Whilst around me, I thought, echo'd
murmurs of *death*.

And now, whilst the *winds* of the
mountain are howling,
O *father!* thy *voice* seems to
strike on mine ear;
In air whilst the tide of the *night-*
*storm* is *rolling*,
It breaks on the pause of the elements' jar.

On the wing of the *whirlwind*[2] which
roars o'er the mountain
Perhaps *rides* the *ghost* of my sire
who is dead;
On the *mist* of the *tempest* which
hangs o'er the fountain,[3]
Whilst a wreath of *dark* vapour
*encircles* his head.

(*Julian*, V, 123)

H. Buxton Forman first noted the metrical and verbal similarities
between the first two lines of both poems as printed above,[4] but the
similarities do not end there. In eight lines of anapestic tetrameter,
Byron depicted a stormy evening in which he heard his ancestors'
voices in the wintry gales and imagined their souls riding the blasts
above Loch na Garr. In the same meter, Shelley expanded his vision to
sixteen lines: Megalena, the fictional writer of these verses, addressed

only one ancestor, her father; but as in Byron's stanza, she heard the voice of her sire through the howling winds and she imagined his "ghost" riding the whirlwind above the mountains. Even the conclusions to these two scenes are identical: the forms of Byron's ancestors were encircled by clouds; and Shelley depicted Megalena's father with a wreath of dark vapor encircling his head.[5]

II

Whether Shelley read *Childe Harold* I-II before he wrote *Queen Mab* in 1812/13 is difficult to determine. We do know that Shelley had access to *Childe Harold* just before he and Mary Godwin eloped to the continent in July 1814, for Mary at that time inscribed upon the flyleaves of a copy of *Queen Mab* two quatrains that were paraphrases of Byron's "To Thyrza" (ll. 29-32) and "If sometimes in the haunts of men" (st. 5), both of which poems were included in all but the first editions of *Childe Harold* I-II.[6] That Mary was at least responsible for bringing Byron to Shelley's attention at this time is suggested by Shelley's entry in her journal for 3 August 1814: "Mary read to me some passages from Lord Byron's poems. I was not before so clearly aware how much of the colouring our own feelings throw upon the liveliest delineations of other minds" (*MSJ*, p. 5).

Shelley, however, may have read *Childe Harold* I-II during the summer or fall of 1812 after he returned from Wales to England for a few months. Because he spent some of October and November in London, his familiarity with *Poems: Original and Translated* and *English Bards and Scotch Reviewers* probably prompted him to read *Childe Harold*, especially since it was the rage of London and had gone through four editions since the spring. Such a reading would explain his renewed interest in the Spenserian stanza, which he used for his poem "On Leaving London for Wales" in November 1812. There appear to be no direct borrowings from *Childe Harold* in "On Leaving London for Wales," but its second stanza embodies the spirit of Byron's expressions:

> With joy I breathe the last and full farewell
>     That long has quivered on my burdened heart,
> My natural sympathies to rapture swell
>     As from its day thy cheerless glooms depart,
> Nor all the glare thy gayest scenes impart
>     Could lure one sigh, could steal one tear from me,
> Or lull to languishment the wakeful smart
>     Which virtue feels for all 'tis forced to see,
> Or quench the eternal flame of generous Liberty.[7]

III

Shelley's avowed interest in Byron's poetry before 1816 probably caused him to read Byron's tales, including *The Giaour, The Bride of Abydos, The Corsair,* and *Lara*—all written and published between the summers of 1813 and 1814. When *Lara* was published in August 1814, Shelley, Mary, and Claire Clairmont were on the continent, but four days after their return Claire recorded in her diary that she was reading "the Lara of Lord Byron."[8] Five months later, Shelley recorded in Mary's journal that "We read, and are delighted with, 'Lara,' the finest of Lord Byron's poems" (*MSJ*, p. 38). Shelley's use of the superlative suggests that he was familiar with Byron's other tales, but there is no record of such familiarity prior to 1816.[9]

IV

Because Shelley was interested in Byron, he also sent a copy of his *Queen Mab* (printed in May 1813) to the author of *Childe Harold.* Byron later recalled that he did not see *Queen Mab* until "some time after its publication" (*L&J*, VI,, 387) but I am inclined to believe that he received it in 1813. However, it is possible that Shelley did not send it until shortly before or after Claire Clairmont met Byron in the early spring of 1816. In a letter describing the contents of the *Alastor* volume (published February 1816), which Claire or Shelley himself provided for Byron, Claire explained to Byron that it "was Shelley who sent you *Queen Mab*; I know not wherefor" (*L&J*, III, 432). Part of this "wherefor" was explained by Thomas Moore when commenting on the first meeting between Byron and Shelley in Geneva:

> It was the first time that Lord Byron and Mr. Shelley ever met; though, long before, when the latter was quite a youth,—being the younger of the two by four or five years,—he had sent to the noble poet a copy of his Queen Mab, accompanied by a letter, in which, after detailing at full length all the accusations he had heard brought against his character, he added, that, should these charges not have been true, it would make him happy to be honoured with his acquaintance. The book alone, it appears, reached its destination,—the letter having miscarried,—and Lord Byron was known to have expressed warm admiration of the opening lines of the poem.[10]

## APPENDIX B: SHELLEY'S "ONE MIND"

In Chapter 6 of this study (see especially n. 21), I argued that Prometheus represents the "one mind" (lower case) but only insofar as that representation relates to individual consciousnesses considered abstractly. Because this interpretation radically differs from Wasserman's consideration of the "One Mind" as an ontological universal of which individual minds are only partial modes, I judge it necessary to explain the basis of this difference.

In his *Shelley: A Critical Reading*, Wasserman correctly explained Shelley's "intellectual philosophy" as an idealism that reduces existence to ideas and things to thoughts, but I cannot agree with his extension of that reasoning to a conclusion that "Shelley does not accept even the real existence of a plurality of unitary minds" (p. 146). Wasserman himself had some difficulty with this conclusion (which is identical to his judgment that, according to Shelley, only the One Mind exists) because he was forced to consider the "paradox" and "ambiguous" acceptance by Shelley of the "illusory" separateness and existence of different and individual minds (pp. 147-49). To resolve this Shelleyan paradox, I suggest that it does not exist: that is, Shelley nowhere, not even in *On Life*, denies the real existence of other human minds and nowhere subsumes individual minds into a universal One Mind.

In defense of this position, I cite Shelley's judgment in *Speculations on Metaphysics* that "we are intuitively conscious of our own existence, and of that connection in the train of our successive ideas, which we term our identity. *We are conscious also of the existence of other minds*; but not intuitively. Our evidence, with respect to the existence of other minds, is founded upon a very complicated relation of ideas, which it is foreign to [the] purpose of this treatise to anatomise" (my italics).[1] This judgment about the existence of other human minds does seem to contradict the all-important essay *On Life*, where Shelley concludes, just before admitting the inadequacy of language to express his intellectual philosophy, that he is only a "portion" of the "one mind" and that "the words *I* and *you*, and *they* are grammatical devices invented simply for arrangement, and totally devoid of the intense and exclusive sense usually attached to them." Wasserman persuasively argued that these "personal pronouns are relational, not substantive, terms" (p. 147). I agree; however, they are relational not to the universal One Mind but instead to the "assemblage of thoughts" (*On Life*) that constitutes the whole of one particular human mind or identity. In other words, Shelley uses the phrase "one mind" to designate not the ontological unity into which all human minds are subsumed, but rather the epistemological unity of thoughts in an individual human mind. And this unity was the first principle of his intellectual philosophy: as he explained in his *Speculations on Metaphysics*, there may be a "specific difference" between thoughts because of their "force"—that is, because of the "variety and irregularity of the occasions on which they arise in the mind"; but there can be no "essential difference" or "essential distinction" between thoughts because "the principle of the agreement and similarity of all thoughts, is, that they are all thoughts." Shelley further affirmed the unitary nature of the human mind and denied any *distinction* among thoughts when he explained in *On Life* that there can be no "essential difference" between "thought" and what we ordinarily judge as "thing": because "nothing exists but as it is perceived" (Shelley here reducing existence to ideas), "the *difference* is merely nominal between those two classes of thought, which are vulgarly *distinguished* by the names of ideas and of external objects" (my italics). Once more Shelley affirmed that there may be a "specific difference" but there can be no "essential distinction" between thoughts in the human mind.

But when Shelley pursued this "same thread of [epistemological] reasoning" to the concept of the "one mind" in the following sentences of *On Life*, he was "on that verge where words abandon[ed]" him and his "dizziness" occasioned a verbal and syntactical ambiguity which made Wasserman believe that Shelley's "one mind" was an ontological universal rather than an epistemological particular. Shelley wrote as follows:

> Pursuing the same thread of reasoning, the existence of distinct individual minds, similar to that which is employed in now questioning its own nature, is likewise found to be a delusion. The words *I, you, they,* are not signs of any actual difference subsisting between the assemblage of thoughts thus indicated, but are merely marks employed to denote the different modifications of the one mind.

In the first sentence above, Shelley is *not* denying the *existence* of other human minds different from his own, and he is not therefore contradicting his judgment in *Speculations on Metaphysics* that other human minds exist. Because perception determines existence in Shelley's intellectual philosophy and because a perceiver can have an idea of other human minds, it would have been absurd for Shelley to deny the existence of other human minds. What Shelley is questioning here, relative to his own "assemblage of thoughts," is the "existence of *distinct* individual minds" (my italics), because there can be no "essential distinction" within the unity of an individual's thoughts (including thoughts of other minds) according to his intellectual system. Thus relative to the "assemblage of [necessarily identical] thoughts" unified into a "one mind"—that is, a single consciousness or human identity (e.g., Shelley's, here questioning its own nature)— the self-conscious thought expressed by the word *"I"* and the object-conscious thoughts expressed by the words *"you"* and *"they"* are identical and *essentially undistinguishable.*

Such a conclusion merely reinforces Shelley's judgments in *Speculations on Metaphysics* and *On Life* that there can be no "essential distinction" between the class of thought called "ideas" and the class of thought "called *real, or external objects.*" And any "apprehension of distinction" between these two classes of thoughts or even between the so-called *"things"* of the second class does not alter the judgment that they are all identical because they are all thoughts. Because Shelley believed that any such "distinction" between *"external* and *internal"* was "merely an affair of words" which deluded us, he could conclude that "the words *I, you, they,* are not signs of any actual [essential] difference subsisting between the assemblage of [these three] thoughts thus indicated" by the "words *I, you, they.*" These pronouns, then, are merely words or "marks employed to denote the different modifications" [i.e., specific differences, not essential differences or distinctions] of the one mind," the one mind here being Shelley's, which questions itself and the unitary nature of all thoughts, including the thought of self.

That the perceiver or self is equal to the assemblage of unified thoughts is, Shelley continues, absurd. "Let it not be supposed that this doctrine conducts to the monstrous presumption that I, the person who now write and think, am that one mind. I am but a portion of it." This means that relative to an individual mind's total assemblage of thoughts, the existing individual mind itself (or more precisely, the thought of *"I"* which exists because it is perceived) is but one of the perceptions or thoughts making up the one mind and therefore is neither distinct from nor inclusive of the other thoughts expressed by the words *"you"* and *"they."* Thus, Shelley can conclude, "the words *I* and *you,* and *they* are grammatical devices invented simply for arrangement [of specific differences among thoughts by virtue of their "force"], and totally devoid of the intense and exclusive sense [of essential difference or essential distinction] usually attached to them." By this conclusion, Shelley does not deny the real existence of other minds; rather, he only denies the "existence of distinct [thoughts of] individual minds" in the assemblage of thoughts that makes up his or any other man's human consciousness. Thus the "one mind" is not the One Mind or the universal Existence which obliterates the real existence of individual minds that Wasserman judged to be merely modes or factors of the One Mind. Rather, the "one mind" is the assemblage of unified thoughts within a particular or individual mind which does exist by reason of the subject's ability to make itself the object of thought. That is to say, the "one mind" is a particular or individual mind in which all thoughts, including those of self and those of other minds, are judged to be unified because of their identity as undistinguishable thoughts, and are judged to be existing because existence is determined by thought.

The metaphysical assumptions of Shelley's intellectual philosophy, therefore, are epistemological rather than ontological. And because the "one mind" is a particular and unified individual mind rather than an ontological universal, Shelley in *On Life* and *Speculations on Metaphysics* affirms rather than questions the existence of individual human consciousnesses. Furthermore, the perfection of these individual human consciousnesses, symbolized immediately through Prometheus who in the abstract represents them all, rather than mediately through Prometheus who represents the One Mind subsuming all human consciousnesses, is the subject of Shelley's drama *Prometheus Unbound.*

# SHORT TITLES AND ABBREVIATIONS

| | |
|---|---|
| *Blessington's Conversations* | *Lady Blessington's "Conversations of Lord Byron."* Ed. Ernest J. Lovell, Jr. Princeton: Princeton University Press, 1969. |
| *Cain Variorum* | *Lord Byron's "Cain": Twelve Essays and a Text with Variants and Annotations.* Ed. Truman Guy Steffan. Austin: University of Texas Press, 1968. |
| *DJ Variorum* | *Byron's "Don Juan": A Variorum Edition.* Ed. Truman Guy Steffan and Willis W. Pratt. 2d ed. 4 vols. Austin: University of Texas Press, 1971. |
| *Julian* | *The Complete Works of Percy Bysshe Shelley* (The Julian Edition). Ed. Roger Ingpen and Walter E. Peck. 10 vols. London: Ernest Benn, 1926-1930. |
| *L&J* | *The Works of Lord Byron. Letters and Journals.* Ed. Rowland E. Prothero. Rev. and enl. ed. 6 vols. London: John Murray, 1898-1901. |
| *LBC* | *Lord Byron's Correspondence.* Ed. John Murray. 2 vols. London: John Murray, 1922. |
| *Medwin's Conversations* | *Medwin's "Conversations of Lord Byron."* Ed. Ernest J. Lovell, Jr. Princeton: Princeton University Press, 1966. |
| *MSJ* | *Mary Shelley's Journal.* Ed. Frederick L. Jones. Norman: University of Oklahoma Press, 1947. |
| *MSL* | *The Letters of Mary W. Shelley.* Ed. Frederick L. Jones. 2 vols. Norman: University of Oklahoma Press, 1944. |
| *PBSL* | *The Letters of Percy Bysshe Shelley.* Ed. Frederick L. Jones. 2 vols. Oxford: At the Clarendon Press, 1964. |
| *Poetry* | *The Works of Lord Byron. Poetry.* Ed. Ernest Hartley Coleridge. Rev. and enl. ed. 7 vols. London: John Murray, 1898-1904. |
| *Revised Life* | Medwin, Thomas. *The Life of Percy Bysshe Shelley: A New Edition* . . . Ed. H. Buxton Forman. London: Oxford University Press, 1913. |
| *Shelley and His Circle* | *Shelley and His Circle: 1773-1822.* 6 vols. to date: I-IV ed. Kenneth Neill Cameron; V-VI ed. Donald H. Reiman. Cambridge: Harvard University Press, 1961-73. |
| *TL Variorum* | Reiman, Donald H. *Shelley's "The Triumph of Life": A Critical Study—Based on a Text Newly Edited from the Bodleian Manuscript.* Urbana: University of Illinois Press, 1965. |
| *To Lord Byron* | Paston, George, and Quennell, Peter, eds. *"To Lord Byron": Feminine Profiles Based Upon Unpublished Letters, 1807-1824.* New York: Charles Scribner's Sons, 1939. |

| | |
|---|---|
| *Williams* | *Maria Gisborne & Edward E. Williams, Shelley's Friends: Their Journals and Letters.* Ed. Frederick L. Jones. Norman: University of Oklahoma Press, 1951. |
| *BNYPL* | *Bulletin of the New York Public Library* |
| *ELH* | *Journal of English Literary History* |
| *ELN* | *English Language Notes* |
| *K-SJ* | *Keats-Shelley Journal* |
| *KSMB* | *Keats-Shelley Memorial Bulletin* |
| *MLN* | *Modern Language Notes* |
| *MLQ* | *Modern Language Quarterly* |
| *MLR* | *Modern Language Review* |
| *N&Q* | *Notes and Queries* |
| *PMLA* | *Publications of the Modern Language Association of America* |
| *RES* | *Review of English Studies* |
| *SIR* | *Studies in Romanticism* |
| *SP* | *Studies in Philology* |

# NOTES

Chapter 1. *Creators and Creations: The Spirits and Forms of Shelley and Byron*

1. *Julian*, II, 174, my italics. Unless otherwise noted, Shelley's poetry and essays are quoted from *Julian* with the exception of *The Triumph of Life* (from *TL Variorum*); Byron's, from *Poetry* and *L&J* with the exceptions of *Don Juan* and *Cain* (from *DJ Variorum* and *Cain Variorum*). See preceding list of short and abbreviated titles.

2. Two fabricated notices incorrectly place Byron and Shelley together at Great Marlow in 1817 or 1818 (see Edward Dowden, *The Life of Percy Bysshe Shelley* [London: Kegan Paul, Trench & Co., 1886], II, 181n.-182n.); and on a voyage to Corsica and Sardinia in 1821 (see Samuel C. Chew, *Byron in England: His Fame and After-Fame* [New York: Charles Scribner's Sons, 1924], pp. 165-66; and G. E. Bentley, Jr., "Byron, Shelley, Wordsworth, Blake, and *The Seaman's Recorder*," *SIR*, 9 [1970], 21-26).

3. For a discussion of this debate, see Sylva Norman, *Flight of the Skylark: The Development of Shelley's Reputation* (Norman: University of Oklahoma Press, 1954), pp. 87-89. Cambridge and Shelley were represented by Richard M. Milnes, Arthur Henry Hallam, and Thomas Sunderland.

4. For some spirited comparisons between the two poets, see "Byron—Shelley," *The Examiner*, no. 870 (3 October 1824), p. 635; *The Autobiography, Times, Opinions, and Contemporaries of Sir Egerton Brydges* (London: Cochrane and M'Crone, 1834), I, 329; G. H. Lewes, *Westminster Review*, 35 (1841), 311-16; Charles Kingsley, "Thoughts on Shelley and Byron," *Fraser's Magazine*, 48 (1853), 568-76; George Gilfillan, *Modern Literature and Literary Men: Being a Second Gallery of Literary Portraits*, 3d Amer. ed. (New York: D. Appleton & Company, 1854), p. 58; Adam Storey Farrar, *A Critical History of Free Thought in Reference to the Christian Religion* (New York: D. Appleton and Company, 1866), p. 203; W. Archer Cocke, "Byron and Shelley," *The Southern Magazine*, 11 (1872), 496-506; "Byron and Shelley," *Temple Bar*, 34 (1872), 30-49; E. Schuyler, "Shelley with Byron," *The Nation*, 48 (1889), 113-16; M. Zdziechowski, "La poésie de Shelley considérée dans ses rapports avec celle de Byron," *Bulletin International de L'Académie des Sciences de Cracovie*, 1891, pp. 54-64; and Karl Marx as quoted by Benjamin P. Kurtz, *The Pursuit of Death: A Study of Shelley's Poetry* (New York: Oxford University Press, 1933), p. 27.

5. New York: Harcourt, Brace & World, Inc., 1968, pp. x, 45. Preceding Buxton's book were Isabel C. Clarke, *Shelley and Byron: A Tragic Friendship* (London: Hutchinson & Co., Ltd., 1934); and A. B. C. Whipple, *The Fatal Gift of Beauty: The Final Years of Byron and Shelley* (New York: Harper & Row, Publishers, 1964). For other twentieth-century comparisons not mentioned in subsequent notes, see Frank Clyde Brown, "The Literary Influence of Byron on Shelley" (Master's thesis, University of Chicago, 1902); Pelham Edgar, "The Nature Poetry of Byron and Shelley," *The Canadian Magazine of Politics, Science, Art and Literature*, 19 (1902), 18-24; Lane Cooper, "Notes on Byron and Shelley," *MLN*, 23 (1908), 118-19; Manfred Eimer, *Die persönlichen Beziehungen zwischen Byron und den Shelleys*, Anglistische Forschungen, no. 32 (Heidelberg: Carl

Winter, 1910); Llewellyn M. Buell, "Byron and Shelley," *MLN*, 32 (1917), 312-13; Friedrich Dannenberg, "Byron und Shelley in ihrer Begegnung," *Germanisch-Romanische Monatsschrift*, 18 (1930), 211-31; Paul Siegel, "'A Paradise Within Thee' in Milton, Byron, and Shelley," *MLN*, 56 (1941), 615-17; Robert Sencourt, "Byron and Shelley at the Lake of Geneva," *Quarterly Review*, 284 (1946), 209-21; D. G. James, *Byron and Shelley* (Nottingham, England, 1951); C. L. Cline, *Byron, Shelley, and Their Pisan Circle* (London: John Murray, 1952).

6. Chapel Hill: University of North Carolina Press, 1935, pp. 132-33.

7. As quoted from "Conversations of an American with Lord Byron," *New Monthly Magazine and Literary Journal*, 45, pt. 3 (1835), 196. For reports of Byron's plagiarisms, see *The Gentleman's Magazine*, 88 (1818), 121-22, 389; and 91 (1821), 349-55. See also A. A. Watts, "Lord Byron's Plagiarisms," *The London Literary Gazette*, nos. 214-17 (24 February-17 March 1821), pp. 121-24, 137-39, 150-52, 168-70; no. 219 (31 March 1821), pp. 201-3; and "Letter from Paddy," *Blackwood's Edinburgh Magazine*, 11 (April 1822), 461-65.

8. Cf. Shelley's similar protestations in the Preface to *The Revolt of Islam* (*Julian*, I, 244) and in his letter to Charles Ollier, 15 October 1819 (*PBSL*, II, 127).

9. Byron's words according to Edward John Trelawny, *Records of Shelley, Byron and the Author* (London: Pickering and Chatto, 1887), p. 29. For a further consideration of this remark, see Chapter 9.

10. My judgments here reflect not only Coleridge's distinction between the primary and secondary imagination in *Biographia Literaria* (Chapter 13) but also D. G. James's analysis of that distinction in *Scepticism and Poetry: An Essay on the Poetic Imagination* (London: George Allen & Unwin Ltd., 1937).

11. Lincoln: University of Nebraska Press, 1954, pp. 7-8, 41.

12. Edward Wayne Marjarum, *Byron as Skeptic and Believer* (Princeton: Princeton University Press, 1938), p. 44.

13. *Speculations on Metaphysics* (*Julian*, VII, 63, my italics).

14. Shelley writes this in *Peter Bell the Third* (IV.31-33) to discredit Wordsworth, from whose non-imaginative center "Nothing went ever out, although/Something did ever enter" (34-35). For similar remarks on the center and the circumference, see Shelley's *On Life* and *Defence of Poetry* (*Julian*, VI, 194; VII, 135).

15. For Byron's note on the *Academical Questions*, see *Poetry*, II, 422n.-423n. It is possible that Shelley first introduced this volume to Byron in Geneva. For his later praise of it, see *Blessington's Conversations*, pp. 139-40.

16. *Julian*, VI, 195-96.

17. Quotations from Wordsworth and Coleridge are from *The Poetical Works of Wordsworth*, ed. Thomas Hutchinson and Ernest de Selincourt, rev. and reset (London: Oxford University Press, 1950); and *The Poems of Samuel Taylor Coleridge*, ed. Ernest Hartley Coleridge (London: Oxford University Press, 1912).

18. *The Statesman's Manual* in *The Collected Works of Samuel Taylor Coleridge, 6: Lay Sermons*, ed. R. J. White (London: Routledge & Kegan Paul, Bollingen Series LXXV, 1972), p. 29.

19. *PBSL*, II, 152.

20. McGann, *Fiery Dust: Byron's Poetic Development* (Chicago: The University of Chicago Press, 1968), p. 270; Gleckner, *Byron and the Ruins of Paradise* (Baltimore: The Johns Hopkins Press, 1967), p. 205.

21. *Blessington's Conversations*, pp. 49, 114-15.

22. *The Metamorphoses of the Circle*, trans. Carley Dawson, Elliot Coleman, with the Author (Baltimore: The Johns Hopkins Press, 1966), p. 77.

23. Letter to John Gisborne, 18 June 1822 (*PBSL*, II, 434).

24. *Defence of Poetry* and *On Love* (*Julian*, VII, 135; VI, 202).

25. *L&J*, V, 456.

26. *On the Devil, and Devils* (*Julian*, VII, 87).

27. *Defence of Poetry* (*Julian*, VII, 118, 137, 135).

28. M. G. Cooke, *The Blind Man Traces the Circle: On the Patterns and Philosophy of Byron's Poetry* (Princeton: Princeton University Press, 1969), p. 99.

29. *Blessington's Conversations*, p. 49.

30. Byron to Murray, 27 June 1816 (*L&J*, III, 335); Shelley to Peacock, 12 July 1816 (*PBSL*, I, 485). I am indebted to Ernest J. Lovell, Jr., *Byron: The Record of a Quest* (Austin: The University of Texas Press, 1949), p. 97, for suggesting this contrast. Charles I. Elton, *An Account of Shelley's Visits to France, Switzerland, and Savoy, in the Years 1814 and 1816* (London: Bliss, Sands, & Foster, 1894), pp. 57-58, similarly contrasted Byron and Shelley's descriptions of the same storm on Lake Geneva (see the same letters cited above, *L&J*, III, 335-36; *PBSL*, I, 483-84).

31. *The Poems of Percy Bysshe Shelley*, ed. C. D. Locock (London: Methuen and Co., Ltd., 1911), I, 559.

32. *The Romantic Ventriloquists: Wordsworth, Coleridge, Keats, Shelley, Byron* (Seattle: University of Washington Press, 1963), p. 254.

33. Shelley's letter to Peacock, 18 December 1818 (*PBSL*, II, 58); and Byron's statement to Medwin (*Medwin's Conversations*, p. 235).

34. As reported and quoted in *The Life, Writings, Opinions, and Times of the Right Hon. George Gordon Noel Byron, Lord Byron* (London: Matthew Iley, 1825), I, 366.

*Chapter 2. With the World All before Them: Byron and Shelley in Geneva*

1. See *The Diary of Dr. John William Polidori, 1816*, ed. William Michael Rossetti (London: Elkin Mathews, 1911), for recorded meetings between 27 May and 2 July; and *MSJ*, between 21 July and 29 August. Mary's remark on the "many . . . conversations" is from her Introduction (1831) to *Frankenstein; or The Modern Prometheus*, ed. M. K. Joseph (London: Oxford University Press, 1969), p. 8.

2. That Byron and Shelley first met in England has been conjectured by John Cordy Jeaffreson, *The Real Shelley: New Views of the Poet's Life* (London: Hurst and Blackett, Publishers, 1885), II, 280-81; and by John C. Roe, *Some Obscure and Disputed Points in Byronic Biography* (Inaugural-Dissertation Presented to the University of Leipzig, 1893), pp. 22-24. But no evidence supports this conjecture with the exception of Claire Clairmont's purported remarks that she, Mary, and Shelley met Byron in 1815!—see William Graham, "Chats with Jane Clermont [*sic*]," *Nineteenth Century*, 34 (November 1893), 762-64, afterwards reprinted in Graham, *Last Links with Byron, Shelley, and Keats* (London: Leonard Smithers & Co., 1898), pp. 20-22. Richard Garnett questioned Graham's (and Claire's) reliability in two letters to Dowden, *Letters About Shelley: Interchanged by Three Friends—Edward Dowden, Richard Garnett, and Wm. Michael Rossetti*, ed. R. S. Garnett (London: Hodder and Stoughton, 1917), pp. 184-85, 187. Claire herself wrote a letter stating that Mary first met Byron during the settlement of Shelley's Chancery suit, i.e., during the spring of 1816—see *To Lord Byron*, pp. 207-8. Mary dated Claire's first meeting with Byron in the spring of 1816—see *PBSL*, II, 398. And so did Byron—see his letter to Kinnaird, 20 January 1817, as quoted by Doris Langley Moore, *Lord Byron: Accounts Rendered* (New York: Harper & Row, Publishers, 1974), p. 302.

3. *Julian*, V, 243.

4. E. H. Coleridge's conjecture that Byron's dedicatory stanzas, "To Ianthe," were "responsible for the Ianthe of *Queen Mab*" (*Poetry*, II, 13n.) is incorrect. Shelley had published and Byron had read *Queen Mab* before "To Ianthe" appeared in 1814, and Robert F. Gleckner, *Byron and the Ruins of Paradise* (Baltimore: The Johns Hopkins Press, 1967), pp. 88-90, argues instead that Shelley's Ianthe was responsible for Byron's title.

5. Letter of ?19 April 1821 (*Williams*, pp. 158-59).

6. *L&J*, IV, 49.

7. *Medwin's Conversations*, p. 194.

8. *Fiery Dust: Byron's Poetic Development* (Chicago: The University of Chicago Press, 1968), pp. 305-6.

9. See his letter to Leigh Hunt (*L&J*, III, 239).

10. McGann, *Fiery Dust*, p. 310. McGann notes that the "manuscript evidence will not sanction the discovery of [Shelley's] influence in any of the first fifty-seven stanzas [with the exception of stanza xxxiii], and it argues strongly (though not conclusively) against Shelley's influence upon any of the first seventy-one stanzas as well," but the last stanza that he can with certainty date prior to 26-27 May is stanza lxii (pp. 305-6, 310).

11. *Diary*, p. 121 (entry for 8 June 1816).

12. Either Shelley or Byron brought a copy of *Queen Mab* to Geneva, for Polidori (*Diary*, p. 107) was reading it on 30 May 1816.

13. See McGann, *Fiery Dust*, p. 305 and n.

14. On 27 June, Byron wrote Murray that one hundred and seventeen stanzas were completed (*L&J*, III, 336-37), that is, six more than he had reported to Hobhouse on 23 June (*LBC*, II, 11). Also see McGann, *Fiery Dust*, p. 305.

15. Mary's "Note on the Poems of 1816," *Julian*, III, 128.

16. That Shelley wrote some of this note (printed in *Poetry*, II, 303-6) is suggested by its Shelleyan conception of love as well as by its parallels with Shelley's own narrative description of this journey to Peacock. For example, compare Byron's "If Rousseau had never written, nor lived, the same associations would not less have belonged to such scenes" with Shelley's "but Meillerie is indeed enchanted ground, were Rousseau no magician" (*PBSL*, I, 483); and Byron's "the 'Bosquet de Julie' . . . long ago cut down by the brutal selfishness of the monks of St. Bernard . . . [is] enclosed into a vineyard for the miserable drones of an execrable superstition" with Shelley's "'the bosquet de Julie' . . . was now utterly obliterated. . . . the land belonged to the convent of St. Bernard, and . . . this outrage had been committed by their orders. . . . a system of prescriptive religion has an influence . . . inimical to natural sensibility" (*PBSL*, I, 486-87).

17. *L&J*, III, 364.

18. From Byron's MS note to *Churchill's Grave*, in which Byron consciously imitated Wordsworth's "*style*" (*Poetry*, IV, 46n.-47n.).

19. See *Poetry*, IV, 57n.

20. Here and elsewhere, quotations are from *John Milton: Complete Poems and Major Prose*, ed. Merritt Y. Hughes (New York: The Odyssey Press, 1957).

21. George M. Ridenour did not use the allusion to *Paradise Lost* in his analysis of the unreconciled "antitheses" to be found in *Epistle to Augusta*; see his "Byron in 1816: Four Poems from Diodati," in *From Sensibility to Romanticism: Essays Presented to Frederick A. Pottle*, ed. Frederick W. Hilles and Harold Bloom (New York: Oxford University Press, 1965), pp. 455-58.

22. Letter to Murray, 15 February 1817 (*L&J*, IV, 54-55).

23. Gleckner, *Ruins of Paradise*, p. 251.

24. Claire-Elaine Engel, *Byron et Shelley en Suisse et en Savoie: Mai-Octobre 1816* (Chambéry: Librairie Dardel, 1930), p. 56n.

25. Ernest J. Lovell, Jr. (*Byron: The Record of a Quest* [Austin: The University of Texas Press, 1949], p. 135n.) and H. W. Piper (*The Active Universe: Pantheism and the Concept of Imagination in the English Romantic Poets* [London: The Athlone Press, 1962], p. 179n.) have suggested that Byron owed the idea of *Darkness* to Shelley, because Shelley in a letter to Peacock on 26 July 1816 referred to "Buffons sublime but gloomy theory, that this earth which we inhabit will at some future period be changed into a mass of frost" (*PBSL*, I, 499). This suggestion is supported by Cyrus Redding: "I happened to know,

from a friend whom I met in Paris, in 1817, and who had seen Byron and Shelley in the south the year before, that with Byron the poem of 'Darkness' originated in a conversation with Shelley, as they were standing together, in a day of brilliant sunshine, looking upon the Lake of Geneva. Shelley said, 'What a change it would be if the sun were to be extinguished at this moment; how the race of man would perish, until perhaps only one remained—suppose one of us! How terrible would be his fate!' or words to the same effect"—see Redding, *Literary Reminiscences and Memoirs of Thomas Campbell* (London: Charles J. Skeet, Publisher, 1860), I, 301; and his earlier version of the same story in *Fifty Years' Recollections, Literary and Personal* (London: Charles J. Skeet, Publisher, 1858), II, 288. Donald H. Reiman has also recently cited this same evidence in *Shelley and His Circle*, V, 198n.-199n.

26. *Fiery Dust*, pp. 166-67, 172; *Ruins of Paradise*, p. 191.

27. *Medwin's Conversations*, p. 156.

28. See *A Vindication of Natural Diet* (*Julian*, VI, 6).

29. For the opposite reading of the evidence and conclusion that Byron renewed Shelley's interest in the myth, see Samuel C. Chew, "Byroniana," *MLN*, 33 (1918), 308-9; and Peter L. Thorslev, Jr., *The Byronic Hero: Types and Prototypes* (Minneapolis: University of Minnesota Press, 1962), pp. 123-24.

30. Letters of 17 July 1816 and of 17 or 18 December 1818 (*PBSL*, I, 491; II, 58).

31. "Note on *The Revolt of Islam*," *Julian*, I, 409.

32. *PBSL*, II, 152.

33. Donald H. Reiman, *Percy Bysshe Shelley* (New York: Twayne Publishers, Inc., 1969), p. 36. Reiman, passim, refers to the frequent union of reason and love in the metaphors of Shelley's poetry.

34. *Julian*, VII, 65, 75-76.

35. *PBSL*, I, 493, 494-95.

36. Also compare *Mont Blanc*, ll. 44-47 and 71-73 with *Childe Harold* III.v and xciii. These and other similarities undoubtedly reflect Shelley's reading of this third canto in MS before he wrote his poem.

37. In *On Life*, Shelley wrote that "the difference is merely nominal between those two classes of thought, which are vulgarly distinguished by the names of ideas and of external objects. . . . By the word *things* is to be understood any object of thought, that is, any thought upon which any other thought is employed, with an apprehension of distinction" (*Julian*, VI, 196).

38. See Polidori's *Diary*, pp. 127-28; and *L&J*, IV, 296-97.

39. For a description of the meeting between Byron and Coleridge at which time *Kubla Khan* was recited, see *The Autobiography of Leigh Hunt*, ed. J. E. Morpurgo (London: The Cresset Press, 1949), p. 288. For Coleridge's reaction to this meeting, see *Collected Letters of Samuel Taylor Coleridge, IV: 1815-1819*, ed. Earl Leslie Griggs (Oxford: At the Clarendon Press, 1959), pp. 636, 641. For Coleridge's letters to Byron and Byron's replies, see pp. 559-63, 597-606, 622-23, 626-28.

40. *PBSL*, I, 490. Joseph Raben, "Coleridge as the Prototype of the Poet in Shelley's *Alastor*," *RES*, n.s. 17 (1966), 278-92, offers a convenient but incomplete listing of Shelley's acquaintance with Coleridge's works prior to Geneva.

41. *PBSL*, I, 504. Shelley's source for this quote may be found in *The Collected Works of Samuel Taylor Coleridge, 4: The Friend*, ed. Barbara E. Rooke (London: Routledge & Kegan Paul, Bollingen Series LXXV, 1969), II, 70. For further information on Shelley's reading of *The Friend*, see my article, "The Shelley Circle and Coleridge's *The Friend*," *ELN*, 8 (1971), 269-74.

42. See Bloom, *Shelley's Mythmaking* (New Haven: Yale University Press, 1959), pp. 11-35; and Raben, "Coleridge as the Prototype," pp. 286-87. If Byron possessed a copy of *The Friend*, he probably received it from Coleridge when they met during the week of 10-15 April. That they at least discussed

*The Friend* is suggested by John Murray's interest in republishing it (see Coleridge's *Collected Letters*, IV, 650 and n.).

43. According to *MSJ*, p. 61, the Coleridge volume arrived on that day.

44. According to *Medwin's Conversations*, p. 178, Byron in Pisa once "began spouting 'Kubla Khan.'"

45. *Shelley: His Thought and Work*, 2d ed. (Teaneck, N.J.: Fairleigh Dickinson University Press, 1971), p. 71.

46. *PBSL*, I, 494.

47. See Newman Ivey White, *Shelley* (New York: Alfred A. Knopf, 1940), I, 456, 714; and Leslie A. Marchand, *Byron: A Biography* (New York: Alfred A. Knopf, 1957), II, 647 and *notes, 70*.

48. In "The Byron Poetry Manuscripts in the Library of the University of Texas," *MLQ*, 8 (1947), 204, T. G. Steffan suggested that "the copy may have been made by Augusta Leigh." Nevertheless, Willis W. Pratt, *Lord Byron and His Circle: A Calendar of Manuscripts in The University of Texas Library* (Austin, Texas, 1947), p. 25, believed the poem to be of "doubtful authorship." So did E. H. Coleridge (*Poetry*, III, xxi) and Samuel C. Chew (*Byron in England: His Fame and After-Fame* [New York: Charles Scribner's Sons, 1924], p. 185 and n.), the latter also noting that among the Galignani editions, "All hail, Mont Blanc" appeared only in 1826. For this slightly different third version, see *The Works of Lord Byron Including the Suppressed Poems* (Paris: A. and W. Galignani, 1826), pp. 715-16.

49. After Shelley delivered this MS to John Murray, Byron's publisher, Claire wrote to Byron: "Shelley mentions likewise Murray presenting him with a copy of your *Poems*, bound in blue and gold" (as quoted in *To Lord Byron*, p. 218). That Shelley retained this and many of Byron's volumes is suggested by "an account book kept by Trelawny from October 29, 1820, to some date in early 1821" in which is found a list of books that Walter Edwin Peck judged to be in Shelley's library in Pisa. For this list, which includes Byron's *Poems, Suppress'd Poems, Don Juan, Childe Harold, Prisoner of Chillon*, and *Curse of Minerva*, see Peck, *Shelley: His Life and Work* (London: Ernest Benn Limited, 1927), II, 265-67.

*Chapter 3. More Things on Heaven and Earth:*
Manfred *and* Alastor

1. Letter to Murray, 17 September 1817 (*L&J*, IV, 174).

2. *L&J*, III, 352, 355, 364, my italics.

3. See letters to Moore on 28 January, to Murray on 15 February, and to Moore on 25 March 1817 (*L&J*, IV, 49, 54-55, 80).

4. *PBSL*, I, 499, my italics. Byron may actually have read this letter, because Shelley carried at least two copies of it when he stopped at Diodati for three hours upon his return from Mont Blanc, and he kept the letter "some days" before sending it to Peacock (see *MSJ*, pp. 53, 55; *PBSL*, I, 502). Because of Shelley's reference to Ahriman and because of the parallels between *Manfred* II.iv.1-12 and Peacock's fragmentary *Ahrimanes*, Kenneth Neill Cameron conjectured that "Shelley either had a manuscript of Peacock's two-canto version of *Ahrimanes* with him in Switzerland and showed it to Byron or he remembered some stanzas well enough to be able to recite them" (see *Shelley and His Circle*, III, 239-40). Byron chose "Arimanes" as the name of his spirit of evil and enthroned him on the summit of the Jungfrau rather than Mont Blanc.

5. Letter to Trelawny, ?19 April 1821 (*Williams*, pp. 158-59).

6. *PBSL*, I, 556-57.

7. Also compare Tasso's "Love,—which did pervade/And mingle with whate'er I saw on earth" (ll. 150-51) with Shelley's apparently later definition of love as "the bond and the sanction which connects not only man with man, but with

every thing which exists" (*On Love, Julian*, VI, 201; Reiman in *Shelley and His Circle*, VI, 639, recently dated this essay between 20 and 25 July 1818).

8. In one of Claire's letters to Byron before 25 April 1816 (as quoted in *L&J*, III, 431-33), she acknowledged his "approbation" of the *Alastor* volume, praised *Alastor* as if he had already praised it, apparently answered his question about the " 'Demon of the World,' " and transcribed Dante's Italian sonnet in order for Byron to judge the accuracy of Shelley's translation of it in the *Alastor* volume. This volume was published by February 1816 (see Cameron, *Shelley and His Circle*, IV, 626), and it is possible that Byron, to whom Shelley had already sent a copy of *Queen Mab*, received one of the two hundred and fifty copies of *Alastor* that Shelley had printed by 6 January 1816, the date he sent one copy to John Murray, Byron's publisher (see *PBSL*, I, 438-39).

9. Letter of 23 November 1811 (*PBSL*, I, 189). See letters of 8 and 16 October (I, 144, 150) for similar references.

10. Frankenstein "saw the image of [his] former self" in Clerval and "the living spirit of love" in Elizabeth. Needing at least one of these friends for psychological completion (" 'we are unfashioned creatures, but half made up,' " he told Walton), Frankenstein in effect destroyed his gentler self (in the persons of Clerval and Elizabeth) when he procrastinated "all that related to [his] feelings of affection" while creating the monster, the latter's physical ugliness serving to mirror Frankenstein's psychological deformity. Frankenstein himself considered the monster "nearly in the light of [his] own vampire, [his] own spirit let loose from the grave, and forced to destroy all that was dear to [him]," and when the monster actually killed Clerval and Elizabeth, he merely externalized what had already occurred within Frankenstein. After Frankenstein described his history to Walton (a psychological equivalent in whom he saw the image of his former self, " 'Unhappy man! Do you share my madness?' "), Walton was prevented (albeit against his will) from irreversibly destroying his affections and killing himself in the manner of Frankenstein. Quotations are from *Frankenstein; or, The Modern Prometheus*, ed. M. K. Joseph (London: Oxford University Press, 1969), pp. 158, 38, 28, 55, 77, 28.

11. Chew, *The Dramas of Lord Byron: A Critical Study* (1915; rpt. New York: Russell & Russell, Inc., 1964), pp. 66, 79-80; Bloom, *The Visionary Company: A Reading of English Romantic Poetry*, rev. and enl. ed. (Ithaca: Cornell University Press, 1971), p. 250; Elledge, *Byron and the Dynamics of Metaphor* (Nashville: Vanderbilt University Press, 1968), p. 83. Chew (pp. 63-64), by the way, ably discredits Heinrich Gillardon's interesting but unfounded belief in *Shelley's Einwirkung auf Byron* (Karlsruhe: n.p., 1898), pp. 89-114, that Shelley's novel *St. Irvyne* was the source for *Manfred*.

12. For useful summaries of these antecedents, see Chew, *Dramas of Lord Byron*, pp. 60-66, 74-80; and Peter L. Thorslev, Jr., *The Byronic Hero: Types and Prototypes* (Minneapolis: University of Minnesota Press, 1962), pp. 166-76. Shelley himself may have been responsible for some of these antecedents, for he translated *Prometheus Bound* for Byron in 1816, and Byron had read the translation of Schubart's "Der Ewige Jude" in the notes to *Queen Mab*. For Byron's possible indebtedness to this translation, see Thorslev, p. 170, and especially compare Manfred's "the cold hand/Of an all-pitiless Demon held me back,/ Back by a single hair, which would not break./. . ./. . . I dwell in my despair—/ And live—and live for ever" (II.ii.137-39, 149-50) with Ahasuerus' "alas! alas! the restless curse held me by the hair,—and I could not die!" in Shelley's note to *Queen Mab* (*Julian*, I, 151).

13. In his footnote to *Nightmare Abbey*, in *The Works of Thomas Love Peacock*, ed. H. F. B. Brett-Smith and C. E. Jones (London: Constable & Co., Ltd., 1924-34), III, 32n., Peacock apparently sensed some relation between *Manfred* and *Alastor*, for in this note he called Byron's "Ahrimanes [*sic*] . . . the great Alastor, or Κακος Δαιμων, of Persia."

14. *Julian*, VI, 202.

15. See *Poetry*, IV, 105n., for this story as narrated by Eunapius. Because this same story is "found in Taylor's *Proclus*, which is the evident source of much of the symbolism in *Prometheus Unbound*," Carl Grabo, *"Prometheus Unbound": An Interpretation* (Chapel Hill: University of North Carolina Press, 1935), pp. 11-12, guessed "that Byron got the episode from Shelley" in 1816.

16. See *Memoirs of Percy Bysshe Shelley*, in *The Works of Thomas Love Peacock*, VIII, 100.

17. *Byron and the Dynamics of Metaphor*, p. 91.

18. Manfred also likened himself to the destructive aspects of Nature: "To be thus—/Grey-haired with anguish, like these blasted pines,/Wrecks of a single winter, barkless, branchless,/A blighted trunk upon a cursèd root" (I.ii.65-68). These lines and a similar description in Byron's Journal to Augusta (*L&J*, III, 360) strongly echo Shelley's description of the Poet's "thin/And white" (ll. 534-35) hair which has its correlative in Nature: "tall spires of windlestrae/Threw their thin shadows down the rugged slope,/And nought but knarled roots of ancient pines/Branchless and blasted, clenched with grasping roots/The unwilling soil" (ll. 528-32).

19. Letter of 12 August 1817 (*L&J*, IV, 157).

20. "Byron and the Mind of Man: *Childe Harold III-IV* and *Manfred*," *SIR*, 1 (1962), 107.

21. Letter to Byron, 9 July 1817 (*PBSL*, I, 547).

22. Edward John Trelawny, *Records of Shelley, Byron and the Author* (London: Pickering and Chatto, 1887), p. 29.

23. Letter to Moore, 1 June 1820 (*L&J*, V, 37).

24. Byron sent this epigraph (with "your" rather than Hamlet's "our") to Murray on 9 April 1817, at which time he also judged his third act (forwarded to Murray a month before) to be only "so so." Five days later, he decided to revise this "certainly damned bad" third act (*L&J*, IV, 100, 110). According to George [*sic*] Brandes, *Main Currents in Nineteenth Century Literature, IV: Naturalism in England* (New York: The Macmillan Company, 1906), p. 301, and to Edward Wayne Marjarum, *Byron as Skeptic and Believer* (Princeton: Princeton University Press, 1938), p. 32, Byron rewrote Act III of *Manfred* at Shelley's "advice." No evidence supports this judgment, and I assume that they both confused Shelley with William Gifford, who did advise revision.

*Chapter 4. Preparations for a "Colossal" Argument between the Snake and the Eagle: The Revolt of Islam and Childe Harold IV*

1. See Shelley's letters to Byron on 8, 11, and 29 September 1816 (*PBSL*, I, 504-8). For his reaction to *Manfred*, see letter to Byron, 9 July 1817 (*PBSL*, I, 547).

2. See Shelley's letters to Murray on 2 and 30 October, and to Byron on 20 November 1816 (*PBSL*, I, 508-9, 511, 513-14).

3. *PBSL*, I, 530.

4. *Julian*, VI, 87, my italics; Mary Shelley, *Frankenstein; or, The Modern Prometheus*, ed. M. K. Joseph (London: Oxford University Press, 1969), p. 14.

5. Shelley thus described his epic in a letter of 13 October 1817 (*PBSL*, I, 564).

6. Letter to Peacock, 17 or 18 December 1818 (*PBSL*, II, 58). Shelley's remarks on Byron in this letter will be frequently quoted in this and the next chapter.

7. *PBSL*, I, 557.

8. Bodleian MS. Shelley adds. e. 19, p. 3; also quoted in *Verse and Prose from the Manuscripts of Percy Bysshe Shelley*, ed. Sir John C. E. Shelley-Rolls and

Roger Ingpen (London: Privately printed, 1934), p. 12.

9. Shelley's familiarity with *Childe Harold* III was extensive: he read it in MS by 18 July and quoted from it on 22 July 1816 (*PBSL*, I, 493, 495); he read it aloud to Mary during the summer of 1816 (see *MSJ*, p. 80); he carried it from Geneva to John Murray and expected to revise the proofs in the fall of 1816; and he praised it during and after his writing of *The Revolt* (*PBSL*, I, 547, 557). For a discussion of *Mont Blanc* in relation to *Childe Harold* III, see Chapter 2.

10. In his letter to Leigh Hunt on 3 August 1817, Shelley announced that he had "arrived at the 380th stanza of my Poem" (*PBSL*, I, 551).

11. See *The Revolt* V.xlix ff. for these allegorical equivalents.

12. The full title is *The Conspiracy and Tragedy of Charles, Duke of Byron*. For a summary of the "Byronic" egotisms in this drama, see G. Wilson Knight, *The Golden Labyrinth: A Study of British Drama* (New York: W. W. Norton & Company, Inc., 1962), pp. 93-95. Because Knight could judge that Byron's *Manfred* was a "successor" to Chapman's *Byron* (p. 232), it is possible that Shelley made the same association.

13. Bodleian MS. Shelley adds. e. 10, p. 182. On p. 181, above the stanza numbered 411 (*The Revolt* XI.xiv), Shelley had first written, "This incident somewhat resembles an incident from the Corsair." That Shelley intended to use this as a footnote is confirmed by the asterisk he placed next to number 411 and by his rewriting the note in longer form at the top of p. 182 before he continued writing the following stanza. Ben W. Griffith first published this longer note, although with some errors, in "'The Revolt of Islam' and Byron's 'The Corsair,'" *N&Q*, 201 (1956), 265.

14. As early as 1821, A. A. Watts suggested that "the *transit of the wild horse* is imitated" from Shelley's *The Revolt* ("Lord Byron's Plagiarisms," *The London Literary Gazette*, no. 214 [24 February 1821], p. 122n.). Byron first referred to *The Revolt* in a letter of 24 November 1818 (*L&J*, IV, 272-73), but he probably received a copy from Shelley by 1 June, by which time Shelley had sent him Hunt's *Foliage* (see *L&J*, IV, 237-38), one of a number of books including *The Revolt* and *Frankenstein* that Shelley had been promising to send to Byron (see *PBSL*, II, 5, 13). Although Byron may not have read *The Revolt* until soon after Shelley visited him on 23 August 1818 and resumed their dialogue on "literary matters" (including Hunt's *Foliage*), *Mazeppa* was not completed until after 24 September (see *PBSL*, II, 37; *L&J*, IV, 264).

15. Shelley probably did not write his Preface until after he completed his poem in September, by which time he had read *Manfred*. For evidence that the Preface was completed by 13 November, see Reiman, *Shelley and His Circle*, V, 146.

16. Compare *The Prisoner of Chillon*, ll. 37-40, 148, 240, and 366-69 with *The Revolt* III.xiv, xix, xxiv, and VII.xxvi. Also compare *The Prisoner of Chillon*, ll. 301, 370-71, with Shelley's *Rosalind and Helen*, ll. 934-36.

17. Letter to Byron, 29 September 1816 (*PBSL*, I, 506).

18. See Leslie A. Marchand, *Byron: A Biography* (New York: Alfred A. Knopf, 1957), II, 699.

19. See Shelley's letters to Byron, 9 July and 24 September 1817 (*PBSL*, I, 547, 557).

20. 1 (1817), 289.

21. Although I do not reproduce the cancellation of "clouds" for "light" in l. 3, I print this poem as it was transcribed by Reiman from Shelley's holograph on the address page of William Godwin's letter to Shelley on 29 April 1817. Reiman (*Shelley and His Circle*, V, 205-14) follows his transcription with a useful collation, dating, and discussion of Shelley's three holograph drafts for this poem, to which I can add only two more particulars: that in the third draft (?1821/22), which appears in Bodleian MS. Shelley adds. e. 8, p. 139 reverso, the seventh line is "Mighty Eagle thou whose dwelling" rather than "thou whose <?shrieking>"

in Reiman's collation; and that when Mary Shelley copied this third draft into Bodleian MS. Shelley adds. d. 7, p. 99, she, despite her other errors, copied line 7 as "Mighty Eagle thou whose dwelling." Although Reiman argues that "there is no need to suppose that 'Mighty Eagle' was addressed to any particular person" (p. 211), I still believe that Byron was the subject in each draft. The possible datings (1817; then 1818/19; and finally 1821/22) of these three separate drafts (in the order suggested by Reiman) in which Shelley attempted to expand his portrait of the "Mighty Eagle" correspond to the times in which Byron appeared under various guises in Shelley's other poetry. In 1821/22, at which time Shelley was called "the Snake" by Byron, Shelley frequently referred to Byron as an "eagle": see *PBSL*, II, 289, 442; and Edward John Trelawny, *Records of Shelley, Byron and the Author* (London: Pickering and Chatto, 1887), p. 22.

22. *PBSL*, I, 591.

23. *L&J*, IV, 153, 155.

24. Shelley listened to Byron reciting parts of *Childe Harold* IV on 23 August 1818, read it by 25 September, and condemned it in his December letter to Peacock (see *PBSL*, II, 37; *MSJ*, p. 105; *PBSL*, II, 57-58).

25. See Jerome J. McGann, *Fiery Dust: Byron's Poetic Development* (Chicago: The University of Chicago Press, 1968), pp. 129-30, 133.

26. I differ from most explicators of these stanzas (vi-vii) by equating "overweening phantasies" not with Art produced by the creative mind, but with the ideal "form[s]" (vii), these being the ideal "things whose strong reality/Outshines our fairy-land" of Art (vi). In my judgment, Byron did not mean empirical reality when he referred to these *things*; rather, he was discriminating between the "aesthetic" (phantastic) and the "metaphysical" (over-weeningly phantastic) products or *things* of the mind.

27. Both Byron and Shelley eulogized Princess Charlotte following her death in childbirth in November 1817, but their separate remarks are quite dissimilar. Unlike Byron, who judged that even "Peasants bring forth in safety," desired that death would have spared the Princess and instead laid "low/Some less majestic, less beloved head," and envisioned a national mourning from "thy Sire's to his humblest subject's breast" (clxix, clxviii, clxxii), Shelley in his *Address to the People on the Death of Princess Charlotte (Julian*, VI, 73-82) sympathized instead for these less majestic women who had also died in childbirth, and then denied the Princess' right to a public mourning because she had not been a political figure acting on behalf of England's people. Rather, Shelley argued, the public should grieve for Brandreth, Ludlam, and Turner, three laborers who had been executed as a result of England's oppressive and unjust aristocratic system. Shelley's republican indignation here was not matched by Byron, for while the latter grieved that "Circumstance" had destroyed the Princess, one beloved by "Freedom" (clxix), the former indicted man for his submissive complicity in a tyrannical government and for his murder of "LIBERTY." But with typically Shelleyan logic, the *Address* concludes with a plea to "follow the corpse of British Liberty slowly and reverentially to its tomb" and with a hope that Liberty would arise from its grave and "make its throne of broken swords and sceptres and royal crowns trampled in the dust."

28. In these last lines, Byron may have been trying to correct Shelley's belief that man can escape Promethean agony. In a letter to Byron on 23 April 1817, Shelley explained that the "horrible circumstances" described in his last letter were behind him and added that "*all human evils either extinguish or are extinguished by the sufferer*, and I am now living with my accustomed tranquillity and happiness" (*PBSL*, I, 539, my italics). Byron received this letter at least by 27 May (see his reference to its substance in a letter of that date, *L&J*, IV, 124; also see Reiman, *Shelley and His Circle*, V, 199-200); and at the end of June, while writing the early stanzas of his fourth canto, Byron appears to echo Shelley's

statement deliberately by writing, "*All suffering doth destroy, or is destroyed,/ Even by the sufferer—and, in each event,/Ends*" (xxii), and then contradicts such an opinion by judging in the next stanza that suffering will return to plague the human spirit. Such an influence of a letter on a poem is not unusual, for Shelley in *Adonais* borrowed portions from Byron's letters about Keats; see Chapter 7.

29. *Fiery Dust*, p. 48.

30. See *MSJ*, p. 111. "The Coliseum" and "Notes on Sculptures" are printed in *Julian*, VI, 299-332.

31. McGann, *Fiery Dust*, p. 43.

*Chapter 5. Tangled Boughs of Heaven and Ocean:
Two Genii and a Maniac*

1. *PBSL*, II, 36-37.

2. Letter to Peacock, 20 April 1818 (*PBSL*, II, 8).

3. These remains are printed in *Julian*, III, 201-3, 336, the "Scene from Tasso" having only twenty-seven lines. For the dating of these remains and an expansion of the "Scene" to fifty lines, see G. M. Matthews, "A New Text of Shelley's Scene for *Tasso*," *KSMB*, 11 (1960), 39-47.

4. Baker, *Shelley's Major Poetry: The Fabric of a Vision* (Princeton: Princeton University Press, 1948), pp. 124-38; Matthews, "'Julian and Maddalo': the Draft and the Meaning," *Studia Neophilologica*, 35 (1963), 57-84; see also Raymond D. Havens, "*Julian and Maddalo*," *SP*, 27 (1930), 648-53.

5. *PBSL*, I, 556-57.

6. Letter to John and Maria Gisborne, 10 July 1818 (*PBSL*, II, 20). Matthews' remarks are from "A New Text of Shelley's Scene for *Tasso*," pp. 44-45.

7. Letter to Peacock (*PBSL*, II, 47).

8. Letters to Peacock, 20 April and 6-7 November 1818 (*PBSL*, II, 8, 47, my italics).

9. It has been conjectured that Shelley abandoned his drama because he did not wish to enter into competition with Byron—see *Relics of Shelley*, ed. Richard Garnett (London: Edward Moxon & Co., 1862), p. 26; Edward Dowden, *The Life of Percy Bysshe Shelley* (London: Kegan Paul, Trench & Co., 1886), II, 238n.; and Helen Rossetti Angeli, *Shelley and His Friends in Italy* (London: Methuen & Co., Ltd., 1911), p. 47. Actually, Shelley began his drama because of Byron's *Lament*. Although Reiman has also suggested that Shelley abandoned the Tasso drama because the subject had been preempted by Byron's *Lament* and *Childe Harold* IV.xxxv-xxxix and by Hobhouse's *Historical Illustrations of the Fourth Canto of Childe Harold*, he later conceded that "Shelley already knew from the publication of Byron's *Lament of Tasso* that his ideas differed sharply from Byron's on the significance of Tasso's life. Shelley may, therefore, have attempted to embody his views on Tasso in the dramatic form of a debate between himself and Byron" (*Shelley and His Circle*, VI, 592, 863).

10. Cf. Byron's Tasso, an "eagle-spirit of a Child of Song" (l. 2).

11. From Bodleian MS. Shelley adds. e. 11, p. 86, as quoted by Matthews, "'Julian and Maddalo,'" p. 72.

12. Shelley had access to the *Ode on Venice* while Mary copied it and *Mazeppa* between 1 and 3 October, after which she returned both to Byron (see *MSJ*, p. 106; and *MSL*, I, 58). Shelley probably did not begin *Julian and Maddalo* until November 1818, and Matthews argues from manuscript evidence that "substantial additions were still being made to *Julian and Maddalo* as late as March 1819, if, indeed, the whole poem were not composed then" ("'Julian and Maddalo,'" pp. 65-66).

13. Letter to Peacock, 17 or 18 December 1818 (*PBSL*, II, 57-58, my italics).

14. From MS. Shelley adds e. 11, p. 85; also quoted by Matthews, "'Julian and Maddalo,'" p. 82.

15. *Shelley: A Critical Reading* (Baltimore: The Johns Hopkins Press, 1971), pp. 75-76. Compare Matthews' judgments on the "composite" Maniac, "'Julian and Maddalo,'" p. 75. For discussions of Shelley as the Maniac, see Arabella Shore, "Shelley's 'Julian & Maddalo,'" *The Gentleman's Magazine*, 263 (1887), 329-42; H. S. Salt, "A Study of Shelley's 'Julian and Maddalo,'" *The Shelley Society's Papers*, pt. 2 (1891), pp. 325-42; John Harrington Smith, "Shelley and Claire Clairmont," *PMLA*, 54 (1939), 785-814; Smith, "Shelley and Claire Again," *SP*, 41 (1944), 94-105; and Newman Ivey White, *Shelley* (New York: Alfred A. Knopf, 1940), II, 42-50, 558-62.

16. See Baker, *Shelley's Major Poetry*, pp. 129-35; Matthews, "'Julian and Maddalo,'" p. 82; Knight, *Lord Byron: Christian Virtues* (New York: Oxford University Press, 1953), pp. 250-59; Saveson, "Shelley's *Julian and Maddalo*," *K-SJ*, 10 (1961), 53-58. For a nonbiographical approach, see James L. Hill, "Dramatic Structure in Shelley's *Julian and Maddalo*," *ELH*, 35 (1968), 84-93.

17. From Shelley's letter to Peacock, 6-7 November 1818 (*PBSL*, II, 47).

18. Shelley's Maniac, who refrained "'From that sweet sleep which medicines all pain'" in order to make his Lady "'less desolate'" (ll. 499, 497), had a more selfless motive than Byron's Tasso, who did not wish to "sanction with self-slaughter the dull lie/. . . and with the brand of shame/Stamp Madness deep into [his] memory" (ll. 214-16).

19. Knight (*Lord Byron: Christian Virtues*, p. 253) and Saveson ("Shelley's *Julian and Maddalo*," p. 56) mistakenly believed this "'child'" to be a veiled reference to Byron's daughter, Ada. That the Maniac is merely addressing his Lady as "'child'" is demonstrated by Shelley's first version of l. 398 in MS. Shelley adds. e. 11, p. 102: "*Child* [canceled] Nay was it I who wooed thee to this breast." This line is also quoted by Matthews, "'Julian and Maddalo,'" p. 81.

20. For this insight, I am indebted to Wasserman's analysis of *Julian and Maddalo* in *Shelley: A Critical Reading*, p. 77. In MS. Shelley adds. e. 11, p. 99, this phantasm was initially called "Laura" and she was introduced "*as if* [canceled] deaths dedicated bride." Matthews ("'Julian and Maddalo,'" pp. 77 ff.) ignores this "*as if*" in his attempt to distinguish the "dead" Laura from the scornful Lady and from the spirit's mate.

21. See in particular stanzas 2-4 of Shelley's "Song for Tasso" (*Julian*, III, 202-3) where Tasso, mixing "love" with "despair" and "the present with the past," sees in the dungeon's "vapour hoar" the "form" of Leonora. This same mixing and phantasmal vision was reproduced in the Maniac's monologue.

22. Shelley's remark to Byron in a letter of 9 July 1817 (*PBSL*, I, 547).

23. MS. Shelley adds. e. 11, p. 96; also quoted by Matthews, "'Julian and Maddalo,'" p. 81.

24. Shelley's acquaintance with stanza ix of *Childe Harold* IV is confirmed by his other allusions to it—see later in this chapter and n. 29.

25. By 8 October 1818, Shelley had heard Byron read the "Dedication" and "the first Canto of his 'Don Juan' a thing in the style of Beppo" (*PBSL*, II, 42). Shelley had read *Beppo* before he left London in March 1818—see his and Claire's letters to this effect (*PBSL*, II, 13; and *To Lord Byron*, p. 238).

26. Cf. *Manfred* I.i.153-57.

27. Shelley's hopes for Allegra are projected into the conclusion of *Julian and Maddalo*: "After many years" (l. 583), Julian returns to Venice, meets Maddalo's daughter, and discovers that her "transcendent worth" (l. 591) has preserved her from the influences of Maddalo and the Maniac.

28. Letter to Peacock, 17 or 18 December 1818 (*PBSL*, II, 58, my italics).

29. These same lines appear to be echoed in a canceled opening to *Julian and Maddalo*: "I rode one evening with Count Maddalo/—*Who knows him not has little need to know*/From me what our land's tongue can teach him not" (MS. Shelley adds. e. 11, p. 63, ll. 2-3 canceled).

30. *Lord Byron: Christian Virtues*, p. 254.

31. This fragment is untitled in Bodleian MS. Shelley adds. e. 12, p. 204 reverso, the top of the page (where Shelley may have written a title) having been torn away. In the first line, Shelley initially wrote "Mighty *spirit*," the second word canceled for "Mind." To both forms of this apostrophe, compare the "Mighty Eagle" fragment (possibly addressed to Byron in 1817—see Chapter 4) and the description of Byron as "Mighty spirit" in *Euganean Hills*, l. 204. In the third line, Shelley appears to have written "rule" rather than "curb," the latter word printed in the three-line transcription of this poem in *Julian*, III, 217. In the fourth line, Shelley first wrote and then canceled "*And stamp upon thy work some.*" Between the fifth and sixth lines of this fragment, there is a draft in a much larger hand of *Prometheus Unbound* II.i.145-47. That this sixth line belongs to the "O Mighty Mind" fragment is suggested by its syntactical compatibility to line 5, by its "giddy chasm" developing the image of "deep stream" in line 1, and by its being written in the same hand and ink as the rest of the fragment. The fragment then was written after this draft for *Prometheus Unbound.*

32. See Wasserman, *Shelley: A Critical Reading*, p. 201 and n. for a similar judgment that Shelley inverted Byron's symbolism.

33. In addition to the borrowings cited in the following paragraphs, compare *Euganean Hills*, ll. 229-32 with *Childe Harold* IV.x and cxxiii; and ll. 321-26 with IV.xxvii-xxviii.

34. Also compare with these lines, Byron's opening lines to *Ode on Venice*: "Oh Venice! Venice! when thy marble walls / Are level with the waters, there shall be / A cry of nations o'er thy sunken halls, / A loud lament along the sweeping sea!" Shelley had access to these lines just before he wrote *Euganean Hills*— see n. 12 above.

35. In 1819, "the tangled boughs of Heaven and Ocean" would result in the construction, not the destruction, of clouds—creative "Angels of rain and lightning" (*Ode to the West Wind*). In that same year, Byron would be termed one of the "forerunners of some unimagined change in our social condition" and asked to join the "cloud of mind [which] is discharging its collected lightning" (Preface to *Prometheus Unbound*)—see Chapter 6, n. 2.

36. Letter to Peacock, 17 or 18 December 1818 (*PBSL*, II, 58).

37. The draft for *The Two Spirits* occupies pp. 13-17 in MS. Shelley adds. e. 12, a notebook containing many draft passages of *Prometheus Unbound*, the draft of "The Coliseum" (pp. 201-187 reverso) and "To Byron" (p. 204 reverso), Mary Shelley's transcription of ll. 1-107 of *Julian and Maddalo* (pp. 177-171 reverso), and among the other 1818/19 poems two that seem to reflect Shelley's relationship with the "spirit" of Byron—"Lift not the painted veil" (pp. 22-23) and "My head is wild with weeping" (p. 24). *The Two Spirits* appears to have been written before March 1819 because the drafts for Act II of *Prometheus Unbound* are scattered through the early pages and occupy the then available space. For example, before the draft of *Prometheus Unbound* II.ii.1-23 was written on p. 33, Shelley apparently wrote an earlier version on the bottom halves of two pages (p. 24 for ll. 1-13; p. 28 for ll. 14-23), the top of each page already occupied by "My head is wild with weeping" (p. 24) and by the last three lines of "Alas! this is not what I thought life was" (p. 28), the last poem mistakenly placed among the 1820 poems in *Julian* but obviously predating the *Prometheus Unbound* draft. If any of the preceding pages had been vacant (specifically, if *The Two Spirits* had not occupied pp. 13-17), Shelley could have written II.ii.1-23 without the awkward separation of l. 13 on p. 24 and l. 14 on p. 28, the intervening pages being already occupied by drafts for Act I of *Prometheus Unbound*, for the fragment "Flourishing Vine," and for "Alas! this is not what I thought life was." It is possible that *The Two Spirits* was written before Act I of *Prometheus Unbound* and "as early as the summer of 1818" as suggested by Judith Chernaik, *The Lyrics of Shelley* (Cleveland: The Press of Case Western Reserve University, 1972), p. 239; or even as early as 1815/16 as

suggested by Wasserman, *Shelley: A Critical Reading*, p. 42 and n. But its many parallels with *Julian and Maddalo* and its position in the notebook argue for the more probable date between September 1818 and March 1819.

38. My text for *The Two Spirits* is that printed by Chernaik, *Lyrics of Shelley*, pp. 239-42, although I here reproduce the canceled epigraph to the poem as it appears in MS. "Genii" may well be the plural of "genius," and Shelley had already written of Byron's "most consummate genius" in the Preface to *Julian and Maddalo*. In support of Byron's being one of these "spirits," compare Shelley's description of Byron as a "Mighty spirit" both in *Euganean Hills*, l. 204, and in the canceled first line of "To Byron." Also compare the apostrophe in another 1818 fragment ("Great Spirit whom the sea of boundless mind"), which may have been addressed to the poet of Ocean who gave "a voice to its mysterious waves." Finally, compare in yet another 1818 fragment ("My head is wild with weeping for a grief") Shelley's concern "that a chief/*Among* [canceled] Like the wild spirits, should be cold & blind" (MS. Shelley adds. e. 12, p. 24). Shelley similarly lamented that Byron's pride had struck "his eagle spirit blind" in *Julian and Maddalo* (l. 51), and the first line of "My head is wild with weeping" seems to reproduce Shelley's response to Byron's *Lament of Tasso*, parts of which made Shelley's "head wild with tears" (*PBSL*, I, 557).

*Chapter 6. Transcendence and Immanence:*
*Shelley's* Prometheus Unbound

1. *Speculations on Metaphysics* (*Julian*, VII, 342). This passage was canceled in Shelley's MS.
2. Compare Shelley's similar views in his Preface to *The Revolt of Islam* and in his letter to Charles Ollier, 15 October 1819 (*PBSL*, II, 127). Shelley alludes to the recent charges against Byron in the periodicals when he refers to the censure of plagiarism over "poems far more popular." Also, Shelley's references to his contemporaries' "uncommunicated lightning of . . . mind" and to the "cloud of mind . . . discharging [eliminating rather than releasing?] its collected lightning" (Preface to *Prometheus Unbound*) may look back to Byron's "Lightning," an uncommunicated or "voiceless thought" which is "sheath[ed] . . . as a sword" in *Childe Harold* III.xcvii; and look forward to Shelley's description of Byron as the "Pilgrim of Eternity . . . veiling all the lightnings of his song" in *Adonais* (xxx). Shelley may also have recalled Byron's "sheathing . . . as a sword" the "Lightning" of his poetry when he wrote the contrary opinion in *A Defence of Poetry* that "poetry is a sword of lightning, ever unsheathed, which consumes the scabbard that would contain it" (*Julian*, VII, 122). See Chapter 9 for a discussion of Byron's "thunder."
3. From Huntington MS. 2177, as quoted by Lawrence John Zillman, ed., *Shelley's "Prometheus Unbound": The Text and the Drafts—Toward a Modern Definitive Edition* (New Haven: Yale University Press, 1968), p. 38.
4. Compare Earl Wasserman's judgment that Shelley's borrowings from Aeschylus' *Prometheus Bound* were reestablished "in a contrary ethical and theological context so as to transform their meanings radically" (*Shelley: A Critical Reading* [Baltimore: The Johns Hopkins Press, 1971], p. 284).
5. *A Defence of Poetry* (*Julian*, VII, 137).
6. *Speculations on Metaphysics* (*Julian*, VII, 65, my italics).
7. *Julian*, VII, 75, the bracketed words canceled in Shelley's MS.
8. *A Defence of Poetry* (*Julian*, VII, 118).
9. *Speculations on Morals* (*Julian*, VII, 75-76, my italics).
10. Letter to Leigh Hunt, ?14-18 November 1819 (*PBSL*, II, 152).
11. For this and Coleridge's contrary definition of a symbol (quoted later in this chapter), see *The Statesman's Manual* in *The Collected Works of Samuel*

*Taylor Coleridge, 6: Lay Sermons*, ed. R. J. White (London: Routledge & Kegan Paul, Bollingen Series LXXV, 1972), p. 30.

12. See, for example, the "statues three" on the Altar of Federation in Canto V.xl-lii: Laon aligns himself with the winged figure who represents triumphant "Wisdom"; Cythna is to be aligned with the woman who represents "Pity and Peace and Love"; and together, Laon and Cythna (represented by the winged figure and the woman) will awaken the sleeping Giant who represents "divine Equality!/Wisdom and Love are but the slaves of thee."

13. This aesthetic judgment, that imagery functions within a drama to give form to human passions, *exactly* summarizes the action of *Prometheus Unbound*. Prometheus or the imagination is "as . . . God" (i.e., each is divine but neither is God, as will be explained shortly in my text) who became incarnate or "assume[d] flesh for the redemption" of man. That Shelley's Prometheus experienced an "incarnation" is frequently ignored, even though he has been compared to Christ. But Shelley's drama is intelligible and the many contradictions therein resolved only if we recognize that Prometheus is portrayed paradoxically as an "immortal" (I.150) who also suffers mortal pain and temporal frustration. Otherwise, Mercury's temptation that Prometheus escape his "slow years" of "torture" by plunging "Into Eternity, where recorded time,/. . ./Seems but a point" (I.416-23), is meaningless. Asia herself suggests to Demogorgon that Prometheus was first an immortal who, in pity for man, came into this temporal world to wake man's hopes, send Love, tame fire, and give speech (II.iv.59-73); and this incarnation is explicitly described by Earth, Prometheus' "Mother," within whose veins "Joy ran, as blood within a living frame,/When [Prometheus] didst from her bosom, like a cloud/Of glory, arise, a spirit of keen joy" (I.156-58). Granted, Shelley always denied that Christ was the God-man as defined by orthodox Christianity, but he ironically used this orthodox myth so that Prometheus, both divine and human, could function as a symbol of man's own divinity. Shelley thus inverted the logic of Christian theology and proved that Christ was divine because he was a man. For additional parallels between Christ and Prometheus, see Wasserman, *Shelley: A Critical Reading*, pp. 291-305.

14. *Essay on Christianity* (*Julian*, VI, 229).

15. *Julian*, VI, 230. Strictly speaking, Shelley here describes Christ's conception of God. However, that Shelley agreed is demonstrated by two factors: he sympathetically acknowledged that Christ had a "conception widely differing from the gross imaginations of the vulgar relatively to the ruling Power of the universe"; and when Shelley chose to disagree with Christ's conception of God, he at least implied that disagreement (see my discussion of the "will" of God and Demogorgon later in this chapter and in n. 35).

16. *Julian*, VI, 232, 231.

17. *Julian*, VI, 239.

18. *Speculations on Morals* (*Julian*, VII, 80).

19. *A Defence of Poetry* (*Julian*, VII, 118).

20. In support of Jupiter's function as Prometheus' "second" or perverted self, consider Shelley's judgment in *Speculations on Morals* that "selfishness is . . . the offspring of ignorance and mistake" (*Julian*, VII, 76). This symbolic identity between Jupiter and Prometheus, whether claimed because both are abstractions of man's actions (his "selfishness" and his "ignorance") or because within the drama itself Jupiter is the creation ("offspring") of Prometheus, is further suggested by the simultaneous liberation of Prometheus and dethronement of Jupiter: the latter being a metaphor of the former; i.e., the imagination restored necessarily being co-instantaneous with selfishness eliminated. For further discussion of Jupiter as Prometheus' "second" self, see Ross Greig Woodman, *The Apocalyptic Vision in the Poetry of Shelley* (Toronto: University of Toronto Press, 1964), pp. 109-16; and Wasserman, *Shelley: A Critical Reading*, pp. 258-61, 287-91. Also consider that Prometheus' vain posturing in his "Know ye not me"

speech (I.112-30) confirms that he sees *his own* "gestures proud" (I.258) in the Phantasm of Jupiter, who repeats Prometheus' curse.

21. *Speculations on Morals* (*Julian*, VII, 75). Wasserman argued in *Shelley: A Critical Reading* that because the Spirits come *to* Prometheus "from the Human Mind," he "cannot be the Human Mind." I disagree, as my previous analysis indicates. True, Prometheus does not allegorically represent all aspects of the human mind including both the "most imperial" quality and the "inferior portion of its mechanism" (*Essay on Christianity*, *Julian*, VI, 231), but he is, in the abstract, a symbol for the "imperial" or divine imagination, that faculty of the human mind by which man perfects himself. As a symbol for man's imagination, he necessarily undergoes the same changes that man himself experiences. Therefore, the consolation he receives from the Spirits of human thought who bear his "prophecy" merely demonstrates that he is indeed a symbol, which, as Coleridge observed, *"always partakes of the Reality which it renders intelligible"* (my italics).

Professor Wasserman, however, would not have accepted this approach to Shelley's metaphysical drama, for he believed that Prometheus is not a "fictional abstraction of earthly man or of his faculties or ideals. . . . he is not a fiction abstracted from what exists, but Existence itself" (pp. 256-57). As "Existence," Prometheus is also defined as "Life" or the "One Mind," into which "all individual minds are subsumed" (p. 146). I can agree that Prometheus represents the "one mind" (lower case), but only insofar as he symbolizes individual human consciousness considered abstractly and not, as Wasserman argued, the universal consciousness of the One Mind. For a defense of this position, see my analysis of Shelley's *On Life* and Wasserman's theory of the One Mind in Appendix B.

22. Shelley read *Childe Harold* IV while writing Act I of *Prometheus Unbound*, and he seems here to be echoing Byron's description of "The skies which rain their plagues on men like dew—/Disease, death, bondage—all the woes we see,/ And worse, the woes we see not—which throb through/The immedicable soul, with heart-aches ever new" (IV.cxxvi).

23. As Shelley similarly stated in his *Essay on Christianity*, "the perfection of the human and the divine character is thus asserted to be the same: man by resembling God fulfils most accurately the tendencies of his nature, and God comprehends within itself all that constitutes human perfection" (*Julian*, VI, 239).

24. *Julian*, VII, 87. In some ways, Shelley appealed to the "vulgar" in Canto I of *The Revolt of Islam*, but even there he undercut the Manichaean hypothesis by making the "Twin Genii, equal Gods" creations or personifications of man: the two principles "burst the womb of inessential Nought" only *"when* life and thought/Sprang forth" (I.xxv, my italics). That these principles were man's creations is also suggested by the next stanza: the "earliest dweller of the world" gazed not at two principles but only at "A blood red Comet and the Morning Star/Mingling their beams in combat," and in "dreadful sympathy" the "thoughts within his mind waged mutual war"; when the "fair Star fell, he turned and shed his brother's blood" (xxvi). Thus if the "darkness lingering o'er the dawn of things,/Was Evil's breath and life" (xxviii), that "darkness" was a consequent, not an antecedent, of man's evil actions. Similarly, the "Snake [of Good] and Eagle [of Evil] meet" only *"when* priests and kings dissemble" and *"When* round pure hearts, a host of hopes assemble" (xxxiii, my italics).

25. *Essay on Christianity* (*Julian*, VI, 235).

26. Letter to Murray, 15 February 1817 (*L&J*, IV, 55).

27. *Shelley: A Critical Reading*, p. 64. Shelley appears to have questioned this "corrective version," for he canceled "There" in the first line above which he wrote "Is there"; thus the final version would read: "Is there more on earth than we/Dream of in our philosophy" (Bodleian MS. Shelley adds. e. 6, p. 5). Although the epigraph from *Hamlet* did not appear until the third issue of the first edition of *Manfred*, which was published on 16 June 1816 (see Thomas James Wise, *A Bibliography of the Writings in Verse and Prose of George Gordon Noel, Baron*

*Byron* [1933; rpt. London: Dawsons of Pall Mall, 1963], I, 120-23), we may assume that Shelley was aware of this epigraph by the time he wrote his "corrective version." Shelley himself may have purchased this third issue, for it appeared soon enough after 16 June to be reviewed (with mention of the epigraph) in the *Critical Review*, 5th ser., V (June 1817), 622.

28. See pp. 59 and 65 for my discussions of the epigraphs to *Manfred* and to *The Revolt of Islam*.

29. *Tusculan Disputations*, trans. J. E. King, Loeb Classical Library (London: William Heinemann, 1927), p. 215 (II.xxv.60).

30. *Shelley: A Critical Reading*, p. 283. When Shelley recorded his epigraph for *Prometheus Unbound* in Bodleian MS. Shelley adds. e. 11, p. 115, he entitled it "To the Ghost of Aeschylus"—see Wasserman, p. 282.

31. Wasserman himself (p. 283n.) refers to Byron's "mocking use" of Dionysius' apostasy in his letter to R. C. Dallas, 21 January 1808 (*L&J*, I, 173). The epigraph, *"Audisne haec, Amphiarae, sub terram abdite,"* could then have been addressed to two apostates: "the Ghost of Aeschylus" and Byron. Furthermore, because Shelley recorded his epigraph in a notebook containing the draft of *Julian and Maddalo* and because he recognized that Byron's defiant Promethean poems were figuratively descendants of Aeschylus' *Prometheus Bound*, it is not unreasonable to conjecture that, in Shelley's mind, Byron was indeed the "Ghost" of Aeschylus. It is also possible that the two poets discussed this epigraph and Dionysius' apostasy when Byron read Shelley the "Dedication" to *Don Juan* in which Southey was attacked as an "Epic Renegade" who "turn'd out a Tory at/ Last": "Apostasy's so fashionable, too,/To keep *one* creed's a task grown quite Herculean;/Is it not so, my Tory, ultra-Julian" (sts. 1 and 17). Byron read these lines to Shelley before 8 October 1818, i.e., during the writing of Act I of *Prometheus Unbound*.

32. *Shelley: A Critical Reading*, p. 284.

33. H. W. Piper, *The Active Universe: Pantheism and the Concept of Imagination in the English Romantic Poets* (London: The Athlone Press, 1962), pp. 198-99. G. Wilson Knight also argued that "Jupiter is a precise duplication of Arimanes" (*Lord Byron: Christian Virtues* [New York: Oxford University Press, 1953], p. 257).

34. Also contrast this lyric to the song of the Fifth Spirit (*Manfred* I.i.100-7), who determined by means of the wind, storm, hurricane, and lightning that a fleet would "sink ere night be past."

35. When Shelley wrote in the *Essay on Christianity* that "Jesus Christ attributes to this power [God] the faculty of will," he indicated his disagreement by the following sentence: "How far such a doctrine in its ordinary sense may be philosophically true, or how far Jesus Christ intentionally availed himself of a metaphor easily understood, is foreign to the subject to consider" (*Julian*, VI, 235).

36. *L&J*, V, 451.

37. *Conversations on Religion, with Lord Byron and Others* (London: John Murray, 1830), pp. 55, 189.

38. *Blessington's Conversations*, p. 114. Byron's remarks on the predestined suffering of man may have prompted Lady Blessington's very Shelleyan rejoinder in 1834: "Destiny is a phantom of our own creation, like the Monsters children imagine, and tremble at. Our Conduct forms our Destiny, and that conduct is much more frequently guided by our weaknesses, than by our Vices" (quoted from her "Night Thought Book" by Lovell, p. 87).

39. *Julian*, VI, 194.

40. Letter to Peacock (*PBSL*, II, 58).

41. For other possible echoes of *Childe Harold* IV in *Prometheus Unbound*, see n. 22 above and compare *Prometheus Unbound* I.24-30 with *Childe Harold* IV.cxxxv; I.450-51 with *CH* IV.clviii; III.i.36 with *CH* IV.clxxxiii; and IV.483-

87 with *CH* IV.cxvii. For the remaining echoes of *Manfred* in Shelley's drama, compare *Prometheus Unbound* I.24-30 with *Manfred* I.ii.7-12; II.iii.47-50 with *Manfred* I.ii.85-89; II.v.89 with *Manfred* I.i.121; and IV.286-87 with *Manfred* I. ii.61-63.

42. *Julian*, VII, 118.

43. Ibid. In attempting to explain himself further, Shelley wrote that poetry strengthens the imagination "in the same manner as exercise strengthens a limb." Just as a limb must be used in order to exercise and thereby strengthen the same limb, the imagination must be used in order to create poetry and thereby strengthen the imagination.

44. Letter to Byron, 8 September 1816 (*PBSL*, I, 504).

*Chapter 7. Some Penetrable Stuff: Shelley and*
*Byron Differing More Than Ever on Politics, Drama,*
*Morality, and Keats*

1. "Extracts from a Diary," 18 February 1821 (*L&J*, V, 205).

2. Letter to Byron, 17 September 1820 (*PBSL*, II, 236).

3. *PBSL*, II, 317, 322.

4. See Byron's "Address to the Neapolitan Insurgents," Appendix V, *L&J*, V, 595-96.

5. Letter to Byron, 4 May 1821 (*PBSL*, II, 291); letter to Hobhouse, 26 April 1821 (*LBC*, II, 169).

6. Letter to Leigh Hunt, 26 May 1820 (*PBSL*, II, 201).

7. *Julian*, VII, 48, 54, 43.

8. *PBSL*, II, 322-23, 330.

9. Letter to Charles Ollier, 14 May 1820 (*PBSL*, II, 196). Compare Byron's "wandering with pedestrian Muses" in his "Dedication" to *Don Juan* (st. 8).

10. In the following stanza is a self-conscious and outlandish double rhyme so characteristic of *Don Juan*: "climate" and "rhyme at." Shelley had been reading the *ottava rima* in Forteguerri's *Ricciardetto* at this time, but his poetic ear was equally conditioned by Byron's use of the verse form. He had read *Beppo* and had heard Byron reading the "Dedication" and first canto of *Don Juan* by October 1818 (*PBSL*, II, 42), and he read the published *Don Juan* (Cantos I-II) by 3 January 1820 (*MSJ*, p. 127). And on 26 May 1820, a few months before he finished his translation of the *Hymn to Mercury* (entry of 14 July in *MSJ*, p. 136) and wrote *The Witch of Atlas* (August), he praised Byron for "the beauty and the wit" of *Don Juan* (*PBSL*, II, 198). Shelley also commended Byron for the "strange and terrible storm . . . at sea" in Canto II, and John Buxton suggests that this storm scene may have prompted Shelley to write *A Vision of the Sea* (April 1820)—see *Byron and Shelley: The History of a Friendship* (New York: Harcourt, Brace & World, Inc., 1968), pp. 116, 120.

11. *Julian*, VII, 103-4. In this same essay (p. 101), Byron is described as "a great modern poet" who in *Manfred* had called "a comet 'A wandering Hell in the eternal space' [I.i.46]." According to Kenneth Neill Cameron, *Shelley: The Golden Years* (Cambridge: Harvard University Press, 1974), pp. 601-2, this essay was probably written in January 1821.

12. *L&J*, V, 495-96.

13. This stanza on Queen Caroline was omitted at Byron's request (see *L&J*, V, 320) from *Don Juan* when Cantos III-V were published on 8 August 1821, but it would have been in the MS version that Byron read to Shelley by 10 August.

14. *Poetry*, VII, 63-64. Byron also ridiculed *Peter Bell* in *Don Juan* III.98-100, stanzas written between 30 November 1819 and 17 January 1820; and on 31 August 1820, he referred Kinnaird to "Mr. Turdsworth's Peter Bell" (as quoted by Leslie A. Marchand, *Byron: A Biography* [New York: Alfred A.

Knopf, 1957], II, *notes*, 95). For other derogatory references to *Peter Bell*, see Byron's "Some Observations upon an Article in *Blackwood's Magazine*"; and his Dedication of *Marino Faliero* to Goethe (*L&J*, IV, 485-86; V, 101-2).

15. "Shelley's Complete Poetical Works," *The Spectator*, 23 November 1839, p. 1119. Mary Shelley's reaction to this review needs no comment: "*But* the Spectator!—its editor must be both a goose and a coxcomb—the notion that L[ord] B[yron] had any hand in the Peter Bell is half-witted" (*MSL*, II, 143).

16. Carlos Baker, *Shelley's Major Poetry: The Fabric of a Vision* (Princeton: Princeton University Press, 1948), p. 171.

17. See *PBSL*, II, 42, 198. Despite Shelley's disapproval of the "Dedication" to *Don Juan*, he was probably indebted to Byron's description of Coleridge as "a hawk encumber'd with his hood" (st. 2) when he wrote in July 1820 that Coleridge was a "hooded eagle among blinking owls" (*Letter to Maria Gisborne*, l. 208).

18. Letter of 6 September 1819 (*PBSL*, II, 117).

19. *PBSL*, II, 317, 345.

20. Byron did, however, speak to Shelley about his intentions to write *Marino Faliero* when the two poets were together in Venice in 1818 (see letter to Byron, 16 April 1821, *PBSL*, II, 283). But Byron did not begin his drama until April 1820, he concluded it by 17 July (*L&J*, V, 7, 52), and he had not seen *The Cenci* by the middle of May (see Shelley's reply to Byron, 26 May 1820, *PBSL*, II, 198). Some time between May and 10 September, when Byron complained about *The Cenci* being "sad work" (*L&J*, V, 74), i.e., perhaps while he was finishing or copying *Marino Faliero*, he did read Shelley's drama. On 6 September 1819, Shelley had requested Ollier to send copies of all of his books to "Lord Byron (at Murrays)" (*PBSL*, II, 118), and it is possible that Murray received and forwarded *The Cenci* in one of the parcels Byron received by 17 July, 12 August, or 7 September (*L&J*, V, 52, 64, 72).

21. *L&J*, V, 268. Shelley had not yet seen *Marino Faliero* and therefore could not "revenge" himself in his reply to Byron on 4 May 1821. Instead, he deferentially misrepresented his own feelings about *The Cenci*: "I am aware of the unfitness of the subject, now it is written, but I had a different opinion in composition. I wish I could believe that it merited—or that anything of mine merited—the friendly commendations that you give them" (*PBSL*, II, 290).

22. *PBSL*, II, 317, 345. Edward Williams read *Marino Faliero* on 22 October and criticized it in terms similar to Shelley's (*Williams*, p. 104).

23. Letter to Byron, 4 May 1821 (*PBSL*, II, 290).

24. See Samuel C. Chew, "Shakespearean Echoes in *Marino Faliero*," Appendix III, *The Dramas of Lord Byron: A Critical Study* (1915; rpt. New York: Russell & Russell, Inc., 1964), pp. 179-81; Stuart Curran, *Shelley's "Cenci": Scorpions Ringed with Fire* (Princeton: Princeton University Press, 1970), p. 48; and David V. Erdman, "Byron's Stage Fright: The History of His Ambition and Fear of Writing for the Stage," *ELH*, 6 (1939), 219-43. Compare Erdman's argument with Medwin's: "Byron pretends that his Tragedies were not intended for the Stage—but who can believe him—and his disappointment at the failure of *Marino Faliero*, and attributing that failure to the acting rather than the demerits of the work, proves [*sic*] that he was not sincere in his assertion" (*Revised Life*, pp. 256-57).

25. *L&J*, V, 323. This passage explains the Shakespearean echoes in Byron's non-Shakespearean drama and repeats what Byron had written about his "*regular* tragedies*" to Murray on 4 January 1821 (*L&J*, V, 217-18).

26. *L&J*, V, 244.

27. See Ernest Sutherland Bates, *A Study of Shelley's Drama "The Cenci"* (New York: Columbia University Press, 1908), pp. 50-52 for a treatment of the time scheme in *The Cenci*. In spite of Bates's conjecture that Act III, scene i, occurs the "same day" as Act II, it must be at least the following day. Bates

ignored Giacomo's meeting with Orsino in II.ii and his later description of that meeting as the "other day" in III.i.339.

28. In September 1821, Shelley believed that Byron would "soften down the severe and unharmonising traits of his 'Marino Faliero'" (*PBSL*, II, 349). Byron's *Cain* proved Shelley right, and one of the reasons Shelley so ecstatically praised it was Byron's dramatic representation of conflict between Cain and his antagonists, Adah, Abel, and especially Lucifer.

29. I here give to Shelley, Byron's purported complaints about *Hamlet*, as reported in "Byron and Shelley on the Character of Hamlet." For a discussion of this essay, see the following paragraph and n. 30.

30. 29, pt. 2 (1830), 327-36; reprinted in abbreviated form by Walter Edwin Peck, *Shelley: His Life and Work* (London: Ernest Benn Limited, 1927), II, 421-32; reprinted in complete form by Bruce R. McElderry, Jr., *Shelley's Critical Prose* (Lincoln: University of Nebraska Press, 1967), pp. 143-57; translated into French and discussed by René Rapin, "Byron et Shelley: Dialogue et commentaire sur Hamlet," *Etudes de Lettres* (l'Université de Lausanne), 3d ser., 6 (janvier-mars 1973), 3-24. For discussions of the authenticity of this dialogue, also see Reiman, *TL Variorum*, p. 100n.; and Wasserman, "Shelley's Last Poetics: A Reconsideration," in *From Sensibility to Romanticism: Essays Presented to Frederick A. Pottle*, ed. Frederick W. Hilles and Harold Bloom (New York: Oxford University Press, 1965), pp. 505-8 and nn. Wasserman cited a similar (or the same) dialogue overheard by Samuel Rogers in Pisa (see *Recollections of the Table-Talk of Samuel Rogers; to which is added Porsoniana* [London: Edward Moxon, 1856], pp. 239-40); and according to *Williams*, p. 144, Rogers was in Pisa on 20 and 21 April 1822. That Mary Shelley authored and published this dialogue is suggested by a number of facts: her association with Cyrus Redding, working editor of the *New Monthly* to which she submitted an article as early as 1826 (see my article, "Mary Shelley and the Roger Dodsworth Hoax," *K-SJ*, 24 [1975], 20-28); her knowledge of Byron's dislike for Shakespeare (see Edward John Trelawny, *Records of Shelley, Byron and the Author* [London: Pickering and Chatto, 1887], p. 22); her familiarity with *Defence of Poetry* (not published until 1840), the judgments in which are echoed by Shelley's remarks in this dialogue; and her predilection at this time to begin articles and stories with a description of "over-canopying chesnut trees": compare the opening paragraph (in terms of diction, syntax, and setting) of this dialogue with the opening paragraph in her review article "Modern Italy," *Westminster Review*, 11 (July 1829), 127-40; and with the second paragraph of her story "The Mourners," first published in *The Keepsake* for 1830. If Mary actually wrote this article, she would not have signed her name, but she would have broken her vow "never to make money of [her] acquaintance with Lord Byron" (see *MSL*, II, 13, 20). If Shelley himself authored this article (as Wasserman suggested) and Mary merely prepared it for the press, it may have grown out of Shelley's earlier attempt to record in dialogue his and Byron's contrary opinions on the quality of Keats's poetry. This earlier dialogue may be found in Bodleian MS. Shelley adds. e. 8, pp. 72-73, and in a transcription by Neville Rogers, *Shelley at Work: A Critical Inquiry*, 2d ed. (Oxford: At the Clarendon Press, 1967), p. 257. Rogers believes that this dialogue on Keats and an accompanying one on "Lionel" (transcribed on pp. 16-17) are between Shelley and himself. The one on Keats, however, anticipates Shelley's arguments with Byron after the death of Keats.

31. Letter to Byron, 9 July 1817 (*PBSL*, I, 547).

32. Knight, *The Golden Labyrinth: A Study of British Drama* (New York: W. W. Norton & Company, Inc., 1962), p. 235; Erdman, "Lord Byron: Life and Works," in *Shelley and His Circle*, III, 320-21; Johnson, *MLQ*, 3 (1942), 420, 423.

33. *L&J*, IV, 410; V, 67; *LBC*, II, 156. Compare Byron's remark on the "butcher's cleaver" to his judgment that the Cato Street Conspirators were

"butchers" (*LBC*, II, 138); and to Faliero's regret that Israel Bertuccio goes "to this butcher-work/As if these high-born men were steers for shambles" (III.ii. 506-7).

34. *Julian*, VII, 19-20. Shelley repeated these judgments, in nearly the same words, in his conclusion to *A Defence of Poetry* (VII, 140).

35. Letter to Marianne Hunt, 29 October 1820 (*PBSL*, II, 240). Compare Shelley's observations to Byron on 26 May 1820 that the "bitter mockery of our common nature" in *Don Juan* is redeemed by "the power and the beauty and the wit . . . —chiefly because they belie and refute it" (*PBSL*, II, 198).

36. Shelley, however, doubted his own faith in Byron, for in *A Philosophical View of Reform* he canceled Byron's name from a list of political reformers including Godwin, Hazlitt, Bentham, and Hunt—see *Julian*, VII, 52, 340n.

37. *Julian*, VII, 121-22.

38. Letter to Peacock, ca. 25 July 1819 (*PBSL*, II, 102; see *Shelley and His Circle*, VI, 897, for the dating of this letter).

39. *PBSL*, II, 190, my italics.

40. *Shelley's "Cenci,"* p. 139. For slightly different judgments about the "supposed" conflicts between Shelley's Preface and drama, see Bates, *A Study of Shelley's Drama "The Cenci,"* pp. 74-77; and Joseph W. Donohue, Jr., *Dramatic Character in the English Romantic Age* (Princeton: Princeton University Press, 1970), pp. 179-81.

41. *The Deserted Stage: The Search for Dramatic Form in Nineteenth-Century England* (Athens: Ohio University Press, 1972), pp. 21, 23. Compare Earl Wasserman's judgment that "Beatrice herself accepts this myth of a punitive theology as the pattern for human conduct and commits herself to the belief that God assigns man . . . the duty of enforcing His system of rewards and punishments" (*Shelley: A Critical Reading* [Baltimore: The Johns Hopkins Press, 1971], p. 93).

42. "The Unpastured Sea: An Introduction to Shelley" (1965) in *The Ringers in the Tower: Studies in Romantic Tradition* (Chicago: University of Chicago Press, 1971), p. 104.

43. *L&J*, V, 232.

44. *Julian*, VII, 13-14.

45. *PBSL*, II, 324-25. The quote from Aeschylus, *Agamemnon*, 759-60, is translated by Jones as follows: "The unrighteous action breeds many others for the future like to its own race."

46. *L&J*, V, 554, 559.

47. *Julian*, VII, 117-18.

48. *L&J*, V, 554, 559, 142.

49. *L&J*, IV, 485, 486, 493.

50. *L&J*, V, 93, 109, 117, 120. The omissions in these letters in *L&J* are supplied by Marchand in *Byron: A Biography*, II, 886; and in *Byron: A Portrait* (New York: Alfred A. Knopf, 1970), p. 335.

51. *L&J*, V, 559. In the fall of 1821, Byron repeated that "the present is not a high age of English Poetry" in his "Detached Thoughts" (*L&J*, V, 441).

52. From *"Further Addenda for insertion in the letter to J. M., Esq., on Bowles's Pope, etc.,"* which is incorrectly attached to Byron's *Second Letter to John Murray* in *L&J*, V, 586-92. Because the *Addenda* was sent to Murray on 12 March (see *L&J*, V, 258-60)—that is, *before* he wrote (25 March) or sent (21 April) the *Second Letter*—Byron must have intended it for the first *Letter* on the Bowles/Pope controversy. Murray, however, attached the *Addenda* to the second *Letter* in his proofs (see *L&J*, V, 337-38). E. H. Coleridge also prints "'Additions to the passages from Keats'" as a suppressed note to the *Addenda* (see *L&J*, V, 588n.-589n.), but its syntax and form ("'Further on we have'" followed by a quote from Keats) suggest that it was intended as an insertion in "Some Observations Upon an Article in *Blackwood's Magazine*" after the passage, "'A little before'" followed by a quote from Keats (*L&J*, IV, 492). Byron had

delayed the publishing of "Some Observations."

53. *L&J*, V, 267-68. Byron was correct, for Shelley did not like this pamphlet when he read it in Ravenna in August; he wrote Mary that Byron offered "some good things—but he ought not to write prose criticism" (*PBSL*, II, 332).

54. *Julian*, VII, 140; *PBSL*, II, 290.

55. *PBSL*, II, 284.

56. *L&J*, V, 267.

57. *PBSL*, II, 289-90.

58. For my analysis of these two stanzas here, I am indebted to Frederick L. Jones, "*Adonais*: The Source of XXVII-XXVIII," *MLN*, 46 (1931), 236-39.

59. For this one comparison, I am indebted to Peter J. Manning, "Byron's 'English Bards' and Shelley's 'Adonais': A Note," *N&Q*, 215 (1970), 380-81. Byron apparently quoted "penetrable stuff" from *Hamlet* III.iv.36, and he reused the phrase in *The Prophecy of Dante* (written in 1819 but not read by Shelley until after he wrote *Adonais*) when he noted that poets, as "birds of Paradise," were "formed of far too penetrable stuff" (III.168-69).

60. Shelley's interest in White is confirmed by an early draft of his Preface to *Adonais*, wherein he condemned Southey as one who had formerly "edited the remains of Kirke White" but who by 1821 failed to see that Keats's poetry promised as much as White's (*Julian*, II, 407). For Shelley's quarrel with Southey, see Chapter 8.

61. As transcribed in *Verse and Prose from the Manuscripts of Percy Bysshe Shelley*, ed. Sir John C. E. Shelley-Rolls and Roger Ingpen (London: Privately printed, 1934), p. 38. A second rejected stanza (p. 41), beginning "His words were wingèd arrows, every one/Barbed with that fire . . ./The lightnings, which the Arch-Sagittary sun/Pours from his quiver," may also have described Byron as a satirist. These two stanzas are located in Bodleian MS. Shelley adds. e. 9, pp. 15, 28.

62. *PBSL*, II, 308-9.

63. Letter of 5 June 1821 (*PBSL*, II, 294).

64. Letter to Leigh Hunt, 26 August 1821 (*PBSL*, II, 345).

65. *L&J*, V, 331.

66. As transcribed by Lyle H. Kendall, Jr., "Byron: An Unpublished Letter to Shelley," *MLN*, 76 (1961), 709.

67. *L&J*, V, 337, 338. Also see above, n. 52.

68. Letter to Murray, 4 September 1821 (*L&J*, V, 357); and *Williams*, p. 110. Compare Shelley's reaction to Byron's first *Letter* on the Bowles/Pope controversy, n. 53 above.

69. *L&J*, V, 472-73; IV, 491n.-492n.

70. *Medwin's Conversations*, p. 238; *Blessington's Conversations*, p. 52.

*Chapter 8. The Trees of Knowledge and of Life:*
*Shelley's Response to* The Prophecy of Dante, Don Juan,
The Vision of Judgment, *and* Cain

1. For the circumstances described in this paragraph, see *PBSL*, II, 194 and n., 197-99, 283 and n., 289-91, 308; and *L&J*, V, 266-69, 498-500.

2. These lines are found in Bodleian MS. Shelley e. 4, fol. 6 verso, but with the exception of my conjectural "her?" are quoted from A. H. Koszul, *Shelley's Prose in the Bodleian Manuscripts* (London: Henry Frowde, 1910), p. 10. C. D. Locock, *An Examination of the Shelley Manuscripts in the Bodleian Library* (Oxford: At the Clarendon Press, 1903), p. 73, was the first to publish this note. On fol. 43 verso, Locock also discovered a virtually illegible note, which he conjecturally transcribed as "To remember that Albi's babies to kept secret from William." Shelley may have written both of these notes as early as April 1818, when he complained about his "invidious office of mediator" in this "painful

controversy." By May 1820, he still resented his role "as the mediator, or rather the interpreter, of a dispute" (*PBSL*, II, 11, 199).

3. "The Planet-Tempest Passage in *Epipsychidion*," *PMLA*, 63 (1948), 953.

4. Letters to Mary, 7 and 15-16 August (*PBSL*, II, 316-19, 336-39—in the footnotes to these pages, the letters by Hoppner, Byron, and Mary are also quoted). Because Mary's letter of refutation to the Hoppners was found among Byron's papers after his death, it is possible that he was too embarrassed to forward it as he had promised. For arguments that Byron did inform the Hoppners of the Shelleys' denials, see *LBC*, II, 189-94; Leslie A. Marchand, *Byron: A Biography* (New York: Alfred A. Knopf, 1957), II, 925n.-926n.; and Doris Langley Moore, "Byron, Leigh Hunt, and the Shelleys: New Light on Certain Old Scandals," *KSMB*, 10 (1959), 27-29. Also see Doris Langley Moore, *Lord Byron: Accounts Rendered* (New York: Harper & Row, Publishers, 1974), pp. 255-57, 487-95.

5. Earl Wasserman, *Shelley: A Critical Reading* (Baltimore: The Johns Hopkins Press, 1971), pp. 461, 460.

6. Letter to Byron (*PBSL*, I, 504).

7. *Julian*, II, 375.

8. Letter to John Gisborne, 18 June 1822 (*PBSL*, II, 434).

9. Reiman recently suggested in *Shelley and His Circle*, V, 145, 423, that Urania (the Muse addressed by Milton in *Paradise Lost* and the mother of Keats in *Adonais*) was the *widow* of Milton. Although this interpretation respects Shelley's description of Milton as "the Sire of an immortal strain" (iv) as well as the notion that Keats was an imitator of Milton, I believe that Shelley intended to depict Urania, not widowed until *after* the birth of Keats (described in st. vi as the "nursling of [her] widowhood" and as her "extreme hope, the loveliest and the last"), as the *mother* of all inspired poets from Milton to Keats. Having once mourned at the death of her son Milton, Urania is called upon in *Adonais* to "weep again" for Keats. Although Shelley in effect withdrew himself from the ranks of inspired poets when he was not recognized by Urania in stanza xxxiv, he did not do likewise for Byron, Moore, and Hunt, the other mourners at the bier of Keats. Apparently, Shelley believed that these three still served the interests of poetry, but he doubted that they would be sufficient to bring on the "memorable age" he had promised to celebrate in the "second part" of *A Defence of Poetry*. With himself unrecognized, with Keats dead, and with Urania widowed, Shelley had no more reason to write this "second part."

10. Letter to John Taaffe, 4 July 1822 (*PBSL*, II, 306).

11. Shelley's ambivalence in the conclusion to *Hellas* parallels Byron's conflicting hopes and fears for Hellas' future in "The Isles of Greece," his lyric in Canto III of *Don Juan*. Shelley read this canto by 21 October 1821 and he was "just finishing" *Hellas* on 22 October (*PBSL*, II, 357, 363). Shelley's indebtedness to Byron is further suggested by the similarities between the stanzaic pattern of "The Isles of Greece" (six lines of iambic tetrameter, rhyming *ababcc*) and that of his final choric song in *Hellas* (four lines of alternating iambic tetrameter, trimeter followed by an iambic tetrameter couplet, rhyming *ababcc*).

12. See, for example, analyses of Shelley's 1821/22 poetry by Harold Bloom, *Shelley's Mythmaking* (New Haven: Yale University Press, 1959); Milton Wilson, *Shelley's Later Poetry: A Study of His Prophetic Imagination* (New York: Columbia University Press, 1959); Ross Greig Woodman, *The Apocalyptic Vision in the Poetry of Shelley* (Toronto: University of Toronto Press, 1964); Jerome J. McGann, "The Secrets of an Elder Day: Shelley After *Hellas*," *K-SJ*, 15 (1966), 24-41; and Wasserman, *Shelley: A Critical Reading*.

13. *PBSL*, II, 363.

14. *PBSL*, II, 347. Compare Byron's remark in a letter to Murray on 23 March 1820: *The Prophecy of Dante* is "the best thing I ever wrote, if it be not unintelligible" (*L&J*, IV, 422).

15. *PBSL*, I, 507.

16. It is possible that Byron received and read the *Euganean Hills* (published with *Rosalind and Helen* in the spring of 1819) before or while he was writing *The Prophecy of Dante* (begun late June 1819, practically finished by October, and sent to Murray in March 1820). In May 1820, Shelley offered to send Byron a copy of *Rosalind and Helen* if he had not yet seen it, but Byron never refers to this volume, to the *Euganean Hills*, or even to *Julian and Maddalo* in his extant correspondence. However, that Byron read at least part of *Julian and Maddalo* in MS is suggested by *Medwin's Conversations*: " 'Shelley, I remember, draws a very beautiful picture of the tranquil pleasures of Venice in a poem which he has not published, and in which he does not make me cut a good figure. It describes an evening we passed together' " (p. 119).

17. *L&J*, V, 65.

18. Letter to Murray (*L&J*, V, 8, 10).

19. Byron's successful use of terza rima, which he was "not aware to have seen hitherto *tried*" in English poetry (Preface to *Prophecy of Dante*), may have influenced Shelley's use of terza rima in *The Triumph of Life*, but Shelley had himself written in this meter (e.g., in *Prince Athanase* and *Ode to the West Wind*) a few years before he read Byron's poem.

20. Shelley's remarks on Byron were made to Peacock in December 1818 and to Gisborne in October 1821 (*PBSL*, II, 58, 363).

21. *Julian*, VII, 112, 137.

22. *A Defence of Poetry*, *Julian*, VII, 131, 124.

23. *PBSL*, II, 42.

24. Letter of 26 May 1820 (*PBSL*, II, 198, my italics). Shelley began to read *Don Juan* at least by 3 January 1820 (see *MSJ*, p. 127).

25. *PBSL*, II, 283-84. By the "curse" in *Manfred*, Shelley probably meant the "Incantation" (I.i.192-261); by the "stanzas in Chillon," probably the stanzas on Clarens (*Childe Harold* III.xcix-civ) or *The Prisoner of Chillon*, both of which he took to Murray in 1816.

26. *PBSL*, II, 309.

27. Letter to Mary, 8-10 August (*PBSL*, II, 323, my italics).

28. *PBSL*, II, 357-58, my italics. Shelley's concluding remark, "I am content— You are building up a drama . . . and the task is sufficiently noble & worthy," indicates that he knew of Byron's decision to continue writing dramas rather than *Don Juan*. Thus Shelley supports Steffan's suggestion that we "should not take too seriously Byron's avowal [see *L&J*, V, 320] that he gave up *Juan* solely at Teresa's request. At the time, he was primarily interested in his dramas and probably found Teresa's aversion an amusing pretext to spread about London" (*DJ Variorum*, I, 39).

29. Letters to Ollier, 16 February and 25 September 1821 (*PBSL*, II, 263, 354, my italics).

30. As quoted by Edward John Trelawny in *Records of Shelley, Byron and the Author* (London: Pickering and Chatto, 1887), p. 79. In the editions of his *Recollections of the Last Days of Shelley and Byron*, Trelawny mistakenly began this statement, " 'Yet at Ravenna. . . .' "

31. Letter to Medwin, 22 August 1821 (*PBSL*, II, 342).

32. Quoted in *DJ Variorum*, II, 7. For a convenient listing of the dates of composition of *Don Juan* (including reference to the accretive stanzas), see *DJ Variorum*, I, 299-310.

33. "Rise and Progress of Popular Disaffection" appeared in the *Quarterly Review*, 16 (January 1817), 511-52, and Shelley seems to be attacked especially on pp. 538-41. For an analysis of this review, its authorship, and Shelley's probable reading of it, see Kenneth Neill Cameron, "Shelley vs. Southey: New Light on an Old Quarrel," *PMLA*, 57 (1942), 489-512.

34. These remarks are from Shelley's letter to Leigh Hunt, ?20 December 1818

(*PBSL*, II, 66) and Byron's letter to Murray, 24 November 1818 (*L&J*, IV, 271-73). The review of *Foliage* in the *Quarterly Review*, 18 (January 1818), 324-35, actually appeared in June and was written by John Taylor Coleridge. But in 1822, Byron and probably Shelley still believed Southey to be the author (see *Medwin's Conversations*, pp. 150-51). After *Conversations* was published in 1824, Southey wrote a letter to the editor of the *Courier* and publicly explained, "*The reviewal in question I did not write*" (letter of 8 December 1824, quoted in *L&J*, VI, 395-99).

35. For Shelley's letters and Southey's replies, see *PBSL*, II, 203-5 and n., 230-33 and n. The review of *The Revolt of Islam* in the *Quarterly Review*, 21 (April 1819), 460-71, was also written by John Taylor Coleridge.

36. *PBSL*, II, 251-53. The review of *Endymion* in the *Quarterly Review*, 19 (April 1818), 204-8, actually appeared in September and was written by John Wilson Croker.

37. *PBSL*, II, 284.

38. *Julian*, II, 407.

39. *PBSL*, II, 309.

40. *L&J*, V, 352-53, 357, 385, 386. For Byron's resumption of his satire on 20 September, see *Poetry*, IV, 525; for his note in the Appendix to *The Two Foscari*, see *L&J*, VI, 387-89.

41. *Poetry*, IV, 482. Compare Byron's remarks to Moore on 4 March 1822 that Shelley is "the *least* selfish and the mildest of men—a man who has made more sacrifices of his fortune and feelings for others than any I ever heard of" (*L&J*, VI, 32-33).

42. Not understanding Byron's purpose in these matters, Medwin in 1824 wrote to Mary Shelley that he could not easily forgive Byron for "not mentioning" Shelley by name in the note in the Appendix to *The Two Foscari*. Medwin's letter is quoted by Ernest J. Lovell, Jr., *Captain Medwin: Friend of Byron and Shelley* (Austin: University of Texas Press, 1962), pp. 168-70.

43. Letter from Horace Smith to Shelley, 30 August 1821 (quoted in *PBSL*, II, 348n.).

44. *Williams*, p. 111; *PBSL*, II, 376, 444.

45. See *PBSL*, II, 357, 198.

46. Shelley's remark as quoted in *Williams*, p. 109. Mary Shelley read *Cain* on 2 November (*MSJ*, p. 161).

47. *PBSL*, II, 373, 376, 388. Byron, according to Medwin, reported that "'Shelley . . . says (what is not the case) that "Cain" is the finest thing I ever wrote, calls it worthy of Milton'" (*Medwin's Conversations*, p. 126).

48. Letter to Horace Smith, 14 September 1821 (*PBSL*, II, 349).

49. See Shelley's remarks on *Manfred* in a letter to Byron, 9 July 1817 (*PBSL*, I, 547). Byron frequently referred to the "metaphysical" quality of *Manfred* and of *Cain* (*L&J*, IV, 54-55; V, 189, 361, 368; *LBC*, II, 43, 197).

50. Trelawny, *Records of Shelley, Byron and the Author*, p. 36; "Queen Mab; Cain, a Mystery; and a Royal Reviewer," *The Republican*, 8 February 1822, p. 192; *Blackwood's Edinburgh Magazine*, 11 (April 1822), 463; and *The Letters of Thomas Moore*, ed. Wilfred S. Dowden (Oxford: At the Clarendon Press, 1964), II, 503-5.

51. Letter to Horace Smith, 11 April 1822 (*PBSL*, II, 412, my italics). On 4 March, Byron himself responded to Moore's deprecation of Shelley's influence: "With [Shelley's] speculative opinions I have nothing in common, nor desire to have" (*L&J*, VI, 33). Compare Arnold's Byronic distaste for "speculative opinions" in *The Deformed Transformed*, begun in Pisa in 1822: "I was not born for philosophy,/Though I have that about me [?Shelley] which has need on't" (I.i.228-29).

52. *L&J*, V, 357; VI, 387.

53. *Revised Life*, p. 334; *The Shelley Papers: Memoir of Percy Bysshe Shelley*

(London: Whittaker, Treacher, & Co., 1833), p. 72n. Byron's portrayal of the pre-Adamite world may have been influenced by similar visions in *The Revolt of Islam* II.x-xii and *Prometheus Unbound* IV.270-318. Unlike Byron, however, Shelley argued in *The Revolt* that "Such man has been, and such may yet become" (II.xii).

54. Robert F. Gleckner (*Byron and the Ruins of Paradise* [Baltimore: The Johns Hopkins Press, 1967], p. 88n.) suggests that "*Cain* might well be regarded in some ways as a reversal of the *Queen Mab* pattern." That Byron intended *Cain* as a "reversal" and for that purpose reread *Queen Mab* in 1821 is suggested by my text that follows and by the considerable number of verbal similarities between these two poems: *Cain* I.138-56 and *QM* VI.103-17; *Cain* I.526-39, III.53-68 and *QM* VIII.206 together with Shelley's note on "time-destroying infiniteness" (*Julian*, I, 156-57); *Cain* II.i.29-43, 98-109, III.180-83 and *QM* I. 249-63, II.70-90; *Cain* II.ii.145-52 and *QM* VII.109-11; *Cain* III.26-30, 338 and *QM* I.37-40, 1-2; *Cain* III.180-83 and *QM* VI.39-41. Also see *Cain Variorum*, pp. 301-2. Byron's *Sardanapalus* (IV.i.1-9, 65-66), another 1821 drama, also echoes *Queen Mab* (I.1-8; II.211-12).

55. *Julian*, I, 146, my italics.

56. Brian Wilkie, *Romantic Poets and Epic Tradition* (Madison: The University of Wisconsin Press, 1965), p. 127.

57. *Julian*, VII, 87.

58. *Essay on Christianity*, *Julian*, VI, 239. For a discussion of this important judgment, see Chapter 6.

59. Shelley was "just finishing" *Hellas* on 22 October (*PBSL*, II, 363); he read *Cain* between 1-4 November (*MSJ*, p. 161; *Williams*, p. 109); Williams, who proposed "Hellas" as the title on 25 October, fair copied Shelley's drama from 6-10 November (*Williams*, pp. 106, 110-11); and Shelley sent the MS to Ollier on 11 November (*PBSL*, II, 365).

60. In this same note to the Chorus in *Hellas* (ll. 197-238), Shelley explained that he himself used *some* of the "popular notions of Christianity," but argued that they were "true [only] in their relation to the worship they superseded, and that which in all probability they will supersede" and that he was not "considering their merits in a relation more universal" (*Julian*, III, 56). In other words, Shelley argued that he was not suffering from the "delusions of Christianity."

61. This version of *Sonnet to Byron* is taken from Mary Shelley's fair copy in Bodleian MS. Shelley adds. d. 7, pp. 95-96. Mary's headnote ("Lines to —— Jan^y 22-1822"), the differences between this fair copy and the other MS drafts, and especially the regular rhyme scheme (*abababab cddcee*) all suggest that Mary copied from another MS draft now lost. (In *Julian*, IV, 117, lines 8-11 of this sonnet differ in rhyme, position, and substance.) Because of the separate drafts for this sonnet, we cannot accept Medwin's claim that Shelley wrote it "one day after reading *The Corsair*" (*Revised Life*, p. 258). Shelley may have begun the sonnet in November shortly after reading *Cain* and *The Vision of Judgment*, two of the "late works of this spirit of an angel" (*PBSL*, II, 376), for we find the first three lines of the sonnet drafted in Bodleian MS. Shelley adds. e. 7 (p. 228 reverso), a notebook containing the rough draft for *Hellas*. And Mary's 22 January 1822 provides a satisfactory terminal date, for in Bodleian MS. Shelley adds. e. 17, consecutive lines (III.66-67 and 68-69) of the fragmentary *Charles the First* (which Shelley stopped writing in January—see *PBSL*, II, 380, 388, 394) are drafted on pp. 95 reverso and 93b reverso, that is drafted around p. 94 reverso, on which appears a twelve-line draft of *Sonnet to Byron* (entitled "To ——" and prefaced by "Im afraid these verses will not please you but"). Byron, however, probably never read this sonnet—see *Revised Life*, p. 258.

*Chapter 9. Serpents in the Deep and Gods in the Heaven: The Triumph of Life-in-Death*

1. *PBSL*, II, 339.

2. *PBSL*, II, 367-68.

3. In a January letter to Peacock, Shelley wrote that he and Byron were "constant companions" (*PBSL*, II, 373), a fact supported by Medwin (*Revised Life*, p. 329) and Teresa Guiccioli (*My Recollections of Lord Byron; and Those of Eye-Witnesses of His Life*, trans. Hubert E. H. Jerningham [New York: Harper & Brothers, Publishers, 1869], p. 472). For specific references to the two poets' meetings, see the diary entries in *MSJ* and *Williams*. According to *Williams* (entries for 11 November 1821 and 18 February 1822, pp. 111, 131), the two poets were engaged in such diverse activities as preparing an edition of "Spinoza's Theologico-political tract" (Shelley would translate and Byron would write Spinoza's life) and "getting up Othello" for the amusement of their circle. Although both projects were apparently abandoned, Shelley completed his translation and Byron at least cast the characters for *Othello* (see *MSL*, I, 196, 316). The two poets' association was also responsible for Byron's lines on Dr. Nott, *The New Vicar of Bray* (see Medwin, *Revised Life*, pp. 362-64) and possibly for his *Stanzas to a Hindoo Air* (see Trelawny as quoted by Iris Origo, *The Last Attachment: The Story of Byron and Teresa Guiccioli as Told in Their Unpublished Letters and Other Family Papers* [New York: Charles Scribner's Sons, 1949], pp. 298-99).

4. *PBSL*, II, 323-24, my italics.

5. *PBSL*, II, 331.

6. Letter of 26 August 1821 (*PBSL*, II, 344, my italics). Thomas Medwin once observed that *The Liberal* was originally Shelley's idea: "the influence Shelley had over Byron, was proved in nothing more than his being persuaded to join in that review, the first idea of which was suggested by Shelley for the benefit of Mr. Hunt" (*The Shelley Papers: Memoir of Percy Bysshe Shelley* [London: Whittaker, Treacher, & Co., 1833], p. 82). For a discussion of "the exact authorship of the proposal," see William H. Marshall, *Byron, Shelley, Hunt, and "The Liberal"* (Philadelphia: University of Pennsylvania Press, 1960), pp. 22-28.

7. Letter of 25 September (*PBSL*, II, 354).

8. *PBSL*, II, 251.

9. *PBSL*, II, 283-84, 289-90, 308-9.

10. *PBSL*, II, 344, 356 (my italics), 388.

11. H. Buxton Forman, ed., *Note Books of Percy Bysshe Shelley: From the Originals in the Library of W. K. Bixby* (Boston: The Bibliophile Society, 1911), I, 171-72; and Neville Rogers, *Shelley at Work: A Critical Inquiry*, 2d ed. (Oxford: At the Clarendon Press, 1967), pp. 223-24. Both printings are taken from the Bixby-Huntington Notebook I, *14$^r$, *14$^v$, *15$^r$ (the asterisk representing reverse foliation). In *Julian* (IV, 120-21), ll. 1-13 are separately printed as "Laurels" and incorrect variants of ll. 14, 16-18 are printed as "And That I Walk Thus Proudly Crowned." For a transcription of the Bixby-Huntington rough draft and of Mary Shelley's fair copy in Bodleian MS. Shelley adds. d. 9, see Irving Massey, *Posthumous Poems of Shelley: Mary Shelley's Fair Copy Book* (Montreal: McGill-Queen's University Press, 1969), pp. 293-95, 188-91.

12. *Shelley at Work*, p. 264.

13. *PBSL*, II, 384-86.

14. An interpretation offered on p. 2 of *Retsch's Series of Twenty-Six Outlines, Illustrative of Goethe's Tragedy of Faust, Engraved from the Originals by Henry Moses, and an Analysis of the Tragedy* (London: Printed for Boosey and Sons, 1820), which arrived in Pisa by 12 January 1822—see below, n. 26.

15. This and subsequent quotations are taken from the bilingual edition, *Goethe's "Faust,"* trans. Walter Kaufmann (New York: Doubleday & Company, Inc., 1961).

16. Letter to Ollier (*PBSL*, II, 354). In this letter, Shelley also complained

that he had failed in his search for "something nobler and better"—i.e., the same "Vision" of human perfectibility that he lamented in "The serpent is shut out from Paradise."

17. *PBSL*, II, 379. Compare similar protestations ("I have neither curiosity interest, pain or pleasue in [or] for any thing good or evil [the reviews] can say of me") in Shelley's letter to Leigh Hunt also written on 25 January (*PBSL*, II, 383).

18. Letters to Joseph Severn, Claire Clairmont, Peacock, and Ollier (*PBSL*, II, 366, 368, 373-74, 372, my italics).

19. *PBSL*, II, 380-82.

20. As quoted in Forman, *Note Books of Percy Bysshe Shelley*, III, 104.

21. For Shelley's reading of these works, see *PBSL*, II, 347, 358, 373, 376; according to Mary, she read *Cain* on 2 November, Shelley read *Heaven and Earth* on 14 December, and Mary read *Werner* on 16 January, *Sardanapalus* on 24 January, and *The Two Foscari* on 26 January (*MSJ*, pp. 161, 163, 165); according to Williams, Shelley praised *Cain* on 4 November, Shelley read aloud *Heaven and Earth* on 14 December, Mary read aloud part of *Werner* on 8 January, and Williams read *Werner* on 23 January (*Williams*, pp. 109, 117, 123, 126).

22. *Medwin's Conversations*, pp. 5, 156. But see *Revised Life*, p. 333, where Medwin reported that Shelley was "much struck by the choral parts" of *Heaven and Earth*.

23. *Medwin's Conversations*, pp. 153-54. Medwin repeated this story in *Revised Life*, pp. 334-35. When *The Deformed Transformed* was published in 1824, it did not contain the lines from Southey.

24. Trelawny's remarks, from a letter to John Murray on 15 January 1833, are quoted in *Medwin's Conversations*, p. 155n.

25. No later than 9 March when Medwin left Pisa (see *Williams*, p. 133).

26. See *L&J*, V, 488; and *PBSL*, II, 376.

27. Byron could have read this scene (ll. 1840-2050) in the *Retsch* volume or in John Anster's alternating translation and summary of *Faust* which had appeared in *Blackwood's Edinburgh Magazine* (7 [1820], 235-58), a copy of which Byron and Shelley apparently had in Pisa. For Shelley's criticism of these translations in *Retsch* and *Blackwood's*, see *PBSL*, II, 376. For Byron's "buffoonery" based on Mephisto's statement in the Prologue ("Wie meine Muhme, die berühmte Schlange," l. 335) and possibly in the scene with the student ("und meiner Muhme, der Schlange," l. 2049), see his letter to Moore (?December 1821): "Goethe's Mephistofilus calls the serpent who tempted Eve 'my aunt, the renowned snake;' and I always insist that Shelley is nothing but one of her nephews, walking about on the tip of his tail" (*L&J*, V, 496).

28. Letter to Peacock, ?11 January 1822 (*PBSL*, II, 373).

29. "The Devil as Doppelgänger in *The Deformed Transformed*: The Sources and Meaning of Byron's Unfinished Drama," *BNYPL*, 74 (1970), 177-202. In this article, I detail the various influences (including Shelley's) on Byron's drama and print in full Medwin's "unpublished note" (as transcribed by Irving in 1825) on this "Unwritten Drama." This "unpublished note" has also been printed by Walter A. Reichart, *The Complete Works of Washington Irving: Journals and Notebooks, Volume III, 1819-1827* (Madison: The University of Wisconsin Press, 1970), pp. 710-12.

30. Williams reports both the wager and the news of Lady Noel's death (*Williams*, pp. 119, 130), and Medwin reports Williams' annoyance at Byron's failure to pay the debt (*Revised Life*, p. 375). Shelley's own annoyance may have been responsible for his desire on 10 April "to make a new will" (*PBSL*, II, 408) and thus change his will of 24 September 1816, which contained a two-thousand-pound bequest to Byron (see Frederick L. Jones, "Shelley's Revised Will," *MLN*, 59 [1944], 544; but also see Reiman, *Shelley and His Circle*, V, 115). Upon Shelley's death, Byron refused this bequest, perhaps in lieu of the

wager he lost to Shelley. For an exoneration of Byron's actions in this wager, see Doris Langley Moore, "Byron, Leigh Hunt, and the Shelleys: New Light on Certain Old Scandals," *KSMB*, 10 (1959), 22-23.

31. See Shelley's letters to Byron on 15 February and to Hunt on 17 February (*PBSL*, II, 389-90).

32. Letters to Hunt on 2 March and 10 April (*PBSL*, II, 393-94, 405).

33. Edward Dowden, *The Life of Percy Bysshe Shelley* (London: Kegan Paul, Trench & Co., 1886), II, 486-87. Elizabeth Parker's letter continues with an amusing anecdote: "'Afterwards [Shelley] said, "It is foolish of me to be angry with [Byron]; he can no more help being what he is than yonder door can help being a door." Mr. Tighe then said, "You are quite wrong in your fatalism. If I were to horsewhip that door, it would still remain a door; but if Lord Byron were well horsewhipped, my opinion is he would become as humane as he is now inhumane. It is the feeble character or the subserviency of his friends that makes him the insolent tyrant he is." This observation Mr. Shelley repelled; he said others were free, of course, to use the law of coercion; he disapproved it, and the only law that should ever govern his conduct should be the law of love. The discussion appeared to be getting warm, these two think so differently; therefore Lady Mountcashell carried Mr. Shelley off to read Euripides, and the subject dropped.'" Because this letter "is known only through Miss Clairmont's copy," Dowden observed that this whole story must "be taken with caution."

34. Letters to Claire, 20 and 24 March 1822 (*PBSL*, II, 397-99, 400).

35. *PBSL*, II, 391-92. Jones tentatively dated this letter in February 1822, but added that it "could have been written late in March or early in April" (II, 392n.). Its similarities with the other March letters to Claire argue, in my judgment, for March. When Claire was over seventy years old, she accurately described for Trelawny Shelley's final judgments about Byron: "Shelley as you know adored Genius—Lord Byron possessed it undoubtedly—at that period this was sufficient to decide Shelley to think no ill of him. Three years later he altered his opinion and became convinced that Lord Byron's genius was a fatal gift that developed in him inordinate pride and a dryness of heart and fierceness of feeling most dangerous in theory as in practice" (as quoted by Ivan Roe, *Shelley: The Last Phase* [New York: Roy Publishers, 1955], pp. 77-78).

36. Leslie A. Marchand, *Byron: A Biography* (New York: Alfred A. Knopf, 1957), III, *notes, 108*.

37. Letters to Trelawny on 16 May, to Claire on 30 May, to Horace Smith ca. 21 May, and to John Gisborne on 18 June (*PBSL*, II, 422, 429, 423, 434-36). Shelley's distinction above between Byron's former "coarse music" and his recent "perfection" recalls Byron's own distinction, in a 20 May letter to Shelley (*L&J*, VI, 67), between his former "exaggerated nonsense" and his recent "things which shd 'not willingly be let die.'" If Shelley recognized this quotation from Milton's "Second Book" of *The Reason of Church Government* (*John Milton: Complete Poems and Major Prose*, ed. Merritt Y. Hughes [New York: The Odyssey Press, 1957], p. 668), he had even more reason to equate Byron with Milton during May and June 1822.

38. Letter to Horace Smith, 29 June 1822 (*PBSL*, II, 442).

39. *Williams*, p. 147.

40. From Mary's description in a letter to Maria Gisborne, 15 August 1822 (*MSL*, I, 180).

41. Medwin also links Calderón's doppelgänger drama to Shelley's vision, but he mistakenly conflates two of Shelley's visions into one (*Revised Life*, pp. 404-5).

42. See *Faust*, ll. 1699-1706; and James Rieger, *The Mutiny Within: The Heresies of Percy Bysshe Shelley* (New York: George Braziller, 1967), p. 233. Rieger's last chapter, "Motes of a Sick Eye," argues the possibility of Shelley's suicide on 8 July 1822.

43. *PBSL*, II, 433. By replacing Milton's *Virtue* with *prussic acid* as the "golden key," Shelley made evident, at least to himself, that death rather than the morally directed imagination provided the only liberation from life's enthrallments. But because he had read Gray's *Progress of Poesy* (see *PBSL*, II, 221), wherein Gray rephrases Milton so that not Virtue but Poesy offers "these golden keys . . ./This can unlock the gates of Joy;/Of Horrour that, and thrilling Fears,/ Or ope the sacred source of sympathetic Tears" (ll. 91-94 in *The Complete Poems of Thomas Gray: English, Latin and Greek*, ed. H. W. Starr and J. R. Hendrickson [Oxford: At the Clarendon Press, 1966]), Shelley also seems to say that *death* is superior to either *Virtue* or *Poesy*. That is, he repudiated both the ethic of *Prometheus Unbound* and the aesthetic of *A Defence of Poetry*, where he had asked for the "poetry of *life*" that "withdraws *life's* dark veil" (*Julian*, VII, 134, 137, my italics). According to Gray, life was worthy of poetical description because its "Horrour" and "Fears" were at least balanced by "Joy" and "sympathetic Tears"; according to Shelley, life was a deceitful enchantress whose capriciousness was matched only by Byron's (see *PBSL*, II, 435)—and both, he hoped, could be escaped in death.

44. *MSJ*, p. 124.

45. "Notes on Shelley's 'Triumph of Life,'" *MLR*, 9 (1914), 441. Bradley called the sixth *Trionfo* that "of Divinity," but I have followed the more modern designation, *The Triumph of Eternity*: see, e.g., *The Triumphs of Petrarch*, trans. Ernest Hatch Wilkins (Chicago: The University of Chicago Press, 1962); and D. D. Carnicelli's edition, *Lord Morley's "Tryumphes of Fraunces Petrarcke": The First English Translation of the "Trionfi"* (Cambridge: Harvard University Press, 1971), p. 24.

46. See Rogers, *Shelley at Work*, pp. 176-79.

47. Richards, *Principles of Literary Criticism* (New York: Harcourt, Brace & Company, Inc., 1924), p. 217; Reiman, *TL Variorum*, p. 29.

48. From Richard Garnett's translation in *Julian*, VI, 284, 286, my italics.

49. Shelley's use of *Comus* in 1821/22 was extensive: see quotations from it in his letters of 26 August 1821 and 18 June 1822 (*PBSL*, II, 344, 433); his paraphrase of the attendant Spirit's opening speech in "Fragments of an Unfinished Drama," ll. 15-27; and his other uses of it in *The Triumph of Life* as cited by Reiman, *TL Variorum*, passim.

50. Cf. *Comus* where the "human count'nance,/. . . is chang'd/Into some brutish form of Wolf, or Bear,/Or Ounce, or Tiger, Hog, or bearded Goat,/All other parts remaining as they were" (ll. 68-72). In Shelley's version, these animal phantoms "'fell from the countenance/And form of all'" (ll. 536-37). Because Shelley by 25 January 1822 had received an edition of Calderón (*PBSL*, II, 378), he probably had also read Calderón's elaborate drama on the Circe legend, *El Mayor Encanto Amor* (see *Love the Greatest Enchantment*, in *Three Dramas of Calderon, from the Spanish*, trans. Denis Florence Mac-Carthy [Dublin: W. B. Kelly, 1870]). In this drama, Circe "made as vassals mine/All these tree-trunks, all these wild beasts" (p. 45). And she was also addressed as the Sun by Ulysses: "After thee,/Sun, whose sun-flower I must be;—/Till thy sweet light from above/ Dawns on me no life I know;/Therefore where thou shin'st, I go" (p. 70)—compare Rousseau describing himself "'as a shut lily, stricken by the wand/Of dewy morning's vital alchemy,/I rose'" (ll. 401-3).

51. Letter of 20 January 1821 (*PBSL*, II, 258).

52. The incident in which Rousseau (who was not seen until he spoke to Shelley, ll. 180-90) identified himself as a poet from whom there did "'rise/A *thousand beacons* from the *spark* [he] bore,'" the "'*spark* with which *Heaven* lit [his] spirit'" (ll. 206-7, 201, my italics) is obviously based on the scene in which Statius (who was not immediately seen until he spoke to Dante and Virgil, xxi.12-13) identified himself as the poet whose "*sparks* . . . from the *divine flame* whereby more than a *thousand* have been kindled were the seeds of [his] *poetic*

*fire"* (xxi.94-96, my italics). Also, Shelley's description of the chariot's procession as a "jubilee" of a "triumphal pageant" in "Imperial Rome," and as an intense light which "obscured . . ./The Sun" (ll. 111-18, 78-79) may have derived from Dante's description of the Chariot of the Church: "Not only did Rome never gladden an Africanus or an Augustus with a chariot so splendid, but even that of the Sun would be poor to it" (xxix.115-17). Quotations are from *The Divine Comedy: Purgatorio (1: Italian Text and Translation)*, trans. Charles S. Singleton (Princeton: Princeton University Press, Bollingen Series LXXX, 1973).

53. *TL Variorum*, passim.

54. Letters to Peacock and Hogg (*PBSL*, I, 486, 494).

55. Cf. Shelley's remarks to Horace Smith on 29 June 1822: "The destiny of man can scarcely be so degraded that he was born only to die: and if such should be the case, delusions, especially the gross & preposterous ones of the existing religion, can scarcely be supposed to exalt it" (*PBSL*, II, 442).

56. See Shelley's letter to Mary on 4 July (*PBSL*, II, 444); Edward Williams' letter to Jane on 6 July (*Williams*, pp. 162-63); and Byron's letter to W. Webb on 2 September (*LBC*, II, 229).

57. See Byron's letters to Murray, 3 and 8 July 1822 (*L&J*, VI, 93, 94).

58. *PBSL*, II, 445; *Williams*, p. 161.

59. To support Steffan's well-reasoned "conjecture" that Byron began to write Canto VI about the middle of April and finished it and Canto VII at least by the end of June" (*DJ Variorum*, I, 384n.-385n.), see Trelawny's statement to Shelley on 22 June 1822 that "Two more cantos are written of *Don Juan*" (as quoted in *His Very Self and Voice: Collected Conversations of Lord Byron*, ed. Ernest J. Lovell, Jr. [New York: The Macmillan Company, 1954], p. 296). Shelley communicated this information to Horace Smith on 29 June (*PBSL*, II, 442).

60. *L&J*, VI, 387. Byron seems to have reported the substance of this note to Medwin at Pisa: "'I disowned the other day that I was of Shelley's school in metaphysics, though I admired his poetry; not but what he has changed his mode of thinking very much since he wrote the Notes to "Queen Mab," which I was accused of having a hand in'" (*Medwin's Conversations*, p. 80).

61. *L&J*, V, 435; *L&J*, VI, 32-33; George Bancroft, "A Day with Lord Byron," *History of the Battle of Lake Erie, and Miscellaneous Papers* (New York: Robert Bonner's Sons, 1891), p. 200; *Medwin's Conversations*, p. 235; James Hamilton Browne, "Narrative of a Visit, in 1823, to the Seat of War in Greece," *Blackwood's Edinburgh Magazine*, 36 (1834), 395; and George Finlay's letter on 31 May 1824 to Stanhope, quoted in Colonel Leicester Stanhope, *Greece, in 1823 and 1824; Being a Series of Letters and Other Documents, on the Greek Revolution, Written During a Visit to That Country. A New Edition . . . to Which Are Added, Reminiscences of Lord Byron* (London: Printed for Sherwood, Gilbert, and Piper, 1825), p. 513. For similar remarks on Shelley after his death, see *L&J*, VI, 99, 157; *Blessington's Conversations*, pp. 52-53; and James Kennedy, *Conversations on Religion, with Lord Byron and Others* (London: John Murray, 1830), pp. 197-200.

62. From Thomas Moore's translation of Guiccioli's Italian, as quoted in Moore, *Letters and Journals of Lord Byron: With Notices of His Life*, 3d ed. (London: John Murray, 1833), III, 359-60; and from Byron's letter to Mary Shelley, ?December 1822 (*L&J*, VI, 175; see also *LBC*, II, 242).

63. Edward John Trelawny, *Records of Shelley, Byron and the Author* (London: Pickering and Chatto, 1887), pp. 28-29. For a denial of Byron's selfishness in this respect, see Doris Langley Moore, "Byron, Leigh Hunt, and the Shelleys: New Light on Certain Old Scandals," p. 21.

64. For an explanation of this, see Chapter 8 (including n. 42).

65. Byron to Moore, 27 August 1822 (*L&J*, VI, 108).

66. *DJ Variorum*, IV, 205. For the dating of these cantos, see I, 306-7.

67. Byron read *Hellas* by 12 April 1822 (*MSL*, I, 167).

68. In this stanza, Byron rejects Love as "Selfish" and "a mere Insanity" in a manner similar to his rejection of Shelleyan Love in *Childe Harold* IV.cxx-cxxv.

*Epilogue: An Island Paradise*

1. Further investigation of *Don Juan* yields only incidentals: Juan being likened to the "plants called Sensitive" (X.37) recalls Shelley's *The Sensitive Plant*, which Byron read in the *Prometheus Unbound* volume in 1821; the ridicule in *Don Juan* VIII.9 of Wordsworth's infamous "Carnage is [God's] daughter" may have been prompted by Shelley's similar parody in *Peter Bell the Third* (VI.177-83), with which Byron was supposedly "well acquainted" (*Medwin's Conversations*, pp. 194-95 and n.); and certain stanzas of *Don Juan* strongly echo Shelley's poetry—compare, e.g., *Don Juan* VIII.137 and X.38 with *Prometheus Unbound* III.iv.164-79 and *To Jane: The Invitation*, ll. 33-38.

2. Letter to Murray, 3 August 1822 (*L&J*, VI, 99).

3. See *L&J*, VI, 164-65; *LBC*, II, 252-53; and *Poetry*, V, 581.

4. *Politics in English Romantic Poetry* (Cambridge: Harvard University Press, 1970), p. 227.

5. "'Neuha's Cave,'" however, was initially inspired by the description of a cave in the ninth chapter of John Martin's *An Account of the Natives of the Tonga Islands* (1817), the second of Byron's acknowledged sources for *The Island* (see *Poetry*, V, 629n.-630n.).

6. For Byron's reading of *The Revolt*, see *L&J*, IV, 273 and V, 74; of *Prometheus Unbound*, see *PBSL*, II, 345; of *Euganean Hills*, consider Shelley's intent to send Byron the *Rosalind and Helen* volume (*PBSL*, II, 198-99); and of *Epipsychidion*, consider Byron's understanding of Shelley's description of Emilia Viviani as his "convent friend" (*PBSL*, II, 347). Note also that Byron's question in *The Island*, "what can our accomplished art/Of verse do more than reach the awakened heart?" (II.101-2), parallels Shelley's concern for the "more essential attribute of Poetry, the power of awakening in others sensations like those which animate my own bosom" (Preface to *The Revolt*).

7. This epithet, perhaps coined by Byron, applies to Claire, Mary, and especially Shelley and can be found in Claire's letter of May 1816 to Byron announcing that the "'whole tribe'" would shortly join him in Geneva (quoted in *To Lord Byron*, p. 211).

8. For this as a quotation from Bligh's *Narrative of the Mutiny on board His Majesty's Ship Bounty*, see *Poetry*, V, 592n.

9. Contrast the opposite in *The Corsair*: "The Sun hath sunk—and, darker than the night,/Sinks with its beam upon the beacon height/Medora's heart—the third day's come and gone—/With it he comes not—sends not—faithless one!" (III.iii.1234-37).

*Appendix A: Some Literary Relations between Byron and Shelley from 1810 to 1816*

1. Hogg, *The Life of Percy Bysshe Shelley*, ed. Edward Dowden (London: George Routledge & Sons Limited, 1906), p. 179.

2. Byron had similarly described the whirlwind elsewhere in *Poems: Original and Translated*: "the gleaming form, through the mist of the storm,/Was borne on high by the whirlwind's wing" ("Oscar of Alva," *Poetry*, I, 145); and "he rolls his form in the whirlwind, and hovers on the blast of the mountain" ("The Death of Calmar and Orla," *Poetry*, I, 177).

3. Compare "Or the mist of the tempest that gather'd below" ("When I rov'd a young Highlander," *Poetry*, I, 192).

4. *The Works of Percy Bysshe Shelley in Verse and Prose* (London: Reeves

and Turner, 1880), V, 185n. John Cordy Jeaffreson used this plagiarism from "Lachin y Gair" to argue that the verses in *St. Irvyne* "are chiefly noteworthy for their evidence that the *Hours of Idleness* [actually *Poems: Original and Translated*] may be styled 'the hornbook,' from which Shelley acquired the rudiments of the art of poesy" (*The Real Shelley: New Views of the Poet's Life* [London: Hurst and Blackett, Publishers, 1885], I, 166). Shelley's plagiarism from "I would I were a careless child" was first discovered by Richard H. Shepherd, ed., *The Prose Works of Percy Bysshe Shelley: From the Original Editions* (London: Chatto and Windus, 1888), I, 174n., but he failed to identify the name of Byron's poem.

5. A close reading of Shelley's 1810 poetry against Byron's *Poems: Original and Translated* would reveal additional borrowings on Shelley's part: compare, e.g., ll. 5-8 of Shelley's "Song: *Sorrow*" in *Original Poetry; by Victor and Cazire* with ll. 21-24 of "I would I were a careless child."

6. Mary's inscription is quoted by Roger Ingpen, *Shelley in England: New Facts and Letters from the Shelley-Whitton Papers* (London: Kegan Paul, Trench, Trubner & Co. Ltd., 1917), pp. 434-35. It is also printed, with minor variations, in Edward Dowden, *The Life of Percy Bysshe Shelley* (London: Kegan Paul, Trench & Co., 1886), I, 430-31.

7. As quoted from *The Esdaile Notebook: A Volume of Early Poems*, ed. Kenneth Neill Cameron (New York: Alfred A. Knopf, 1964), p. 53. Cameron suggests that Shelley's reading of Spenser was responsible for the Spenserians of this poem (p. 193).

8. *The Journals of Claire Clairmont*, ed. Marion Kingston Stocking (Cambridge: Harvard University Press, 1968), p. 44 (entry for 17 September 1814).

9. In 1817, Shelley imitated a scene from *The Corsair* in *The Revolt of Islam* (see Chapter 4); and in February 1818, Mary read *The Giaour, The Corsair,* and *Lara,* and she saw *The Bride of Abydos* performed in London (*MSJ,* p. 92).

10. Thomas Moore, *Letters and Journals of Lord Byron: With Notices of His Life,* 3d ed. (London: John Murray, 1833), II, 238.

*Appendix B: Shelley's "One Mind"*

1. Quotations from *On Life* and *Speculations on Metaphysics* are from *Julian,* VI, 196; VII, 59-61, 65.

# INDEX

*284*

The Johns Hopkins University Press

This book was composed in Baskerville text and display type by Horne Associates, Incorporated, from a design by Susan Bishop. It was printed on 50-lb. Publishers Eggshell Wove paper and bound in Holliston Roxite vellum cloth by Universal Lithographers, Inc.